P9-CFT-839

SHANGHAI

When I first visited Shanghai shortly after the Cultural Revolution, Communism had fallen on the city like a sandstorm, burying and preserving. The international community who had made Shanghai great between the wars might have been scattered across the world but their edifices remained largely untouched. Even the light switches had not changed since the 1930s. Now Shanghai is one of the most exciting economic centres in the Far East. The place is booming, with new investment and new building projects. There is no place for sprung dance floors or an Art Deco swimming pool and no sentimentality at their loss. On the other hand Shanghai is not the spiritually dead city that I first explored. The highly charged atmosphere of the Twenties and Thirties, what the Chinese described as '*jenao*', a perpetual 'hot din' of the senses, has returned. It seems entirely possible that Shanghai will overtake Hong Kong and Tokyo to become once again the leading city in the Far East and an Asian international capital. Shanghai's former inhabitants would have approved.

Harriet Sergeant is the author of *Between the Lines: Conversations in South Africa* and *The Old Sow in the Back Room: An Englishwoman in Japan*. She lives in London.

By the same author

BETWEEN THE LINES: CONVERSATIONS IN SOUTH AFRICA

THE OLD SOW IN THE BACK ROOM:
AN ENGLISHWOMAN IN JAPAN

SHANGHAI

Harriet Sergeant

JOHN MURRAY
Albemarle Street, London

For my father
who first took me to Shanghai

© Harriet Sergeant 1991

First published in 1991

First published in paperback in 1998
by John Murray (Publishers) Ltd,
50 Albemarle Street, London W1X 4BD

Reprinted 1998

The moral right of the author has been asserted

All rights reserved. No part of this publication may be
reproduced in any material form (including photocopying or
storing it in any medium by electronic means and whether or
not transiently or incidentally to some other use of this
publication) without the written permission of the copyright
owner, except in accordance with the provisions of the
Copyright, Designs and Patents Act 1988 or under the terms of
a licence issued by the Copyright Licensing Agency,
90 Tottenham Court Road, London W1P 9HE. Applications for
the copyright owner's written permission to reproduce any part
of this publication should be addressed to the publisher.

A catalogue record for this book is available from the
British Library

ISBN 0-7195-5713-5

Printed and bound in Great Britain

Contents

List of Illustrations

PLATES

ACKNOWLEDGMENTS

The author and publisher wish to thank the following for permission to reproduce photographs:

Plate 1, Uta Schreck; 2, 26, Culver Pictures Inc., New York; 7, 8, 20, 21, 24, 25, Illustrated London News Picture Library; 9, Taeko Wada; 10, 11, Koichi Okawa; 12, 32, Sir William Hayter; 13, Patricia Maddocks; 14, George Stewart; 15, 17, 18, Lady Chancellor; 16, Lady Keswick; 19, Hongkong and Shanghai Bank Archives; 22, 23, 36, 37, 38, 39, John Hillelson; 28, Emily Hahn; 29, Wang Baolian; 30, 31, Tony Rayns.
    The cartoons which appear on chapter opening pages throughout the book are from the work of Georgi Sapojnikov (Sapajou), chief cartoonist for the *North China Daily News* from 1925–49.

Acknowledgments

Two people have inspired this book. Irene Kuhn, my next-door neighbour in New York worked as a journalist in Shanghai during the 'twenties and gave me the idea. Jean Tan de Bibiana left Shanghai after the Communist Revolution at the age of three and came back for the first time to explore the city with me.

I am indebted to Calliope Caroussis, my research assistant in London, Ruth Price who helped me in Washington and Emma Hart who checked the manuscript. I am also grateful to Antonia Lloyd Jones for braving the Russian section of the Bibliothèque Nationale in Paris, Odile Emery who checked my French translation, Keiko Imai, Kayoko Takai and Hideko Martin for their help with the Japanese research, the Bank of China for their care of me in Shanghai and the Hong Kong and Shanghai Bank for their assistance. My research has led me far and wide and I have met with nothing but kindness, especially from the following institutions: the School of Oriental and African Studies, University of London; the New York Public Library; Bancroft Library, California; the Hong Kong University Library and the Bibliothèque Nationale, Paris. Lastly, I wish to thank my family, friends and acquaintances who introduced me to Shanghai's diaspora of former residents. Without them this book could not have been written.

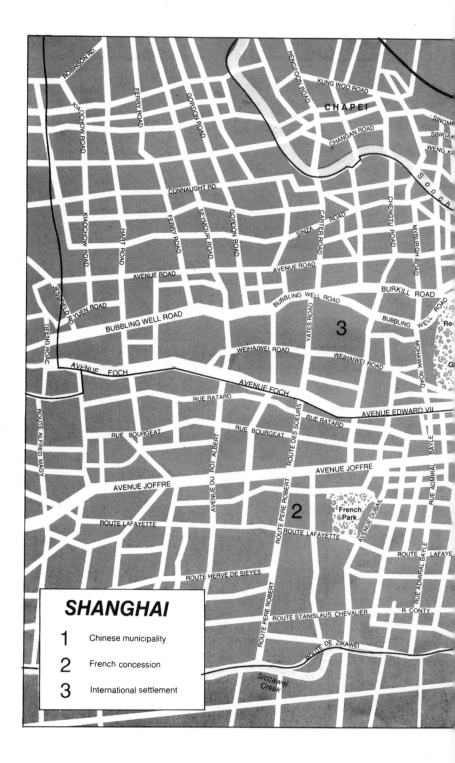

SHANGHAI

1   Chinese municipality

2   French concession

3   International settlement

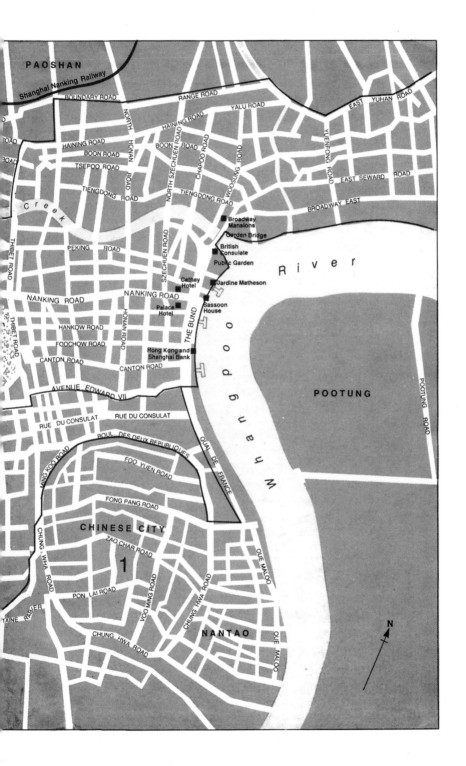

PAOSHAN

Shanghai Nanking Railway

BOUNDARY ROAD   RANGE ROAD

NORTH

HONAN

ROAD

ROAD

Creek

HAINING ROAD   YALU ROAD   EAST YUHAN ROAD

HAINING ROAD

BOON ROAD

TSEPOO ROAD

TIENGDONG ROAD

BOON ROAD

CHAPOO ROAD

WOOSUNG ROAD

NORTH SZECHUEN ROAD

YUENFONG ROAD

EAST SEWARD ROAD

TIENGDONG ROAD

BROADWAY EAST

PEKING   ROAD

River

Broadway
Mansions

Garden Bridge

British
Consulate

Public Garden

Cathay
Hotel

Jardine Matheson

SZECHUEN ROAD

NANKING ROAD

NANKING ROAD

HONAN ROAD

Palace
Hotel

Sassoon
House

THIBET

ROAD

THE BUND

HANKOW ROAD

FOOCHOW ROAD

Hong Kong and
Shanghai Bank

THIBET ROAD

CANTON ROAD

CANTON ROAD

AVENUE EDWARD VII

RUE DU CONSULAT   RUE DU CONSULAT

BOUL. DES DEUX REPUBLIQUES

QUAI DE FRANCE

Whangpoo

POOTUNG

POOTUNG ROAD

MING KOO ROAD

FOO YUEN ROAD

FONG PANG ROAD

CHINESE CITY

1

ZAO CHAR ROAD

CHUNG WHA ROAD

PON LAI ROAD

VOO MING ROAD

CHUNG HWA ROAD

TAINE RIVER

CHUNG HWA ROAD

NANTAO

QUE MALOO

QUE MALOO

N

Introduction

ONE AFTERNOON IN 1932 Lord Bangor was taking a stroll in the Chinese countryside outside Shanghai.

I was staying on a houseboat with friends. We had gone on a walk carrying a gun in the hopes of getting a pheasant or a duck. Colonel Hayley Bell, the grandfather of Hayley Mills, was one of the party. He had lagged behind to examine an old shrine. Suddenly the rest of us were charged by a water-buffalo. They were very dangerous and hated foreigners, I suppose we smelt different, but any Chinese child could control them. They let their animal loose on the foreign devil then demanded a dollar to drive the brute off.

I was up a tree and my two friends in a shed. The buffalo was snorting and flicking his tail. A Chinese boy arrived and asked for his dollar. I was eager to pay when Hayley Bell appeared on the scene. The beast stamped a foot and lowered its head. Hayley Bell walked straight up to it and kicked it hard on the nose. The astonished animal turned tail and lumbered off followed by the urchin. 'Shock tactics is what it's about,' said Hayley Bell as I climbed out of the tree, 'I am not going to be blackmailed by some snotty-nosed Chinese infant. Just go up to the animal and show it who's master.'

So had the foreigner tackled China in 1842, won Shanghai and turned a Chinese town on the coast of the East China Sea into the largest port and industrial centre of the Far East. From that date Shanghai opened to the West. The Chinese authorities designated certain areas outside the city for foreign use and granted the new inhabitants special rights and privileges. Shanghai's potential as the entrepôt for the Yangtze basin attracted American, British and French traders. They hastened to set up trading companies,

I

banks and, after the arrival of the Japanese in 1895, factories. To protect their interests they formed their own municipal councils and police forces. In pursuit of profit they created the most international metropolis the world has ever seen.

From its inception as a foreign enclave, Shanghai emerged a free city. New arrivals required neither visa nor passport to enter. To the dispossessed, the ambitious and the criminal, it offered a fresh start. Lady Jellicoe, who was brought up in the city, recalled, 'One never asked why someone had come to Shanghai. It was assumed everybody had something to hide.' Shanghai's approach to law and order proved equally attractive. The foreign traders believed in self-government and the minimum of regulation. Over the years they protected people as varied as American conmen, White Russian tarts, Japanese jazz players, Korean tram conductors, Jews fleeing from the Nazis and Chinese revolutionaries fleeing from each other. Like New York today, its diverse society created a taut, compelling atmosphere as well as innovation and financial success. Life there was a highly charged affair, what the Chinese call *'jenao'*, a perpetual 'hot din' of the senses. Sir Harold Acton wrote of the city then, 'Everywhere one jostled adventurers and rubbed shoulders with people who had no inkling how extraordinary they were: the extraordinary had become ordinary: the freakish commonplace.'[1]

By the 'twenties and 'thirties Shanghai was as much a Chinese as a Western creation: a place where, as one historian has put it, two cultures met but neither prevailed.[2] Architecturally, Shanghai recalled a city in northern Europe or America. Neo-Grecque skyscrapers and department stores lined the business centre. Fake Tudor houses and Spanish-style villas filled the suburbs. The weather reinforced the impression. Bitter winters and hot, humid summers made any New Yorker feel at home. At the same time Greater Shanghai and the old, walled city remained under Chinese control. By 1932 the Chinese population exceeded three million. The foreigners numbered fewer than 70,000. Shanghai saw the birth of the Chinese Communist party and the political struggles which shaped China's future. Like Shanghai's foreign inhabitants, the majority of Chinese came from elsewhere. The city offered Chinese from the interior contact with the West and an escape from a rigid social system. They associated Shanghai with the stylish, the new, the audacious in everything from dress to politics. The Chinese believed that Shanghai represented China's future and saw its glittering modernity infecting China with twentieth-century life. No one suspected the reverse might happen. No one dreamt China's future lay in that great sprawling back land of droughts, floods, famine and brigands. Shanghai's foreign and Chinese inhabitants might depend for their wealth on the interior but they dismissed it as a poor thing until Mao Zedong made it his own.

In the 'twenties and 'thirties Shanghai became a legend. No world cruise was complete without a stop in the city. Its name evoked mystery, adventure and licence of every form. In ships sailing to the Far East, residents enthralled passengers with stories of the 'Whore of the Orient'. They described Chinese gangsters, nightclubs that never closed and hotels which supplied heroin on room service. They talked familiarly of warlords, spy rings, international arms dealers and the peculiar delights on offer in Shanghai's brothels. Long before landing, wives dreamed of the fabulous shops: husbands of half an hour in the exquisite grip of a Eurasian girl.

For the new arrival Shanghai surpassed its reputation. The city stands on the Whangpoo, a tributary of the Yangtze. Passenger liners would moor off the Bund, Shanghai's most eminent street and the hub of the city. As you stepped ashore Shanghai's inimitable odour of expensive scent and garlic overwhelmed you. A dozen different languages assailed your ear. Beggar children tugged at your clothes. American cars hooted at your rickshaw puller. Trams hurtled past. Above your head the foreign buildings of the Bund thrust into the sky. At your feet Chinese beggars picked at their sores. Down a side street a middle-aged Russian woman and a pubescent Chinese girl fought over a sailor. On the pavement Chinese dragging wheelbarrows of silver swore at immaculately dressed Englishmen stepping from their club. In the road a Sikh policeman in a red turban blew his whistle as two Chinese girls ran through the traffic on very high heels, their cheong-sams flipping open to the hip. Even blindfolded, you would have recognized Shanghai by the sheer, almost hysterical energy of the place.

Shanghai offered equally varied entertainment. You could visit the racetrack in the centre of the city, bet on a game of *hai-alai* introduced by the Portuguese in the French part of town or attend a baffling production of Chinese opera. There were military parades to enjoy, foreign battleships floating on the Whangpoo, newspapers from every major capital and films in a variety of languages. In the evening an invitation to a formal English dinner party might be followed by a visit to a nightclub to watch a Japanese dancer who called herself a Filipino princess undulate to the music of a German Jewish band. At one point if you fell ill you could choose your doctor from twenty-eight nationalities including two Romanians, one Armenian, one Egyptian, one Mexican and ten exceptionally competent Hungarians.

You could buy luxuries from every Western country as well as Japanese wedding kimonos and silk underwear embroidered by small, Chinese boys. Brave visitors explored the old Chinese city, its narrow streets choked with beggars, babies peeing through split pants as well as fortune-tellers and letter-writers. Chinese barbers squatted on the pavement as they cleaned out customers' ears with a ball of fluff fixed to a handle. Old men, taking their pet birds out for an airing, might have held up bamboo cages with dwarf siskins or a Japanese nightingale for you to admire. Impoverished intellectuals wrote their autobiographies in chalk on the pavement and invited the charitable to lay money on the incident that particularly moved them. Dark, cramped specialist shops lined the streets – shop, workshop and home all together. One might sell only silk umbrellas: another porcelain from inkpots to spittoons. In a third the owner carved ivory and pig's bone into mahjong pieces, sunshade handles, mouthpieces for pipes, cigarette holders, dice, carved hands with long handles to scratch the back and even circular combs to relieve itchy heads. The ritual of Chinese life spilt over from here into the French Concession and International Settlement. To the sound of gongs, wedding processions made their way between the overhanging houses. The bride dressed in red sat concealed in a red lacquer sedan chair shouldered by servants. Behind followed more servants carrying the dowry of freshly varnished furniture, new quilts, vases and even several live geese. At Chinese New Year the city was resplendent with fireworks and Chinese in new clothes. In early spring Chinese children celebrated the Feast of Lanterns by appearing at dusk with a lantern in the shape of a rabbit, dragon or flower and lit with a candle. The foreign tourist looked on stupefied. 'So much life, so carefully canalised, so strongly flowing – the spectacle of it inspires something like terror', wrote Aldous Huxley in 1926.[3]

Celebrities like Huxley filled Shanghai's hotels. They too wanted to see for themselves what one ambassador described as 'this unreal, fantastic creation'.[4] Shanghai was where Noel Coward caught flu, Mary Pickford bought her shoes, Bertrand Russell gave a lecture and

4

Bernard Shaw ate two lunches in one day. Christopher Isherwood, W. H. Auden and André Malraux wrote about it. Mussolini's son-in-law, Count Galeazzo Ciano pursued Chinese beauties in its nightclubs ('To such an extent', one man murmured to me, 'that Mussolini's daughter, Edda, had the greatest difficulty catching her husband's attention long enough to get pregnant'). Wallis Simpson was rumoured to have appeared in a series of dirty postcards, posing in nothing more than a lifebuoy.[5] Charlie Chaplin and Paulette Goddard arrived in love. Eugene O'Neill, travelling as the Reverend William O'Brien, chose to have a nervous breakdown accompanied by a lady who described herself as a Swedish masseuse. Hollywood set a Busby musical in a Shanghai bar while Josef Von Sternberg, the director of *Shanghai Express* spent 'a pulsating three hours'[6] in a Shanghai amusement hall.

The Shanghai of the 'twenties and 'thirties offers a tour of the pre-war era. It reduces a period of great complexity to a manageable itinerary. In a city where the protagonists of the Second World War sat on the same council and went to the same nightclub, it displayed the issues of the day on the scale of municipal politics and street battles. Its end summed up an era of violent change and pointed to a disturbing future. At the time Shanghai was dismissed as a freak city. Sixty years later its messy, multi-racial society, its random violence, demonstrations and displaced people are all too familiar. It set the pattern for the success of Far Eastern cities like Singapore and Hong Kong but also proved a paradigm for a peculiarly modern way of living.

When Shanghai fell in 1949 to the Chinese communists a door was shut. During the Cultural Revolution the door was bolted for good. A world had gone. I first went to Shanghai just after the Cultural Revolution and was planning my last trip when the tanks arrived in Tiananmen Square. Nothing appears to have altered since the pre-war era. Shanghai is bigger, there are more people and a few new skyscrapers but otherwise communism has fallen on the city like a sandstorm, burying and preserving. The street names are different but not the buildings, from the office blocks and hotels on the Bund to the villas in the suburbs. Even the interiors are untouched. The marble lobbies and art-deco swimming pools are pre-war as are the light switches. Communism has mummified Shanghai's appearance in a manner inconceivable to a Westerner. Shopping centres, over-passes and subways are all missing. So, despite the carefully preserved wrappings, is Shanghai's spirit.

To write about a spiritually dead city presents difficulties. I walked down roads where stirring events had taken place and into houses famous for their occupants but the Shanghai I sought remained elusive. I visited a former pawnbroker whose back room, now closed to the Chinese, was stacked with the debris of fifty years ago. Fur coats from the 'thirties hung next to Chinese opera costumes. Greedy for the past I examined carriage clocks, a set of silver grapefruit spoons and a gold Hunter watchcase with a Russian inscription on the back. I laid out certain objects and tried, like the children's party game, to guess the connection and make a coherent story. I could find nothing in them of the Shanghai I was looking for.

I eventually tracked down Shanghai's past several hundred miles away in a Tokyo bar. The owner was a diminutive woman of seventy-six in gold hoop earrings. When she heard what I was writing about she took me into a corner and ordered whisky and water for us both.

Her name was Manuela and she had been a famous dancer in Shanghai's nightclubs. Her parents had separated when she was a child, her father replacing his wife with a geisha. He disapproved of Manuela's dancing career and disowned her when she chose a *nissei*, a half-Japanese, half-American, for her second husband. The marriage lasted two years. At the age of twenty-four Manuela sought a new life in Shanghai. She acquired an American journalist as an agent whose best friend ran a famous Shanghai restaurant called 'Jimmy's Kitchen'. Sometimes he treated her to a meal. Other times she visited a gambling club which provided free noodles and cigarettes. She took the cigarettes home to pay her room boy.

After a short time Shanghai's most successful nightclub owner gave her a regular spot and launched her career. On the first night, eleven bouquets of flowers fell at her feet. Ten came from her agent and one from Jimmy. Face, she explained to me, was all important in Shanghai.

From beneath the bar, she pulled out an album of old newspaper cuttings. They showed Manuela in a number of exotic poses advertising her show. Hawaiian skirts, oriental pants, tight bodices and split skirts appeared barely able to restrain her small, compact body from bursting into movement. She pointed out her favourite, a

6

velvet dress cut like a second skin with an immense ruffle exploding from beneath the bottom. It came from a German Jewish homosexual who played in her band. His 'cousin' had worked as a transvestite in the Moulin Rouge. When he fled from Paris the cousin brought the dress with him and gave it to Manuela.

I asked what made her dancing special. She held up her tiny, strong hands, the fingers splayed like starfish. People liked the expression she put into them, she explained. Otherwise the most important thing was spirit. She described her most famous dance. A white man comes into the jungle, falls in love with a native and they have a child. The child, Manuela, is brought up Tabu. No native man will touch her. She started the dance by praying to the moon, 'My face is so lovely, my breasts so nice, my hips so warm . . . ' The old lady in front of me began slowly to run her hands over her body as she relived the past. With eyes half-closed and head thrown back, she moaned, 'Why can't I make love? I want to make love. Please moon send me a sweetheart!' The Tokyo bar was suddenly still. Manuela lowered her head, took a sip of whisky and smiled at me. 'It was a great success. The moment a band saw me arrive in their club, they burst into that tune.'

She leaned across the table towards me, suddenly sad. 'You would never have wanted to leave if you had been in Shanghai then. Now it's all changed. It's so dirty and the taxi drivers don't know the old street names.' She sighed. 'Sometimes I sit at home on my own, drink whisky and remember. Then I just cry and cry.'

People like Manuela made Shanghai. I realized that if I wanted to find the past, I had to ransack the memories of its former inhabitants. My search took me from the Far East to America and Europe. Nearly everyone I interviewed was in their eighties and nineties. Some were senile. One died the day before our appointment. Their recollections were usually inaccurate, nearly always slanderous and sometimes just unbelievable. As the past overwhelmed them they confided what had stayed brightest in their minds: a thirteen-year-old sing-song girl who wrapped naked legs around a man's neck and beat on his back tiny, bound feet encased in red silk; the enchantment of opium, a favourite nightclub, a Hungarian boy who kept a pet chicken called Smosch or, simply, the man next door, a bit-part player like Mr Sutton who, Lord Kadoorie remembered with a smile, had a series of cupboards in his apartment.

Every morning he asked his boy, 'How hot is it?' If the temperature was seventy-eight degrees, the boy said 'seventy-eight', and he would open cupboard number seventy-eight and there was a complete set including bowler hat, clothes, shirt, everything for that temperature. So he would put a flower in his button hole and go out looking splendid and that was that.

I interviewed many Chinese who still live in Shanghai today. They presented me with a special challenge. When I first went to the city, it was almost impossible, unless under the protection of a host organization, to book a seat on a plane, find a hotel room or even catch a taxi. Local calls took an hour to make. If I did finally get through and the person I wished to interview was there, they expressed polite regret. Unless I belonged to an organization they could not see me.

Through a combination of luck and bluff, I persuaded the Bank of China to take pity on me. Life became much easier. They reserved a suite for me in Shanghai's finest guest house, drove me around and even provided two young chaperons. My interviews turned into impressive affairs and assumed a certain ritual. I would arrive with my chaperons and greet the old man I had asked to meet, he flanked by an interpreter and a party official. Sitting in huge, coffee-coloured armchairs complete with lace antimacassars, we would exchange compliments and sip tea poured from a thermos. The old man would look at the official and, after receiving a nod from him, recite his sufferings during the Cultural Revolution. This formed a set piece, delivered by everyone I met as it was well received by foreigners. When he finished, I asked my first question about the 'thirties. He replied evasively and we would both glance at the party official. As I came low on the list of important assignments, he or she was usually young with no knowledge or interest in the past. I would try another question. Tentatively the old man opposite me would lay down the lightest of clues as to what he might discuss. Sometimes I caught sight of it through the thick hedge of translation, more often not. Even if I did, one stupid question or clumsy translation saw my quarry withdraw behind impenetrable platitudes. Occasionally I was lucky. The pleasure of remembering proved too tempting. The old man would talk as if in a dream until the past opened up like a sunny, secluded spot. Together we would sit and bask, the official and the chaperons left far behind. When we parted he might shyly squeeze my hand or slip me a small treasure, a photograph or a book.

By my third visit I had made friends in Shanghai. The central government now encouraged foreigners and a few people were willing to talk when I went up to them in the street or park. An old lady shelling peas outside her house told me about working in a silk factory. An elderly engineer invited me to his room for a dish of sweet fungus soup and read me love poems he had written in French. A man in a bar introduced me to Mao Zedong's former doctor. A series of chance encounters led to an invitation to eat dim sum with Shanghai's richest businessman. Another evening I was approached in the street by a tough-looking Chinese in a blouson jacket. As we strolled, I asked the standard question; had he suffered during the Cultural Revolution. He looked perplexed. He said he had been a Red Guard. He had enjoyed himself very much.

My encounters with the city's former foreign and Chinese inhabitants took on more and more importance for me. They conferred on Shanghai a tangible personality. For this reason I have included many of these meetings in my book. Under their influence and with the help of municipal files, diplomatic records and old newspapers I began to investigate Shanghai as one would the subject of a biography. I sought out information and gossip. I observed the city's behaviour in its moments of crisis. I relied on the people who told me about Shanghai and the events which reveal its character. The result is a book divided between the nationalities who contributed most to the city and the battles of 1927, 1932 and 1937 which destroyed it. Above all I have tried to identify the trait which places Shanghai among the great cities and which makes any history of it relevant today. In 1926 Aldous Huxley summed up Shanghai's secret as, 'Life itself . . . dense, rank, richly clotted life . . . nothing more intensely living can be imagined.'[7]

· ONE ·

A Simple Equation
The Rise of a Great City

ON A SUNNY afternoon I took the lift up Shanghai's tallest pre-war building. Broadway Mansions, now renamed Shanghai Mansions, stands at the confluence of the Soochow Creek and the Whangpoo. From across the old Garden Bridge, it looms over the Bund, a sixteen-storey cliff face of red brick with terraces rising in uneven steps up its sides. In the 'thirties the Foreign Correspondents' Club occupied the top floors. Drink in hand, journalists watched from its heights the bombing of Shanghai. During the war the Japanese made it their headquarters after they had conquered the city. The lift stops in a glass corridor opening on to a terrace. I walked out, looked around and understood something of the excitement of the Japanese generals. Shanghai extends to the horizon in every direction. Distance bestows a sense of intimacy and power on the onlooker. I felt I only had to stretch out my arm, pry open a window or lift off a roof to understand Shanghai.

It is a grey city: grey slate, grey stone, grey scuttling figures and the wide, lazy loop of the grey Whangpoo river. It is a busy city. On the river floats every shape and size of boat down to the smallest tug equipped with a clothes line, charcoal stove, wife and children. Directly below me and bordering the Whangpoo curved the Bund, Shanghai's most important street and as busy as the river with bicyclists breaking in waves around cars and buses, the persistent tinkling of their bells rising through the hooting of the motorists and the deeper boom of the ships' horns. Away to the south-west ran the French Concession, its tree-lined avenues gashes of green through the grey roofs. Between it and the river lay the misshapen circle of the old Chinese City of Nantao, the city wall long since gone,[1] the narrow, stone streets now clean of the beggars, pimps and street-hawkers that used to infest its gloom. To the north of Soochow Creek stretched Hongkew and Yangtzepoo, once part of the International Settlement and home to the poorer foreigner before it was destroyed by Japanese and American bombs. Between the modern buildings I could still glimpse areas of grey-tiled, Chinese roofs curling at the corners like burnt paper. Beyond was the working-class district of Chapei and to the east, across the river, Pootung. They reached the horizon in a botched landscape of factory and dockland; grey and very busy.

In the 'thirties Shanghai covered 20 square miles, 12½ square miles of which was under foreign control. It was a small, densely packed city. In 1932 its population stood at over 3,000,000. At the same time Greater London contained 7½ million people spread over 70 square miles. Shanghai was almost three times as crowded.

Most of all Shanghai is a river port. The Whangpoo dominates the city. All Shanghai's grandest foreign firms and banks built their offices along the Bund, looking out over the Whangpoo. In autumn when fog shrouded the Bund, the sound of fog-horns echoed between the buildings and reverberated up and down the streets to join with the low, muted note of a conch shell blown from a junk or the thrash of propellers. The smell of Whangpoo, a mixture of sewage, seaweed and coal, infiltrated the city. It caught people unawares as they left nightclubs or restaurants, reminding them that however big and sophisticated Shanghai had become, it was still a river port.

The river always appeared busy. Small ships travelled fussily, letting off steam, their sirens screaming. Steam launches chugged back and forth dragging six or seven barges. Bobbing in and out among the liners, sampans propelled by an '*ulow*' took passengers and sailors to and from their ships. Junks with sails spread wide drifted past on the current. Foreign cruisers, moored midstream, gleamed in the sun, guns protruding beneath their awnings. Further down, against a backdrop of factories and godowns, dredgers churned slime from the river bed. In the wet docks men, balancing on sampans while holding brushes several yards long, splashed the side of a passenger liner orange. Dirty, old coasters, trailing black smoke but still jaunty under names like *Amelia* and *Aphrodite*, made their way out to sea.

A few minutes' walk from the East Gate of the Chinese city lay the junk anchorage. Here junks crowded up against each other in different shapes and sizes. Some were built to cross the ocean. Others worked just one river. All shared square bows, brown sails patched in bright colours and poops painted with a gigantic eye. On every poop you might catch a glimpse of potted plants, perhaps a cat asleep, washing hanging on a bamboo pole, a bird in a cage and someone fanning the charcoal while the rice boiled.

Wharves lined the river right through the centre of the city. On the Bund itself ships loaded and unloaded, their hatches open wide while cranes ground overhead. Coolies rushed back and forth across gangplanks, loads of cargo on their heads. As they ran, they half-sang and half-called together, the foreman shouting out whatever inspired him: 'Look at that fat, white foreign woman coming past now'; the others taking up the chant: 'Oh, look at her, look at her.' The foreman continuing, 'Imagine getting lost up her Jade Gate'; the others replying, 'What a fate! What a fate for a poor man!' Country people loaded up flat-bottomed boats with jars of soya sauce, baskets of chickens, rolls of mats and then turned to make their way back up the river and into the interior.

You could not escape the river. At the end of every east-bound road, out of every window on the Bund, there it was, an open expanse in a city with no open spaces, reflecting the sky, catching the light and coiling its way around Shanghai like a great, silver snake. 'If it were not for this river there would be no Shanghai', mused a local paper in 1931.

The inhabitants would not be able to breathe in the smoky atmosphere without the fresh sea breezes: there would be no money to build her houses, her hotels and her firms, if it were not for this stretch of water that spells commerce and links her with the outside world. The river flowed between these banks long, long before anybody ever thought of building a city and calling it Shanghai.[2]

The river had attracted Shanghai's very first Western visitor. Mr Hugh Lindsay, an agent of the East India Company, arrived in Shanghai in 1832. Since 1757 the Chinese government had restricted the foreign trader to Guangzhou (Canton) and business to one small guild of merchants, the Cahong. Mr Lindsay was on the lookout for an alternative to Guangzhou. He found it, he was sure, in the small, walled city of Shanghai.

What Mr Lindsay saw were junks. He counted an average of four hundred entering Shanghai weekly in one July which, if representative of the whole year, made Shanghai one of the leading ports in the world. Some junks came from Guangdong and Manchuria, a few from Java, Indochina and Siam but the majority arrived down the Yangtze. This great river, as Mr Lindsay quickly appreciated, was the reason for Shanghai's importance. The Yangtze Watershed drains half of China reaching one-tenth of the world's population. Ocean-going vessels travelled inland as far as Hankou, river steamers to Suifu and smaller craft still further, not only up the Yangtze, but also to its tributaries, providing almost thirty thousand miles of waterway. In Mr Lindsay's time rafts transported most goods. They carried up to twenty tons, stayed afloat in one foot of water and transported whole villages including the local barber and tinsmith down to the city.

Shanghai is a great city because it stands at the tip of the fertile and populated, lower Yangtze basin. The Chinese had been building waterways across the area for two thousand years. Goods travelled to and from Shanghai by an estimated half a million miles of artificial waterways. Almost no roads existed. The Chinese erected single-span, humpbacked bridges in order to allow boats to pass under rather than anything more than a wheelbarrow to go over. When the British arrived Shanghai was China's largest native port. 'The advantages which foreigners would derive from the liberty of trade with this place are incalculable,'[3] mused Mr Lindsay.

Shanghai offered the foreigner position. It stood midway on the coast between north and south China and near to Japan with which the West began to trade in 1853. Barely a hundred miles east lay the great circle route of ships travelling between the west coast of North America, Japan, China and south-east Asia. Shanghai formed the natural centre of Far Eastern shipping and was midway between Atlantic Europe and America. It was to become, as Mr Lindsay foresaw, the seaport of the Yangtze River and the principal emporium of Eastern Asia.

The Yangtze made Shanghai. Nowhere else in the world did such a vast area and so many people depend on one river and one city for their trade. It meant opportunities for foreign importers as well as exporters and set Mr Lindsay to dreaming of the Chinese snug and happy in Lancashire textiles.

The city depended on the interior for its wealth but could not control it. Shanghai never became a state city. The Shanghai businessman showed little interest in administration. Within his city he could do what he liked because in the nineteenth century the Chinese government was inept, and, after 1911, non-existent. Beyond the city limits Shanghai's influence proved diffuse rather than direct and about progress rather than politics or power. Shanghai became the centre and disperser of novelty. Winding slowly up into the smallest tributaries went stories of what the floating villagers had seen and heard; kerosene street lamps, the first rickshaw, unbound feet, bobbed hair, escalators and communism.

Reluctantly I took the lift down from the top of Shanghai Mansions and joined the flow of Chinese pressing home from work. In the aqueous light of dusk, the crowds spread over the pavements and on to the roads silent but for the swish of bicycle wheels and the tinkling of bells. Most had moved into the city from the countryside during the 'fifties. They showed little curiosity about Shanghai's past or the foreign buildings they lived and worked in. Some even suggested the city should be razed and started again. They represented the vast indifference of the country to Shanghai's qualities and reminded me that Shanghai's development depended as much on its relationship with China as with the Whangpoo.

The one hundred years that saw Shanghai emerge as an international port witnessed the disintegration of the Middle Kingdom (as the Chinese referred to their country). Shanghai's independence relied on China's weakness. This swung both ways. The revival of a strong, central government in China put an end to Shanghai.

The years between 1842 and 1949 saw China all but taken over by the West, turned into an informal colony and shared out between Europe and the United States. To foreigners and Chinese alike, Shanghai symbolized foreign aggression and its impact on China. Even its inception as an international city followed the first, disastrous encounter between East and West.

China in the eighteenth century suffered the characteristics of an island state. Its four thousand years of compulsively, repetitive history, its dynasties overthrown by peasant rebellions which created dynasties to be overthrown in their turn, its rigid, social order, despotic Emperors, extraordinary literature and art had unfolded in relative isolation. The deserts, mountains and icy plains to the north and west and the Pacific to the east cut off contact with other civilizations. China had nothing to compare itself with but the primitive people on the fringes of its vast empire. The Chinese believed themselves the centre of the civilized world and their civilization the only one in existence.[4]

The arrival of the foreigners in the eighteenth century coincided with the decline of China's rulers. The Manchu who siezed power in 1644 had dissipated their former vigour with a passion for intrigue and display. They treated Westerners as just another tribe of upstarts and rejected Western overtures for trade and diplomatic contact as ludicrous. This compared unfavourably with the foreigners' experience in India where local rulers had agreed to draw up trade agreements and honour treaties. India proved part of the Indo-European tradition. China most emphatically was not. The country operated a policy of total exclusion. It was even a crime for a foreigner to learn Chinese while demands for a foreign consul in Beijing were viewed as a gross insult. A British mission led by Lord Macartney in 1793 to establish contact with the elusive Manchu government ended in humiliation and failure. Chinese intransigence compelled the foreigner, if he was to act at all, to act with force. As one American put it, 'Diplomatic intercourse can only be had with this government at the cannon's mouth.'[5]

This particularly irked the British who held the bulk of China trade. British merchants sold English textiles to India, shipped Indian cotton to China and Chinese silk, tea and porcelain back to the United Kingdom. The policies of the Manchu government ensured the East India Company, Britain's sole representative in the East until 1834, sold less than it bought. The British exchequer had to make up the balance with precious hard currency in the form of silver bars until they discovered the one commodity the Chinese wanted:

opium. In the 1760s China imported 1,000 chests a year, each one weighing 133 pounds. By 1838 the total had risen to 40,000 chests and the addicts could be counted in their millions. Opium, grown in India and sold in China, had saved British trade in the Far East and created fortunes for British and American merchants. Taxes on opium made up one-seventh of the revenue of the British government in India while the tax on tea, now paid for by opium, accounted for one-tenth of the total revenue of the United Kingdom.

China's desire to call a halt to 'an infamous traffic', as Gladstone called it, coincided with British determination for greater trade opportunities. In 1840 the First Opium War broke out between the countries which ended in defeat for China two years later. The British happened upon Shanghai towards the end of the fighting. It was June 13th, 1842. Three days later the appropriately named *Nemesis*, a British armed paddle steamer, towed two British frigates and three sloops opposite the crescent-shaped fort of Woosung which guarded the entrance of the Whangpoo from the Yangtze. The Chinese, believing their defences impregnable, cheered the visitors good-humouredly. It took a day's firing to vanquish them. The Chinese garrison stared in amazement at the British 'cannon balls innumerable, flying in awful confusion through the heavenly expanse'.[6]

The Treaty of Nanjing, forced upon the reluctant Manchu under the guns of a British man-of-war, opened Shanghai and four other ports, Guangzhou, Xiamen, Fuzhou and Ningbo, collectively known as the Treaty Ports, to the foreigner. It signified the start of China's humiliation at the hands of the West. The Chinese had either assimilated or expelled earlier invaders. For the first time in its four-thousand-year history this proved impossible. The problem of how to establish China's independence and self-esteem in the modern world haunted the country, and Shanghai Chinese in particular, for the next hundred years.

Other countries immediately hurried to China to share the spoils. France, Belgium, Sweden, Norway and Russia put forward their demands while setting up businesses in the Treaty Ports. In a supplementary agreement the British had included the somewhat euphemistically named 'most-favoured-nation' principle. This meant that any 'favoured nation' could automatically assume all privileges granted by China to another 'favoured nation'. The United States, Britain's biggest rival in the China Trade, had remained neutral during the First Opium War, berating Britain for its action while profiting from the suspension of Anglo-Chinese trade. Now President Tyler dispatched a Massachusetts politician, Caleb Cushing, in order to 'save the Chinese from the condition of being an exclusive monopoly in the hands of England'.[7] The President expressed his concern in a letter to the Emperor couched in terms thought appropriate for addressing a Red Indian Chief. Cushing signed a treaty with the Chinese at Wangxia in July 1844 which included a clause placing Americans in China under consular jurisdiction. It meant that the Chinese had no power over foreigners of the 'most-favoured-nation' variety, whatever the crime they committed. They could only be tried in their own courts and by their own consulate. This proved crucial to Shanghai's development. Shanghai's traders took up the clause as the basis for a curious piece of law known as extraterritoriality. For the next hundred years it ensured the safety of the foreigner, his property and his business. China and its troubles could not touch him.

Cushing's clause formed the basis of Shanghai's constitution. It established Shanghai as a state within a state. On the strength of it, the city's foreign inhabitants made a series of bold decisions. They refused to pay Chinese taxes except land tax and maritime dues which they themselves collected while imposing taxes on all Chinese who came to live in the Settlements. They claimed the right to land troops while excluding Chinese troops from the Concessions. Finally in 1854 they drew up the Land Regulations which laid down elementary principles for local self-government. It removed the Settlements from the control of the Chinese and the Consuls stipulated in the original treaties, and put authority into the hands of every tax-paying foreigner. On July 11th, 1854, a committee of these, described as the most 'unconventional municipality in the world',[8] held the first annual meeting of the Shanghai Municipal Council. Furious foreign offices warned the traders that they had no right to administrative independence from China. They had no rights at all and certainly no legal precedent. All they had, as Rhoads Murphey has put it, was 'bluff, manœuvre, and force majeure'.[9] It was to be the Municipal Council, the businessmen, who now ran the city.

For both foreigner and Chinese, extraterritoriality established Shanghai as the symbol of their unequal relationship: an insult to China and confirmation to the West of its superiority. The first few hours after the city's capture by the British saw an example of this attitude. British sailors had viewed the killing of soldiers who carried fans and sent monkeys with fire crackers tied to their backs to set ships ablaze as 'a kind of sport'.[10] One British officer recalled coming across two British sailors and a soldier in a paddy field. They were standing about fifty yards apart in a triangle. Between them, half a dozen Chinese ran helplessly back and forth. The officer wrote, 'Our three men were loading and firing at them as coolly as if they were crows, and bayoneting to death those who fell wounded. I endeavoured to stop them but they paid no attention.'[11] For their part the Chinese ignored the lessons of the war. The Manchu officials withdrew to the splendours of the Forbidden City where they pretended their defeat and even the foreigner himself simply did not exist. Their subjects continued to exhibit the same attitude well into the twentieth century. When I asked Chinese from Shanghai if they had Western friends, they looked puzzled. They appeared to regard the foreign invasion of their city as a meteorological freak, both harmful and beneficial but, I was made to understand, a background event, unimportant and so unworthy of comment. For the next hundred years, despite living side by side, foreigner and Chinese conducted a campaign in mutual contempt. The friendship and respect which spasmodically existed between India and Britain never had its counterpart in China.

The Opium War also dictated Shanghai's unique topography. The foreigners divided the land set aside by the Chinese into three Settlements, each with frontage on the Whangpoo. The French Concession lay between the walled Chinese city and Yang-ching-pang Creek, later filled in and called Edward VII Avenue. The British Settlement stretched from Yang-ching-pang to Soochow Creek while the American settlement consisted of a piece of land fronting the river to the north-east of Soochow Creek. In 1863 the Americans joined with the British to create the International Settlement. The Chinese controlled the original walled city and all the land bordering the Settlements. Each section of the city made up a separate political unit with its own municipal council and police force. In the 1920s and '30s the various authorities required drivers to hold three licences. The Treaty of Nanjing had failed to fix the Western boundaries of the International Settlement and the French Concession, and the foreigner used every excuse to extend them into the Chinese countryside. The original area was leased in perpetuity from the Chinese. The Chinese, at least, regarded it as part of China.

In its early years as an international city, Shanghai resembled a colonial outpost. After the Treaty of Nanjing in 1842 trading houses like Jardine Matheson and Dent & Co. dispatched young and healthy men to open branch offices. Along the edge of the Whangpoo, on land covered with mulberry trees and ancestral graves, they built comfortable houses with arched verandas and red-tiled roofs. They planted their compounds with tulip trees, roses and magnolias. Behind lay the merchants' godowns (warehouses) and homes for the Chinese assistants. The larger firms had two or three partners, eight or ten foreign clerks and fifty or sixty Chinese staff. They dealt principally in silk, tea and opium. Opium clippers arrived from India and, as a gesture to the drug's illegality in China, discharged their contents into hulks lining the Whangpoo before clearing customs. Chinese dealers distributed the opium from the hulks. The firms employed a tea expert, usually a foreigner, whose job it was to visit the tea centres of Jiujiang, Huzhou, Hankou, Xiangtan and Hangzhou in late April and early May. Chinese merchants brought silk to Shanghai. For two months of the year the trader worked day and night, seven days a week buying, transporting, packing and shipping the tea and silk. Otherwise he led a leisurely existence, a few hours in the office interspersed with long lunches in the mess.

The rural appeal of the outpost vanished for ever in one of the greatest of China's many peasant revolts. The Taiping Rebellion lasted from 1850 until its defeat in 1864 and was responsible for the death of probably twenty million Chinese. It changed the composition of the Settlements and defined their relationship with the Chinese interior.

The humiliation of the Manchu provoked a crisis among an already irate peasantry. China's agriculture was in disarray due to a massive growth in population from about 142 million in 1741 to about 400 million by 1840. The lack of cultivated land had been aggravated by the slow but persistent policy of China's landowners to concentrate their holdings. The peasants proved ready to rally to a man even as unprepossessing as Hong Xiuquan, a teacher from a small town outside Guangzhou who had failed the civil service examination and been refused baptism by a foreign missionary. Hong declared himself Christ's younger brother and proposed to establish a Heavenly Kingdom in China, make all men brothers and evict the demon Manchu. Hong's egalitarian vision attracted able leaders and a fanatical following. The Taipings captured Nanjing, known as the

Southern Capital and, but for the intervention of the foreigners on the side of the Manchu, might have taken all of China.

In September 1853 the Chinese city of Shanghai fell to a Triad offshoot of the Taipings called the Small Swords Society. The fighting had devastated the surrounding countryside. Only the foreign enclave remained untouched and to it for safety and protection came Chinese refugees. Since 1845 the foreigner had forbidden the Chinese to live in the Settlements but these refugees arrived with gold and wanted houses. Suddenly, the ground on which foreign Shanghai stood proved more precious than tea, silk or even opium. The price of an acre jumped from about £74 before the Rebellion to as much as £12,000 in the early 1860s. The traders pulled down their compounds, bought land from the Chinese farmers (conveniently extending the Settlements) and built over their recreation ground. Even the British Consulate with its prime position overlooking the Soochow Creek and the Whangpoo felt tempted to let go a few acres in the city's first real-estate boom. Streets, shops and two-storey houses now covered the countryside behind the foreign warehouses on the Bund. The foreigners named the streets running from north to south after Chinese provinces and those from east to west after its cities. The Chinese living in Shanghai called the streets by number rather than name. Nanking Road was known as First Street, Jiujiang Road as Second and Hankow Road as Third.

The refugees set a precedent. Chinese saw the advantages of living at a distance from their own government, protected by the foreigner from arbitrary taxation and arrest as well as from the hazards of war. The number of Chinese in Shanghai jumped from 500 in 1850 to 70,000 in 1872. They were not allowed to vote in the Municipal elections even though their taxes formed the bulk of Municipal income. Their money made possible such future civic improvements as gas lamps, a post service and macadamized roads. Their presence in the Settlement showed Shanghai had learnt not just to survive but to profit from China's upheavals. Its prosperity depended on the country's vicissitudes.

The second half of the nineteenth century supplied plenty of these. Shanghai continued to grow and prosper as China fell apart. Chinese and Westerners alike identified Shanghai with the increasing success of the foreigner. 'What a change has come over the scene', observed one missionary with satisfaction in the 1860s. 'The foreigner is present and prominent everywhere; he is regarded, and with reason, as the depository and source of all wealth, influence and power ... in fact, foreigners are everything.'[12] This proved most evident in Shanghai's brothels. Sex, that otherwise great leveller, remained in the traditional colonial position of white male on top of yellow female. Chinese experiments in the other direction exemplified the attitude of East and West, fear on one side, contempt on the other and incomprehension all round. Foreign prostitutes, the Chinese reported, 'have big teeth and tousled hair' and 'are as ugly as devils and as frightful as lionesses. They freeze the hearts of beholders.' When the Chinese male finally plucked up courage to buy one, he discovered a contempt to rival his own. One Chinese was perplexed to find himself presented, as the *Shenbao*, Shanghai's leading Chinese newspaper reported on May 24th, 1872, with a naked foreign woman, 'lying on the couch with a handkerchief over her face'.[13]

China's complete subjection to the West allowed foreign domination of Shanghai. Even China's history at this point is of the foreigner in China rather than of China itself. The most important foreigner, both in Shanghai and China, was Great Britain. The First Opium War had coincided with a massive expansion of British colonial ambitions throughout the world. Strategically placed conquests stretching from Gibraltar to Hong Kong allowed the British to fuel boats and transport men with greater efficiency than any other Power in China. France for example had nothing between China and itself but Martinique and Algeria, until it acquired Madagascar in 1881. Britain always regarded China as an informal colony. It took what it could make money from and defend easily and left the hinterland untouched. In terms of investment the United States proved a distant second to Great Britain until the start of the new century. Absorbed in a civil war, it had been slow to move into China. By the 1900s it had acquired Hawaii and the Philippines and built up a large Pacific fleet. Its principal interest was mission work. American missionaries, inept at converting Chinese in any number, proved extraordinarily successful at influencing American public opinion and foreign policy.

Great Britain's approach set the tone for the occupation of China. Each of the Great Powers had their sphere of influence in which the others agreed not to trespass. This scene of cosy rapacity was brought to an end by the arrival of two new players. Russia and Japan profoundly affected Chinese history and the foreigners' position in China.

Since the fall of Napoleon, Russia had replaced France as Great

Britain's principal enemy. Russian territorial gains over the same period had matched Britain's. By the mid-nineteenth century their interests conflicted in a number of places. As the British lacked the army or resources to crush on land, they resorted to guile. They constructed a territorial washing line around Russia starting from the Baltic looping through Turkey, Iran, Afghanistan and China. Each country acted as a piece of washing to distract Russia from its firm march down the path of imperialism. As Russia tugged one country out of its way, the British would cunningly wave another at its head. China did not appear on the line until the last decade of the nineteenth century when Russia began collecting pieces of Manchuria. In 1896 the Tsarist government proposed extending the Trans-Siberian Railway across Manchuria with a supplementary line from Haerbin to Port Arthur. The Chinese Eastern Railway completed in 1903 had enormous significance. It allowed Russia economic penetration of Manchuria and the entire north of China. As the British saw to their disgust, not only goods but soldiers could be transported within weeks from the heart of Russia.

Russia's move startled the other Powers into a hasty scramble for first railway and then mining rights. At the same time Britain cast around for a means of putting the Russians in their place, which, for the British was the other side of the Amur River. The British had always relied on a surprise show of naval force in China, sufficient against the Chinese but inadequate for the Russians. The Americans declined to fight unless it proved easy and inexpensive. It was at this critical point that Japan asserted itself against the Chinese.

Japan had found contact with the West more fruitful than China (partly because the Japanese had successfully resisted any form of colonization, informal or otherwise). The arrival of the American navy under Commodore Perry in 1853 had forced Japan out of a self-imposed isolation and had started a fashion for the Occident. Japanese travelled to Europe and America to study factories, banking systems, armies and political institutions. They created a modern, industrial country with one of the highest literacy rates in the world and, by the 1920s, almost universal male suffrage. The country's first act, after shaking off its unequal treaties with America in 1894, was to copy the Western example and impose just such treaties on others, namely China. The two countries fought over Korea, a vassal to the Manchu for two hundred years. The Sino-Japanese War of 1894–5 ended with China's humiliating defeat at the hands of a neighbour it had always considered vastly inferior to itself. China and Japan concluded a peace treaty in Shimonoseki on April 17th, 1895. Two clauses guaranteed recognition of Japan on the same level as the Western powers and freedom for the Japanese to manufacture in the Treaty Ports.

The treaty transformed Shanghai from a trading port into an industrial city. Foreign traders soon copied the Japanese and built their own factories along the Whangpoo. Electricity and coal were cheaper and interest rates lower than in the rest of China while the inflated price of land allowed foreign and Chinese landlords to raise credit with ease. Continual unrest in the interior provided a labour force willing to work long hours for a small wage. The Japanese became an important member of the International Settlement.

They also saw themselves as a rival to Russia's holdings in Manchuria. Britain, envisaging a limited Japanese operation against its enemy, made a considerable loan to Japan. Thus encouraged the Japanese attacked the Russian fleet in Port Arthur in February 1904. Fifteen months later the Japanese defeated the Russian army and destroyed the Russian Baltic fleet after its painful journey half-way across the world. For the first time an Oriental had soundly trounced the West. The damage to the Tsar's prestige proved far-reaching in Russia. The discontent which swelled into the Russian Revolution of 1917 began the very summer Russia was forced to withdraw and leave the Chinese Eastern Railway to the Japanese. The battle was Japan's first venture into an area whose resources it used for the next four decades to fuel its military operations in China and the Far East. The British, despite warnings from America, continued to view Japan as their tool to take out or put away at will.

Japan's victories over China and Russia marked the lowest point in China's foreign relations. The Russo–Japanese war had been fought on Chinese soil without either side considering it necessary to ask China's permission. In the two Opium Wars and the Boxer Rebellion of 1900 a small foreign force had defeated large numbers of Chinese. The Manchu court under the Empress Dowager Ci Xi showed imagination and flexibility only in its choice of punishment for those advocates of reform. The Chinese living in Shanghai could see for themselves the urgent need for change if ever they wished to evict the foreigner from China. From the walls of the Chinese city they watched in awe the achievements of the International

Settlement, from the building of hospitals to the drilling of a well-disciplined, well-armed Volunteer Corp. In December 1872 the foreigners gave a demonstration of their new fire brigade to a Chinese crowd accustomed to frightening away the fire devil with drums and cymbals. The *Shenbao* reported it was a spectacular sight. Ten years later the same paper concluded sadly, 'In starting great projects, we Chinese lack the resolve of the Westerners.'[14]

The Chinese in Shanghai absorbed and finally set out to emulate. In 1905 the Chinese gentry, merchants and traders who lived outside the Settlements and fell under the jurisdiction of the Peking government, set up a city council. It was the first of its kind in China. Many Chinese had acquired a Western education at the schools and universities run by missionaries in the city. Others had benefited from foreign study in America and Europe and had chosen to settle in Shanghai on their return. It was these Western-educated Chinese who called with increasing strength for an overhaul of China's moribund institutions. They exerted tremendous influence on China's history during the first thirty years of this century – in 1929 four members of the new Chinese government had studied in American universities. As one British newspaper in Shanghai put it, 'The returned student can no longer be ignored. They have become the most hopeful force in the country . . . the foundation of reconstruction in China.'[15]

Shanghai, as the most Western city in China, attracted China's would-be reformers. The International Settlement and the French Concession offered protection and an alternative to the rigid social system many Chinese now despised. Their increasing identification with the city moved Shanghai from the position of foreign enclave on the edge of China to the centre of events shaping the country's future.

The first and most important of these events was the overthrow of the Manchu in 1911. The instigator and ideologist of the Chinese Revolution was Sun Yat-sen, still revered today by communist Chinese and Nationalists on Taiwan alike. The son of poor peasants from Guangdong, he grew up in an area imbued with the Taiping tradition. The success of his brother who had emigrated to Hawaii paid for a medical education in Hong Kong. As the most famous and influential of Western-educated Chinese, it is appropriate that he should have lived in Shanghai. I visited his house in the French Concession, now preserved with its contents as a shrine to his memory. It helps explain the attraction of Sun's message and the influence the city's eclectic mix of East and West had on him. Built in red brick with a small garden at the back, the house itself looks transposed from an English suburb. On the lawn, where China's leading left-wing intellectuals gathered, I almost expected to see a garden gnome thoughtfully fishing. Inside a hodgepodge of furnishings, a traditional Chinese chair, an American record player and a Samurai sword evokes the style of the Treaty Port Chinese. Sun's library is in the same vein. He stored manuscripts on Chinese history next to a biography of Washington, a complete Dickens and six volumes of Havelock Ellis including *Studies in the Psychology of Sex*. Even a photograph of Sun himself, taken on his return to Shanghai from Europe in 1911, contains these seemingly contradictory elements of East and West. Below the amused and sensual eyes of an Oriental is an Edwardian moustache, a high, stiff collar and a small, tightly knotted tie. This diversity of thought and taste was a prominent feature of the new Chinese approach to culture and politics. It owed much to Shanghai and the opportunities the city provided. It proved a strictly urban phenomenon, fascinating but finally too diffuse a message to impress the Chinese peasant after 1949. The influence of the Western-educated Chinese lasted just as long as the city.

The absence of any central government from the downfall of the Manchu in 1911 to the advent of the Communists in 1949 increased Shanghai's prominence. The period is characterized by the attempts of various Chinese leaders to exert physical control over the country. An almost continuous state of civil war existed with armies constantly on the move. The principal contestants fell into two categories: those who intended to rule China in traditional fashion and those who wished to experiment with Western ideologies. Sun Yat-sen, dismissed by Lenin as a man of 'inimitable – one might say virginal – naïveté', was soon supplanted by the more ruthless Yuan Shikai who tried to restore the Imperial tradition with himself as the new dynasty's first Emperor. His death in 1916 was followed by ten years of confused fighting between the military governors or warlords of the various regions, and a return to almost medieval conditions of squalor and terror for the populace.

As China collapsed into chaos during the 'twenties, Shanghai enjoyed some of its best years. The fighting affected neither the trade nor the river traffic on which the city depended. Refugees from the interior provided labour for Shanghai's factories while the better off enriched the city with their savings. An increasing confidence and a growing political awareness was revealed in a spate of new Chinese business ventures and the founding of the Chinese Communist party in 1921 in a Shanghai's girls' school located propitiously at Joyful Undertaking Street. Initially attracted by the city's large and unhappy proletariat, the party demonstrated its popularity three years later on May 30th, 1925 when the Settlement police fired upon a crowd of Chinese students, killing twelve. The communist-led, Shanghai Trade Union immediately called a strike. On June 1st 200,000 workers refused to go to work. They were joined by 50,000 university and secondary school students. Even Chinese businessmen, much to the discomfort of the International Settlement, had taken up the student slogan of, 'No taxation without representation!' The impressive display of anti-foreign feeling deeply disturbed the foreigner. The years of China's abasement appeared to be over.

As if to confirm this, a new spirit of nationalism spread through the country. In Guangdong, Sun Yat-sen's political party called the Guomindang or Nationalists, founded shortly after the revolution, had survived despite harassment from the local warlord. A year after Sun's death in 1925, his successor Chiang Kai-shek, in uneasy co-operation with the Chinese communists and with training and advice from the new communist regime in Russia, led a well-equipped force north. Its purpose was to unite the country and evict the foreigner. In the spring of 1927 he arrived in Shanghai where, with foreign help, he snatched the Nationalist party from the communists, in a battle which left many of his former allies dead in the city streets. By October 1928 Chiang Kai-shek had defeated a sufficient number of warlords to justify a tentative National government with its capital in Nanjing. He now set about convincing the West, especially Britain and America, that he was the best leader for China and a sound man to lend money to. He chose Shanghai where his carefully considered actions might have the maximum of publicity from Western journalists. He converted to Christianity and in a highly public wedding in the Western style married the girl with the right background for his plan. Song Meiling's father had been the close friend and financial backer of Sun Yat-sen. Her sister was Sun's second wife and she, educated in America, was the darling of the powerful missionary lobby in Washington. Chiang continued to impress Washington from his new capital in Nanjing where

26

his government issued a multiple of reforms, from factory acts to divorce. In Shanghai the foreigners were forced, among other things, to allow Chinese into the International Settlement's parks and to vote in Municipal elections.

Chiang had failed to eradicate all the Chinese communists in Shanghai. They regrouped and civil war broke out. In 1931 Japan invaded Manchuria and Chiang found himself fighting on two fronts. He abandoned his country to the Japanese and retreated west in order to save himself for a final confrontation with the communists whom he always considered the greater threat. A traditionalist at heart, his rule took on all the Manchu characteristics of despotism and incompetence. He all but destroyed Shanghai's Chinese business community in his efforts to extract money from the city. Even Meiling fell out of favour and was replaced, at least in private, with a young and docile concubine.

The success of the Japanese army in Manchuria encouraged the Japanese navy to try something similar in Shanghai. In 1932 and 1937 the city found itself the setting for two battles between the Chinese and Japanese. The destructive high spirits of each country's new-found nationalism coincided with the Depression in America and Europe and a loss of will to interfere in China's affairs. Shanghai could no longer depend on foreign intervention for its survival or prestige. After the defeat of the Chinese army in 1937, the Japanese invaded the Yangtze valley. Trade on the river was disrupted and access to the interior became almost impossible. Shanghai finally lost its source of wealth. By the time the Japanese seized the International Settlement in 1941 and marched the British into camps, it was a dead city.

Shanghai briefly revived in 1945 with the defeat of the Japanese only to fall to the communists in 1949 when Mao Zedong, in the ancient Chinese tradition of the peasant leader, restored central authority to China. Under communist slogans that recalled those of the Taiping rebels, he consolidated his grip on the country in a fashion reminiscent of a new emperor founding his dynasty. When his peasant generals marched into Shanghai they were disgusted by its squalor and sophistication and appalled by its independence. They soon showed that they preferred a dead city in their control to a prosperous one out of it. One can imagine a similar reaction from Chinese communists to Hong Kong today. Shanghai's individuality became its undoing. The interior, so long despised for its backwardness, nevertheless proved to be the true China. Shanghai was not and never could be. Without foreign protection, it was powerless to withstand the Chinese peasant. In the end, neither dollars nor a well-aimed kick could hold off the water-buffalo.

*   *   *

Brief history

1637	The first English trading ships arrive in Guangzhou
1757	The Chinese government restricts Western traders to Guangzhou
1839	The start of the First Opium War between China and Britain
1842	British forces plunder Shanghai The Opium War ends with the Treaty of Nanjing Shanghai is opened to international trade
1843	Treaty of the Bogue sets out 'most-favoured-nation' principle
1844	Sino–American Treaty of Wangsia includes clause on extraterritoriality
1850	Outbreak of the Taiping Rebellion
1853	Shanghai is occupied by the rebels Chinese seek refuge in the foreign settlements
1854	Shanghai's foreign inhabitants draw up the 'Land Regulations' First annual meeting of the Shanghai Municipal Council
1863	The British and Americans join to form the International Settlement
1864	End of the Taiping Rebellion
1894–5	The Sino–Japanese War concludes with the Treaty of Shimonoseki The Japanese build the first factories in Shanghai
1904–5	The Russo–Japanese War The Chinese in Greater Shanghai set up the first city council in China

1911   The Chinese Revolution, inspired by Sun Yat-sen, results in the overthrow of the Manchu dynasty

1912   Yuan Shikai is elected President of the Republic of China

1918   The Chicherin Declaration drawn up between the Bolsheviks and the Chinese government renounces extraterritoriality for Russians in China

1919   Chinese students demonstrate in Beijing against the decision of the Paris Peace Conference to award Shandong, previously held by Germany, to Japan. This demonstration marks the start of the May 4th Movement

1920   Civil war breaks out in China between the various warlords

1921   The first National Congress of the Chinese Communist party is held in Shanghai

1924   In Guangzhou the Guomindang and the Chinese Communist party, with assistance from Russia, form a united front

1925   A general strike by Chinese workers against Britain and Japan begins after a demonstration on May 30th in Shanghai
       Sun Yat-sen dies

1926   The army of the Guomindang sets out from Guangzhou with Chiang Kai-shek in command to seize China back from the warlords
       Chinese representatives are elected on to the Shanghai Municipal Councils of the International and the French Settlements

1927   Chiang Kai-shek splits with his communist allies in Shanghai

1928   Nanjing is made the capital of China after the success of the Northern Expedition and the defeat of the warlords

1931   Japan occupies Manchuria

1932   Japan invades Shanghai

1937   The outbreak of the second Sino–Japanese War
       The bombing of Shanghai

1941   The Japanese take over the International Settlement

1949   Shanghai falls to the Chinese communists

TWO

The White Russians

IN THE SPRING of 1927 a fictional group of young Chinese, all children of rich parents, sat in a Shanghai tea-house discussing China's future. Mao Dun, the eminent author, described in his novel, *Midnight*, how they had spent an exhilarating morning marching in demonstrations. Nothing like this had happened to them before. Now, the novelty of workers' rights and shabby tea-houses was wearing thin. They grew restless and argumentative until one young man exclaimed,

'I say, everybody, why do we have to bury ourselves in this god-forsaken hole on such a glorious day? I know a wonderful new pleasure-garden run by a White Russian – Rio Rita's. They've got good wine and good music, and there are White Russian princesses, princes' daughters, imperial concubines and ladies-in-waiting to dance attendance on you. Green, shady trees and lawns as smooth as velvet. And then there's a little lake for boating ... ah, it reminds me of the happy hours I spent on the banks of the Seine ... lily-white bosoms and thighs . . . and the burning passions of the French girls!'[1]

The young Chinese wanted to get back to normal and in Shanghai that meant crumpling up the revolutionary pamphlet and trying out the latest White Russian nightclub. Shanghai was famous for its nightclubs. In a city of numerous nationalities, they offered neutral ground on which to meet. Dancing, like sport and gambling, proved a pleasant way for people to socialize who had little else in common. Shanghai night life ranged from the ballroom of the Majestic Hotel, built in the shape of a four-leaf clover, to the sailors' bars in Blood Alley, where the price of a beer paid for a twelve-year-old behind a dirty curtain. The evening might begin with dinner and a cabaret at the Ambassador, the Casanova, or the Venus Café. It continued with high-balls at the Saint Anna Ballroom on Love Lane with its Filipino orchestra; or an absinthe at the semicircular bar of the French Club on Rue Cardinal Mercier, where I took a turn on the sprung dance floor. Hot nights were passed at the outdoor Pleasure Palace with its lighted walks, lined with trees and flowering shrubs. Late nights ended in the Little Club where a negro band played beneath a tent of grey velvet. 'All rather dim,' as one woman remembered, 'but deliciously romantic and very exciting.'

In nearly every nightclub, from the lowest in Blood Alley to the most expensive, worked the White Russians. They played in the orchestra or danced with customers, charging from ten cents to a dollar for a dance ticket depending on the place and their age. Their glamour and wildness created the mood which overtook Shanghai at night.

The Standard Shanghai Guidebook of 1934 estimated the city's White Russian community at about 25,000. They formed the largest foreign community after the Japanese. The White Russians originally came from Russia and belonged to that country's upper and middle classes, destroyed or dispersed by a succession of calamities. The survivors of the First World War trenches had returned to the upheaval of the Russian Revolution and the outbreak of civil war shortly after. They then had to make a choice between communism under Lenin or loyalty to the Tsar. Those who remained loyal were known as White Russians. The Bolshevik victory forced the White Russians to flee. The Europeanized nobility who spoke a foreign language and possessed a foreign bank account went to Europe. The less fortunate journeyed east across Siberia to Vladivostok on the Sea of Japan. After it fell to the Bolsheviks in 1920, they crossed into Manchuria to settle in Haerbin or continued south into China and the Treaty Ports of Tianjin and Shanghai. Other Russians came to China from Siberia itself. Between 1909 and 1913 350,000 families, many of them Jewish, had settled or had been exiled along the newly completed Trans-Siberian Railway. As the Bolshevik army moved across Russia, Siberia offered the last escape route.

The Bolshevik victory deprived the White Russians in Shanghai of citizenship and the benefits of extraterritoriality. Their uncertain status left them neither accepted by the Chinese and the foreign community nor wholly rejected. They, like the nightclub, represented neutral ground and a good time. Anyone would take them on for a tango, at least until the music stopped – beyond that was a different matter. The Russian temperament, it was generally agreed, disqualified them from the everyday world of business and matrimony. Their ambiguous position meant they could mix freely. Their lives extended into the poorest and richest parts of the city. They got everywhere and nowhere.

Their arrival profoundly affected the city. No one could think of Shanghai as a colony of white privilege while White Russians pulled rickshaws, begged for alms, died in the streets or became the favourite concubine, as one Chinese told me, of his wife's uncle. Their absorption into the city was complete. Shanghai was their home. They identified with and impressed their personality upon the city. How much Shanghai was them or how much they were Shanghai is hard to say. Unstable, corrupt, sentimental, brave and romantic; the attributes of the city and the race are interchangeable. I believed that if I understood the White Russian, I would understand Shanghai.

The previous experience of many White Russians partly explains their impact on the city. They had lost their families and homes and had travelled through some of the wildest areas of the world to escape. People had been indifferent and the cold unendurable. In San Francisco I met Olga whose father was an officer in the Imperial Army. She recalled the journey she made at the age of three from her home on the Volga far more vividly than her later years in Haerbin. Her family came two thousand miles by camel and it took three months to traverse the Steppes. For days they went without food or water, Olga's mother trying desperately to find something to boil.

Peasants charged them five gold roubles for a piece of bread. When they reached Lake Baikal in Siberia, they crossed on a sledge pulled by horses. The ice was twelve feet thick and the lake sixty miles wide. Olga huddled among the straw and sheepskins between her mother's legs to keep warm. Half-way across they rested and changed horses at a wooden cabin built on the ice. 'It was a trip through hell,' said Olga.

Many Russians never recovered. I met men and women in their eighties who talked of the past in the present tense. Photographs of the Tsar and Tsarina hung in their sitting-rooms. Each night they asked God to send Russia an Orthodox Tsar. It was as if their experience resembled a battered suitcase which they had never thought to unpack or throw away.

The majority of White Russians who reached Shanghai were former merchants, ex-army officers, rich peasants and university teachers. In the city's nightclubs they often claimed to be generals, counts and princesses but it was their very ordinariness which disturbed their foreign hosts. In background and education the White Russian reminded the foreign trader of himself. The similarity emphasized the gulf now between them. The White Russian had seen his brother put up against a wall and shot for wearing a white collar. He had to endure his wife giving French lessons and his daughter dancing with strangers. His predicament summed up the precarious existence of life for the foreigner in China. Sir William Keswick, whose family owned Jardine Matheson, put it in perspective. When news of Britain's defeat at Dunkirk reached him in Shanghai, he realized, 'My God, if the Germans invade England, that will be my fate!'

Citizens of Nowhere

Before the advent of the White Russians, Shanghai offered the foreigner little culture besides the occasional new film, attended by the foreign consuls and taipans in evening dress, or a performance of amateur theatricals. On summer evenings the Municipal Orchestra gave concerts in the park on the Bund. Rich foreigners drifted past in their houseboats. The less well-off arrived with their Chinese servant bearing a favourite wicker chair and a cocktail shaker.

From the 'twenties, nearly all the big hotels employed Russian orchestras and singers. Russian theatres like the Pribytkova and the Tomsky put on ballet and opera. Russian ballerinas danced before hotel guests. For the culturally ignorant came the opportunity for self-improvement. Impoverished Russians taught languages, horse-riding, fencing or how to play a musical instrument. White Russian artists and poets argued in cafés, founded societies and printed their controversies. By 1937 more Russian books were published in Shanghai than in Paris or Berlin. The famous journal, *Sovremenniye Zapiski*, transferred its printing from Paris to Shanghai in the same year. The Russian community supported two White Russian newspapers, the *Shanghai Zaria* (Shanghai Dawn) and *Slovo* (The Word) as well as countless literary clubs. A poet called Spurgot started the most popular in the autumn of 1933. Its members included painters, writers, actors, musicians and journalists. Elirov, the master of ceremonies and an eminent ballet dancer, gave each meeting a theme. 'The Fight Against Boredom',[2] the title of a poem dedicated to the association, describes the aim of these occasions and reveals an exercise in wishful thinking. The sentiment it expressed was more redolent of leisured, pre-revolutionary days than the harsh existence of Shanghai.

A Russian even penetrated the *North China Daily News*, Shanghai's most important foreign newspaper and the mouthpiece of the British community. In 1925 the editor appointed Georgi Sapojnikov, an officer in the Imperial Army, as the paper's cartoonist. He had originally been inspired by Christmas on the Front during the First World War. Under the signature of 'Sapajou' he produced a cartoon each day until 1949 when the paper closed. Every four years he took four months' leave when no pictures appeared. The *North China Daily News* apologized to its readers but admitted he was irreplaceable.

34

Everyone I interviewed spoke of him with affection and admiration. Many still kept Christmas cards drawn by him. He had the gift of reducing the complexities of Chinese politics to a single image and of capturing the ebullient, chaotic nature of Shanghai without sentimentality or cynicism. He appears in his own cartoons, a tall, thin man wearing a raincoat and looking overwhelmed or bemused by the events of the day. After the communist take-over in 1949 he joined the White Russian evacuation to the Hawaiian island of Tubabao where he died of cancer. A friend explained that he did not want to leave Shanghai and simply lost heart. Throughout his life he received tempting offers from newspapers around the world but preferred to stay in Shanghai. In one cartoon he imagines himself a dictator with the power to sort out the city's traffic, noise and overcrowding. Finally he sits back and smiles. 'We would change nothing,' he says. 'We like Shanghai as she is.'[3]

Russian musicians also improved the Municipal Orchestra. Enid Saunders Candlin, author of an evocative book on Shanghai, *The Breach in the Wall*, was the daughter of a tea merchant. A vital old lady in bright orange lipstick, she now lives in New York where she told me about her music teacher, a Mr Leibensohn from the St Petersburg Conservatory. Hardly five foot tall, he always appeared exhausted. She could not understand how he had had the will to leave everything he loved or survive the journey to China.

The White Russians built several Orthodox churches, famous for their choirs. At the midnight mass of the Easter cycle, the crowd of foreigners and Russians, each carrying a tall, white taper, was so great that annexes were erected to hold the overflow. At midnight arose the cry: 'Christos voskresi!' answered by the congregation, 'Vo istinu voskresi!'

Music meant everything to the White Russians. Hilary Wadlow recalled as a child visiting White Russian musicians in Avenue Joffre. They lived in tiny, damp cellars with nothing else in the room but a grand piano, a cello or a violin. Her White Russian piano teacher, who wore too much make-up and, 'stank like a badger', nagged Hilary to practise more. She said Russian children practised all day.

Russian children also outdid all others at the Christmas Carol service in the Town Hall. Every year Shanghai's schools entered their best singers; the British girls from the Cathedral School in their neat uniforms, the casually dressed Americans, the solemn, stiff-backed pupils of the Kaiser Wilhelm Schule and the French children from the Lycée. The White Russians, who looked the smallest and shabbiest, despite polished shoes and bows tied in the girls' hair, performed last. Without any fidgeting, they stepped forward, the conductor lifted his baton and at once the children sang out in four parts. Foreigners had little respect for the White Russian community but this performance always won admiration.[4]

White Russian women opened dress salons and beauty parlours and brought a sense of style and luxury to the city. Madame Garnet ran the most expensive dress shop in town on the ground floor of the Cathay Hotel. Lady Jellicoe described the White Russian owner as 'staggering'. She was married to a 'dashing' Italian naval officer and looked like Evita Peron. Pencil-slim with blonde hair, she refused to make clothes for anyone over a certain width. Lilo Philips, a German who lives in Tokyo and is still pencil-slim herself, recalled that Madame Garnet's customers had no say in the design except to mention for what occasion they wanted the dress. Madame Garnet used only French silks and jerseys and hand-stitched everything. Lilo Philips still wears her things. Once she took a friend whom Madame Garnet disliked on sight. She said nothing but produced, as Lilo said, 'an ugly garment covered in sequins and bows which my friend adored'. Every evening Madame Garnet took the lift to the ballroom on the top floor of the Cathay Hotel with its views across the Whangpoo. There she danced the tango with her husband. He was a dark, handsome man; she was always exquisitely dressed, her hair pulled back into a heavy chignon. They danced beautifully together. No one could take their eyes off them.

The heart of the White Russian community was Avenue Joffre in the French Concession, known as 'Little Russia'. Day and night, unemployed Russians dawdled here, many poorly dressed. Girls who had just arrived still wore their hair in plaits. Shop signs in Cyrillic script swung above their heads. The smell of fresh bread and cakes from famous White Russian bakeries like De De's tantalized. From the numerous Russian restaurants and bars drifted the sound of music and singing. Even in the smallest place, a violinist made his way from table to table.

The lack of extraterritoriality affected every newcomer to Avenue Joffre, including the most prosperous. Michael Schiller's family were Russian Jews. His father, a music graduate from St Petersburg Conservatory, played the cello in Shanghai's famous orchestra. Michael attended the Shanghai Public School, one of the best in the city. The

British boys often talked of Home. He told me bitterly, 'Home was always somewhere else, never the playing fields of Shanghai. The city was my only home and it rankled.' Michael Schiller, unlike his classmates, lacked an official identity except for a piece of worthless paper issued by the League of Nations. He did not possess a passport until he arrived in the United States in 1946.

The White Russians were subject to Chinese laws, courts and prisons. George Gladky was arrested in the French Concession during a drunken brawl and sentenced to seven days' imprisonment by the Chinese Second Special District Court in the middle of June 1932. He arrived in prison with dysentery. At first the Chinese guards laughed at his repeated demands for water; then they became angry, entered the cell and beat him with the butts of their rifles. Gladky did not resist and only occasionally screamed when they poked his chest with bamboo stakes. The guards left him lying on the floor covered in blood. When he came to, he called for a doctor. The guards returned and thrashed him again, this time more severely and from that he died. Learning of his illness, George's brother rushed to the jail. The Chinese prison authorities said that they had never heard of a George Gladky. After some persuasion they promised to look for the body and let him have it for burial. But first he had to complete a form – in Chinese. As one Russian remarked to me, 'We were under Chinese law: that was all right but we were also under Chinese whim and that wasn't.' In 1931 the Japanese invaded Manchuria and made the happy discovery, as Peter Fleming witnessed, that 'you can beat White Russians up till you are blue in the face, because they are a people without a status in the world, citizens of nowhere'.[5]

Lack of status affected their relationship with the other foreigners in Shanghai. At first the White Russians were treated with respect. On November 11th, 1922, the Captain of the S.S. *Corestan* called on the British Consul in Haerbin. Three days before sailing, White Russians fleeing the communists inundated his ship. He was unable to take them all. Even if he did, would he get them off again? The British Consul guaranteed their landing rights in Shanghai and told the Captain to accept as many as possible. In his report, the Consul described the Russian refugees as a better class of person with considerable quantities of gold roubles, unlikely to become destitute for some time.

When the roubles ran out and other refugees arrived with no

roubles and not even a change of clothes, the foreign community panicked. They had always depended on an aura of superiority to make up for their lack of numbers. How could this continue, one British newspaper demanded, when white women, driven by unemployment and the need to support their families, offered themselves to the Chinese of the lowest classes? It was a spectacle to affect 'the prestige of the white nations in the Orient' and converted the problem into an international issue of 'considerable' importance.[6]

Some foreigners turned a cold shoulder. One White Russian recalled that the British behaved worst of all. 'A couple of servants and they thought they were God Almighty.' Young men arriving at the British Country Club with a White Russian girl received a severe set-down. White Russian women caused further embarrassment when they wished to wed foreign husbands and acquire that magical attribute, a passport and a country. Most British firms sacked the men who succumbed.

The British considered marriage to a White Russian almost as bad as marriage to an Eurasian. Both were 'mixed' marriages. This appeared still the case as late as 1937 when the *North China Daily News* started a Russian column. By then a White Russian wife did not deprive a man of his job but she was expected to underplay her nationality. She had to stop speaking Russian and seeing her Russian friends. The Russian column in her husband's newspaper served as the only link to her community. The *North China Daily News* thought the column an example of the city's capacity to absorb different cultures, which indeed was a 'valuable quality in these difficult days',[7] but, by 1938, a bit late and beside the point.

People who were children at the time recalled the White Russian as an exotic, somewhat repellent, creature who visited the house but never stayed to dinner. An American woman described a former countess who taught her mother French once a week. The little girl stared in fascination at the woman's dyed, red hair which changed shade with each application until one memorable occasion when it turned purple. Apart from her extraordinary coiffure, the countess always wore a lace jabot. No matter what the weather or the outfit, the jabot remained in place. To the countess it represented a talisman against destitution. She had convinced herself that no one in a lace jabot could starve. Other foreign children remembered White Russians as objects of charity – long, shuffling lines of unhappy people to whom they handed out blankets and oranges at Christmas.

For their part the White Russians complained of exclusion from the good jobs in the Municipal administration. By 1937 the International Police force had failed to promote one of its many White Russian employees to inspector. Municipal commissions lacked a White Russian representative. The Russian community, wrote one of its journalists, was saturated with Shanghai patriotism; many considered the city their second home; yet, in spite of the hard work and sacrifice of the last fifteen years, they were still considered citizens 'not only of the second, but sometimes of the third order'.[8]

Foreigners dismissed the White Russian as emotional, untrustworthy and usually drunk. He could not compare with the diligent and thrifty Chinese. Neither the Chinese nor the foreigner understood the mentality of a man who spent a month's salary on one night out. The poor Chinese and White Russian faced the same problem of daily survival. The White Russian's reaction of desperate gaiety appeared as revolting to the Chinese as gluttony does to the careful eater.

Nothing in the White Russian background had prepared them for survival in Shanghai. Most were from comfortable, middle-class homes. They had attended university or military school. A career as an officer, a businessman or a professor stretched ahead but then came the Revolution and a very different future. Enid Saunders Candlin recalled the White Russian woman who taught French at the Shanghai American School. When the Revolution broke out, she was away helping her sister with a new baby. She never got back to her home, never saw her husband and son again.

Shanghai turned out to be just another in the series of catastrophes for the White Russians. Many gave up, like the starving factory worker described by Malraux in his novel *Man's Estate*, who one day kills himself leaving behind four children and a wife so 'mad with anger' that she slaps the corpse until the children, crouching in the corners of the room, ask, ' "Why are you fighting?" '[9] Others acquired a dazed expression, drank, told lies and had fun. Reality had proved a grotesque joke. Safety, sanity even, lay in fantasy. They brought to Shanghai an air of carnival time but of a carnival that ended too often in tears and rainstorm.

Shanghai in the 'twenties and 'thirties was a place and a time unable to assuage the White Russian need for security and order. Life for them flipped back and forth between Western ease and respectability one moment, Oriental poverty and hopelessness the next. The force that tossed the switch was unpredictable – a new war, a lost job or a stolen wallet. A White Russian bodyguard explained the position: 'Once a year we had a Russian Ball in the Majestic Hotel. It was very popular. If I had my smoking jacket, I went. If it was in the pawnshop, I didn't.'

The Sweetest and Cleanest Girls in the Whole Town

The suffering endured by many White Russians to reach Shanghai shaped their impact on the city. Valentin V. Fedoulenko's story is typical. He served as an officer in the First World War and was in St Petersburg with his regiment when the October Revolution broke out. He managed to escape back to his home town of Kazan on the Volga as yet unaffected by events in the capital. Kazan's legal society invited him to give an after-dinner speech on his experiences. He described the insults to officers, the arbitrary arrests and the beatings. The lawyers clapped politely but refused to believe him. They thought war wounds had affected his brain.[10]

At first it seemed they were correct. By the time the Bolsheviks arrived, Fedoulenko had become a store manager and had acquired a wife. Then the killings began. The Bolsheviks went through the city systematically, arrested anyone of consequence, put them in a basement and shot them. By August the anarchy had spread to the surrounding towns. The Bolsheviks forced businessmen and bureaucrats on to barges on the Volga then blew them up.

Kazan fell unexpectedly and briefly to the White Russian army led by General Kappel. Fedoulenko joined Kappel, fought and lost and found himself in the retreat from Omsk in November 1919. Wives and children accompanied the army. Hundreds died of disease and cold.

Fedoulenko's wife reached Vladivostok separately from her husband and escaped to Shanghai with the help of the captain of a Japanese boat. The White army retook Vladivostok but lacked supplies and pay for its soldiers. Fedoulenko worked with a group of officers as stevedores on the Vladivostok docks. He also fried coffee on the streets. Sometimes he sold mustard and vinegar. Then news came of a communist push on the city. The White Russians, demoralized, half-starved and lacking ammunition, had given up all hope when an Admiral Stark offered them an alternative. The Admiral had acquired the last taxes collected by the Tsar's representatives from the Russian Maritime Provinces. He now bought and provisioned the remaining thirty or forty boats in Vladivostok harbour, mostly mail and messenger ships but also including harbour tugs and even two large ice-breakers. The White Russian fleet set sail for Korea, the first foreign country where they might stop safely.

What went through Fedoulenko's mind as he looked back at Russia for the last time? He said: 'We had no plans, only that we could leave and go any place so as to escape the Bolsheviks. Outside of that we had no plans. Whatever would be in the future, anything would be better than to be caught by them. This is what our thoughts were at the time.'

Admiral Stark sent Fedoulenko ahead to Shanghai to arrange permission for the fleet to enter the harbour. Fedoulenko turned first for help to the small but wealthy Russian community of bankers, tea merchants and consular officials headed by a Mr V. Grosse, Deputy Commissioner for Russian Affairs. Grosse, described scathingly by Fedoulenko as 'a typical Baltic German', passed him on to an assistant. In desperation, Fedoulenko tried the British Port Authorities who gave permission for the fleet to stay two or three weeks. They even provided a welcoming party in the form of a harbour boat and an English officer. A foreign visitor to the fleet was amazed to find the decks cramped with household goods from pots and pans to cots and even nappies hanging on the five-inch guns of one boat. Fedoulenko said the English and other foreigners showed him 'curiosity' and even 'sympathy'. Grosse, on the other hand, remained uninterested. When the fleet arrived, Madame Grosse told the men to return to Russia where the new government would give them work. Fedoulenko said, 'Our sailors almost threw her overboard for this. We were barely able to save her.'

Admiral Stark now badgered the Americans to allow his fleet into Manila harbour. In the end they gave him permission but refused landing rights. As Fedoulenko remarked, 'Admiral Stark said that we would all go ashore and just squat there.' Once again the fleet needed provisions. The indefatigable Admiral turned on the Chinese authorities. He said that Russian soldiers 'would take matters in their own hands', unless something was done. The Chinese hastily assigned him SH$20,000 and ferried food and coal to the ships. The coal turned out to be coaldust supplied by a greedy Chinese contractor. Admiral Stark sent it back with further abuse. The Settlement authorities had to intervene before the ships could depart. At this point Fedoulenko decided to settle for Shanghai rather than risk an uncertain future on a Filipino beach. At Manila the Admiral sold the fleet and divided the proceeds among his men. Fedoulenko received enough to open a pharmacy in the French Concession. The last he heard of Admiral Stark was from Paris where Stark had rejoined his family and found work as a taxi driver. He had refused his share of the boat money and died a poor man.

In Shanghai Grosse reacted to the refugee crisis very differently from the compassionate and resourceful Admiral. Where danger had made a hero of Stark, it reduced the Consul to a small and anxious functionary. He did not understand the refugees and feared they might endanger his position. He was quick to inform the Shanghai Municipal Police when a group disembarked without permission and, unable to resist impressing the authorities, added that he had already found work for them – as labourers on a sugar plantation in the Hawaiian Islands. When the refugees asked for assistance, Grosse informed them that he had nothing to contribute. The refugees, accustomed to Admiral Stark's imaginative use of public funds, pointed out that he possessed 160,000 gold roubles from the former Tsar's treasury. As loyal subjects of the Tsar, and in want, they considered themselves the proper recipients. At first Grosse blustered. When pressed, he admitted that he had already sent the money to the Chairman of the Russian Imperial Ambassadors in Europe. The refugees retired stupefied. As Fedoulenko explained, Grosse held a 'Germanic contempt for us even though he had been a servant of Imperial Russia'. A band of infuriated Cossacks wrote to Grosse, promising, among other things, that 'You shall soon be in the place to which you belong.' This last threat Grosse dared not dismiss with his Baltic disdain. Cossacks were notorious troublemakers. He sent an urgent letter to the Municipal Police begging for protection while directing them to a house in Yangtzepoo Road where 'the most aggressive of the malcontents'[11] took their meals.

Muza Potapoff described to me the kind of future Shanghai offered a cadet from Admiral Stark's fleet. I met her on the doorstep of the Russian Community Centre in San Francisco. On Thursday the centre offers a cheap lunch and entertainment. The week I attended, a middle-aged American woman with spectacles and a T-shirt gave a performance in a Hawaiian skirt. Her undulations failed to impress one group of old men. They picked up their table and carried it to the furthest corner of the room. There they slapped the plastic top and shouted for more tea. Their shaved heads and abrasive manner recalled Grosse's difficult Cossacks. I went up to find out but they waved me aside. They had no time for women, they said. A woman was good for only one thing and they were too old for that now. On my way out, I noticed Muza Potapoff. Despite old age, she wore a smart hat and walked with a straight back, attributes I had learnt to associate with women who once lived in Shanghai. We sat in the sun and she told me about her husband who had been a cadet in Admiral Stark's fleet.

Gregory was eighteen when he left the fleet at Shanghai and he owned nothing but his cadet uniform. The Municipal authorities arranged a billet for him and his fellow cadets near Hongkew Park but failed to make plans for the boys' future. Some days they did not even receive enough to eat. The cadets spent their time walking in the park. One afternoon a child approached Gregory and said in Russian, 'My brother is also a cadet.'

'What's his name?' asked Gregory.

'George,' replied the other.

Wishing to please the child, Gregory exclaimed, 'That's my name too!'

The boy's mother introduced herself and they sat and talked. She and her husband were Russians and had lived in Shanghai for many years. Gregory explained he wanted to work but knew no English. The lady's husband owned a construction business and needed an assistant. The next morning Gregory presented himself and got the job – the only cadet out of his class to find one. The same charm and initiative won him Muza.

Muza was born in Vladivostok where her father owned a large estate on which he bred horses for the Russian army. A year before the communists arrived in 1922, Muza's father had started to sell horses to the Japanese army. When the communists took over the town, the Japanese offered Muza's family a permanent visa to live in North Korea, under their control since the Sino–Japanese war of 1894–5. Few other foreigners were similarly complimented and Muza, now aged fifteen, met only Japanese and Koreans. At twenty, she received a proposal through her Japanese nurse from a descendant of a Samurai. Her father was away at the time but the nurse and Muza's mother pressed her to agree. Outraged – 'I knew how they treated their women' – Muza announced her ambition to live in Shanghai with her mother's sister. Her parents finally consented and her father bought her a light-blue evening dress from Haerbin and a third-class ticket for Shanghai. He must have assumed his daughter's good looks and feisty spirit would do the rest. His judgment was vindicated even before the boat reached China. Norwegian sailors in the third class were causing Muza trouble. One of the ship's servants reported her predicament to the Japanese captain. Her protestations of poverty made in polite Japanese so charmed him that he had her moved into first class at no extra cost.

Muza's aunt lived in the French Concession. She was less well-educated than Muza's mother but good-natured and eager to find Muza a husband. She invited six Russian factory workers to meet her niece. Muza's first encounter with the Russian male proved a disappointment. After they left, she rounded on her aunt.

' "I don't like one of them!" I declared.

' "Well, I can see you are a cut above them," she admitted. Then she said, "A friend of mine has a former cadet living with her. She owes me some money, she can send him instead." '

Muza was sitting on the veranda the evening Gregory walked up to the house. He smiled and she noticed that he had nice teeth and eyelashes. They talked together until midnight. He had heard of her father. Next day he arrived with a box of chocolates and invited Muza to a dance at the Russian ex-officers' club. Her mother had forbidden her to go to parties without a chaperone, Muza explained regretfully. Gregory promptly invited the aunt as well. Muza put on the evening dress and set off with a light heart to discover if waltzing with a man in Shanghai was any different from dancing lessons with her English governess in Vladivostok.

The cadets had rented a hall and an orchestra. They assigned guests to particular tables. People did not move to another without a formal introduction. Muza was deliriously happy. 'It was the sort of evening I had dreamt of in Korea.' She and Gregory married four months later.

The Municipal Council offered Gregory a job with the high salary usually reserved for British employees. They lived in a pleasant house with a number of servants. Every summer Muza visited her family in Korea. Shanghai had treated them well, I said. Her face suddenly puckered and she looked away before saying, 'My husband died at thirty-four from a heart attack. He was an alcoholic. He always worked hard, woke up every morning at five however much he had drunk the night before. I think too much happened to him too young. He never got over it. Neither I nor Shanghai could make up for his loss. That was why he drank.'

In San Francisco I also met Boris Vladimirovitch and his wife Olga. Both in their eighties, they lived on the ground floor of a clap-board house crowded with books, papers and heavy, dark furniture. A marmalade cat slept on top of a box of old files. 'Olga is a poetess,' said her husband in explanation. Whatever time I arrived at, Boris would disappear immediately into the kitchen and prepare pastries, ham, and cods' roe which we ate with sour cream and black bread. Boris poured brandy for us and we toasted Shanghai. As we talked he produced albums, photographs, Christmas cards, a certificate from the Chinese Military School issued by the warlord, Zhang Zuolin, and, finally, his prized possession, a larger and much grander certificate, stamped with red seals which he had received on passing out of cadet school in Russia.

Even in his late eighties, Boris Vladimirovitch is a solid, tough-looking man. When Valentin Fedoulenko was selling mustard on the streets of Vladivostok, Boris was sitting in a train on the border between the Russian Maritime Province and China. January 1922 was very cold, he recalled. At the border station defeated White Russian soldiers, 'in a terrible state', filled every railway carriage. The Chinese forced the men to hand over their weapons and enter internment camps. Boris did not blame the Chinese: 'We had fought in the Great War and then our own Civil War. Some of us had held a rifle in our hands for seven years. What do you do with 17,000 desperate men?'

Manchuria was under the control of Zhang Zuolin, one of China's most powerful warlords. That winter, faced with an uprising in his province and a collection of armed White Russians on his border, he solved both problems with an offer of work. Boris Vladimirovitch shrugged, 'Why did the Russians go into the Chinese army? It wasn't a very nice way of living, that's for sure. We did so because of the foxy way the Chinese General lured us in.' Zhang Zuolin promised to rearm every Russian who served in his army for a certain period and to allow them to return to the Maritime Provinces to fight the Bolsheviks.

A Colonel Chekhov took charge of recruitment. Boris admitted that he did not believe joining up would lead to an uprising against the Bolsheviks but the pay of ninety silver dollars a month proved alluring enough. The Chinese encouraged the Russians to recruit each other with inducements of higher rank. One man emerged a captain because he arrived with sixty experienced cavalrymen. The White Russians supplied Zhang Zuolin with the most efficient fighting force in the country.

The warlord's new followers fought in Chinese greatcoats and Tartar hats. The Chinese called them Tartars after their headware. They campaigned against ill-trained peasant boys. Most Chinese soldiers only fought until they had accumulated enough plunder to return home and buy a decent wife. When they saw Russian hats, they ran away. 'We went through Chinese troops like a knife through butter,' said Boris with satisfaction. He offered to find me a photograph of himself taken at the time. He disappeared into his wife's study, moved the cat and returned with two black and white snaps. The first showed a stunted sapling in a desolate landscape. Next to the tree stood four young men in greatcoats, their faces frowning against the light. Clumps of blond hair shot out from beneath their Tartar hats. The second photograph displayed three Chinese heads hanging by hooks pierced through their ears. The faces grimaced as if with toothache. Boris Vladimirovitch explained that the heads belonged to merchants who insisted they had no provisions. Boris's general decapitated two or three before the others brought out their goods. I stared in bewilderment at the snaps, then at Boris. His story conjured up a mythical past of barbarism and adventure. I almost expected the old man opposite me to admit to dragon-slaying and have a picture to prove it. Boris, sipping his brandy and stroking his cat, appeared unaware of the incongruity. I asked for more photographs. Boris looked amazed. 'What do you expect? We were living in savagery. Two pictures are miracle enough!' But who owned a camera in a warlord's army and why those particular shots? I persisted. Boris said he could not remember, and continued.

The Russian officers taught the soldiers formations and commands according to the old, Russian military manner. They travelled across China in an armoured train equipped with a bakery as they refused to eat Chinese food. Did he have Chinese friends? I asked. He said it was difficult to know what a Chinese was thinking. The White Russians had little contact with them. Russian officers worked out all operational and military details. Beside the interpreters, the only other Chinese in the train were the cooks and they cooked Russian food.

Boris said, 'I was twenty-six, alive and in good health, which was something, but we were living among the Chinese. I missed European society.' A group of his friends decided to subscribe to a White Russian newspaper published by the emigré community in Haerbin. The poems by a woman called Olga Alexeyevna Skopichenko caught their attention. Boris admitted, 'I am not a very understanding man in such a subtle matter as poetry but hers were patriotic and nostalgic so it appealed to me.' He and ten others wrote to her. In the end only Boris continued the correspondence.

In 1926 Boris advanced on Shanghai as part of Zhang Zuolin's Northern Army which was defeated by the Nationalist army under Chiang Kai-shek, trained and equipped by the new Bolshevik regime in Russia. Once again Boris found himself retreating from communists. The collapse of Zhang Zuolin left him out of a job and owed 700 silver dollars. Thankful to be alive (the graves of 2,000 White Russian officers and men lay between Shanghai and Manchuria), he decided to find work in the city.

Shanghai was seriously overcrowded. Chinese willing to labour for no more than a floor to sleep on and a handful of rice performed most manual jobs. Well-paid posts went to foreigners while Eurasians and Portuguese monopolized clerical and shop work. Boris had nothing to recommend him but a youth spent fighting. The owner of a lumber boat took him on as a guard.

On Christmas Eve pirates attacked the boat and shot Boris in the leg. He explained exactly to me how it had happened – the angle of the sun, the position of the boat and the luck of the pirates. An ambulance picked him up from the wharf and took him to the French hospital. The hospital staff were busy looking after students and workers injured in the demonstrations taking place in Chapei. They abandoned Boris in a corridor. Four hours later he was preparing himself for death – 'After all I had survived, it seemed like a sick joke' – when his correspondent, Olga Alexeyevna Skopichenko walked in. During the upheaval of the last six months, they had lost touch. Neither knew of the other's whereabouts until Olga heard friends discuss Boris's accident. Appalled by his condition when she found him – 'They had not even given him a tetanus injection' – she summoned doctors and nurses and bullied them into activity. Boris recalled with pleasure the fuss she made and pulled out another photograph, this time of Olga in a book about Shanghai's most eminent White Russians. A large, voluptuous woman with soft hair and a wide mouth, she continued to visit Boris regularly. I wondered what they talked about. As a leading member of the Russian artistic community and a founder of the Shanghai Churayevka, a literary association which met once a week, her life was a complete contrast to Boris's. Sixty years later she sat opposite him still, smoking steadily, saying little, appearing amused, even soothed by his volubility. By the time Boris left hospital this unlikely couple had fallen in love and they married shortly after. Boris looked for another job and was hired by a Mr Lu as his bodyguard.

The White Russian bodyguard, gun slung over a shoulder or tucked under an arm as he balanced precariously on the running board of a rich man's car, became a familiar sight in Shanghai. For many it epitomized the dangerous, exotic existence offered by the city. Wealthy Chinese employed bodyguards to insure against kidnapping. Shanghai's gangs and secret societies snatched the retired warlords and officials as well as the compradores and businessmen who had chosen to live in the comparative safety of the International Settlement and the French Concession. Many of the rich Chinese I interviewed had been taken. One spent most of his childhood with gangsters. They appeared to view the crime as an acceptable risk of city life, rather like a traffic accident or the typhoon floods in August. Mr Lu was held for three months before the Municipal Police rescued him 'with a great deal of shooting'. A renewed spate of threatening letters convinced him to hire Boris.

A Confucian in the old style, Mr Lu impressed Boris with his gentlemanly attributes. He had inherited his wealth. He shunned ostentation and innovation and lived his life according to the pattern laid down by his forefathers. He never showed anger or raised his voice but expressed himself clearly and quietly. He refused to wear Western clothes, preferring a long, blue Chinese gown lined in winter with red fox. He remained respectful towards his father who was an opium addict and faithful to his wife. Mr Lu's household must have been very reassuring to a White Russian, old-fashioned himself, after the turmoil of the previous eight years. Boris explained, 'When I first arrived in Shanghai I was a rough man out of the army. His example was my education. I regarded him as a philosopher and teacher.'

Boris earned SH$100 a month and received an extra SH$20 a month in tips. (As an employee of the Shanghai Municipal Council, Muza Potapoff's husband had been paid SH$900 a month.) Guests invited to weddings and parties gave three to five silver dollars wrapped in red paper for the bodyguards and drivers. The host also provided them with an excellent dinner.

Boris described for me a typical day in the life of a Shanghai bodyguard. The morning commenced with a round of Mr Lu's businesses. First they visited his exchange shop, one of many scattered about the city offering Shanghai's residents nearly every currency in the world. Mr Lu's shop even dealt in Soviet money. It was a small, shabby outfit with no decoration but for a line of baskets hanging out of holes in the ceiling. The offices, Boris explained, were upstairs, out of sight. The customer placed his money in a basket which immediately disappeared through the hole to return with the new currency and a receipt. While waiting he could help himself to the boxes of matches dangling from a piece of string or pour a cup of tea from the hanging teapot. 'The Chinese knew how to look after their customers,' said Boris approvingly. Despite appearances, Mr Lu's exchange shop made SH$50,000 a day.

From the exchange shop they called on Mr Lu's furniture company, then a paint-supply shop and, finally, a hotel. 'My boss even manufactured his own brand of sheets,' said Boris with pride. During these visits Boris sat outside in order to watch the door and scrutinize the passers-by. He explained, 'If you are living as long in China as me you can tell a gangster by small things,' and, eyes narrowing on a point beyond Olga and me, he spoke as if he were seeing the man once again walk down the street towards him. 'Maybe he tilts his hat, a little to one side, so; or he has turned the wide sleeves of his Chinese gown back and folded his white, silk underwear over the cuff; or maybe he is walking towards you exercising his fingers with two metal balls; or perhaps he has stopped at the corner and is using his fan, that is all right but, as he moves off, he tucks his fan down the back of his collar which is a bad sign; or his cigarette sticks to his bottom lip and he lets it hang there while he speaks to a girl. Any one of these signs made me suspicious and I would watch every move the man made. He was the sort to kidnap my boss again.' I found Boris's description so vivid that a year later, when a former Red Guard approached me on a Shanghai street, I instinctively drew back. Here was Boris's gangster in modern disguise.

At lunchtime Boris returned to his boss's home where Mrs Lu cross-questioned him on her husband's movements. If Boris faltered, she checked up on him as well. Boris shook his head. 'She was a very jealous type even though Mr Lu never visited girlfriends and I should know!' When Boris joined them, the Lus had six sons. Five years later, the family had grown to nine sons and one daughter. A concubine, I said, might have provided a welcome respite. 'Mr Lu believed in restraint,' said Boris severely.

The arrival of the Chinese communists in 1949 put an end to the White Russian community in Shanghai. Boris and Olga, refugees once again, sailed for Tubabao, an island in the Pacific. There they lived in beach huts with their fellow nationals until America took them in. 'The Americans thought we were Red Russians,' explained Boris. 'It took a long time to persuade them otherwise.' Boris now offered to drive me to where I was staying. It was a very old car and Boris preferred the middle of the road. He scolded, 'You should not think of walking. This is a bad neighbourhood. There are very dangerous people around.' In the afternoon sun of a San Franciscan spring it looked peaceful enough. Boris shook his head and honked at a car full of blacks. One waved what appeared to be a knife at us. 'Suspicious types are the same everywhere,' said Boris smugly and turned down a side street.

Boris Vladimirovitch was lucky. He was, at least, qualified for the dangerous jobs on offer. The majority of White Russians in Shanghai had enjoyed a comfortable existence in a semi-feudal society. Shanghai's ferocious capitalism destroyed them. During the first ten years many White Russians took to drink, especially young men with no families. People recalled White Russians and Chinese beggars dying together on the streets.

The difficulties encountered by White Russian men compelled their women to earn a living. Again, Eurasian and Chinese competition made office and shop work unobtainable. Women with families to support were forced to take up 'taxi dancing'. Every evening they sat around the city's dance halls waiting for a man to buy a book of tickets and spend one on them. The work increased their ambivalent status. Some used their job to become prostitutes or acquire a foreign husband. Others returned home to cook breakfast for aged fathers.

The Russian dance hostess, like the bodyguard, formed the quintessential image of the White Russian in Shanghai. One Englishman remarked to me, 'They were beautiful, unstable, haughty and desperate and very, very fascinating.' He was showing me an album of his Shanghai days. The photographs all displayed stiff, overweight English in wicker chairs or at race meetings. I flipped to the last page and found a snap of a lovely girl, half-lying on a lawn, laughing up at the camera. The naturalness of her pose and the vivacity of her expression made me ask if she was a White Russian. The man looked uncomfortable and glanced towards the kitchen where his wife was making us tea. 'Yes,' he said, finally. 'She was in love with a friend of mine,' and he closed the album and put it away.

Hallett Abend, an American journalist based in Shanghai, had a less happy experience. Beneath their prettiness, he found the White Russian hostesses dull, greedy and with a preference for perfume rather than soap. He continued, 'As a class they were indifferent and inexpert harlots, but as mistresses (once their affections were genuinely aroused) they were ardent. And usually unfaithful.'[12]

The best White Russian hostesses worked in Del Monte. A number of men recalled the dance hall for me with affection and nostalgia. By 1927 it had become a grand affair with a wide veranda and a large garden. A few men mentioned rooms upstairs but refused to elaborate. Del Monte had started in the early 'twenties as 'a little café of shoddy dimness' specializing in pre-dawn ham and eggs. There was no upper floor and the girls impressed one American journalist with their good breeding. They danced for a dime a number and supported whole families on their few English phrases of 'Allo,' 'Goodbye, please,' 'You nice' and 'Please buy vun small bottle vine.'[13]

In other dance bars, girls quickly informed their partners, 'You won't find me here next month. I'll be in Casanova or Del Monte's.' The less scrupulous worked in places like the Tumble Inn whose business card ran thus:

TUMBLE INN
No.14, Lane 182 Bubbling Well Road
(Opposite the Union Jack Club)
with the
Sweetest and Cleanest Girls
in the whole town

(Examined once a week by Dr. R. Holper, M.D.)
Shanghai[14]

An English reporter has left a description of a similar establishment in Haerbin which is nonetheless typical of the bars catering to sailors in a port like Shanghai. The inn did not pay the girls a salary but expected them to pick up customers, agree on a price and take them outside. To the reporter the prostitutes appeared like bereaved children, sitting in bevies about the room. Whenever they relaxed, their faces took on a haggard and hungry expression. Half-way through the evening the management proudly announced a parade of nudity. The young women exhibiting themselves bit their lips in constraint and embarrassment. The patrons appeared to have enjoyed the act even less than the girls.[15]

Most business went on in the summer when heat and humidity drove foreign wives and children to seaside resorts like Weihaiwei, a British port on the East coast of China. Lonely husbands visited the brothels in the International Settlement and paid as much as twenty dollars for a girl. The less extravagant frequented the dens in the French Concession along Avenue Foch and Avenue Joffre or joined the soldiers and sailors in Hongkew's dance halls. Competition meant that the girls had to work to titillate. In the 'Victoria' they appeared as ballet-dancers, footballers, nymphs and bathing beauties. At 'Stenka Rasin' they dressed as bandits; in 'Merle blanc' they strutted up and down as Parisiennes while in 'Tchorniye glaza' they wore large gypsy earrings and scarves. If frills failed to attract a man, they fidgeted with a suspender.

Older women moved across Soochow Creek to Hongkew where the bars along Broadway charged much lower prices. They finished in the Venereal Department of St Vincent Hospital or an alley near the Creek. Here pockmarked White Russians with shapeless figures stood in front of every passing male. 'Come to my house,' they begged hoarsely, raising their skirts. If accepted, they led the man to a wooden shed a few yards away. A visitor to Shanghai stopped to offer one woman some Russian cigarettes. Delighted, she told him that she came from Blagovestchensk, a town in the Amur region of Russia. She and her husband had fled eight years before across the frozen Amur with a thousand dollars between them. They were terrified of capture but, she said triumphantly, they had got through. The man, a left-wing intellectual and sympathetic to the Russian communists, wondered if life in the Soviet Union might not have been preferable.

Louise Gerald would have disagreed. Born in New York, her parents brought her at the age of three to Russia where her father, a gold miner, died in 1918. After the Revolution, she escaped to Shanghai and applied to the American Consulate for recognition as an American citizen. They refused her. Eight times she tried to reach America as a stowaway on a Dollar Line ship. When she was discovered on the eighth attempt, she flung herself into the Whangpoo river. She was rescued, taken back on board where she threw herself again into the river and again and again and again, until the crew locked her up in a cabin. She was twenty-two, she explained to the judge, and had no work or money.[16]

For most White Russian girls the choice appeared less straightforward. Sometimes they slept with a man because he knew the right people; other times they did it to pay the rent. The line between self-promotion and prostitution was a thin one. As old ladies, of course, none admit to a colourful past. By chance I was given an introduction to a Princess Lyuba of High Wycombe. She sounded depressingly respectable and I almost refused her invitation to lunch.

Princess Lyuba lived in one half of a large stone house. The shrubs on the Princess's side threatened to take over both house and driveway in contrast to her neighbour's bed of well-pruned roses. The Princess opened the door to me, a tiny woman in her late seventies with narrow hips and slim legs. Beneath dyed-blonde curls, her eyes were small but well shaped and wide apart. She had a straight nose and a Joan Crawford mouth, painted red. Taking my arm with both hands, she led me in and, still holding tight, sat me down on a sofa. Leaning close, she whispered urgently, 'I have to escape from here,' and jerked her head towards the door where I glimpsed a figure in a dressing gown shuffling past. She continued, 'My husband is eighty-five and an old man. It is difficult for me to keep the place, you know, smelling clean.'

This announcement appeared to give relief for she relaxed her grip and offered me a drink. Half-way through our conversation, she moved close again, smiling warmly, and described the restricted life her husband's infirmity forced her to lead. 'How can I escape?' she cried, clasping her hands. I asked why she did not live in London. She wailed, 'But I have no money. Everything is in his name. I gave him everything.' Her hand reached out to stroke mine. 'Last night I was lying in bed pondering how to escape when suddenly I thought, "This Harriet. She will help," and then, you know,' she looked upwards, 'a Great Peace swept over me.' I was seduced and about to offer my spare room when I noticed her hands. She was wearing a quantity of wedding rings. I asked how many times she had married. She replied that she was unsure and we had better count. We found six gold bands. She shrugged, 'In those days one never slept with a man unless one was married; so we got married. I started at sixteen and now I am seventy-six. Six is not so much, don't you think?' She paused, then added, 'Of course, sometimes one forgot to buy a ring.'

The Princess was fifteen and living in Haerbin when the Japanese invaded Manchuria in 1931. The young Lyuba appears to have had a catastrophic effect on the Japanese male. She and her family were enjoying dinner in a restaurant when a group of Japanese men burst in, waving knives and threatening to carry her off. The owner poured drinks all round before smuggling Lyuba's family out the back way. He warned them to keep their daughter hidden if they wished to avoid further incident. Soon after the family left Haerbin for good. The Japanese had discovered a lucrative business in kidnapping wealthy White Russians. If the families could not pay, the Japanese killed the victim and left the corpse on their doorstep. As a jeweller, Lyuba's father felt particularly vulnerable. He abandoned everything and walked to Shanghai.

Lyuba found work as a shop assistant. A White Russian couple befriended the young girl and introduced her to the French Club. The impressive stone building on Rue Cardinal Mercier epitomized the international and stylish image of the city. It had a sprung dance floor, a lovely roof garden and a vast, art-deco swimming pool which I used before a Japanese hotel consortium pulled it down. The club, in contrast to its British counterpart, welcomed White Russian members, especially precocious White Russian nymphets like Lyuba. She felt she had arrived 'in society', as she put it, and resolved to stay there. Her chance came one afternoon by the swimming pool. Lyuba was resting on the edge when a dress designer swam up and asked her to model in his show. 'He wanted someone with a good figure,' she said, her satisfaction still evident. Her first appearance on a catwalk provoked equally warm memories. She recalled the moment in detail. The band broke into a waltz and the audience applauded wildly. As a dress designer had more cachet among her new friends than a shop assistant, she looked around for the means to become one.

When Lyuba first arrived in Shanghai she had come across a relative of her mother's, a Princess Ludmilla who owned a dress salon. Lyuba's mother had refused to receive Ludmilla because she earned her living. This did not stop Lyuba now asking her relative to teach her everything she knew – 'I was quick on the uptake' –

and moving into her house. Ludmilla was a widow with a son of seventeen and a young English lover called Kenneth. Every morning before work Lyuba rode with Kenneth. Every evening she poured Kenneth his first drink. The widow grew jealous of the attention the two men paid the sixteen-year-old girl and regretted her kindness. She told Lyuba to leave. 'So being Russian, I said, "Yes, but I will take your son with me." ' They were married in a Russian church in Chapei. Before the ceremony Lyuba felt suddenly and unaccustomedly afraid, 'but as the street was cobblestoned and I was wearing very high heels, I couldn't run away.' The marriage at least brought her a title, 'which I never used except with the Americans after the war'. As the prince and princess had nowhere to go, Lyuba rang up an old Russian couple who let them stay the night and baked a pie in celebration.

A few days later Lyuba's new mother-in-law, relieved that the girl had ceased to be a rival for Kenneth, invited the couple to live with her. The experience proved a salutary one for Lyuba. The widow's dress salon began to lose money. First Ludmilla took to gambling, then she opened a roulette club in her home. The head of the French police enjoyed dropping in for a game. I wondered what he and the other customers had made of the youthful princess but on this Lyuba refused to elaborate, merely remarking, 'We were happy enough until my relative committed suicide.' Kenneth had exchanged their feckless household for the British Country Club and his older Russian mistress for an English girl who would enhance rather than blight his career. When the widow understood he would never come back, she killed herself. Lyuba showed me a photograph of them both, the widow in sunglasses looking up from a wicker armchair at a tall, young man. Her long neck was stretched back, the smile on her face almost a grimace. Lyuba then passed me snaps taken by her husband of herself at seventeen. They revealed a small-waisted, shapely girl posing in shorts, hands on knees, the face knowing and ebullient. The contrast between the two women was painful. The fate of her mother-in-law convinced Lyuba that a White Russian on her own could ill afford sentiment. She went on, 'After we buried my mother-in-law, I rushed home to remove everything valuable. She owed a lot of money and I wanted to be there before her creditors.'

Lyuba opened a dress salon on the proceeds in a block of flats opposite the French Club now called the Jing Jiang Hotel.

She hired a woman who knew how to book-keep, rented a large house and took on eighty workmen, including a number-one tailor as overseer. (In Shanghai the head of any organization, from the most humble to the largest, was called number one.) She designed everything from the black-velvet drapes in the shop to her outfit for the opening night of blue net and diamante stripes. One friend bought the material in Paris for her, another paid to have it made up and still a third did the carpentry in the changing rooms. Helpful friends now filled Lyuba's life. She hung a huge mirror studded with pearls against the black velvet and a cut-glass ball from the ceiling. The theatricality of the decor and the youthfulness of its owner must have caught Shanghai's imagination. She assured me that 'everybody' came to the opening night. Shortly afterwards Lyuba's business began to make a profit. Twice a year Lyuba held a fashion show at the Majestic Hotel using her clients as models. 'Everybody' came to that too, including Douglas Fairbanks and Mary Pickford on their visit to the city.

I asked about the Prince. She replied, 'Oh, he had gone off with a dancing girl by then. He didn't want to work and I had had enough of him.' She next married a Swiss diplomat in Tokyo, Lyuba wearing a Japanese wedding kimono, and they set off on a world cruise for their honeymoon. By Honolulu the diplomat had still not consummated the marriage. Lyuba lay in bed one morning, playing with an ivory shoe-horn, as her husband came out of the bathroom. She held up the horn. 'You'd be better off using this instead,' she said. At Honolulu, Lyuba left the boat and returned to Shanghai on her own. The diplomat gave her 'a very handsome present' so there were 'no hard feelings'.

The Princess now suggested we have lunch. We went to a pub and ordered whitebait. She appeared to pick at her food yet emptied her plate far faster than me. She wore an elegant, corduroy suit designed by her in the 'fifties. 'I got it out especially to wear for you,' she said. When we returned home, she showed me her possessions incongruously scattered among ugly, modern furniture: antique Chinese chairs, Japanese lacquer boxes and an ancient glass bottle from Egypt stuck to the mantelpiece because 'when one gives big parties, people walk off with things, don't you find?' She wore her favourite, a gold arm-band set with ovals of agate brought back by an archaeologist from his dig in Persia. 'He hated my husband, too,' she said as if this was an attribute.

When I talked about the past, she answered unwillingly, her mind occupied by the present and her schemes for the future. She felt nostalgia for nothing except, perhaps, the seaside town of Positano in Southern Italy where she had lived until a heart attack forced her home to High Wycombe. She baffled me. I could not understand how she was able to recall details such as the ivory shoe-horn but dismissed with a shrug decades of experience. Her life appeared like a series of postcards sent off from a world cruise. She revealed the occasional, colourful incident but left unrecorded the journey and its purpose.

In an effort to pin her down I asked about her departure from Shanghai. The Princess explained that she had contracted tuberculosis just before the war and had taken a train across Russia to Switzerland where she put herself into a sanatorium. Only now did I understand the significance of the Swiss diplomat and why his impotence had not caused more upset. The acquisition of his nationality had been her moment of triumph. It released her from China and her status as a refugee. It also ensured a comfortable war. She stayed in the sanatorium until 1945, enjoying herself with a number of kings and princes as well as an exceptionally charming Austrian count. 'All the best people had T.B.,' she said. At night they attended balls in Davos. She did not explain how she paid for the sanatorium.

After the war she returned to Shanghai to re-open her dress salon. With the arrival of the Chinese communists in 1949 she lost everything for the third time. She said, 'When I was little my father put 25,000 old roubles for me in a Vladivostok bank. By the time I grew up they were worthless. It's no good looking to the past. Shanghai taught me that. It was a city where everybody lived avidly for the present. I had been happy in the sanatorium so I went back there until 1954.' She glanced down at her hands. 'The Austrian count and I did not bother with rings,' she added.

That still left four husbands, I said. She replied, 'Of course, but that is rather a long story and not really to do with Shanghai, don't you think?'

As Princess Lyuba saw me off she cupped her breasts regretfully. 'My bubs have dropped. I never wore a bra, you know.' In the window next door, above the well-pruned roses, a curtain twitched.

I drove away, unsure whether to be relieved or sorry at the

Princess's absence from my spare bedroom. Her sheer pleasure in life had almost proved stronger than her intrigues and greed. She personified the transient, optimistic mood of the White Russian community and of Shanghai itself. I identified her style with the city's. Even after fifty years and in the implausible setting of High Wycombe it still had the power to dazzle.

I am unlikely to have lunch with Mrs Litvanoff much as I would enjoy the occasion. A white-slave trader and one of the city's countless, small-time crooks, she vanished in the communist take-over of 1949. Middle-aged with neither looks nor charm, Mrs Litvanoff survived on her indefatigable will. Her kind usually left no trace of their existence except in the general belief that Shanghai was a wicked city, the 'Yellow Babylon' of the Far East. Victoria Litvanoff did leave a record and in an improbable place.

A former member of the International Settlement's Special Branch told me that his department kept files on all the important people in the city, including his own father-in-law. He knew more about the man's proclivities than either his wife or daughter, but 'Of course, I never let on the full story.' These records are now stored in the Military Reference Branch of the National Archives in Washington D.C. They are held along with other previously classified material, in a baffling section of the building where even the number of floors shifted depending on whom I asked and which lift I took.

After almost a morning's search I found myself sitting opposite Mr Taylor in a small room without a window. Rumours abound about Mr Taylor. Academics approach him with caution. Some spend a year preparing for a meeting. Of this I was unaware. I thought myself clever enough merely to have found this thin man with his shock of white hair who answered my questions in a Southern lisp and wore a Texan tie-pin. Would he have an index? I enquired. Mr Taylor smiled slyly and took me upstairs to a dark, endless room stacked with documents recently handed over by the CIA. I was impressed. The British Secret Service provided nothing of the kind, I told him. Mr Taylor fixed his plump, beanbag eyes on me. 'The CIA pass on their records, but not their indexes. There are no indexes in our archives.' I looked around at the stacks and back at Mr Taylor. How did anyone find anything? I asked. Mr Taylor smiled until his eyes almost closed then said, 'I read it and remember.'

Each day Mr Taylor's tie-pins seemed to grow more elaborate and the checks on his suits louder. Each day he rewarded my presence with a further sheaf of papers which the day before he had assured me did not exist. On my first morning another researcher approached me. A young man with a military haircut and black, shiny trousers, he lectured me on the Jewish conspiracy in America. He added that 'a great and important man', and a good friend of his, knew of the existence of a sensational document. It proved that Roger Hollis, later head of the British Secret Service and allegedly recruited in Shanghai by a beautiful, Russian agent, shared a house with members of the Third International. Hollis had come out to Shanghai as a young man and worked for the British American Tobacco company. Young Englishmen, I knew, lived with other young Englishmen and not with members of the Third International. Intrigued, I set to and found nothing – not even the scandal on my detective's father-in-law. Mr Taylor shook his head and explained that the Americans had carried the files out of Shanghai in 1949. Some were lost at sea, the rest were picked clean by the CIA and then by MI6. The young man said his friend did not want to talk to me. The air in the windowless room grew hot and heavy. I had decided to leave when I read the first report on Mrs Litvanoff.[17] It offered neither spies nor scandal but a rare glimpse into the city's foreign underworld.

In March 1935, Inspector Jones of the Shanghai Special Branch made an appointment with a clairvoyant. Clairvoyance was against the law in the International Settlement and Inspector Jones had come to investigate. The clairvoyant shared an office with a Chinese doctor called Liu (Lew) Ding on the Nanking Road. Like many poor Chinese dwellings, it had been subdivided. The original office now contained an entrance hall, a doctor's surgery and a cubicle for the clairvoyant. She arrived late. The Chinese doctor asked the police inspector to step into his surgery while she went to her cubicle. No doubt, wrote the inspector, to preserve the mystery surrounding the profession which the sight of her in street clothing might destroy. When he entered the cubicle he found it lit by candles set in a brass sconce. On a table in one corner a human skull grinned at him over two thigh bones arranged crosswise. The fortune-teller wore a long black gown and hood, with only her hands and eyes visible. She agreed to help the inspector bed his girlfriend as long as he made it worth her while. She needed to know only the lady's first name as she herself 'was very strong'. The inspector judged her to be about sixty years old. She told him that she was half-Russian and half-French from which he deduced she was a pure White Russian. As Russians fell under the Chinese Criminal Code which contained nothing against fortune-telling, he was unable to prosecute.

The crystal-gazer was Victoria Litvanoff. She may have appeared sixty to Inspector Jones but, born in 1893, she was in fact still in her forties. She claimed to have married four times, each husband, except for the last, expiring in one of the century's catastrophes. The first, a Russian officer died at the Front; Baron Toll, the next, fell in the Russian Revolution; and the third, Captain Koishi Senoo of the Japanese Army, perished in the Japanese earthquake of 1923. She had married her last husband a year later in Shanghai. She had lived in Haerbin and Japan and had visited most of the big towns in China. She would do anything for money. She used the information she gleaned through her fortune-telling to blackmail her clients. She also kidnapped white women and sold them to brothels. A Miss Fuller 'who came under Mrs Litvanoff's influence', as the police report delicately put it, complained that Mrs Litvanoff had taken her money, her clothes and even tried to change her British passport for a Chinese one.

As well as telling fortunes, blackmailing and brothel-keeping under such names as Madam Ganette, Victoria Seou, Madam Dafin Desmond and Dauphine Desmonde she had also tried 'prestidigitation' five years before with a Portuguese called Rosario at the Paris Theatre in Shanghai. A bemused police officer watched her appear in a bathing costume and place herself behind a curtain handcuffed, leg-ironed and hung with chains from which she extricated herself in five minutes. She then proposed some mind-reading and called for volunteers from the audience. The diligent inspector held up his hand. Once on stage he saw that the trunk she used contained a sliding panel while the handcuffs, standard issue of Shanghai Municipal Police, easily slipped over Dauphine Desmonde's hands.

Mrs Litvanoff obviously took pride in her performance for she had a photograph taken of the event. She appears in a sari and high-heeled shoes, one arm held dramatically up, the other resting on a skull and thigh bones arranged beside her on a table. Beneath the veil the face is long and heavy. The brows are straight and the mouth droops under the nose like a Mexican moustache. I wondered if the skull and bones were the same as Inspector Jones had noticed when she promised to make his girlfriend more amenable. It raised all sorts of interesting questions. Where had she found them and how long had they travelled with her during her gypsy existence around the Far East? Did she pack them with her clothes, wrapping them up in her underwear, or did she treat them with more reverence? She was obviously fond of them. I imagined her taking them out and arranging them in each new room she moved to as some women do soft toys or a favourite photograph. They must have acted as inspiration when once again her schemes inexplicably failed; a signal that she was back in business and ready to start anew.

Special Branch wanted to see Mrs Litvanoff in their handcuffs off-stage as well as on but she knew her Shanghai law too well and always just eluded them. They had one means of frustrating her. Mrs Litvanoff planned to take her show to Berlin. When she applied for a visa, the German Consul sought information on her from Special Branch. Their answer confined Mrs Litvanoff to the Far East.

Her crystal-gazing ability did not prevent Mrs Litvanoff's own life becoming irksome after 1936. The year before she had run a successful brothel in the French Concession whose 'evil reputation' became so notorious that it provoked the otherwise lackadaisical French police to make a raid. In her haste to avoid arrest Mrs Litvanoff fell down a flight of stairs and broke her hip. It left her with a limp and the raid meant she had to start again.

In Shanghai this required only a change of name and venue. Extraterritoriality permitted Mrs Litvanoff to escape the law by moving back and forth between the French Concession and the International Settlement. When wanted in both places, she made for the Outside Roads' Area to the west of the city. With its large houses owned by rich foreigners, it appeared like any other suburb except for one difference, or from Mrs Litvanoff's point of view, one attraction. No one knew who had jurisdiction over the Outside Roads' Area. The International Settlement claimed the highways, known as the Municipal Roads, as theirs. They had built them. Houses on these roads paid Municipal taxes and were subject to Municipal Authority and police protection. Houses off the roads fell under the jurisdiction of the Chinese authorities. What lay on or off a road remained undefined. Sometimes the Chinese refused even to recognize the International Settlement's claims to the highways.

Mrs Litvanoff rented a house in an alleyway under Chinese jurisdiction with one side facing a Municipal highway. It was a position of perfect, legal ambiguity. To obtain the keys of the house,

Mr and Mrs Litvanoff paid two months' taxes in advance. After that, like many of their neighbours in Dixwell Road, they defaulted. The Council could do nothing to evict them.

Mrs Litvanoff put up a few perfunctory decorations, hired some girls and opened for business. Then disaster struck. Her husband fell in love. Nikolas Nikolayevich Litvanoff, ten years younger than his wife, had led a fairly typical existence for a White Russian. As a boy he had attended the Khabarovsk Cadet Corps School in Russia. He had joined the White Army at sixteen and fought the Bolsheviks. He must have been a good, if somewhat youthful soldier, for in Vladivostok he became assistant tutor to the Russian Cadet Corps before moving to Guangzhou as a member of the Portuguese River Police. When that proved uncongenial he set up an electrical contractor's business in Shanghai. He had married his wife in 1924 and stopped working in order to help her more lucrative ventures. He appeared to be absolutely under her influence. Then he met Veronica, a White Russian prostitute employed in his wife's brothel. They fell in love, borrowed SH$600 from Indian money-lenders and ran away together to two small rooms on the Weihaiwei Road. That was bad enough, but then he set up his own brothel offering the sort of unusual delights which his former wife had specialized in. The invitation to the opening promised extraordinary entertainment; an exhibition by a Russian male and French female, a lesbian act between two French females and naked dancing. Nikolas considered acquiring a second brothel, but, as the police reported, 'this establishment is an ordinary brothel so it would appear that Litvanoff has not yet assumed control'.

Mrs Litvanoff was heartbroken. First she tried suicide and when that failed she visited the police. Did they know, she said in pious tones, that her husband kept a bawdy house? She pulled out copies of the *Evening Post* and *China Press*. Here he was, advertising himself as 'Miss Helen, electric massage and manicure'. Were the police going to allow this sort of thing to continue? They showed her out politely and made a note that a complaint had been made by Mrs Litvanoff, 'notorious brothel keeper and procurer for all forms of debauchery'.

She let her husband know what she had done and he and Veronica immediately sent off an anonymous letter to the Special Branch. They accused her of working against Great Britain and its agencies in Calcutta and of trying to obtain a passport to get to Hong Kong.

'With a few glasses of drink in she tells lots,' they promised, adding that she was a troublemaker and a Bolshevik as well as a Polish Jew and only 'Rusky' by marriage – the ultimate insult in a notoriously anti-semitic community. Special Branch concluded regretfully that Bolshevism was about the only charge they could not pin on Mrs Litvanoff.

A far more damaging complaint came from an unexpected source. The Russian newspaper, *Novosti Dnia*, published the following under the title 'Yellow Babylon's latest abomination'.

R-r-ring . . . R-r-ring . . . R-r-ring
The telephone receiver is picked up.
– Mrs X?
– Yes.
– I am speaking from the salon.
– What salon?
– The 'Salon of Love'. It is the latest word of the gay Shanghai. Madam, we have here the most handsome men in Shanghai, full of sex appeal. With them you can experience every pleasure. Our address is . . .

Further conversation depends on the character of the lady who receives the call. If she likes exciting thrills, she will make a note of the address and ask again the number of the house in order to make sure. If she is indignant . . . she will hang up . . .

The above . . . is not a fantasy. Unfortunately, it is the dreadful and bitter reality of the dissolute Shanghai. Telephone calls and offers of this nature have by no means been a rarity in Shanghai . . .

Preference is given to Russian ladies who are married to wealthy foreigners . . .

The article ended with the hope that the police would do something about it. Special Branch sent Inspector Ross and D. S. Tcherem-shansky, a White Russian himself and, so far, an unsuccessful recruit. They even had an invitation card. Despite its promise of 'a paradise' of some eighty or more beautiful high-class European and American girls (Mrs Litvanoff offered both sexes), number 237 Dixwell Road did not appear to exist. The two inspectors noticed a Chinese policeman at the entrance to an alleyway. They asked him for directions. Without hesitation, he pointed to the house he was standing guard over. Mrs Litvanoff shared with Princess Lyuba the knack of making the right friends.

The two inspectors entered a room divided in two by a heavy curtain. On their side stood some easy chairs, two small tables and a gramophone player from Chicago. After a brief wait a middle-aged woman hobbled in on crutches. Tcheremshansky had no difficulty in identifying her as the notorious Mrs Litvanoff. She was still suffering from her accident with the French police and a case of slashed wrists over her husband. Neither injury stopped her enthusiastic entertainment of the two men. They ordered some alcohol and filled her glass continually. As her husband had promised, she became talkative after a few drinks and by 'patiently listening to the woman's chatter', the inspectors obtained the information they sought.

The curtain drew back to reveal three harlots, two Russians and a Chinese, reclining on the floor in suggestive postures. Above their heads several rows of coloured lights flickered on and off. The inspectors thought these were meant to conjure up the 'Paradise' promised in the visiting cards. The three prostitutes wore lace skirts which scarcely covered their bottoms and flimsy brassières. An imitation red rose completed the ensemble. As neither inspector appeared eager to get on more intimate terms, the star performers became somewhat restless and began to complain of the cold. The Chinese girl, aged about sixteen, scrambled to her feet, climbed on top of the radiator and sat there shivering. One of the Russian women came over and asked if she could borrow a greatcoat from the men as she too felt a little chilly.

Mrs Litvanoff now began to tell the inspectors what they had come to hear. She boasted of the 'respectable' married women, with husbands 'unable to satisfy their sexual appetites', who visited the gigolos employed in her brothel. These women, stated Mrs Litvanoff, were of American, English and French nationality and wore masks to avoid recognition. She described two kinds of gigolo, the Red and the Blue. Women hired Red gigolos to act as paid companions or entertainers. They did not sleep with their patrons. Blue gigolos were hired either by the hour or the night, 'for the sole purpose of satisfying the lust of female clients', and charged one hundred dollars a night. Mrs Litvanoff hinted that she could cater to almost any perversion provided she was paid enough. The two inspectors left, disappointed not to have seen the 'specially constructed beds and chairs',[18] described on the invitation card.

Inspector Tcheremshansky's visit to Mrs Litvanoff's brothel made his career. 'Shows considerable improvement,' commented his superior. The carefully typed pages of his report reveal a grudging admiration. Mrs Litvanoff became almost a hobby for him. It was he who discovered her history and ensured her immortality. The last note in her file states that she was finally imprisoned for refusing to pay a hotel bill in Guling. After that she vanishes.

The image of Victoria Litvanoff, glaring at us over a skull and crossbones, epitomizes for me the savage, incorrigible vitality of the city. Her life, a black burlesque of perversion, abduction and dead husbands, defies moral judgment. In this she resembles Shanghai itself between the wars. Innate to Shanghai's glamour was poverty and corruption. In the peaceful year of 1935 the Shanghai Municipal Council collected 5,590 dead men, women and children from the streets of the International Settlement. Crime and corruption were endemic. The head of the French Police controlled the city's opium trade. Gangsters, politicians and foreign businessmen ran Shanghai to their mutual advantage. Shanghai's reputation as a place where anything was possible depended on this paradox.

Mrs Litvanoff and Princess Lyuba represent the moral ambiguity at the heart of Shanghai. Listening to the Princess, I discovered that lies melt into legend with deceptive ease. Deception was regarded as a legitimate means of survival not only by the White Russians but, to a lesser extent, by all Shanghai's nationalities. The chaos of China and the precarious position of the city made it difficult to live any other way.

Two final images from the White Russian community sum up its equivocal nature. The first is characterized by the photograph an old man showed me of himself as a child in a sailor suit, standing next to a lady in Edwardian costume. On her head is an enormous white hat, in her hands a parasol. The little boy looks solemnly at the camera. His mother has her head tilted to show off a long, white neck. There is an air of ease, of summer holidays and bright, seaside light. The other is a short item in the *North China Daily News*. Police found a White Russian man frozen to death near the Bund. He had crawled under some warm pipes which cooled off during the night. He lacked identification of any sort. His pockets revealed just seven coppers cash.[19]

The White Russians felt obliged to reconcile these two opposing images of themselves. The effort caused an almost collective insanity in the community. In the end they failed. Neither the time nor the place were propitious and the city they sought to identify with turned out to be as illusory as the lives they tried to recreate. In 1949 they found themselves once again, some for the third, even fourth time in thirty years, penniless and with nowhere to go.

In 1924 such thoughts were far from General Glebov's mind as he surveyed the Bund from the bridge of his boat. Shanghai offered the last chance of survival for him and his band of Cossacks. The Municipal authorities disagreed. They refused to welcome General Glebov as they had Admiral Stark. Fleets of White Russians were less of a novelty and Cossacks, in particular, had proved unsatisfactory citizens. General Glebov and his men rode patiently at anchor for three years. When funds ran low they sold their arms to the local warlord. In January 1927 their luck changed. The Nationalist army, considered by Shanghai's foreigners to be communist, had marched north from Guangzhou and now appeared poised to take the city. The authorities of the International Settlement suddenly saw trouble-makers who hated communists in a different light. Hastily, the General was invited ashore and asked to form a defence detachment. As one Cossack recalled, 'Our only drawback was an over-supply of officers. Some of us had to become juniors or even join the ranks.' On January 21st two companies and a machine-gun platoon presented themselves to the Municipal Council.

The crisis not only provided jobs for the Cossacks but saw Shanghai move into the centre of events which were to determine China's future.

· THREE ·

The Order of the Brilliant Jade
1927 – the First Battle

ON FEBRUARY 19TH, 1927 Shanghai's Chinese workers organized a welcome for the approaching Nationalist army in the form of a general strike. The effect on Shanghai was recalled for me by the oldest person I have ever interviewed. Mr Lord is 101 and lives near Goring-On-Thames. He first went to Shanghai in 1918 at the age of thirty-three where he worked for an insurance company and joined the Pork Pie Club, a society of enthusiastic photographers and pork-pie eaters. Mr Lord specialized in aerial photography. His great friend, Carl Nahmmacher, represented Boeing in China and the two men often flew together in Carl's two-seater aeroplane. On the day of the strike, they took off at about ten in the morning and wheeled across Yangtzepoo to find the industrial district still and silent. Nothing moved around the factories. The chimneys had ceased to belch and not a single coolie chanted on the wharfs. In the streets factory workers played with their children. Carl turned south and followed the Whangpoo through the city. The river flowed peacefully without even a sampan scuttling across its surface. The trams had stopped running on the Bund and the department stores were closed in Nanking Road. A great quiet hung over everything. Shanghai, the busiest city in the Far East, had been silenced. Mr Lord recalled, 'After landing we went straight round to the club for a stiff drink. We knew what had happened in Russia when the communists took over. We were appalled.'

Many of Shanghai's foreign and Chinese inhabitants shared Mr Lord's fear of communism. They saw the Nationalist army as a Red army and their city a potential victim of Red Rape. They imagined their businesses snatched by communist cadres and themselves, like the middle classes in Russia, blown up on barges or shot in cellars.

The man responsible for Shanghai's predicament was Sun Yat-sen. The instigator of China's revolution in 1911, Sun had proved unable to hold on to power after the downfall of the Manchus. By the early 'twenties only Guangzhou remained under his precarious control. The rest of China, including the Chinese areas of Shanghai, fell under the rule of competing warlords. Desperate to regain the initiative in China, Sun first tried America and Europe for help. When they refused to take him seriously, he turned in 1923 to the new communist regime in Russia, his 'last choice',[1] as his wife admitted years later to Edgar Snow in the Chocolate Shop on Nanking Road. Lenin sent Mikhail Borodin, a professional revolutionary with experience in such diverse places as Mexico, Chicago and Glasgow. He transformed Sun's Nationalist party into an effective political and military organization with strong appeal to the ordinary Chinese – but failed to convert all its members to communism. The Nationalist party consisted of two distinct groups, the Guomindang and the Chinese Communist party. Under Sun Yat-sen they had allied themselves uneasily together. The Guomindang, made up of middle-class businessmen and landowners, rejected emphatically the call from radical student members of the newly formed Chinese Communist party for land reform, financial equality and the repossession of the foreign concessions. The students frightened the Guomindang almost as much as they did Mr Lord.

The conservative element of the Nationalist party had a powerful representative in Chiang Kai-shek. In a series of devious moves, Chiang had won Sun Yat-sen's confidence before his death in 1925 and had outwitted Borodin to emerge as military leader by May 1926.

That summer, Chiang Kai-shek and Borodin appeared to make up their differences in order to fulfil Sun Yat-sen's dream of a united China under the Nationalist party. While Sun lived, a Northern Expedition against the warlords seemed overweeningly ambitious. Now, troops trained and equipped by Russia marched smartly out of Guangzhou. Their aim was the Yangtze valley, six hundred miles to the north-east, considered by the British as their particular sphere of interest.

The army moved off in two parts reflecting the split between its leaders. The communists under Borodin made their way to Wuhan while Chiang Kai-shek travelled north-east to Nanchang and Shanghai. Borodin's fifth columnists worked ahead of his units, politicizing the peasants and workers. After a successful engagement, he would redistribute the land and leave the peasants to take revenge on a hapless landlord or unpopular governor. When Borodin and the Chinese communist leaders arrived in Wuhan, ecstatic Chinese let off fireworks in the streets. In nearby Hankou, the second-largest entre-pôt after Shanghai, Chinese mobs seized command of the local British Settlement. Chiang Kai-shek's divisions pursued a rather different policy. They confirmed the landlord in his place and left foreign property undisturbed. Chiang Kai-shek occupied himself less with workers' rights than with his plans to take over the Nationalist party. He chose Shanghai as the place to destroy his communist allies. His decision had serious implications for the city and its future. To the Shanghailander (the name given to a foreign inhabitant of the city), Chiang Kai-shek and Borodin loomed together in their imagination as interchangeable bogey-men. In one way the Shanghailander was correct. Both the Russian and the Chinese understood the impor-tance of Shanghai as the richest city in China. Whoever controlled its revenues would have the resources to master the whole country.

The advent of the Nationalist army concentrated that great, diverse, sprawling mind of Shanghai as nothing else could. It affected everybody and everything in the city. I talked to people who were there at the time. Dotted all over the city, most saw what happened without understanding that this was the end of Shanghai. Their memories are haphazard. It was as if their minds worked like Mr Lord's finger and they had spent the spring of 1927 snapping at whatever caught their fancy. The result, spread out in front of me, appeared a jumble of images and events. They revealed how the city behaved in an emergency. I had wanted the writer's equivalent of an aerial photograph, everything clear and sharp, one glance taking in the whole. Instead I hardly knew what to pick up or where to begin. The confusion was indicative of the city itself. Three Municipal Councils, warlords, gangsters, guilds, international companies, foreign journalists and spies from every country ensured intrigue was as natural as breathing.

The beginning of the year saw the city's institutions prepare themselves in characteristic fashion for the emergency. The Municipal Council ordered the Volunteer Corps on the alert. Set up during the Taiping Rebellion, it consisted of British, American, Italian, Danish, German, Filipino, Jewish (the first independent Jewish unit in the world), Portuguese, Japanese, Chinese, White Russian and Eurasian companies with weapons and a commanding officer courtesy of the British War Office. As well as these part-time soldiers (even in the direst emergency men were allowed time off to see to their business), twenty thousand troops from America, Europe and Japan, including the largest British force ever sent to the Far East, transformed the city into an armed camp. A semicircle of barbed-wire barricades appeared on the streets from the North Station down through Hungjao Road to Siccawei separating the International Settlement and the French Concession from the Chinese territory under the control of the warlord, Sun Chuanfang. On the Whangpoo river floated forty-five warships.

The sight of marching soldiers stirred the editorial staff of the *North China Daily News*, first printed in 1850 by Henry Shearman as a weekly and known affectionately as the 'Old Lady of the Bund'. The paper has long since closed but its office at 17 The Bund still squeezes up between the former Bank of Taiwan and the Chartered Bank to erupt above its neighbours in a splendid if top-heavy, two-tiered roof. It provided thorough coverage of foreign, local and Chinese news while its editorial policy reflected the preoccupations and vanities of the foreign businessman. Even now its yellow pages have the power to conjure up a colonial never-never land where the natives loved and emulated one and gentlemanly virtues were rewarded with money and an interesting life. Beneath the nostalgia, the newspaper formed part of the establishment which ran the International Settlement. A representative of the paper always sat on the Municipal Council. Its leader columns frequently concealed facts that might embarrass the Council beneath a veneer of frankness, while issuing Council propaganda in the form of 'Empire Prose' – the stuff to exhort young men to glory and confirm old men in their prejudices. The manipulative side of the *North China Daily News* came as a shock to me. It is like finding out that one's grand-uncle gave little girls sweets for the wrong reason.

In January 1927 the pages of the newspapers filled with photographs of regiments, such as the Fifth Brigade, 2nd Punjab Regiment (87th) which paraded through Shanghai playing pipes and creating 'a very good impression by their business-like appearance'.[2] In the Settlement, foreigners prepared to entertain the troops arriving from abroad. An unspoken agreement existed to pitch in and provide 'wholesome substitutes', as the *North China Daily News* put it, for the 'unsatisfactory diversions of the street', and the lack of any real fighting to occupy the men. Fortunately, the 87th had come with their hockey gear and this, declared the paper, was the ideal place for hockey. On Jinkee Road the British Women's Association opened a canteen equipped with a bar, billiard table and two gramophones as well as palms and potted plants. Union Jacks and bunting gave the necessary decorative touch. Sir Elly Kadoorie, one of the leading members of Shanghai's Iraqi Jewish community and a great anglophile, lent his magnificent home, Marble Hall, to the troops. The veranda alone accommodated two hundred men. The *North China Daily News* reported how Sir Elly provided the men with pork pies, ham sandwiches, sausages and mashed and chipped potatoes at very low rates. Books were also laid on and once again the ubiquitous game of hockey.[3]

Hockey and books, warned the newspaper, failed to fill the long evenings. Its leaders encouraged people to invite soldiers home to dinner and give them some 'personal acquaintance with Shanghai's generous British qualities of kindliness and hospitality'.[4] The newspaper described the reaction of one foreign family's Chinese servants to the news that five soldiers were arriving for tea. The Chinese considered soldiering as one of the lowest occupations and soldiers as worse than criminals. The servants assumed that neither they nor the family would be alive for dinner. The amah threatened to run away and in fact hid in the bathroom all afternoon. The head servant, a dignified old man, volunteered to open the front door and watched in amazement as the English soldiers wiped their feet on the mat. Gathering confidence he brought in the tea things and, with a deep breath, proffered a plate of sandwiches. One of the sergeants looked up and thanked him. After they left, the old man admitted, 'These soldiers belong very proper, no same Chinese.'[5]

The British army requisitioned Del Monte, the nightclub famous for its White Russian hostesses, and turned it into a convalescent home. In attendance was Dr Fergus McDonnal, a twenty-three-year-old Scot and the only person I interviewed who remembered the place filled solely with young men. Dr McDonnal found himself flooded with dinner invitations especially from wives with daughters. Being handed the address of a stranger and told to put on a dinner jacket, he admitted, was all 'a bit overwhelming'. He celebrated New Year's Eve with the McBains, an old and distinguished Shanghai family banned from the British Country Club after the first Mr McBain married a Chinese. Dr McDonnal recalled a splendid evening with the best of everything. Even the mince pies contained gold sovereigns.

Despite the games of hockey and the bracing talk from the *North China Daily News*, the soldiers found the corrupting influences of the city irresistible. Dr McDonnal gave way to his passion for golf, while still under orders to be armed at all times. After a game Dr McDonnal was walking back to the club house when he caught the eye of an officer sipping a pink gin.

'Where's your weapon?' barked the officer.

Dr McDonnal tipped out his golf bag. At the very bottom lay a pistol.

'Is it loaded?' demanded his superior.

Dr McDonnal had to admit it was not.

'What good is that then?' said the officer before returning to his drink.

The majority of soldiers took advantage of Shanghai's celebrated brothels. The International Settlement alone boasted almost seven hundred. When the army first arrived, it had requisitioned certain brothels and ordered the local police to stop soldiers using any others. In the 'maisons tolerées' as they were called, Dr McDonnal regularly inspected the girls for diseases. He admitted that as an inexperienced and 'relatively pure' young man the weekly visit shocked him and was 'enough to put you off, I can tell you'. He dispatched sick girls to the 'Lock Up' hospital where they stayed until cured. This admirable set-up came to an end after the Chinese accused the British Army of offering under-age adolescents – an odd complaint since China lacked an age of consent and Chinese men preferred prostitutes of thirteen and fourteen. A Labour Member of Parliament raised questions at Westminster and, in the ensuing scandal, the army gave up brothel-keeping. Within a short period the *Lancet*, a leading British medical journal, reported more soldiers had succumbed to venereal disease than to the 'flu.[6] Venereal disease incapacitated Dr McDonnal's entire regiment. Before returning home to their wives and sweethearts, the men were sent to Weihaiwei to recover from the dangers of inactive service in Shanghai.

Shanghai's forthcoming battle also attracted foreign revolutionaries and members of the Third International. Men like Thomas Mann, Earl Browder, the leader of the American Communist party, Manabendra Nath Roy, the Indian Comintern agent and the young André Malraux (who was later to record his experiences in his novel *Man's Estate* and complete an extraordinary career as de Gaulle's Minister of Youth, Culture and Sports) arrived bright with expectation. The Third International, set up by Leon Trotsky to export the Russian Revolution, had tried and failed in Europe. Now China beckoned. Like the missionaries and businessmen before them, the revolutionaries were seduced by China's millions and the desire to 'even scores with the American, British, and other European capitalist-imperialists'.[7] They also needed a success for their own survival. In Russia, Joseph Stalin, who opposed Trotsky and his programme, grew daily in power and popularity. It was in Stalin's interests that the Third International should fail in China.

Shanghai corrupted revolutionaries and soldiers alike. Members of the Third International found themselves seduced. Everything was so cheap. Funds provided by Russia enabled them to give banquets every night. Extraterritoriality protected them from the persecutions of the anti-communist warlord. They were free to enjoy themselves and their politics. American car dealers talked happily of a 'Red Boom' as revolutionaries, accustomed in their own countries to using trams and buses, now bought cars. Only Earl Browder cast a dampener. At dinner parties he insisted on eating black bread and water – the staple of the Russian peasant whose contributions were paying for the Chinese Revolution.

Borodin, the Russian revolutionary responsible for the success of the Nationalist army, settled down in Shanghai and became almost respectable. He put his children, aged nine and eleven, into the Shanghai American School under the name Ginzburg, and gave a series of interviews to the *North China Daily News*. His interviewer obviously found the proximity of the Russian communist overwhelming. He described Borodin as a strong personality, able to erase reason and substitute feeling, adding 'One ceases to think after one has been with him a few minutes and simply vibrates as with an over-dose of a narcotic.'[8]

The soldiers and the revolutionaries changed the look of the city. When you wanted to cross the road, you had to pause for the armoured cars and the howitzers of the Volunteer Corps to march past, led by the commander on a white horse. You might be woken up in the morning by a company of American troops chewing gum as they drilled outside your window. You found your favourite restaurant booked out a week in advance and, when you did get a table, wild-looking men, speaking incomprehensible languages, glared at your husband's gold watch-chain or your wife's fur coat. People complained that Shanghai had become 'an armed camp' and the 'Red GHQ for Asia'.

Meanwhile, at 185 Foochow Road, the Special Branch of the Municipal police force made its own and less obvious preparations. Patrick Givens, the head of Special Branch, a tall, broad-shouldered Irishman, had won the admiration of Irene Kuhn, now in her nineties and living in New York. She was then a pretty, American reporter, recently arrived from Paris. A photograph exists of her in a Chanel coat riding around China on a donkey. She thought Patrick Givens a handsome man 'without a drop of fat on him'. He took her on opium raids and impressed her with his quiet manner, 'not something you associate with a detective', which inspired instant respect.

Patrick Givens principally occupied himself with the suppression of communism. Shanghai with its large proletariat and student population had become the centre of Chinese communist hopes and the scene of their greatest endeavours. Patrick Givens was eager to counter the 'insidious' work of communist propaganda in the International Settlement. Like everybody else he held Chiang Kai-shek responsible and planned a campaign of disinformation against him. In a confidential report, he commented that his Chinese detectives, 'with whom I am in agreement', believed that 'the wickedness' of General Chiang Kai-shek could only be brought home to the uneducated classes by representing him as 'an unscrupulous, avaricious and blood-thirsty traitor'.[9] To this effect Special Branch planned a series of cartoons depicting the General as a tortoise, a cobra, a wolf and even a leech. A scribbled note on the report mentioned that the Nationalists themselves used this form of propaganda, adding, 'It is very effective and is easily understood by those whom it is intended to reach.'[10] The British authorities had no intention of letting Shanghai become, as the *North China Daily News* loftily put it, 'a Tom Tiddler's ground for the sport of these and their fellows'.[11]

The Chinese worker also prepared for the coming fray. Strikes occurred throughout the city. Not far from Mr Givens' office and flanking the Nanking Road, stood the Wing On and Sincere department stores. Striking shop assistants took over the roof garden of one and refused to come down until management cut their working day to twelve hours and their working week to six days. They also wanted more food at lunchtime. The management dismissed their demands as revolutionary. When the shop assistants grew bored, they dropped leaflets and firecrackers over the edge of the roof. The crowds below immediately slowed, looked upwards and caught the pamphlets with eager hands. People shouted, 'Down with British Imperialism!' Indian and Chinese policemen rushed to the scene, blowing whistles, hitting their way through the throngs to arrest people and seize the literature.

Among the crowd strolled a thirteen-year-old Jewish boy from Russia. Sam Ginsbourg had just moved to Shanghai with his family from Vladivostok where his father managed a saw mill and his mother was a dentist. After 1949 Sam stayed in Shanghai and joined the Chinese Communist party. His memoirs, a combination of youthful freshness and official party line, present events from the communist point of view. He and his brother spent the first few months of 1927 exploring the city on foot. They listened to the numerous speakers on Shanghai's streets. Sam liked the workers and students whose slogans, he is keen to tell us, were taken up with enthusiasm by their listeners. Other speakers resembled 'clerks and shop keepers'.[12] They invited their audience to examine photographs of communist atrocities in Wuhan, men forced to eat their own ears, women raped and villages burnt to the ground. Despite such inducements, few people lingered to hear what they had to say. The speakers reminded Sam of actors playing an unfamiliar role. He saw one man rescued by police from an angry group, his gown torn and his picture gallery missing. Sam guessed the 'shop keepers' were plain-clothes detectives spreading anti-communist propaganda for the foreign authorities. One can only wonder if Mr Givens' posters had more success.

In this atmosphere of 'lies and half lies',[13] as one member of the Third International described Shanghai in 1927, rumour became the city's reality. Along the Bund, businessmen accosted each other for the latest whisper. In clubs and restaurants they exaggerated the wildest report and passed it on. Information was traded as a commodity. 'Unless you gave the impression of being satisfied with momentous news and, above all, of being reluctant to part with it, no one bothered you,' recalled one businessman. 'I've found more snoops and gossips to the square inch than I have found in any New England town of a thousand inhabitants,'[14] growled Eugene O'Neill before departing in disgust. In the absence of real information, ordinary foreigners found the situation baffling and saw themselves as the innocent victims of 'a universally outrageous fortune'.[15] The best bet, most agreed, was to stay behind the broad back of a British Tommy and absorb carefully the instructions published in the *North China Daily News* entitled 'How to Spot Communists at Moving Picture Shows and Other Public Gatherings'.

In the narrow streets of Nantao, the old Chinese city, the executioners of the warlord had no trouble doing this. Carrying broadswords and accompanied by soldiers, they seized pickets and students handing out Nationalist leaflets, marched them into the middle of an alley, bent them over and cut off their heads. They then stuck the heads on pointed bamboo poles or piled them on to platters and carried them through the crowded streets to the next scene of execution creating 'a veritable reign of terror'.[16] A Chinese cameraman nicknamed 'Newsreel Wong' filmed these scenes of medieval grisliness for American audiences. Running breathlessly behind the executioners, he recorded the horror on the faces of the Chinese, rushing for protection behind the barbed-wire entanglements. In the French Concession and International Settlement, French and British police refrained from chopping off heads. They merely expelled the arrested from the protection of the Settlements into the districts under Chinese control where the executioners awaited them. For two days there was fighting in the Chinese areas. The army, so long expected, did not arrive. Chiang Kai-shek had halted twenty-five miles outside Shanghai.

Those strikers still alive returned to work. The executioners put the decapitated heads into birdcages and strung them up on telegraph poles. The Settlement continued to wait in fear of an invasion. Foreigners from Hankou arrived at Shanghai's wharves with stories of anti-foreign riots inspired by the success of the Nationalist army, chapels smashed, bibles torn up and homes looted. In Shanghai business came to a standstill. Even if the businessman did escape with his life, what of his city and his investments?

The answer lay in Rue Wagner in the French Concession. Towards the end of February, the Chairman of the Municipal Council, a small, amiable American called Stirling Fessenden, made his way to a house in this street. He went in trepidation. His host was Du Yuesheng, Shanghai's most notorious gangster.

Du Yuesheng proved central to the events of 1927. To understand how the city operated beneath the confusion and misinformation, one has to know the man who led Shanghai's underworld.

I was standing on Foochow Road next to the racecourse when I first heard his name. My informant was Ricky Lu, a dandy in his eighties who had miraculously survived the Cultural Revolution with his pre-war wardrobe of tweed suits and two-tone brogues intact. During the 'thirties he had moved through that lush pleasure world of theatres, brothels and gangsters. Gangsters, he explained, owned Shanghai's entertainment establishments. The city's Peking Opera stars always treated Du carefully. Even the internationally renowned Mei Lanfang (a close friend of Charlie Chaplin) gave private performances in Du's home. Both Ricky Lu and Du were famous for the number and beauty of their girlfriends, Mr Lu relying on charm and looks rather than money and power. Both men had married Peking Opera stars. I asked which role Du's wife specialized in. 'Old men,' said Mr Lu with a smile. He pointed to the apartment block across the road. Du rented it out to the most expensive girls in Shanghai. They entertained politicians and warlords with their singing and well informed, witty conversation. They did not sleep with just anyone. Ricky Lu sighed, overcome, it seemed, with memories of creatures so alien to the gaggle of Chinese girls now emerging from the building. Then he added, 'It was called the Happy Times block.'

Du started life far from establishments like Happy Times.[17] Born in 1888 in a small village called Gaoqiao in Pootung to a poor family, his mother's brother mistreated him after his parents' death. By eighteen, Du had grown into an unattractive youth with a big, shaven head and ears like panhandles who preferred gambling with friends on street corners to work as an apprentice at the Dah Yeu Fruit Hong in Nantao. His boss hesitated to sack him because of his following among the petty criminals in the area. Five years later even they could not help when he was caught stealing. Du did not try for another job. He loafed around Nantao, getting known, under the nickname of Fruit Yuesheng, as a small-time criminal. Then a friend offered to put him up for membership of the Green Gang.

Shanghai had two main gangs known as the Green and the Red. The gang or secret society was part of Chinese tradition and also served depending on circumstances, as a mutual help and revolutionary organization. During times of unrest they came into their own, contributing to the defeat of the Mongol dynasty in the fourteenth century. They became the only opposition party possible in Imperial China where dissent meant an elaborate and painful death. The secret societies attracted men like Du, the marginal and the destitute, dispossessed peasants, bandits, coolies, vagabonds, boatmen and smugglers. They offered an alternative to China's rigid social system. People such as travelling artisans, herb doctors and wandering monks did not fit into traditional Chinese life where the individual was subservient to his family, his clan, his village and his guild. The gangs stood for initiative and choice. In a vast country like China they provided a ready-made organization and a communication system for the prospective revolutionary. The Taiping rebels, Sun Yat-sen, Chiang Kai-shek and Mao Zedong all made use of secret societies.

In Shanghai membership was hierarchical, with the city's riff-raff forming the lowest rung. Peasants, driven off their land by years of warlord activity and revolution, who had made their way to Shanghai's factories only to find themselves alone and unable to speak the dialect, sought support in the *banghui*, or mutual-aid groups linked to the secret societies. Middle-rank members consisted of those whose jobs and corruptibility made them indispensable to the running of a criminal organization. They included detectives and policemen of the French Concession, the International Settlement and the Chinese municipality, military officers in the local garrisons, minor politicians, factory foremen, labour contractors and merchants. The top ranks were reserved for bankers, rich businessmen and politicians.

In the initiation ceremony Du swore secrecy, mingled his blood and learnt the recognition signals members exchanged in teahouses and other public places. He then moved into the Tian Song Lodging House on Nantao Bund. It was something of an anti-climax. Membership gave him the occasional job but not much else. Anything he earned, he gambled away immediately. Four years passed before he got his chance.

A fortune-teller named Pan advised him to move in with his friend Dong Asan. Du did and waited hopefully. After a year Ah San gave him an introduction to Huang Jinrong, better known as Pockmarked Huang. Conveniently for the smooth running of the French Concession, Huang was head of both the the Chinese detectives in the French Sûreté and the Green Gang. Du hung around Huang's house until Gui Song, Huang's mistress and an ex-brothel-keeper from Suzhou pointed out his diligence and perspicacity to her protector.

Huang made Du responsible for transporting opium to and from the hong or warehouse in Hongkew. Du's former influence with the petty criminals of the area ensured his success. After a year, Huang gave Du his own hong to manage on Rue du Consulat in the French Concession. It was then Du put into operation a plan to form a cartel of the city's opium gangs. His success made him the most powerful gangster in Shanghai. He and Huang, to whom Du always remained loyal, now ran the city's underworld.

Success meant Du attracted a different class of business associate who needed somewhere discreet to meet him. In the same road as his hong, he opened the Mei Tsung Hwa Kyi jewellery shop. It was his first step into respectability. Here he entertained junior officers of the Chinese police and the smuggling prevention squad. His friendships increased with every year. By the age of thirty-five he could count on men in the French Consulate, the judiciary and the French police.

Friends need money. Du put together an organization of systemized extortion under the simple but apt name of the 'Black Stuff Company'. Every opium hong in the French Concession paid the Green Gang from $3,000 to $10,000 a month, out of which Du handed $180,000 to his friends in the French authorities. He also organized the 'Opium Pipe Company' which covered all opium dens in the French Concession, south of Avenue Edward VII and west of Mohawk Road. Du taxed each den thirty cents a day per pipe. Du's men collected the money every afternoon and affixed a seal to the den's account books. They fined the owner of the den $50 for each pipe he failed to declare. If a den tried to hide its existence from the Green Gang, Du arranged for the French police to make a raid and deal with the owner according to law. The police never punished owners whose account books displayed the seal of the 'Opium Pipe Company'. The Company made a profit of $100,000 per month.

Du's influence spread into every aspect of the city's life: from the French authorities who, it was generally agreed, Du bribed in a 'tactful' manner, to the post-office union who allowed him to read the mail. His power even extended into the heart of the British community. Colonel Hayley Bell, the resolute kicker of water buffalo, owed Du a large sum of money on his mortgage. Du also brought the same order and method to kidnapping. He organized the snatches then offered his services as mediator, taking fifty per cent of the ransom.

The events of 1927 confirmed Du as one of the most powerful men in Shanghai. Gratitude from Chiang Kai-shek and the foreign authorities brought national power and international respectability. His reputation improved to such an extent that by the mid-'thirties the gangster who delivered new coffins to adversaries found himself described in Shanghai's *Who's Who* as a 'Well-known public welfare worker'. The list of his achievements even makes the claim plausible. He was a prominent member of the French Municipal Council, the president of two banks, a director of various businesses, and the founder and chairman of the Cheng Shih Middle School. Under his influence the criminal and respectable worlds of the city were bound by a history of mutual favours and obscure loyalties. The most unlikely people owed him a good turn, I was told by Baron Rothschild, a Belgian diplomat in Shanghai after the Second World War. The Baron always accepted invitations to Du's famous garden parties because 'it was wise to keep on the right side of him'. At the festivities Du appeared a benign old man in a long Chinese robe of white silk; only his skin, yellow from opium addiction, betrayed him. He spoke no foreign languages. The Baron always tried to give Du a piece of 'juicy' gossip. The old gangster, he explained, lived off inside information and gleefully collected even the tiniest morsel. The Baron added that everyone of importance in Shanghai had contact with Du. It was impossible to avoid him.

Ricky Lu recalled meeting Du in the Ningbo Merchants' Club where the gangster gambled with Ricky's father. Short and slender with large yellow teeth, very long arms, a shaven head and ears that stuck out, the young Ricky Lu thought he looked like a monkey. Years later Ricky found himself working in the same firm as Du's son but, as he put it, 'the boy lacked the balls of his dad'.

Christopher Isherwood and W. H. Auden met Du in 1938, five years from the *Who's Who* entry and by then a government official with an important position on the Red Cross Central Committee. An aroma of his principal activities must still have lingered for Isherwood describes him as 'a Big Business chief after the classic American pattern'. They interviewed Du in his strongly guarded flat where

> at least a dozen attendants were posted in the hall, and, when we sat down to talk, there were others who stood in the background behind our chairs. Tu himself was tall and thin, with a face that seemed hewn out of stone, a Chinese version of the Sphinx. Peculiarly and inexplicably terrifying were his feet, in their silk socks and smart pointed European boots, emerging from beneath the long silken gown. Perhaps the Sphinx, too, would be even more frightening if it wore a modern top-hat.[18]

Du first became interested in the Nationalist party through Sun Yat-sen, a fellow member of the Green Gang and a friend. Du saw the potential of the party and gave Sun protection and support. He befriended Chiang Kai-shek, also a member of the Green Gang and, as Sterling Seagrave described in his excellent book, *The Soong Dynasty*, a 'young ill-tempered bravo'[19] with a police record in the International Settlement which included armed robbery, extortion and murder. The two men cemented their friendship in Shanghai's brothels and gambling clubs. Du's advice and help ensured Chiang's rapid rise in the Nationalist party. Together they planned to destroy the Chinese Communist party in Shanghai.

Stirling Fessenden, chairman of the Municipal Council, described his meeting with Du to a fellow American, J. B. Powell, the courageous editor of the *China Weekly Review* who published the account only after Fessenden's death.[20]

Stirling Fessenden drew up outside an Edwardian villa of arches and balustrades transformed into an armed fortress and drug depot. Armed guards stood at the gates. On each of its three floors, Du kept one of his three wives. Despite the guns, the gangsters and the matrimonial arrangements, the house preserved an atmosphere of Edwardian respectability and managed to look like the secondary school it became after 1949. Fessenden told Powell, 'I could not help but notice that the large entrance hall was lined on both sides with stacks of rifles and sub-machine guns.'

Fessenden joined Du Yuesheng, the French Chief of Police and an interpreter and the three 'got down to business immediately'. The Chief of Police explained that the collapse of law and order in the Chinese section of Shanghai concerned them all. The warlord's troops were in retreat and the Nationalist army still some distance off. Nothing stopped Shanghai's communist trade unions from taking control of those areas of the city under Chinese jurisdiction and formerly in possession of the warlord. From there, Du predicted, they would move against the foreign Concessions. Du made his proposition. He was willing to stop the Reds but under two conditions. He required at least five thousand rifles and ammunition from the French authorities. Then he turned to Fessenden and demanded permission to drive his military trucks through the International Settlement in order to move arms and munitions – a request which the Settlement authorities had always refused to grant any Chinese force.

Fessenden agreed, subject to the approval of the Municipal Council. As he confided to Powell, 'I realised we were taking a desperate chance in dealing with a man of Du's reputation, but the situation was critical.' Du had convinced Fessenden that the communists were plotting to seize the foreign settlements and defend themselves against the arriving Guomindang troops. Fessenden believed Du's story of a split between the communists and the Nationalists. This was a lie. At the time of the meeting in Rue du Consulat, the communists viewed the Nationalists as an army of liberation and on their side. It was Du and Chiang Kai-shek, not the communists, who engineered the split. Meanwhile, Du succeeded in frightening Fessenden. Later, Fessenden talked wildly to Powell of 'widespread disorder and bloodshed', foreigners 'sandwiched between contending forces' and the 'international complications'. In his panic Fessenden appeared to forget the twenty thousand foreign troops defending the Settlement. He accepted everything the gangster told him. Du no doubt found it a pleasant diversion to deal with a man described by the US State Department as one of life's 'feeble creatures', who 'had gone to pieces in the Far East' and was 'conspicuously unfit for his position'.[21]

The advantages for Du were obvious. Under the communists he would lose everything. Already the communist-backed unions had taken over the guilds which formed his power base among the workers. The French Concession consented to his demands because of their mutual business interests. Du used the Concession to export opium to France. His bribes ensured the operation remained free from official interference either from the French government or the French authorities in Shanghai. (His son recalled receiving a hamper of toys every Christmas from his father's Parisian associates.) When he and the French Chief of Police talked of their concern for law and order they meant the breakdown of their drug empire. Du also planned to make a profit. Shanghai's Chinese businessmen contributed millions to pay for the removal of the communists. The French Municipality provided free arms and ammunition. Du only had to wait for the right moment to put his men in place.

The communist trade unions, unaware of the alliance between Du, Chiang Kai-shek and the Settlement authorities, had decided to seize those areas of the city under Chinese control before the arrival of the Nationalist army. From noon on March 21st, about 800,000 workers went on strike. Sam Ginsbourg recalled the unfamiliar silence in Szechuen Road which usually rang with street cars. Armed policemen protected buses from strikers and stone-throwers.

The communist trade unions had their headquarters a short walk from Du's house in a grubby apartment at 29 Rue Lafayette. Here Zhou Enlai, a returned student from Paris and later Minister of China under Mao Zedong, divided his five thousand communists into cadres of thirty backed up by workers and the unemployed. They supplemented their 150 guns, mostly Mauser pistols, with knives, clubs and axes. As they took their positions throughout Greater Shanghai, women carried bowls of food to them from hundreds of small restaurants and street vendors. Zhou Enlai and three hundred of his best men took over the police stations, the arsenal, the Chinese law courts, the telephone and telegraph centres and the power stations. The Ginsbourgs watched their lights blink then dim. Later on their telephone ceased to work.

In the International Settlement the authorities blocked off all main roads leading into Chinese territory with huge, spiked gates. The Volunteer Corps advised foreigners living in the Chinese areas to move into the Settlement. A patrol made up of foreign clerks, accountants and managers visited Sam's family at lunchtime. The officer, a small man with a large moustache and a red nose, told Sam's parents in pidgin English to evacuate quickly: ' "Chop-chop, savvy?" ' His fear made them nervous.

With bullets singing about their home, the Ginsbourgs threw together a few belongings, locked up their flat and joined the crowds of refugees escaping to the safety of the foreign territory. An American druggist on North Szechuen Road lent the Ginsbourgs his attic, four hundred yards from the boundary of the International Settlement. The next morning the boys ran on to the roof to watch the battle.

First Sam looked south across the International Settlement. He saw shops boarded up and streets empty but for a motionless bus in the middle of the pavement and the occasional passer-by. He then turned north and witnessed a scene 'not to be easily forgotten'.[22] A gate and barbed-wire fence guarded the boundary between the International Settlement and the Chinese district of Chapei. Chinese and Sikh policemen, supplemented by a group of foreign volunteers, searched the thousands of Chinese refugees seeking to escape Zhou Enlai and his communist cadres. They searched every refugee, regardless of age and sex and ordered some back for no apparent reason that Sam could see. More than once they separated a family, keeping the children back and allowing the parents through or separating a married couple. When the cries and curses grew unbearable, the police flailed the crowds with their batons. At times they locked the gate and allowed no one in. Thousands of people then pressed against the gate, yelling, begging and crying. Some tried to climb the barbed-wire entanglements only to be hurled backwards by the police. A group of Chinese suddenly squeezed through and ran off down North Szechuen Road. Sam heard shots outside his house and saw a man writhing on the ground in a pool of blood; another lay still. A British officer walked slowly towards the bodies, a pistol in his hand.

A few days later the Ginsbourg family woke to the sound of gunfire. Sam's older brother who had slipped out earlier, returned to announce the arrival of the Nationalist army in the city by way of Longhua, a place famed for its pagoda and execution ground. The soldiers had joined Zhou Enlai's communist cadres against the remnants of the warlord's army, despite Du's prediction to Stirling Fessenden. In the twilight Sam Ginsbourg watched black smoke rise above North Station where the warlord's White Russian troops, whose armour-plated train had successfully held out against the communists' Mausers, finally conceded defeat to the heavy artillery of the Nationalist army. The Ginsbourgs spent the night huddled in fear on mattresses spread across the floor. In the dark, they listened to the sounds of a battle and watched the reflections of a huge blaze from the direction of Chapei. They dared not leave or even fall asleep.

In the early hours of March 22nd, Sam and his older brother crept out without waking their parents to find the city transformed. Zhou Enlai and his men, backed by large segments of the Nationalist army, had taken Shanghai but for the International Settlement and the French Concession. Sam described the general rejoicing. Red flags covered the houses, people wore red armbands, speakers addressed excited crowds and men and women wept. Pushing slowly through the throngs, members of the Volunteer Corps tipped their steel helmets low over their brows.

The fighting appeared over. The Ginsbourgs returned to Chapei and rented an apartment on Range Road not far from the North Railway Station. They still heard gunfire at night. Sometimes from their back window in the early morning they saw corpses in the alleyway. By afternoon the bodies had disappeared. The majority of Shanghai's foreigners refused to venture from the Settlement. They waited in trepidation for the communist attack and took some comfort from the troops and the barricades. Unknown to them, their leaders were making welcome the very man responsible for their predicament.

On March 26th Chiang Kai-shek's gunboat sped smoothly past the forty-five foreign warships on the Whangpoo and tied up at the Bund. Du's successful meeting with Stirling Fessenden accounted for Chiang's easy berthing and the affability of his first foreign visitor, Patrick Givens. No longer did the head of Special Branch wish to depict Chiang Kai-shek as a cobra and a tortoise. On Du's advice, the authorities now regarded Chiang as an ally. Givens presented him with a special pass which allowed him to enter the International Settlement with an armed guard whenever he wished.

Chiang arrived to a Shanghai held by the communists under the traditional authority of Zhou Enlai. Three thousand sympathetic Nationalist troops now supplemented an equal number of workers united behind the General Labour Union, who, as Seagrave remarks, 'imagined a reunification with the Kuomintang [Guomindang], and a glorious future in coalition'.[23] Chiang did not trust his troops, nor the reinforcements at Hangzhou, to march against men whose activities as fifth columnists had contributed to the army's success.

He confronted the same problem as Patrick Givens. How to win the heart of the Chinese worker?

Chiang chose the easiest way. He wooed the potential victims of the workers. Shanghai's Chinese businessmen had heard what had happened in Hankou where, as the Standard Oil Company confided to the American State Department, farmers and labourers had murdered a number of wealthy Chinese, 'the only motives for these murders being the victim's wealth and a planned confiscation of the victim's property'.[24] They had read the posters stuck up by students on Shanghai's streets. They were not happy at all. Wealth remained their only weapon. Chiang, if he was to break with the communists, needed alternative sums of money to replace the Russian funds and the revenues from Guangzhou which the communists controlled. Shanghai's Chinese businessmen had no choice but to back Chiang.

Chiang did not underestimate the difficulty of his task. The workers were well-organized and popular. He chose to play a game of Grand Mother's Footsteps. For every step he took forward he made a feint in the opposite direction in order to confuse his enemy and fudge the issue while all the time preparing for the final blow. The *North China Daily News*, well-informed, even if it did not know quite what to make of its information, declared 'Is the Kuomintang splitting up? ... Events are moving so rapidly here that it is difficult to know all the facts.'[25] A representative of Chiang immediately complained: 'the English Press in China is spreading all kinds of lies on this subject. It ought to be suppressed.'[26]

Du Yuesheng also laid plans to reassert his influence with the workers. On April 9th, 1927 he invited Wang Shouhua, chairman of the Shanghai General Union, to his house. Wang accepted and turned up at the Edwardian villa without a bodyguard – a foolish move in Shanghai. Du, for example, employed four: a bad-tempered blacksmith called Fiery Old Crow; an ex-gardener; a one-time waiter at the Shanghai Club who spoke English and a former chauffeur at the American consulate after whose Stars and Stripes[27] (or Flowery Flag to the Shanghainese) he was nicknamed. Du never paid a visit unless accompanied by two carloads of armed men. On a round of Shanghai's teahouses, steam baths and nightclubs, one car of bodyguards always arrived first to 'case the joint'. Du followed in his bullet-proof sedan with a second car of gangsters. Only when the men had surrounded the car door did he step forth and, safe in the heart of his mob, gingerly cross the pavement. Once settled in the club, his guards arranged themselves about him, their guns out for all to see. Fiery Old Crow and Flowery Flag greeted Wang on his arrival. They failed to mention dinner or even offer a glimpse of Du. Instead they bundled the hapless Wang into a car and drove out of Shanghai through the Western suburbs to a dirt road that ended in a field. There they strangled Wang, rolled him up in a hessian sack and threw him, still groaning, into a grave.

The communists made Du's job easier by their reluctance to exploit their victory, consolidate their hold on Shanghai and break with Chiang Kai-shek. The reason for this lay in Russia. Stalin's drive against the opposition headed by Trotsky had turned into a pogrom. Stalin dismissed with unctuous assurances Trotsky's view that a 'shackled' Communist party in China could only lead to the establishment of a 'fascist dictatorship'.[28] Communists around the world obeyed the official line. Nothing but praise for Chiang Kai-shek appeared in the international communist press. The Chinese workers looked on him as their hero. Factory workers arrived at his headquarters with gifts of kettles, teapots, boxes, baskets and cloth. Stalin instructed the Chinese Communist party in Shanghai to co-operate with Chiang, avoid military conflict and bury their weapons.

In the first week of April Chiang ordered those Chinese troops loyal to the communists to leave Shanghai. Their commander approached the Chinese Communist Central Committee and offered to arrest Chiang Kai-shek as a counter-revolutionary. They hesitated. Could the commander not feign sickness instead? they asked. He left the city in disgust.

The events of April 12th proved Trotsky right without doing either him or the Chinese communists any good. Before dawn a siren blast from Chiang's gunboat answered the plaintive call of a bugle. Almost immediately machine-gun fire spluttered out over the Shanghai night. The communists had gone to bed in control of the city. They woke to bullets from men in white armbands bearing the Chinese character for 'labour'. They did not understand who was attacking them or why. Four hundred died fighting.

The men behind the guns were, as Pan Ling has described in her book, *Old Shanghai: Gangsters in Paradise*, Du Yuesheng's 'hijackers, pensioners, bodyguards, masseurs, manicurists, hawkers and waiters', as well as 'bouncers from the sleazier bars and restaurants'.[29] They shared one great asset. They hated communism and scorned factory workers. The day before they and the troops Chiang still trusted had received weapons, white armbands and instructions to shoot anyone who possessed a gun but not an armband. During the night they took their place stealthily throughout the city.

The gunfire woke the Ginsbourg family. They jumped out of bed and huddled in the dark not daring to turn on the lights. In the morning they glimpsed police patrols and pickets wearing white armbands. They watched police drag manacled students and workers from alleyways and throw them into Red Marias.

The next day the communist trade unionists announced a general strike in protest at the deaths. A hundred thousand workers marched through the rain to the Guomindang headquarters. They called for insane things: no more killings, the killers punished, their weapons returned. They did not seem to understand their situation at all. Women and children marched with them. None of the strikers bore arms. Soldiers loyal to Chiang Kai-shek lined Paoshan Road by San Te Terrace. As the strikers passed, machine-guns suddenly opened fire without warning. Men, women and children scrambled screaming in the mud. The troops charged with fixed bayonets, dragging people out when they fled into houses to hide, and killing them in the gutters. It took eight trucks and several hours to clear the streets of corpses.

In the White Terror, as it was called, the Guomindang executed 12,000 supposed communists in three weeks. (About the same number as the Red Guards killed in Shanghai during the Cultural Revolution forty years later.) Fifty thousand were put to death or imprisoned within the year. The French Concession and International Settlement co-operated with a series of raids and house-to-house searches. The foreign authorities handed over prisoners to the Nationalist military courts.

To their horror Chinese businessmen found themselves sharing the same cells as communists. They had called on the service of thugs. Now they found the same thugs holding them to ransom. On the pretext of hunting communists, the National Government kidnapped rich Chinese and forced their families to make 'heavy contributions'[30] to military funds in exchange for their release. The Northern Expedition was the reason for the Chinese businessman's discomfort. The leading article in the *North China Daily News* of

July 30th stated Chiang Kai-shek needed SH$20,000 a month to finance his campaign and was indulging in an 'orgy of taxation' as well as more 'insidious methods' to raise it. It is not difficult to guess who made himself responsible for the latter.

Chiang Kai-shek had taken Greater Shanghai. The Chinese leader and the foreign authorities mutually congratulated themselves. The Municipal Council promoted Stirling Fessenden to Secretary-General and increased Patrick Givens' pension. Chiang Kai-shek rewarded Du Yuesheng by making him Chief of the newly established Bureau of Opium Suppression, an irony much enjoyed by Shanghai's inhabitants, and decorated both Du and Givens with the Order of the Brilliant Jade. Only Sam Ginsbourg remarked on the bizarre state of affairs which resulted in the head of Special Branch receiving the same distinction as the city's leading gangster.

The ordinary Shanghailander still felt perplexed. Exactly who had saved Shanghai, even the newspapers found hard to say. The China Press talked of Nationalist troops. The *North China Daily News* wrote about 'armed Kuomintang labourers'.[31] Even the Shanghai Municipal Police Report appears uncharacteristically vague, describing Du's men as 'merchants' volunteers'.[32] The *North China Daily News* reports the march and the shooting of the demonstrators 'many of them women and children' but makes no mention of a massacre.[33] Foreign journalists appeared to have overlooked eight truckloads of corpses. It is possible the authorities were attempting to hide the massacre; or the massacre itself might have been just another of those 'gross distortions and exaggerations' that the Chinese Communist party put about, as a disillusioned Harold Isaacs later complained.

An elderly Chinese businessman who had invited me to dinner in the Yale Club had the last word: 'It is no good trying to find out what really happened. No one ever did.' After all, what was important? Shanghai had survived.

The events of 1927 placed Shanghai 'before the world; Shanghai has become a world problem'.[34] Large investments both in human and financial terms forced Britain and America to formulate a policy towards the maverick city. The rise of Chiang Kai-shek and the Nationalist party appeared to herald a new era for Shanghai. The governments of Great Britain and the United States noted the nationalist sentiment infusing China. They agreed with the Inter Missionary Council that the Chinese 'heartily support the purposes and aim of the Nationalist Government',[35] and rejected as impracticable attempts to fight it. They instructed the foreign authorities in Shanghai to make concessions to the Chinese from the momentous to the trivial. The foreigners allowed Chinese into the parks of the International Settlement from which they had previously been excluded and even talked of ending extraterritoriality. When the incensed Shanghailander petitioned home for the weapons and soldiers to keep the Chinese in their place, Clarence E. Gauss, the American Consul-General for Shanghai dismissed such demands as 'antiquated'. The days of bluff, he believed, were over. 'A suggestion of force in China at the present juncture must be backed by sufficient force and the authority and intention to use that force.' It would require 'tens of thousands' of men and would mean war. He summed up, 'I do not believe the powers are prepared to face that contingency.'[36]

American missionaries had provoked this new mood in the United States. The Americans had originally come to Shanghai, like everybody else, to make a quick fortune. They had settled in Hongkew to the north of Soochow creek known euphemistically by the Chinese as 'The Rainbow's Mouth'. The Chinese authorities had never officially given it to the Americans. It has 'just growed'[37] as one resident put it, to finally merge with the British (the Americans wanted to use the British jail) into the International Settlement. East Coast merchants like Heard & Company, Wetmore's, Olyphant's, Wolcott, Bates & Company and most important of them all, Russell & Company, linked to the Yankee merchant clans of Roosevelt, Delano and Forbes, traded opium alongside their British counterparts. Frederick Townsend Ward of Salem, Massachusetts, the first in a long line of American adventurers and conmen attracted to the city, led foreign sailors against the Taiping rebels in the 1860s, married a Chinese, enriched himself on loot and even collected the title of brigadier-general of the 'Ever Victorious Army' from the Manchu Emperor. It was, however, missionary work, which as one American newspaper reported, formed 'the chief feature of American enterprise in respect to China'.[38]

China's vast numbers had set American missionaries to dreaming of the same fantastic possibilities as American businessmen. Here, as a missionary wrote in the nineteenth century, was a docile and kindly race, 'wedded by custom to foolish idolatry but never willing seriously to defend its practice'.[39] They imagined obedient millions under their sway. In Shanghai, missionaries set up schools and universities for the Chinese, the most famous of which was St John's College. Dr Hawk Potts, the president of St John's University, recalled, at a Shanghai Rotary Club dinner in 1934, the pleasant existence enjoyed by the missionary in the city: 'everybody had his own residence, with a large garden, and a retinue of servants.'[40] Their style of living hardly matched their success at conversion. In 1898, for example, China boasted 3,900 Protestant missionaries to 700 Catholic missionaries. Despite lack of funds and people, Chinese Catholic converts stood at half a million. Protestant converts numbered less than 200,000. The Chinese found the French Jesuits rather more impressive than the Americans with their wives, their houses and their 'very comfortable, easy sort of life'.[41]

In Chiang Kai-shek the missionaries saw hope for China's future and an extension of their own power and influence. An after-dinner speech by Fletcher S. Brockman reported by the *St Louis Globe Democrat* in March 1927 typifies missionary propaganda in the United States. The administrative secretary of the Y.M.C.A. for the Far East and the man who had established the organization in China in 1898, Brockman took pains to stress how 'profoundly American in spirit' was the new Nationalist party. The Nationalist leaders were graduates of American universities – 'I knew the fathers of most of them nearly as well as they did themselves.' He warned his audience in Henry James style not to be misled by radical elements, 'thrust in from Europe'. The Nationalist army 'is the spirit of our own fathers marching down the Yangtzse'.

The need for propaganda was great. At the end of the nineteenth century cheap Chinese labour had led to horrendous race riots in the United States ('kill 'em lots,' advised the editor of the *Montanian*), and numerous local laws and ordinances against the Chinese culminating in the Exclusion Law of 1882 forbidding entry of Chinese into the country except for teachers, students, merchants and tourists. Chinese already in America were refused U.S. citizenship. Hollywood was still making 'Yellow Peril' films in the 'twenties and in California it was illegal for a Caucasian to marry a Chinese until after the Second World War.[42] The missionaries won sympathy for the Chinese by association however far-fetched. They created an illusion which they themselves fell for. They believed Shanghai, for example, to be like 'an American country town',[43] whose inhabitants would exhibit, with only the minimum of encouragement, all the small-town virtues Americans believed made America great.

Missionary success in the United States, if not in China, meant that missionaries dictated American foreign policy. A display of arms against Chiang Kai-shek in 1927 would 'inevitably inflame' all China against the thousands of American missionaries in the interior, stated the Secretary of the Navy in Washington.[44] Anything more than a naval force for defence and evacuation risked 'very strong public condemnation here both in Congress and out'.[45] As the *North China Daily News* admitted: 'It is a plain fact that public opinion in America is very largely based upon and influenced by missionary information. Government action follows public opinion . . . '[46]

Britain objected to the expense. Homer Brett, the America Consul for London, reported that taxation in the United Kingdom was 'believed to be at the limit of endurance'. The government accounts had closed for the year revealing a deficit. New expenditure would be looked upon 'with a feeling of despair as many hold that trade cannot possibly revive until the tax burden is lightened'. He quoted a popular newspaper joke: ' "Coldstreams for China" runs the headline: "Gold streams for China" groans the taxpayer.'[47]

Shanghailanders spent the years before the outbreak of the Second World War trying to persuade their governments that Shanghai was worth the streams of gold. Their failure, they knew, meant the end of Shanghai. The city survived because the gunboats on the Bund and the threat of troops from home protected their businesses and investments. It explains their keenness to present Shanghai as a city worth saving, not vice-ridden but an honourable place and of good cheer. This was why they so eagerly provided distractions for the troops. They did not want the sort of articles in the *Lancet* or questions in Parliament which might make an order to send the boys back to Shanghai an unpopular political move. At a pinch you could ask the public to sacrifice a son – but not to syphilis.

The Shanghailander forgot it had not been the British Tommy who had saved Shanghai but a Chinese gangster. The foreign soldiers hardly fired a shot.

A year later the troops pulled out. The offices of B Defence Force presented the Shanghai Club with three silver fruit dishes. Dr McDonnal's regiment, now cured of disease, left in November 1928, the privates disconsolate at the prospect of Singapore. They had to say goodbye to the White Russian women they had met in Shanghai's cabarets and bars, who boasted of fabulous pasts, of fathers who were generals and princes, of knives and forks made of gold, of palaces and sable coats. As one soldier put it: 'But what I 'ates about leaving Shanghai is that down below, we won't meet the women we've known 'ere. Now tikes me for instance, I haint no Don John, but I just been looking around here a month or so and already I can sign on the dotted line with a Princess, no less.' Now in Singapore 'acorse they might be alright, but is there any Princesses among'em? Hi'll wager there ain't.' His friends agreed: 'Artie's right, the lad's got it. No fear, there's no royalty awaiten fer us in Singapore.'[48]

The attitude of the Chinese to the foreign invasion of their city is aptly caught by an incident witnessed by a Shanghailander in Medhurst Road. He found the servants, cooks and coolies of the area gathered around a boiling pot. Into this they threw 'what at first sight appeared to be parts of a human body'[49] but which were in fact a head, hand and a leg fashioned from flour or rice to look like the real thing. When questioned the Chinese announced that they were 'eating an Englishman'.[50]

I asked Dr McDonnal for a particular incident that summed up 1927 for him. On an early morning stroll in Jessfield Park, he recalled encountering a British officer of the Volunteer Corps arguing with a Chinese commander. The commander and his troops wanted to cross the bridge into the Settlement. The lone British officer showed equal determination to stop them. 'He knew not a word of Chinese so he tried some Arabic. Finally he said, "Fuck Off" and they turned and walked away.'

The officer epitomized the British attitude in Shanghai. They did not want change. They wanted time and their city to stand still. The pact with Du Yuesheng had been an attempt to do just that. As their desire determined Shanghai's future, it is important to understand their contribution to the city and what exactly they wished to preserve.

· FOUR ·

The British

BEFORE THE SECOND World War the British arrived in Shanghai by boat after a six-week voyage through a Far East both exotic and familiar. The ports of call – Colombo, Penang, Singapore and Hong Kong – all fell under British rule. The traveller could admire the minareted buildings in Singapore and go to church. He could be amused by the monkeys in Penang's streets and ask the way from a policeman. The ports represented a British Far East, contained and clipped at the edges. Outside lay jungle and wilderness when the ship steamed for days past nothing but green coasts, a fishing boat or a few huts on stilts. The smell of this other East drifted off the land and into the cabins. The heat took hold of shipboard life. Electric fans, ice cream, cold drinks and even a makeshift canvas pool appeared on deck. The women bared their arms and legs in dresses of white voile. People slept during the day and sat out at night, listening to the same record over and over again, talking until late or embracing in the shadows beneath a lifeboat.

Hours before the passengers caught their first glimpse of China, its mud came streaming towards the ship, turning the Pacific blue to a brownish yellow. From the mouth of the Yangtze stretched countryside straight out of a China guidebook; rice fields, the occasional pagoda and water-buffaloes with boys on their backs. As the ship turned into the Whangpoo the scenery changed. Billboards advertising chewing gum, cigarettes and Tiger Balm now soared over the mud huts on wooden struts. The countryside gave way to factories, godowns and docks. Twelve miles up the Whangpoo the ship rounded Pootung Point. The traveller found himself facing not China nor anything remotely Chinese. The 'Liverpool of the East' lay before him.

The visitor's first sight of the city was the Bund, a 7½-mile curve of grand eloquent waterfront. Originally a tow-path along which coolies pulled the Emperor's annual rice tribute, under foreign occupation the Bund had developed into Shanghai's most prestigious road and commercial centre. Its foreign buildings soared above the traveller's head, an architectural hymn to white omnipotence. Façades of bronze and granite erupted against the Chinese sky. Each possessed the authority of a public building without achieving it. For the Bund symbolized Shanghai's obsession with business. Its magnificence belonged to the city's most important firms, banks, hotels and clubs. The Hongkong and Shanghai Bank, the *North China Daily News*, the Shanghai Club, the Chartered Bank, Sassoon House, Bank of China, Yokohama Specie Bank and Jardine Matheson & Co., all displayed their success along the Bund. Their neo-classical domes and columns aimed to reassure rather than to delight. This, they declared, was no mirage on the edge of China, a modern phantasmagoria of elevators and air-conditioning. It was here to stay, a future taken care of and worth investing in. Like the monuments of ancient empires, the purpose of the Bund was to inspire awe and a sense of permanence in the onlooker.

The British contribution to Shanghai appeared as solid and durable as the Bund. The British owned the largest bank and trading firms. They administered the trams, the police force, the gas company and water works as well as the courts and Municipal Council on British lines. It is easy to forget that the British never colonized Shanghai as they did Hong Kong. Nightclubs in Shanghai did not close at midnight to the tune of the British National Anthem. The city had neither a Governor who was the Queen's Plenipotentiary in China nor the status of China station to the Royal Navy. Shanghai boasted only a Municipal Council and its businessmen. As one remarked,

'We just thought out what we wanted to do, and went ahead and did it.'[1] The Bund, like the British in Shanghai, is deceiving. A few blocks away from the water, the splendid edifices give way to two storeyed shops. As Christopher Isherwood noted when he arrived, 'The biggest animals have pushed their way down to the brink of the water: behind them is a sordid and shabby mess of smaller buildings.'[2] The Bund stood as a statement of strength. It also represented an almighty bluff. For the British never managed to be as solid as they seemed. In themselves, their institutions, even in their hold on the city, the squalid and the shabby lurked just around the corner.

The Spoiling Life

Young men hired in Britain and sent out to China for a four-year stint received the plum jobs in Shanghai's trading firms and institutions. Those who combined ability with upbringing found themselves privy to the city's political secrets. They moved easily up the Long Bar of the Shanghai Club where a man's job dictated at which spot on the polished wood he took his drink.

These are the people to take you on a tour of the best that Shanghai had to offer. Young and well connected, they demonstrate the good life enjoyed by the British without its accompanying dark side. For them Shanghai was merely a posting. They lacked a financial and emotional investment in the city. Their interests were not on the line. They could afford to be tolerant. Their interlude in the Far East remained a bizarre, sometimes dangerous but, most of all, carefree time. Lady Jellicoe who grew up in Shanghai summed up the attraction: 'It wasn't China really. It was the new world. It was vibrant, it was alive, there were people doing things and making a lot of money. It was a marvellous mixture of people all the time and then of course it was the spoiling life, let's face it, it was idiotically spoiling.'

For these men Shanghai initiated a distinguished career. Now in their eighties, vestiges of the Far East still decorate their English country homes; an embroidered panel from a Mandarin robe, a Hiroshige view of Mount Fuji or a portrait of an eighteenth-century concubine posed in the attitude of a Fragonard shepherdess. On arrival, I was seated in front of a fire, offered sherry then lunch. It was always pleasant. An atmosphere of ease and deliberate shabbiness pervaded. Sofas appeared dog-haired, curtains grand but faded. In winter pots of freesias or azaleas from the hot-house decorated the rooms. The men I interviewed were tall and impressive. They presented an ideal Shanghai, a vast amusement park of thrills without spills where soldiers fired but were never shot and bandits fled at the sound of a British voice. I believe their memories, like themselves, to be true if somewhat exclusive. Their youth and the later war years cast a golden light over their Shanghai interlude. They recalled only happy times; an exciting ride, a good party, an amusing incident. What about the corruption and the politics, I demanded? They looked vague and shook their heads. The stuff of their working lives now lay unpacked and scattered. Their recollections centred on unconnected incidents, stored in the memory like spotlit paintings. Casual moments of pleasure had turned out to be more durable than anything else. 'If you had asked me about that ten years ago, I could have told you,' said Sir Christopher Chancellor whose job as Far Eastern correspondent for Reuters made him one of the most well-informed men of the time. 'Now I just can't remember.' He paused then asked, 'Was it so important?'

The journey to Shanghai began with a job interview in London. George Stewart is a large-faced, kindly and immensely shrewd man who finished his career as senior manager of the London branch of the Hongkong and Shanghai Bank. I once sat next to a man at dinner who remembered an interview with him. He told me, 'George Stewart terrified me. We discussed my first posting. He announced I was off to Cambodia. I asked why. He said it would do me good.'

George Stewart joined the Hongkong and Shanghai Bank in 1929 at the age of twenty. His uncle, Dr Marshall, practised as the bank's doctor in the city. Like many school-leavers, George did not have much idea of what he wanted to do. His uncle persuaded a partner of Jardine's to propose him for a job. He recalled, 'In those days getting into the bank was rather like getting into Eton; it was very, very difficult.' The bank interviewed him in London and gave the impression that the young man would have no trouble passing the exam. George Stewart concluded they had decided to take him. The bank set competitive exams in order to turn down the socially suspect with grace. The interview stressed the importance of regarding the bank as a career rather than a job. 'They wanted people to come in and stay the course.' It ended in very British fashion with a discussion on rugby.

After four years in London, the bank dispatched George Stewart to Shanghai by boat. He looked on the journey as an unexpected holiday. Nearly everyone travelled then by P. & O. and George Stewart enjoyed the social life. At the various ports of call a representative from the bank came down to meet him and take him out.

In the same year as George Stewart set sail for the Far East, Edward Ward, later to inherit the title of Lord Bangor but not much else, journeyed to Shanghai on the Trans-Siberian Railway. Lord Bangor is a journalist and broadcaster. Tall and charming, he has married a number of times and now lives in a flat with an antique collection of fairground paraphernalia. 'My present wife's,' he said, picking his way between a life-size lion and a wooden angel to offer me not the usual sherry but a glass of champagne.

An introduction from his first fiancée landed him a job in Reuters and a posting to China. The Trans-Siberian train was by then the fastest and, at £60 from Moscow to the Manchurian frontier, the cheapest method of travel to the Far East. It also proved the least popular as most people felt disinclined to try out the world's first communist railway. Lord Bangor found the journey 'curiously enough, very enjoyable'. Reuters provided him with a 'second-category' ticket. First category boasted its own washroom while second shared with the next-door compartment. Whoever first arrived locked the other's door. The carriages were pre-Revolutionary and came upholstered in red plush with mahogany and brass fittings. The 'Express' seldom travelled at more than thirty miles an hour. When it pulled uphill Lord Bangor took his exercise by jumping off and running alongside. At the frequent stops peasants met the train, selling eggs and chickens and other produce. All the stations showed Moscow time, hours out by the time the passenger reached Siberia. Every night people held parties in the different compartments. The Commissar for Vladivostok gave the most splendid. For several evenings he served his excellent champagne to Lord Bangor, a German commercial traveller, an English sea captain, an American newspaperman and a Moscow taxi driver and his wife. They watched the Commissar drink half a tumbler of straight vodka chased with a glass of champagne five or six times an hour and then gently collapse in his corner. The others drunk a last toast before calling the provodnik to pull off the Commissar's boots and put him to bed. After a week of heady living, Lord Bangor admitted even caviare began to pall, 'when you could eat as much as you liked when you liked'.

George Stewart arrived in Hong Kong to be 'rather overcome by the whole thing'. It was May, very hot and he had to work harder than he had expected. He found the bank's dominant position in the colony overpowering for a junior employee and the regulation mess life uncongenial. After two months the bank transferred him to Shanghai which he much preferred. It lacked the nanny atmosphere of Hong Kong and he could live with whom he liked.

Eight days from Moscow, Lord Bangor's train pulled into the Manchurian frontier town of Manzhouli. From there he changed to the Chinese Eastern Railway for the port of Dairen where he took ship to Shanghai. He started work and moved into a flat in the French Concession. His living costs halved while he earned twice as much as he had in London. He recalled, 'Old China Hands talked of a Golden Age in the early 'twenties . . . maybe they thought it had sunk to around nine-carat gold but it was golden enough for me.'

The work proved long and arduous. Office hours included Saturday mornings and few firms gave holidays apart from a Long Leave of six months every four years. Lunch, however, lasted two hours which allowed time to catch up on sleep or play a sport. George Stewart wondered how he packed so much in. 'We all had to work hard, yet I was up early to ride and after a very active night life. I don't understand how I did it. Was it the climate or just youth?'

Most young men arriving in Shanghai followed Lord Bangor's example and settled in the French Concession with its spacious houses and pleasant, tree-lined boulevards. Lady Hayter whose husband, Sir William Hayter, worked at the British Embassy, recalled renting a villa with lattice windows and fake timbering, 'just like a dentist's home in Woking except that the garden flooded every typhoon season'. A Shanghai apartment block provided an alternative. The Cathay Mansions, now the Jing Jiang Hotel, on the former Rue Cardinal Mercier offered a roof garden with a view to the river. Suites were rented already furnished. Bedrooms came equipped with Irish linen sheets monogrammed by hand and bathrooms tiled in black and white. Chinese linen was considered inferior and only used in the restaurant at lunchtime. The building possessed its own bakery and printed menus daily on the twelfth floor. One man recalled a children's dining-room with animals painted around the wall; blue, child-sized furniture; and carefully planned meals for sickly or overweight children. Many British, accustomed to houses without central heating and only the occasional bathroom, found the luxury a revelation. They put it down to the American influence on the city.

After accommodation, the question of which club to join preoccupied the new arrival. Shanghai abounded in clubs. Nearly every nationality and most activities necessitated a club. The British offered three: the Country Club, sixty-five acres of landscaped gardens on Bubbling Well Road with its own ballroom, tennis courts and swimming pool, the Shanghai Club and the Shanghai Race Club. An employee of the Hongkong and Shanghai Bank recalled, 'You had to be introduced to a committee and we were thankful to be taken on as a new member.'

The Shanghai Club, at Number 3 the Bund, was notorious for its snobbishness, its martinis and the hundred-foot Long Bar – the longest, it said, in the world. Lord Bangor, forced to undergo a grilling from members of the committee, told me he found it 'quite a business to join'. The Shanghai Club banned Chinese and women from membership. Its members even blackballed a Chinese prime minister. I found an old Shanghai cartoon pasted into one man's album which summed up the club's attitude to women.

Beneath the title of 'Club Regulation' a Chinese servant is on the telephone in the Shanghai Club. The female voice at the other end asks in pidgin English: 'That belong Hall Porter? Well, my wantie savvy s'pose my husband have not, no got?' (Is that the hall porter, I want to know if my husband is there?)

The Hall Porter replies: 'No missy, husband no got.'

The wife says angrily: 'How fashion you savvy no got, s'pose my no talkee name?' (How do you know he is not there when I haven't told you his name?)

To which the Porter says, 'Maskee name, missy any husband no got this side anytime.' (The name doesn't matter, madam, nobody's husband is ever here, at any time.)

The Shanghai Club first appeared in the late 1860s after the Taiping Rebellion on a lot previously occupied by Hiram Fogg's store. Members could relax on the porch with a pink gin and watch the junks go by. At the turn of the century a splendid new structure with Greek columns replaced the old building. Members were able to stay in rooms on the top floor. In the morning they enjoyed a breakfast of kedgeree, bacon and eggs, porridge in winter and toast and Oxford marmalade. The newspapers came freshly ironed.

Lord Bangor had imagined it 'a raffish place' and 'a haunt of sailors and international adventurers, drug traffickers, white slavers, beautiful women and all that'. His first visit proved a terrible disappointment. The place looked as sedate as anything in St James's. The Long Bar impressed him, especially before lunch on Saturdays when business flowed for the weekend. He recalled Chinese barmen in white jackets elbow to elbow as they served members standing eight deep down its length. At one end the bar turned a corner and ran for a short distance parallel to the Bund. The heads of the big banks and firms reserved this section for themselves. Nobody took a drink there unless invited.

Today the club is the Dongfeng Hotel where Chinese in blue overalls enjoy lemonade and noodles. The series of partitions dissecting the bar reminded me of hatchets breaking the back of some mythical serpent whose death no one wanted to take a chance on. They appeared an act of revenge by the Chinese on a place which saw them serve but never order a drink. One regulation remained unchanged. When I asked for a lemonade, the attendant turned leisurely to one side, spat, faced me again and jerked his thumb in a universal gesture. Women, it seems, are still unwelcome.

George Stewart dedicated his free time to riding, a decision he never regretted. Many people recalled the charm of the Chinese countryside and the character of China's horses. One man confided he had fallen in love with a White Russian and bought a pony during his first winter in Shanghai. At five every morning he left the Russian girl for his pony. Half an hour later he was galloping over the frozen paddy fields with the whitening sky and the air like knives on his face. He remembered the name of his pony but not that of the girl.

'Pony, pony, pony! that's all you talk about,' exclaimed one exasperated French woman over a lady's lunch in November 1932. She expressed her irritation accurately. In Shanghai they did not ride horses, they rode ponies. The ponies were driven down once a year from the grasslands of Mongolia and sold in horse fairs as far south as the Yangtsze. The horses came pony-sized but strong. One of twelve or thirteen hands could carry a man weighing 140 pounds.

You tamed your pony yourself. It was not easy. The ponies feared people and the Chinese grooms, known as *mafoos*, feared both pony and foreigner. It took a month to subdue the pony sufficiently to mount. Even then two men had to grapple with the pony's head while a third held on to a hind leg to stop it bolting. Once in the saddle anything could happen for the Mongolian pony had a mouth of iron. The function of the rider was to stay upright despite a bite on the shin or a sudden buck that sent one man into a double somersault before he hit the ground. If a rider fell off, his pony savaged him. 'Europeans galloping wildly in no special direction, resolutely concentrating only on staying aloft, were a common feature of life in China,'[3] recalled Austin Coates in his excellent book *China Races*. The same happened when the ponies were harnessed to carriages: 'A galloping carriage in a narrow Shanghai lane was no joke, not least to those inside the carriage.'[4]

People persevered because, as the *Official History of the Shanghai Paper Hunt Club* recorded, the pony exhibited all the qualities sportsmen admire, 'undoubtable pluck, staying power, amazing cleverness over a country, and the determination from start to finish to get home first'.[5] Their stamina became legendary. Lieutenant-Colonel Souvoroff of the Haig Riding School rode a white pony called Almas at the end of August 1929 from Shanghai to Nanjing and back in sixteen days. He covered 700 miles with an average of 45 miles a day. Captain W. F. Adair owned a champion called Betha, rumoured to lack a tongue (no one had dared check), which the captain once rode twenty-four hours without stopping. The animals also performed well as racers and jumpers.

Lord Bangor, who had become a life member of the Shanghai Race Club, 'for what that turned out to be worth', attended the sales eager to pick a winner for the new year's Shanghai Derby. The horses arrived from Mongolia resembling small, woolly bears. 'Subscription griffins' (a griffin was the nickname for a British newcomer to India) cost about £25. Two or three people might club together to buy one. They drew their ponies by lot and the lucky man finished with an exceptional racer. At the worst he owned a good riding pony for only £25. A pony's feed and stabling cost less than £5 a week. Lord Bangor recalled that most of his friends could afford a racehorse and even win an important race.

A few months' training turned the shaggy animals into miniature racehorses with powerful, well-ribbed bodies, strong backs and shapely legs. A short neck appeared their only defect. They walked as they galloped with their necks stretched out in a straight line. The Griffin's Plate at the spring meeting saw the new ponies race for the first time. If the horse proved a winner, its owner could ask ten times what he paid. 'Very satisfying,' said Lord Bangor, 'except you then had to break in another pony.'

At the centre of the International Settlement lay the racecourse. Now it is divided up between the People's Square, a desolate stretch of concrete and the People's Park. Here elderly Chinese sit on benches or stroll about the paths, gossiping, playing chequers or practising their t'ai chi. Over the treetops rise the skyscrapers, built with such optimism fifty years before and a reminder of the past most working-class Shanghainese said they preferred to forget. In one corner the authorities had placed a rockery, the size of a small hill. I walked up to look at the view. An old lady hesitated then followed me. When she thought no one could see us, she grabbed my arm and asked, 'Are the foreigners coming back? When they were here before they took the best of everything. Life was so bad, so bad. We suffered so much we didn't care if our children lived or died.' From behind a fence in a corner of the People's Square, I saw the empty tiers of the former grandstand still intact. She followed my gaze. On impulse I asked her if she had ever attended a race. After a moment, she admitted she went regularly as a child when her father earned good money as a nightwatchman for a foreign godown. 'Those years whole families go to races.' She enjoyed the acrobats and the food stalls selling specialities from all over China. On one occasion, 'My father's Number Two brother lost a heap of money and my aunty hit him in front of whole crowd of people. She hit him many, many times until everyone was laughing and some men started to bet whether he fall down or not.' She shook her head. 'Long, long time since I thought of that,' she said and tottered off on half-bound feet down the rockery path.

Next to the grandstand stood the Shanghai Race Club with its clock-tower known as 'Big Bertie'. As ornate and exclusive as the Shanghai Club, it included a marble staircase, teak-panelled rooms, oak parquet floors, bowling alleys, a Turkish bath suite and a separate staircase for lady guests. The coffee room with its huge, brick fireplace covered the area of a tennis court and a half. The club held legendary Christmas parties. Lord Kadoorie recalled overhearing as a boy the scandalous details of one in particular. The guests had dined at a long table set in the centre with a magnificent silver bowl filled with flowers. The bowl appeared so large it inspired one man to make a daring bet with a lovely Shanghai socialite. She immediately accepted and ordered the servants to throw out the flowers and water and fill the bowl with champagne. 'Then, in front of everyone, she stepped on to the table and plunged in.'

The Race Club is now a public library. I paid a visit one lunchtime to find it empty but for a bemused Chinese librarian who spoke to me in French. He did not know it had been a race club. He showed me his office on the top floor. Its floor-to-ceiling windows displayed a view of Renmin Park. He was fond of the view, he told me. We explored other floors. Book-stacks filled some rooms. Others stood empty and unused. Nearly all still had their original teak panelling.

On the staircase the librarian and I paused in a stream of sunshine to admire the Art Deco balustrade rising upwards in wide sweeps. I tried to imagine what kind of men had climbed its steps. I had seen photographs of club members leading winners off the racetrack. They wore soft hats, well-cut overcoats and smoked cigars. Their faces looked hard and heavy under a veneer of geniality. I had hoped to find some trace of them in a place they must have recalled with pleasure. The librarian and I waited but no ghostly groups drifted past. The sight of us, a Chinese man and an English woman, must have sent them back in a state of celestial apoplexy to a heaven no doubt as exclusive and well-equipped as their club.

Shanghai's earliest plans show provision for a racetrack. For-eigners organized races from 1844, the year they arrived in the Settlement. During the cooler months heats took place for two hours on Saturday afternoon. The first recorded Shanghai race meeting occurred on 17th and 18th April, 1848. It appears to have been a jolly and informal occasion. The jockeys called a lap, 'Once round from the Willows', after a convenient clump. Roman Nose (which every Mongolian pony had) beat Kiss-me-quick in the Hack Stakes. One horse bolted into the countryside. The meet fin-ished with The Native Purse. The riders, mainly mafoos, raced in Chinese cavalry dress with bells, high saddles and bamboo whips. The winner, appropriately enough, bore the name of Tattersall. As one enthusiast summed up when addressing the committee in April 1853, 'sport and nothing but sport should be our object, even though some of our arrangements might astonish the ideas of the knowing men of Newmarket, as much as a whirl round Fives Court Turn might astonish their nerves'.[6]

As early as 1861 the Spring and Autumn Meetings could be described as 'the grand festival of Shanghai'.[7] All business closed down for a week. Chinese and foreigners dressed up in their best. The Chinese wore silk robes. The British ladies put on long-sleeved gloves while the men sported grey top hats and elaborate waistcoats. Bets were large but discreet with young men keeping books in a corner of the grandstand. Ladies did not bet, at least not with money. Instead they wagered fans, bonnets, cigar boxes and even umbrellas. They did not restrict themselves to one fan or one bonnet. At the Spring Meet of 1861 a husband told his wife that, until business improved, ten dozen gloves was her limit.

The Meets turned into a Chinese as much as a foreign festival.

The Chinese loved gambling and lined the course. Ten thousand watched the Spring Meet of 1861. The Chinese understood the prestige involved in racing and the very grandest Chinese attended. Even the Emperor's representative, the Daodai, arrived for an hour and met the European ladies. His guard brandished four flags, two spears, two servitors and one umbrella and howled when the Daodai arrived and left the grandstand.

In 1911 two Chinese millionaires, tired of exclusion from the Race Club, started their own course three miles north of the Settlement at Kiangwan. They encouraged an international membership and co-ordinated their meets with the Shanghai Club. Before long racing enthusiasts attended both.

The Shanghai races became an integral part of Shanghai business life and the ideal place for a man to display his wealth and compete for prestige. (John Fairbank, the eminent China historian, recalled the wife of the American Consul wearing purple furs to the races.) Shanghai's dirty linen was raced in public. The bitter rivalry between the two trading firms of Jardine Matheson and Dent, Beale & Co. was ridden out in front of the intrigued and amused spectators until Dent's went suddenly and mysteriously bankrupt in 1867. Generation after generation of Shanghai's most prominent families took part. Formidable jockeys and owners included Harry Morriss and his brother Hayley, the sons of Mohawk Morriss, the founder of the *North China Daily News*; Eric Moller of the Moller Line and his sons; the Ezra brothers, grandsons of Isaac Ezra, the Iraqi Jewish opium trader and property tycoon; J. A. S. Alves, a descendant of one of the first Portuguese families to come to Shanghai; S. P. Ma, T. L. and H. F. Hu and T. N. and T. U. Yih, all sons of great Chinese merchant families. Big firms like Jardine Matheson and the Arnhold brothers took promising jockeys on to their payroll. As George Stewart recalled, 'In theory the jockeys were amateur but it was sometimes not too easy to discover what benefit to the firm of the owner the jockey gave during office hours.'

Eric Cumine was one of the most famous of these jockeys. After 1949 he moved to Hong Kong and became a Steward of the Happy Valley Race Course as well as a celebrated architect. He is a reminder of how much Hong Kong racing owes to the Shanghai tradition. His racing box is lined with photographs commemorating fifty years of racing triumphs. He told me that he excelled at every sport; 'Even though I am small, there was nothing I did not win a cup for.' His riding career began inauspiciously, for Eric Cumine is a Eurasian ('my grandmother was Chinese, both my parents were Scottish while my father spoke eight Chinese dialects') and no one trusted him with a decent horse: 'So I rode these donkeys, always at the back of the field but it was a marvellous place to be. I saw everything.' He learned how to 'read' races and how his rivals behaved in a given situation. The Mollers gave him his first chance on a good horse and after that he went on to win ten out of twelve races that meeting. 'What the hell. Everything I rode cantered into the straight. Everybody riding his heart out, and I was holding. A dream situation.'8

Newcomers like Lord Bangor enjoyed the parties in the boxes and the intense rivalry between owners and jockeys who had ridden against each other for a generation or so. 'It made for heady entertainment. Racing in Shanghai was on an immense financial scale. I don't think anything compared with it until Hong Kong.'

Both Lord Bangor and George Stewart recalled with affection that other great sporting institution of the city, the paper hunt. It summed up much of the pluck and eccentricity of the British in Shanghai. *The History of the Shanghai Paper Hunt Club 1863–1930* declared confidently:

> If it were possible to attend a gathering and listen to the talk of those adventurous spirits who, in days gone by, left their homes for the Far East to carve out a career, make a fortune, lay the foundations and build this great cosmopolitan city, we should probably find that a great deal of that talk was about the Shanghai Paper Hunt Club.

The Shanghai Paper Hunt Club grew out of the British need to hunt wherever they found themselves. In India they pursued jackals, the hunt lasting from four in the morning until six followed by a good breakfast and a drive into town and the office. Shanghai lacked any relevant animal to hunt and an attempt to chase one member with a red cowl on his head was not a success. Instead the British thought up the paper chase. The first recorded hunt occurred in December 1863 and was won by Augustus Broom on a pony called 'Mud' with 'Bogtrotter' second, the names of both ponies appropriate for the 'dismal swamp' the riders found themselves riding over. The Chinese dismissed these exploits as 'rank madness' as the leader of the *North*

China Herald commented in December 1866 and, unable to resist a dig at the Chinese, it went on, 'The idea of the same man studying for a degree of *xiucai* in the morning and going paperhunting in the afternoon is utterly beyond his comprehension and because it is so, China is the stagnant country it remains.'

The actual sport, as Lord Bangor recalled, was a cross between hunting and point-to-point racing. After a checkpoint, about two miles from 'home', it became a race. The winner had the privilege of laying the paper for the next week's hunt, wearing a pink coat and a top hat. Lord Bangor admitted to failure: 'The first time out I was chased by an enraged Chinese peasant, wielding a formidable thornbush. The second time I fell off my pony miles out in the country and had to walk home.'

Lord Bangor's boss and the 'blue-eyed boy' of Reuters in the Far East was Sir Christopher Chancellor, a great paper hunt enthusiast despite an embargo imposed by his Managing Director 'because it was so dangerous'. He and his wife, Sylvia, are both now in their eighties and live in an old, stone house in Wiltshire. I went to meet them and to find out about paper hunting.

Lady Chancellor greeted me in her gardening clothes. 'Don't look at me, don't look at me,' she called, waving energetically in my direction as if I was a chicken who might, with a little luck and exertion, go and peck elsewhere. Later, while her husband poured sherry, Lady Chancellor showed me photographs of him as a young man, lounging on a houseboat with Tony Keswick, the heir apparent of Jardine Matheson. They had just returned from a bird shoot and behind them rose rack upon rack of dead snipe. The photograph revealed a slight, dark man with an almost androgynous beauty. His wife explained his size and colouring accounted for his popularity with both Japanese and Chinese and his ability to extract information from them. Large, blond Anglo-Saxons provoked feelings of unease.

I picked up a clipping from a Shanghai newspaper lying loose in the album. Dated November 22nd, 1931, it praised Christopher Chancellor for combining 'sound intellectual equipment' with 'a marked ability for penetrating the unknown'. I handed it to him. He turned it over slowly as if examining a fossil or piece of ancient pottery. Glancing up at me, he nodded with sudden recognition and said, 'Shanghai? What fun we had! It was the best time of my life. We were all young men with top jobs. I was only twenty-seven.'

He and Tony Keswick had attended the same college at Cambridge together and Tony's brother, John, fagged for Christopher at Eton. When Christopher first arrived in Shanghai, Tony invited him to stay. In later years the two men still lunched together once a month. Riding gave him the most pleasure in Shanghai. He never owned fewer than ten ponies and adored paper hunting.

We were sitting by the fire in a large room on the ground floor. The windows looked out over a lawn, a gravel drive and fields. Suddenly five hounds appeared and bayed at a distant tree. The rest of the pack followed, eddying over the grass and under the window before streaming off towards a ditch where they came to a halt. The hunt arrived shortly after. They saw the hounds had lost the scent and pulled up on the Chancellors' drive. I had never been close to a hunt before and was dazzled by the sheer production of it. Everything looked bigger and brighter than I had imagined, the shine on the horses, the stiffness of the clothes, the women's hair in immaculate buns beneath bowler hats. The horses' limbs shivered from exertion, their riders panted. I had expected the picturesque but not the energy. It was a powerful and frightening combination of formal appearance and bloodthirsty intent. I understood now the reaction of the Chinese farmer as he watched horse and rider trample his fields – and not just the paper hunt. A well-turned-out British regiment marching down a Shanghai street must have produced the same, disturbing impression. A member of the hunt rode to the edge of the lawn, took off his hat and bowed to the house. 'Is it to me? Is it to me?' cried Christopher Chancellor with pleasure as he ambled out to wave them on. He stood, lost in delight, as they rode off. 'I don't want them on my lawn,' announced his wife, coming into the room.

Lord Bangor recollected Christopher Chancellor's determination to win a paper hunt. He bought better and better ponies until he finally succeeded. At least, unlike some, he had lacked the confidence to order a pink coat in advance and had nothing to wear for the following week. This was 'extremely mortifying' but Rosemary Meyer, a Danish girl and a fine horsewoman who had won the hunt some time before, lent Christopher hers which, although a tight fit, he wore proudly at the next meet.

The Paper Hunt, unlike other British clubs, attracted a number of different nationalities. Many Chinese rode to the hunt and the club elected Stanley Wang, educated at Cambridge University and a keen hunter and point-to-point enthusiast, as a steward in 1929. The prejudice against women, however, remained entrenched. Regulation 1A of the 1925 Paper Hunt Club Rules, stated that 'Honorary Lady Members shall not have any voice in the management or affairs of the Club'. Nor could they 'enjoy the privilege' of riding in the club Paper Hunt, club Handicap or the club Steeplechase. They might enter ponies but not themselves unless for the Ladies Paper Hunt. From 1929 the club changed its rules and allowed them to ride with the men but only once in every consecutive four weeks or three times in any one season. In a mixed hunt the men found themselves torn between the urge to win or the desire to stop when a beautiful woman fell off, which they did 'in armfuls',[9] and help her back on. Miss Maisie Middleton, the offspring of a famous paper hunt family and Lord Bangor's second wife, needed no such leg up. In January 1930 she won the Christmas Hunt on her pony Rooslan. A month later on February 23rd three out of the first six past the post were women. One can understand the paper hunter's desire to restrict them.

The season began at the end of November after the cotton and bean harvest and finished in March with the start of the new crop. The club did its best to mollify Chinese farmers who disapproved of the hunt, tried to sabotage it and made large financial claims for damage. 'We paid the farmers jolly well to ride over their land. The ground was so hard during winter it was impossible to do any damage,' recalled Willy Grieve, still with the irritation of a true paper hunt enthusiast. The hunt distributed SH$5,000 each year for crop damage and built several wooden bridges which benefited villages as well as hunters. Relations still remained strained. One rider recalled discovering a mantrap in a cabbage patch.

On the eve of the new season's first hunt, the hunt master held open house at the race club for all members. The following day the master laid the trail accompanied by the head paper hunt boy and half a dozen other Chinese carrying bags of different-coloured paper. Green paper indicated bridges where the hunt had to stop, purple signified wades. A club rule demanded that the master and every subsequent winner took the jumps they laid paper over. The club made an exception for Frank Maitland, hunt master between 1887 and 1897 and, at 224 pounds, too heavy for any pony to lift. A young member accompanied him as he laid the trail and took the jumps instead. The hunt covered five to ten miles. The Chinese boys threw patches of paper down every few hundred yards, often on grave mounds to catch the eye. A map still exists of paper hunt country, now long since built over, with its creeks, jumps, fields and even a tree, each affectionately and graphically described as Rubicon Creek, The Bath Tub, Coffin Jump, Slough of Despond, Bridge of Sighs, Here and There and the Family Tree.

After a good lunch, a line of limousines made their way from the city and parked at the end of Bubbling Well Road. Men and women climbed out in riding costume, reluctantly discarding their heavy coats to shiver in the cold. Stamping their feet in their cloth-soled shoes, the mafoos held the saddled and waiting ponies. By three o'clock about one hundred paper hunters had gathered, the previous winners in pink jackets, amidst a crowd of spectators and children. The mafoos removed the blankets, tightened the girths and the riders mounted as the senior steward announced, 'Gentlemen, time is up, you may go!' The first jump saw refusals, crashes, tangled bodies and empty saddles for, as one man remarked, the Chinese pony was a cunning animal who preferred his rider to investigate the jump before him. Sometimes the trail disappeared and the hunt fanned out until one rider raised his hat and shouted 'tally-ho'. Then the hunt bunched together and galloped through the flat countryside dotted with innumerable grave mounds, tidal creeks and lagoons fringed with willows. They jumped the small creeks and crossed larger ones, like the Rubicon, on arched bridges no wider than a paving stone. They passed frozen paddy fields, villages of grey-tiled houses enclosed with moats and red or yellow temples surrounded by bamboo corpses and clusters of juniper, elm and ginko. Through the trees the riders caught an occasional glimpse of a junk, gliding along the wider creeks; or a man fishing with a line of cormorants sitting on the gunwales of his sampan, their necks ringed with a metal band to prevent them swallowing the catch. Magpies circled overhead.

Despite the cold, riders took the wades even if it meant a soaking. The alternative, as I. A. Toeg discovered, could be worse. His pony refused the water for an exceptionally high, single-stone bridge. The paper hunt stewards decided against penalizing him as they judged the shock to his nerves punishment enough. Sometimes the wade turned into a swim and the front riders realized the Chinese had tricked them. Willy Grieve explained that Chinese farmers would often re-route the trail then sit and watch the hunt's confusion, laughing their heads off. They particularly enjoyed sending the riders into a cold and stinking creek.

It was a dangerous sport, even without farmers. Christopher Chancellor described the risk of riding at full gallop over the half-moon bridges and recalled a surgeon always in attendance. It was easy to come off and fall into the water below; to misjudge the leap over the numerous small creeks; or to be fooled by a grave mound, a small hillock with a stone slab set in one side. Enid Saunders Candlin remembered her pony knocking aside a bone which looked 'horridly familiar'. Grave mounds near the winning post sometimes decided a race. Riders had to make a split decision whether to jump or go round. Some mounds turned out far wider than they appeared.

Other mishaps could only have occurred in China. On the third Ladies Paper Hunt in the winter of 1927 a Miss Cohen's pony barged into a bamboo waterwheel shelter, 'causing his rider some discomfort', while a Miss McCloskey mislaid her bowler hat, eventually returned by a Chinese who demanded the same rate as for a lost pony. Willy Grieve remembered another hazard of enjoying the Chinese countryside. He was riding behind the hunt because his Australian horse, brought over from Hong Kong, had proved 'less handy on its feet' than the Chinese ponies. Too late he noticed a crowd had stopped ahead of him. 'I rode right into an ambush laid for the hunt by these filthy Chinese brigands on their wretched-looking ponies.' They had a couple of old-fashioned pistols between them which they waved at Mr Grieve. 'Get off your horse. Have you any money?' they demanded. 'Of course that was a ridiculous question. One never went riding with money. Was I worried? Not a bit. But I was afraid they would take my horse. Well, there was a lot of argy bargy. None of us had any money.' The irritated brigands dispatched Teddy and Marion Arnold home to get some. A couple of Chinese who were with the hunt suggested to the brigands that perhaps the Arnolds had gone for the police instead. Dumbfounded at such perfidy, the brigands fired a few shots into the air and took off.

After six miles the hunt quickened, the leaders watching each other nervously until they caught sight of the crowd and the flags which marked the finish. They took the last water jump and raced to the line. As they came into view their names were shouted out and the spectators cheered and applauded. They dismounted amidst congratulations and back slapping. One gallant old paper hunter who had only just beaten a lady on 'Bonzo' declared she ought to have won, not only for her hard riding but because her head looked as neat at the finish as when she started. The joy, she recalled, of the Eton Crop. Everybody then retired to tea at the race club where they hoisted the new winner on to the bar to the song of the Paper Hunt Club.

After one unsuccessful hunt, George Stewart turned up for a drink at Tony Keswick's covered from head to toe in dust. A young lady looked him up and down. 'Do you do that for fun?' she asked.

George Stewart found he could barely fit everything in. Shanghai had dubbed him eligible. Men with marriageable daughters invited him to endless dinner parties. After dinner sleepy parents delegated one person to take the young out to a nightclub saying: 'It's our party, send the bill to me.' George Stewart recalled, 'Once it was established I could behave properly it was surprising how many girls I did know.' He took girls he liked to the Cathay Ballroom on the top floor of the Cathay Hotel. Every Saturday night a wealthy, middle-aged woman gave a dinner party there accompanied by her gigolo. She impressed George Stewart for she went to only the best places in town and changed her gigolo for a new model every summer. When Ciro's opened, she never stepped inside the Cathay again. George Stewart followed her to Ciro's which boasted a smoke-remover and air-conditioning – 'quite something then'.

The National Balls were the city's grandest social occasions. They took place in the Majestic Hotel which had started life as a private house owned by Captain McBain. Lord Kadoorie told me how the captain had fallen in love with the daughter of the sampan woman who made the deliveries and cleaned his ship. Despite strong disapproval from the British, he had married her. He gave his new wife the best education he could afford. She spoke French, German and English fluently and always dressed with perfect taste. He built what later became the Majestic Hotel so that he, his wife and their nine children could live together under one roof. When he travelled to Europe with his family and retinue of servants, it was in his own private carriage hitched on to the Trans-Siberian Railway. George Stewart remembered the St George's Ball, with the various foreign dignitaries dressed up in colourful uniforms – 'anybody who had a uniform and some medals put them on'. The organizers of the St Andrew's Ball shipped haggis out from Scotland and put on a display of pipers in kilts. At the St Patrick's Ball they played Irish airs.

While at the George Washington Ball you could eat red, white and blue ice-cream and admire a model of Mount Vernon made entirely of sugar. One Englishwoman was particularly impressed by the illuminated American eagle over the bandstand, 'but then I was rather young and in love with an American at the time'.

The British in Shanghai led an intensely social existence. 'Never was the near future more filled with enormous parties,' declared the Women's Page of the *North China Daily News* in February 1937. 'Hectic days are the regular fare with hurried fittings for fancy dress balls and charity programmes, rushing hither and yon to wedge in the smaller affairs like teas and cocktail parties or committee meetings.'[10]

Lord Kadoorie described the 'tremendous competition between the hostesses'. An ordinary dinner party offered two different kinds of soup, fish, entrée of some sort, bird, beef, then a savoury followed by three or four different puddings. At 11.30 people said, 'Let's make an early night of it,' but no sooner had certain guests departed than the hostess announced, 'Well, why not just one dance at a nightclub?' Lord Kadoorie went on, 'And of course you'd see your friends sitting right next to you.' He would regularly stay out until four in the morning, 'with no consideration for my driver', come home, have a bath, sleep for two hours then go riding before leaving for the office: 'We all did it and we thoroughly enjoyed ourselves.'

Shanghai offered an extraordinary variety of entertainment to the enterprising young man. One recalled two parties he attended in the same month. In the summer of 1936 he went to a garden party given by Tony Keswick. Two bands played, the Lancashire Fusiliers and the Jessfield Club Orchestra. It rained continuously. The women wore formal garden frocks, their trains sodden from the rain and their heels ruined by sinking into the mud with each step. A few weeks later a Chinese professor invited him to a dinner party memorable for its mix of Western and Chinese styles. Dr Tai served an excellent Chinese dinner in an English oak-panelled dining-room followed by coffee in the French drawing-room. The doctor then took his guests around the garden to admire the flowering magnolia trees. They sat out on the terrace and listened to an English painter recount his adventures in Laos before putting a few records on the gramophone and dancing in the moonlight.

Less innocent pleasures also beguiled the new arrival. Sir Harold Acton recalled hotels which provided drugs on room service and foreigners who offered narcotics after dinner including one hostess who 'glittered with diamonds and cocaine'. Very occasionally he smoked opium with Chinese friends and was able to explain to me the knack of preparing a satisfying pipe. In the brothels of the French Concession young men could explore every nuance of sexual deviation. On the street corners of the International Settlement eager Chinese girls, their cheongsams split to the waist, overwhelmed passing males. Their presence was the result of a moral welfare campaign led by an American missionary called Dr Frank Rawlinson which forced the Municipal authorities to close its brothels. Before Dr Rawlinson's misguided crusade, young men saved up to spend an evening at The Line, the city's most famous, foreign brothel and the creation of Gracie Gale, a well-built San Franciscan who belonged to a long tradition of American madams in the city. Gracie had a loud, throaty laugh and decided views. She refused entry to Chinese, 'dope pedlars' and 'hopheads', adding, 'I won't stand for any of that French stuff either.'[11]

Today you can still visit The Line's former home at 52 Kiangse Road. It stands in a quiet street behind the Bund. During the 'twenties it was a convenient stroll from the business centre of the city. The streets along Soochow Creek were notorious for American brothels and makeshift drug factories. From the outside The Line advertised its presence by a discreet brass plate on the front door. Inside, Gracie Gale had furnished the house with Chinese Chippendale, Oriental rugs and, as Irene Kuhn, an American journalist for the *North China Daily News*, recalled, the most extensive foreign library in the city. Gracie only served French champagne and employed a famous Chinese chef called Fat Lu who had cooked for the Imperial Russian Legation in Beijing and could prepare anything from fried Chicken Maryland to Chicken à la Kiev.

Gracie encouraged men to drop in for a brandy and a gossip after work or a boring dinner. Irene Kuhn told me of her frustration when she discovered where her male colleagues received their information on the stock market or the latest warlord manoeuvres. 'There was just no way I could compete with the stories they picked up at The Line,' she said.

Gracie only employed foreign girls. She specialized in demure-looking Americans, like Big Annie who took up her knitting when business turned slack and reminded a man of home. Percy Finch, an American journalist, also recalled the not-so-nice Lotus, a redheaded nymphomaniac at her best at four in the morning, 'doing the cancan on a polished table top with a champagne bottle hugged to her bare breasts and her magnificent hair shimmering halfway to her pink-nailed toes . . . her audience in a state of exhausted appreciation'.[12] His favourite was Agnes who later married a French diplomat and possessed, apart from a pair of melting, brown eyes, a body, 'as electrifying as softly stroked velvet'.[13]

Gracie, like everybody else in the city, used the chit system. Her customers signed for their entertainment and at the end of the month Chinese shroffs collected payment from their offices. It made Shanghai the only place in the world where a man could get a woman on credit. Very occasionally a customer tried to cheat Gracie. Once a shipping owner, one of the city's civic leaders, treated his friends to a night at The Line. The next morning when he saw the bill, he refused to pay. Gracie knew the man officiated as vestryman at the Holy Trinity Cathedral. That Sunday dressed 'as prim as my Aunt Eliza'[14] as she later put it, Gracie attended the service. She watched her bad debt, unctuous in his morning suit, pass the collection plate in which members of the congregation placed either money or a chit. With a sweet smile, Gracie contributed his brothel chits and watched 'the old buzzard sweating all the way down the aisle'. She knew he would have to pay the chits for he could not tell the Dean where he'd signed them, 'so at least the good old cathedral got his filthy money'.[15]

When Dr Rawlinson started his campaign, Gracie invited him to The Line. The visit, apart from disconcerting her customers, left the missionary unconvinced. At least Gracie had the Municipal Council on her side. The Council made a great deal of money issuing licences to the Settlement's brothels. Their closure meant a serious loss of revenue but Dr Rawlinson would not give up. Finally the Council agreed to withdraw its licences. A curious ceremony was held every three months in the Town Hall on Nanking Road. Missionaries, puzzled Chinese brothel-keepers and a few foreign madams watched as a policeman put small balls inscribed with the various licence numbers into a drum and mixer (usually reserved for the church tombola), cranked the handle and turned a tap at the bottom to release a ball whose number he yelled out in English and Chinese. The house holding that number had to close. The policeman always failed to call Gracie's number. On a voyage back from San Francisco, she had briefly married an Englishman, later chairman of the Municipal

Council. As she said: 'God knows, he never was any good to me before.'[16]

It was not Dr Rawlinson but the Russian Revolution which finished Gracie. A man could keep a Russian mistress for a month on what one night at The Line cost. Gracie went home to San Francisco, discovered things were not much better there and sailed for the China Coast. Between Honolulu and Japan she attended a party, went down to her room, filled her bath and slit her wrists. They buried her at sea.

Women like Gracie Gale ensured there were no limits to what a young man might enjoy. What mattered in the city was how he did so. You might snort cocaine, sleep with the divine Lotus or buy a Chinese virgin for unnatural acts, but the British made sure you pursued your vices with decorum. The British sense of occasion permeated the city. George Stewart recalled that Shanghai lacked the formality of Hong Kong. It was better, his friends agreed, to live under British protection than under the British flag. But he still paid calls on people, dropped cards and turned up in tails for a quiet dinner party.

The British demanded proper attire at all times. 'Man is at his best . . . when formal,' declared the *North China Daily News* in the middle of one steamy July. It went on to point out the unsightliness of certain parts of a man's anatomy, notably 'the Adam's apple and the back of the knee' which made it impossible for an Englishman to consider wearing shorts even for tennis. 'No man dressed in "shorts" can be entirely oblivious to his ridiculous appearance and this in turn reacts upon his poise in the same way that a knowledge that he is wearing a brass collar stud might easily give him an inferiority complex.'[17] This was particularly true at night. A letter signed 'Etiquette' appeared a few months later in the *North China Daily News* deploring 'the gross breach of manners and lack of breeding' of the younger set in the picture shows and hotel ballrooms. At dinner in the Majestic Hotel, Etiquette saw, to his astonishment, a number of young men dancing in their office suits. Worse followed with the sudden appearance on the dance floor of a 'merry little couple', the young man in a pair of Shanghai Volunteer Corps shorts, khaki stockings, a tennis shirt and a sun resister coat. Etiquette had quite enough of 'damp and soiled' attire during the day. Saturday night was time for 'that distinctive and refreshing change'.[18]

An American witnessed the British passion for formal attire in bizarre combination with the equally British devotion to volunteer organizations. The British had founded and manned the Municipal fire brigade with the help of Chinese assistants since 1866. Their equipment, imported from England years before, resembled museum pieces and they were slow to turn out for an unpopular owner of a burning building – but the Shanghai Fire Brigade formed the city's and, for many years China's, only fire-fighting force. One night the fire alarm went off in the International Settlement near the Bund. The astonished American watched firemen in full evening dress fighting the flames, their black tails waving in the breeze and their white shirt-fronts and ties daubed with soot. The Chinese assistants wore firemen's uniforms, including brass helmets. When he asked why the British fought fire in tails, he was told they had been at a dinner in the Shanghai Club when the alarm went off. There was no time to change. It happened so often that the municipality reimbursed them for all cleaning, pressing and repair bills.

Clubs, wild parties, clean tails and all the paraphernalia of the spoiling life was made possible by the Chinese servant. Cheap, ingenious and good-natured they offered a world of total service and a way of life 'which is, I am sure, what many people most remember when they think of Shanghai', explained Enid Saunders Candlin. They were also 'our friends'.[19] Certainly the majority of British made few other Chinese friends. Their servants became their only contact with the country in which they lived. At best, it resulted in a precious if necessarily flawed relationship.

You talked to your servants in pidgin, a combination of Chinese grammar and English vocabulary. Irene Kuhn remembered her introduction to its 'sublime elasticity' at a cocktail party. The hostess called her Number One Boy to her and said, ' "Boy, go topside; catchee one-piece blow rag, puttee stink water, bring my side," ' which meant, ' "Boy, go upstairs, fetch a handkerchief, put some perfume on it and bring it to me." '[20]

Most foreigners employed more servants than they needed. The Chinese had a saying, 'Never break another man's rice bowl', never take away another man's chance to make a living. Irene Kuhn recalled the ritual which followed a dropped handkerchief. She rang the bell for her headservant known, even if an old man, as Number One Boy, who arrived, heard her request and summoned the coolie. When the coolie came, Number One Boy instructed him to pick up the handkerchief. The Number One Boy refused to pick it up himself. To do so deprived him of 'face' and the coolie of his job.

William Hayter and his wife arrived in Shanghai a few years after George Stewart, Lord Bangor and Christopher Chancellor. A tall, spare man with an ascetic face, Sir William joined the Foreign Office in 1930 after Winchester and New College. Everything about Shanghai failed to impress the couple, ('noisy, provincial-cosmopolitan and corrupt') except for their Number One Boy, Kui. He had previously worked on board the flagship of a British gunboat flotilla whose duty it was to patrol the Yangtsze. Quei had used his position to smuggle opium up and down the river. When discovered and dismissed, he organized a walkout, taking with him all the Chinese who worked on the gunboats and thus effectively immobilizing the fleet. To save face and flotilla, the British gave him a job attached to the embassy which provided less opportunity for opium-smuggling. The Hayters found him 'an elderly gentleman of immense charm and dignity', and started their married life 'with a degree of luxury . . . that we were never to attain again'.

A young man drinking in a bar could telephone his Number One Boy and announce ten for dinner in an hour. A dinner which in Europe took days of preparation would promptly appear. Number One Boy borrowed extra cutlery from his friends who generally worked for friends of his master. Lord Bangor recalled recognizing his own cutlery when he dined in other people's houses.

Lord Bangor, determined to discover how his cook achieved this miracle, paid his first visit to the kitchen, a ramshackle building at the back of the house. He saw no other cooking equipment but baked mud stoves fired with charcoal and a large number of Chinese boys. Who were they, he asked? His cook looked evasive and said they had come to help with the party that evening. Later on, Lord Bangor discovered that the man ran a cookery school at his master's expense. The boys helped as pupils. Lord Bangor fed and housed them in various sheds and corners in the back yard. The cook lost the cost of the school in the household accounts. As Lord Bangor remarked, 'The value of eighty or ninety eggs alone would have been enough to feed half a dozen Chinese.'

Number One Boy ran the foreign household smoothly and efficiently. Once a month 'master' or 'missy' might check the household bills as low wages forced Chinese servants to become creative accountants. Cook and Number One Boy usually took 15 per cent 'squeeze' from every delivery to the house. Jack Crompton owned a houseboat which he used at weekends. Jack kept no cat but every month the same item appeared on the accounts, 'cat chow five dollars'. After a few months he sent for his Number One Boy. 'What thing every month belong five dollar cat chow?' he asked. 'You savee plenty well laota no belong cat this boat side. I no wantchee see any more cat chow five dollar.' ('Why does five dollars for cat food appear every month in the accounts? You know perfectly well we don't have a cat on the boat. I don't want to see this again.') The Number One Boy nodded. Next month Jack read in the accounts: 'Cat chow five dollars. One piece cat ten dollars.' ('Cat food, five dollars. One cat, cost ten dollars.') The houseboat still lacked a cat. Lord Bangor said that Jack gave up after that. He knew when he was beaten.

Hilary Wadlow and Rosemary Dale grew up in Shanghai and recalled the effect of Chinese servants on foreign children. Hilary admitted that she had never dressed herself until she returned to England. Once, when ill in bed on a cold day, she rang for her amah and said, 'I want to do pee pee. Please sit on the lavatory seat and warm it up for me.'

Rosemary Dale explained that Chinese servants rarely took holidays as they were afraid to lose their jobs. Sometimes they pretended a cousin had died and asked to attend the funeral because they felt guilty admitting they wanted a day off. Rosemary's parents enjoyed Shanghai's social life and she spent most of her time with her amah who was 'such fun and never complained about anything'. Rosemary's amah had bound feet and could only totter after her escaping charges. She showed me the sort of shoe her amah would have worn. Only four inches long with a wide arch and narrow toe, it resembled more a silken slipper for a pig's trotter than a shoe. It sat in my hand, a miracle of absurdity and frivolity. A smiling, naked lady embroidered on its side almost made me forget the excruciating pain Rosemary's amah had suffered as a child, slipping her foot into something which barely took two of my fingers.

Hilary Wadlow's amah showed her a side of Shanghai usually hidden from the foreigner. Hilary's mother insisted that she and her amah took a daily walk. As neither enjoyed the exercise the amah introduced the little girl to her relations instead. They lived in a small room with a low ceiling over a market near Siccawei Road. Hilary recalled that it stank like a drain. In one corner the grandmother embroidered slippers for the foreign market while, at the other, a group of men played mahjong. A charcoal stove in the middle of the room filled the place with smoke. Hilary picked up a pair of white, silk slippers from the pile, put them on and pranced about. Everybody stopped what they were doing to watch her. On another occasion, Hilary's amah took her to meet a branch of the family who lived on a sampan in Siccawei creek. The sampan was less than six foot wide and covered with a rattan roof. When Hilary arrived the family were sitting down to eat around a large pot of rice in the centre of the table. They made room for Hilary and filled her bowl with 'marvellous food', eel stewed in oil and garlic, strange vegetable dishes and dumplings followed by fried pastry. She wondered what they thought of her, sitting among them in her grey, rabbit coat with its monstrous fur buttons.

The spoiling life corrupted. Joan Willoughby remembered the dependency it induced in her mother. Born and brought up in Shanghai with only four years schooling at an English boarding school, Joan's mother was a typical 'Shanghai Girl'. At thirty-five her life fell apart when Joan's father announced his intention of retiring to Surrey. Joan's mother hated it. Famous in Shanghai for her clothes and parties, she found no one in Surrey to match her Chinese tailor or cook for either creativity or cheapness. She knew her Number One Boy swindled her but she also knew when to call a halt. English servants required orders. Madam had to be up by 8.15 and downstairs at 9.00 to give the cook her instructions. Joan's mother was unused to nagging or explanations. In Shanghai her servants knew what she wanted before she did herself.

Joan admitted that her mother never learnt to adapt. She recalled a last visit home before her mother's death at the early age of forty-nine. As usual it was chaotic. The hot water did not work. The cook had just given notice and the place looked filthy. ('My mother had never made a bed before she came to England.') At half-past one with no lunch on the table, Joan's mother went to her father in despair. ' "I can't find a book which tells me how long to cook cabbage," she said.'

The paper hunt, club life, the faithful and amusing servant represented a narrow but accurate recollection of happiness. I had expected to hear something of Shanghai's corruption and cruelty but never did. Years of retelling the same anecdote had chipped away all extraneous matter. The polished result more resembled myth than fact. There is nothing wrong with myth. It is a study in wishful thinking and what people want is never irrelevant even if they do not achieve it. The British had simple wants. They revelled in the good life, remembered it best and enjoyed telling me about it. Myth always contains an element of fantasy and even in the prosaic legend of the British there exists the supernatural. It was, of course, a very British version of the supernatural, taking the form of power and money rather than flying horses or dragons. It centred on four Jewish families whose eccentricity and love of display epitomized so much of the city.

They held the right qualifications for mythical beings. They came from Baghdad and possessed fabulous wealth. Most of them were Anglophiles who made their fortune under the protection of the British, sent their sons to British public schools and, in the Second World War, despite threats and bribes from the Japanese and the confiscation of their businesses, remained loyal to the British and followed them into the internment camps. To the British in Shanghai, the Kadoories, Sassoons, Hardoons and Ezras offered the seductive combination of riches and devotion. They appeared larger than life creatures, genie-like in their exotic appearance, their limitless fortune and their willingness to please. People talked about them with a mixture of amazement and condescension. Everybody had a story to contribute. Every story made it clear that the British rubbed the lamp to summon or dismiss. For the British this formed an essential part of the charm. One was, at the end of it, superior to even the supernatural, simply by being British. The teller of the anecdote finished with a distant and, dare I say it, smug expression. I could sympathize. As a gentile it is very gratifying to feel one up on a genie.

In a city used to seeing Chinese and foreign businessmen displaying their success in grandiose mansions, the houses of the Iraqi Jews were legendary. The most magnificent was Marble Hall, the home of the Kadoories. It still stands on Bubbling Well Road, now known as Nanking Road West.

Today Lord Kadoorie lives in Hong Kong, devoting his time to his charitable foundations. He is one of the leading Taipans on the island, and I went to meet him in great excitement. It is not often, after all, one hears the genie's side of the story.

His father, Sir Elly Kadoorie, was born in Baghdad and arrived in Shanghai from Bombay on May 20th, 1880 as an employee of the first Iraqi Jewish firm in Shanghai, David Sassoon & Sons. He left to start up on his own with $500 capital and became a successful merchant banker, real-estate and hotel owner, and rubber grower.

The site of Marble Hall was originally intended for a club but when half-finished it burnt down. Elly Kadoorie bought the land in 1920 and decided to build a house. He then took his family to Europe for three years, leaving the construction to an architect who was the stepson of a famous Hollywood actress. His film star connection had given the architect very grand ideas indeed which only revealed themselves after his patron's departure. The first telegram to the Kadoories in Europe demanded: 'Want to raise ballroom roof fifteen feet.' Lord Kadoorie recalled that his parents had planned a large reception room but nobody had mentioned a ballroom. 'What are you talking about?' they wired back. The telegrams kept coming: 'Must do this, must do that.' Exasperated, Elly Kadoorie sent final and, in the circumstances, possibly unwise instructions: 'Do only what is absolutely necessary.'

After three years, the Kadoorie family returned to Shanghai. They found enraged contractors, the architect an alcoholic in hospital with DT's, and a ballroom 65 feet high, 80 feet long and 50 feet wide lit by 3,600 different-coloured electric light bulbs. With one flick the Kadoories could turn their ballroom from pink to blue to red or have the whole lot on at once. They named it Marble Hall after the extraordinary amount of Italian marble imported for the fireplaces. Despite the expense, Marble Hall remained incomplete. The Kadoories appointed a half-Italian, half-Spanish architect who had just finished work on 'The Wheel', a gambling den which had astounded Shanghai with its decor, including a colossal chandelier. Lord Kadoorie finished, 'What with him and the DT's of the first architect, Marble Hall was produced and there it is.'

It was the first house in the city to have air conditioning. Lord Kadoorie described the 'tremendous fuss' made by the firm who installed it. They had fitted out factories before but never a house. The General Electric Company of America made the light fittings including the 18-foot chandeliers in the ballroom. To change a light bulb, servants lowered the chandeliers to the floor by a winch. The memory made Lord Kadoorie pause and repeat in stupefaction, 'Eighteen feet, each chandelier! Well, it was quite a house, I must say.' When the gas central heating broke down, a servant fixed the problem by connecting a pipe behind the meter. 'We were impressed until we found she'd been stealing the gas for years and my brother was Chairman of the Gas Company! Such was the city of Shanghai. The life there was unique.'

Rabindranath Tagore, the famous Indian poet and twelve disciples paid a visit to Marble Hall. Lord Kadoorie fetched him from their ship anchored at Woosung, some two hours from the city. Throughout the drive, Tagore did not utter a single word. When they arrived at Marble Hall, he retired to his suite and called for pen, ink and paper. Two hours later he reappeared and started, without any preliminaries, an animated conversation with Lord Kadoorie's father.

I wondered how such a fabulous establishment with forty-three servants and visiting Indian philosophers had survived the Cultural Revolution. The Red Guards had turned the ground floor of the Cathay Hotel into a bicycle repair shop. They had removed the dome from the nearby Beth Aharon Synagogue, bricked up its front and installed a factory inside before pulling it down. I went to discover the fate of Marble Hall.

It has survived well. Renamed the Children's Palace and transformed into a school for gifted children, it still looks as Lord Kadoorie remembered it: a white, two-storeyed house with a covered veranda and steps down to a lawn. Even its transformation seems appropriate. Marble Hall is like a child's fantasy. There is nothing real about its appearance. The ornateness and luxury only add to its air of insubstantiality. Two idealized statues of a boy and a girl now stand on either side of the steps. So well do the past and present mesh that, for a moment, I was unsure if I was looking at a dedication to Chinese Youth or Peter Pan and Wendy. Around me played the city's cleverest children. For the first time in China I found myself ignored. I later discovered that the authorities are proud of the Children's Palace. It represents an ideal China which foreign delegates are encouraged to see. The pupils are so accustomed to being on show that they no longer notice their audience.

I walked up the steps to the veranda where, in 1927, British soldiers had munched pies and discussed hockey. Now Chinese children constructed a papier-mâché dragon of monstrous dimensions. 'To which group do you belong?' asked an elderly teacher. I told him I was on my own. 'No unofficial visitors allowed here,' he said and pointed back down the drive. I waited until the children distracted his attention, then slipped inside.

The central room appeared immense, the walls and ceiling covered in white moulding. Framed in stucco, a stage with a piano was set into one wall. At each end of the room a huge, white, marble fireplace stretched almost from floor to ceiling. Dust had collected in the scrolls and furbelows. The room reminded me of a wedding cake which has stood too long in the baker's shop. It was not a display to encourage confidence.

On the staircase, a middle-aged woman stopped and also asked the name of my group. 'I am from England,' I replied, as if this was group enough. She led me upstairs to a sunny landing running the length of the house. In one room overlooking the garden, a class of children sketched the head of a Greek statue. A boy stood facing the wall, 'as punishment', explained my guide. I turned to find myself surrounded by ten middle-aged Caucasians, all coarse-featured and overweight. My guide was delighted. 'Your group!' she said. No one in China can be happy on their own for long. She left me with them.

It was not until one of them spoke that I realized I was meeting my first communist Russians. Their leader was a tall man in a belted, black-leather coat down to his ankles and a face that hung in folds of flesh. The women's clothes looked tight and unflattering. Like Marble Hall itself, I could not quite believe they were real, so much did they resemble the Western caricature of Russians. At any moment I expected a cameraman to roll past, a make-up girl to spring from the wings and the 'Russians' to break into American. Instead the leader tweaked the ear of the punished boy until the child's eyes watered then moved on with a benevolent smile.

When we reached the end of the landing we turned to explore the rest of the house but found ourselves facing a window overlooking a street. Marble Hall lacked depth. This is a feature of Shanghai's grand homes, including the former British Consulate. They were designed like stage sets. Land was expensive and the emphasis was all on that first, sweeping view. As with the Bund, what lay behind seemed unimportant. 'Why spend money on what no one sees?' was how one Chinese businessman put it. Outside the children had gathered to acknowledge us with a farewell song. As they listened, the faces of the Russians slackened with emotion and their eyes glazed. They clapped enthusiastically. Their Chinese guides looked bored and hurried them into the waiting bus. The Russian leader turned on the steps for a last speech but the children had already dispersed with shouts and giggles. Illusion, it seems, is still an important part of Marble Hall.

To the British, Silas A. Hardoon, born in Baghdad in 1852, appeared an even more fantastic creation. The Kadoories, after all, 'were almost one of us', as one Englishman put it. The same could not be said of Hardoon or his wife. Silas Hardoon like the Kadoorie family was fabulously wealthy, charitable and civic-minded. His money built the Beth Aharon Synagogue on Museum Road, one of the most interesting of Shanghai's buildings. He was the only man to win seats, simultaneously, on the Municipal Councils of the French Concession and the International Settlement. He also fulfilled British prejudices of how a Jewish businessman should behave. He had started as a rent collector for E. D. Sassoon and enjoyed it so much that even when he made his fortune from property and public utilities, he continued to visit the Chinese tenements himself. He refused to give up the office which had seen his first success despite its shabbiness and lack of heating. In winter he worked at his cramped desk in an overcoat.

His private life attracted particular interest. His wife, Luo Jialing, was a Eurasian – her father, a French gendarme and her mother a Chinese from Fujian Province. Orphaned at nine, she existed by selling flowers and herself near the Old West Gate of the Chinese city. Down the road from Marble Hall, Silas built Hardoon Park and called it Aili Park, 'Beloved Li', after her. A folly on a grand scale, it resembled a sort of Chinese theme park with a Buddhist hall, ballroom and three separate establishments set among pavilions, rockeries, arched bridges, bamboo groves, artificial hills and a number of lakes. Former eunuchs from the Imperial Palace who had been offered a home after the 1911 Revolution by Luo Jialing, wandered among these glories. Like many ladies of easy virtue Li took to religion in middle age. She became a devoted Buddhist and kept a resident Buddhist scholar who spent his time and her husband's money editing 8,416 rolls of the Buddhist canon. Her picture appears in the preface – rumoured to be a beauty she is revealed as a plump, middle-aged woman with fleshy features and hair in a roll over her forehead like a French beret. She wears a lace collar and a gold locket and looks the incarnation of respectability.

The British could not understand Hardoon's obsession with Chinese culture. At his funeral he chose to have both Jewish and Chinese rites. He bought Chinese paintings and manuscripts and encouraged visiting scholars to debate before him. In 1914 he started a school for Chinese children in Aili Park. He did not approve of the modernization of China and his pupils played ancient Chinese games, studied Confucian ethics and followed a Buddhist vegetarian diet. After this success, he adopted ten children from a Shanghai orphanage (mostly the offspring of sailors and prostitutes) and brought them up speaking English, Hebrew and Chinese. They later attended the Shanghai Public School where Michael Schiller, a fellow pupil, befriended them. They invited him to come and play several times in Hardoon Park. They always issued a formal invitation (the huge, red entrance gates and the guard on duty precluded 'dropping in') and sent a chauffeur to pick him up. Michael Schiller recalled doing nothing in particular, just wandering through room after room of heavy, dark, Chinese furniture. The adults of Aili Park ignored them. The Hardoons had lost interest in the children and the servants took their cue from their employers. The children never received a new toy or pocket money to buy sweets. Once they stumbled into a vast ballroom with a pair of ornate chairs set at one end like a double throne. Here Hardoon and his wife held court. The children sprawled on the floor and offered Michael a swig from a bottle of Napoleon brandy they had found in a cupboard. They had no idea what it was. It was just something to drink.

What happened to them? I asked. Michael recalled meeting one of the girls many years later in San Francisco. By then she was middle-aged, divorced and doing some manual job to pay the rent.

Hardoon's death proved as extraordinary as his life. He left £4 million to his wife, mostly in land and tenement buildings, and appointed her sole executor. A cousin of Hardoon contested the will. He claimed that as Hardoon was an Iraqi national his will should be governed by the laws of Iraq. This called for one-quarter of the estate to go to the wife and for the rest to be distributed among the next of kin. The cousin took Luo Jialing to court. The case, one of the most elaborate in Shanghai's history, lasted six years and raised numerous points of international law. Was Hardoon, who had left Iraq while under Ottoman rule, still a citizen of the modern state of Iraq and did its law apply to him while he lived under the protection of the British in China? This point led to a debate on the exact definition of foreign rights in China followed by a brief digression to establish if Mrs Hardoon was a wife or concubine.

On that subject Luo Jialing had taken no chances. She had been married by the British Consulate-General in 1928 and was, even the cousins had to agree, Hardoon's legal wife. The case, described by the *North China Daily News* as 'one of the most important and certainly one of the longest',[21] decided in favour of Mrs Hardoon. By then the money had gone. The children who were supposed to receive a minimum of one million Shanghai dollars each were left penniless, the house and its contents sold off. Michael Schiller's parents bought some silverware in the auction. A fire broke out during the Second World War and destroyed everything except the plumbing in one fountain.

Sir Ellice Victor Sassoon's influence on Shanghai proved more durable. The Cathay Hotel which he built still dominates the Bund, as Sir Victor, after his arrival in 1931, dominated the commercial and the social life of the city. George Stewart, the Chancellors and Tony Keswick recalled him vividly. In extravagance and unpredictability he surpassed even the British expectations of their Jewish genies.

His family was much grander than that of the average Shanghai businessman. David Sassoon, the founder of the dynasty, had become a British subject and sent his sons to English public schools. One of them, Albert Abdullah David Sassoon, made his name as a philanthropist and was knighted in 1890. His son, Sir Edward Albert, married a Rothschild's daughter, became a friend of Edward VII and a Member of Parliament. In the next generation, Sir Philip Sassoon, in the happy position of inheriting both Rothschild and Sassoon money, distinguished himself as the youngest British M.P. He was a great art collector and the owner of two pet penguins as well as a signed copy of *A la recherche du temps perdu*. Victor's cousin was Siegfried Sassoon, the poet.

Sir Victor Sassoon had arrived in Shanghai at about the same time as Sir William Keswick, known to everyone as Tony, the acknowledged leader of British society in the city. The two men had more in common than either they or their British friends conceded. Educated at Cambridge University, both were groomed to run family firms with a similar background and outlook. Jardine Matheson and Sassoon & Co. were founded within a few years of each other in the 1840s. They made their money from the trade triangle of India, China and Britain, most particularly by the export of opium from India to China. The two companies operated over a number of continents. Almost from their inception, they set up offices in

London, Bombay, Shanghai and Hong Kong. They diversified into industry, real estate and anything else a bright, Jardine nephew or Sassoon son thought interesting. Operations, however daring and far-flung, remained under family control. Both Jardine Matheson and Sassoon & Co. saw nepotism as a virtue. It provided a 'steel frame' and 'a firm, unwritten constitution',[22] for two companies whose members communicated by letters which took three months to arrive if at all. Stanley Jackson's description of Sassoon working practice in his excellent book on the family applies equally well to the Jardine nephews: 'all the brothers acted together by an educated instinct. They sensed infallibly how the others would respond to the prod of crises.'[23]

Both families succeeded in making the transition from drug traders (the disgrace in British society attached to the trade rather than to the drugs) to powerful and respected members of the British community. The Jardines spent their retirement in Parliament promoting the interests of their firm. The Sassoons 'slid smoothly into that social niche in English society reserved for visiting nabobs and lesser rajahs'.[24]

Most British in Shanghai revered the Keswicks almost as royalty. When Tony Keswick married a girl from England it was understood that, like a prince, he had to go abroad to find his equal. As one man remarked, 'No one would have expected him to marry a Shanghai girl.' The attitude to Victor Sassoon was more ambiguous.

Victor appeared to be the only Sassoon in the fourth generation with the commercial ability to carry on the family tradition. He was a captain in the Royal Air Force in the First World War until a plane crash left him crippled, with a permanent pain in his right hip. He could only walk with two sticks. His father, Edward Elias Sassoon, had suffered a number of strokes and Victor was afraid of ending up 'a cabbage'. Sensitive about his handicap, he had no desire to marry. As he said, 'If I had healthy and attractive children I could not help becoming horribly jealous of them.' He did not ride but his horses had made nearly as much history as his business deals. He had raced his thoroughbreds in India, Ireland and China under the pseudonym of 'Mr Eve'. It was he who remarked, 'There is only one race greater than the Jews and that's the Derby.'[25] He was also a champion golfer. Before Shanghai he had lived in Bombay, still the centre of the Sassoon empire, and had held office in the India legislative assembly. In 1931 he announced his intention of leaving India and taking his business with him.

The arrival of this almost legendary creature in Shanghai caused enormous speculation. What would it be like doing business with a man known to bet £10,000 on one horse-race? How would one of the richest and most successful businessmen in the British Empire fit into Shanghai society? As one Shanghailander explained: 'He was Jewish but one couldn't very well snub a man who played golf with the Prince of Wales. It was a perplexing topic at the Club, I can tell you.'

Sir Victor Sassoon blamed the Indian Nationalist campaign for his decision to leave India. In an interview with *The Times of India* in 1931, he said, 'The political situation does not encourage one to launch out in a big way for the time being.'[26] The *North China Daily News* was more informative. In India Sir Victor Sassoon sounded 'a dissenting note' against the introduction of a more compassionate Factory Law favouring 'an even more conservative policy'.[27] That and his desire to avoid British taxes decided him. He looked around and chose Shanghai. The International Settlement had rejected calls for even the gentlest Factory Act. The authorities had no plans to introduce new taxation while the Shanghailander possessed a resistance to change that reassured even Sir Victor. He declared it the place to do business 'on a large scale'.[28]

Once in Shanghai he bought land and built. He organized the Cathay Land Company and the Cathay Hotel Company. He took over Arnhold & Co. with its extensive contracting interests. He controlled the Yangtsze Finance Company and the International Investment Trust. He pulled down picturesque Victorian buildings, like the Majestic, and put up apartment and office blocks, department stores and hotels. His appetite for real estate made a site on the Bund more expensive than the equivalent in New York or London.

He outdid the Shanghai businessmen in everything. A man came to see him with an idea for producing five thousand pairs of shoes a day which involved importing American machinery and mechanizing the Shanghai shoe industry. Sir Victor expressed an interest, provided he owned the cowherds, the tanneries, the shoe factory and the chain of shoe shops. The man went away dumbfounded.

Sir Victor Sassoon's showpiece was the Cathay Hotel on the Bund. Lilo Philips lived there for three months before the Second

World War. She recalled each suite furnished differently with built-in wardrobes the size of rooms. The bathrooms contained marble baths with silver taps and purified water. She liked to eat in the Tower Restaurant on the roof of the hotel where she could gossip with the manager, Freddy Kaufmann, about Berlin in the 'twenties and mutual European friends. She remembered the hustle and bustle around the reception desk; people constantly arriving and departing, the hall piled high with ship trunks. 'You felt at the centre of events in the Cathay Hotel,' she said. The hotel, famous throughout the Far East, set a precedent of luxury and glamour which, like the skylines Sir Victor had created, became associated in people's minds with Shanghai itself.

Opinions were mixed on Sir Victor. Baron Robert Rothschild found him amusing, cynical and very keen on the ladies. He appeared 'a rather romantic figure' who resembled an Indian prince with his dark eyes and swarthy complexion. To the Baron, the limp only increased his charm. He held brilliant parties in his penthouse at the top of the Cathay Hotel. Tony Keswick and Sir Victor insisted, unlike most of their compatriots, on socializing with the Chinese. The Baron was enchanted by the Chinese women – like exotic birds in their jewels and silks. Sir Victor's apartment boasted several sitting-rooms as well as a bathroom containing two baths. Sir Victor confided to the Baron that he liked to share his bed but never his bath. Sir William Hayter had less pleasant memories of Sir Victor's mock-Tudor house on the road that now leads to the airport: 'It was the sort of thing a stockbroker might live in with worm holes drilled into the wooden beams', and of his parties, he said, 'He enjoyed playing practical jokes and once poured *crème de menthe* down the back of my suit. Why it was funny, I can't remember.' Sir Victor also took pleasure in photographing his guests and was rarely without a camera. Sir Harold Acton found him 'a very agreeable fellow if rather a Philistine', who cared little for the arts but kept a large number of women. 'Apparently sex was a bit complicated because of his accident. He married his nurse in the end.'

George Stewart, Sir William Hayter, Tony Keswick, and the Chancellors, all recalled his fancy-dress parties. Like his business deals they dazzled and befuddled. In February 1933 he invited his guests to dress as if caught in a 'shipwreck'. The costumes ranged from pyjamas to tails. Mary Hayley Bell (the mother of the actress, Hayley Mills) wore a flannel nightdress with her hair in curlers, looking, the social column of the *North China Daily News* conceded, 'very much prettier than most girls could in that dress'.[29] By nine o'clock the absurdity of the costumes and the cocktails had loosened tongues and conventions. The guests filed into dinner beneath the astonished gaze of diners unprepared for the sight of Shanghai's most respected citizens walking half-clad into the Cathay dining-room. Mr and Mrs Don Burdick's entrance caused the greatest sensation. They appeared naked except for a shower curtain, above which their heads dripped with water. Sir Victor Sassoon, dangling a hot-water bottle from his waist, snapped away, no doubt adding to his 'interesting collection' of photographs.

The spectacular, fancy-dress parties failed to impress Sylvia Chancellor. 'Victor said to me, "Is it a coincidence that you never come?" I said, "Not entirely!" ' But even she attended his Circus party in January 1935.

Right up to the last moment harassed individuals rang around their friends for inspiration. Sir Victor came as ringmaster in a scarlet coat and top hat. Mrs Winter was the tattooed lady. Another Shanghai matron arrived with her bicycle dressed as a trapeze artist while Irene Dunsford almost completely covered herself in the slippery costume of a performing seal. Mr Harold Watson marched into the ballroom, a self-possessed and beautiful bride leaning on the arm of a blushing 'groom' who refused to remove her mask and remained one of the mysteries of the evening. John Keswick, Tony's brother, and Sylvia Chancellor – 'My husband was away or I wouldn't have dared' – smuggled a donkey into the goods lift of the Cathay Hotel for John in his role of Don Quixote. The animal kicked them both in the lift and cut John's lip. At the top they enticed it on to the dance floor where it stood and brayed at the whirling couples. 'Get it out of here,' said Sir Victor. The donkey then lifted his tail and shat. Sylvia Chancellor admitted, 'John was not easily embarrassed but I think he felt he might have gone a bit far that time.' The donkey and its mess were removed and a number of Chinese guests dressed as acrobats cartwheeled among the dancers. The end of the party passed unnoticed by Sylvia Chancellor: 'I went to sleep in the middle of the dance floor.'

Sir Victor Sassoon also gave fancy-dress parties for children. At the Flower and Vegetable Party held in the Hotel Metropole, Sir Victor Sassoon appeared as Number One Gardener while the children arrived as pansies, forget-me-nots and sweet peas. The room was decorated to look like a garden with the food laid on wooden tables under parasols.

They were not parties for everybody. You had to be somebody, or somebody's child, to receive an invitation. Rosemary Dale whose father worked for the Shanghai Municipal Council said she was not 'smart enough' to be invited. She recalled her more fortunate classmates coming away with marvellous presents and her jealousy when one year they each received a camera. Many of the grown-ups who did merit an invitation sneered at Sassoon for trying too hard. Sylvia Chancellor's lack of interest implies a criticism of his ostentation. Another woman remembered discussing at a dinner the best route Home. Victor started to say something when her friend cut in. 'Don't you go by camel?' he said. 'Well, perhaps it was unkind but how could he talk of England as Home? It was too absurd.'

The same woman showed me a photograph of herself at the Shipwreck party. She and her friends looked very silly. It made me wonder if Sir Victor gave his fancy-dress parties as revenge on those who took his hospitality but abused him behind his back. I imagined him going through his photographs afterwards with amusement and satisfaction. That was what I hoped. I suspected that Sir Victor wanted the approbation of people like the lady at the dinner party. The British in Shanghai had deceived him into thinking their approval a precious commodity. It was the Bund all over again. The man responsible for so much of the Bund's façade had been taken in by its bluff. Did Sir Victor never stroll behind his marvellous hotel and see the shabbiness there? Did he never ask himself who were these people who sneered at him? 'Quite ordinary folk', with 'an exaggerated idea of their own importance' was how one more clear-sighted letter-writer to the *North China Daily News* described them. 'Where else would one see a page of the leading daily devoted to Mrs So and So's tiffin, Mrs Somebody's tea and Mrs Otherboy's cocktail party?'[30] The British accepted his invitations, got drunk and danced until six in the morning but always refused to be won over. It was their one strength and only attraction. Like a plain but crafty virgin, they made the most of it.

Sir Victor Sassoon's parties came to an end with the outbreak of the Second World War. In the spring of 1941 he left Shanghai. When he returned in 1946, he found the Japanese had ripped out all the boilers and radiators from the Cathay Hotel for scrap, the Americans had moved in and General Wedemeyer had taken over his suite. He did not despair. He valued his holdings in Shanghai at £7½ million and the war was over. Three years later the unimaginable happened. Despite a reassuring notice outside the Country Club promising that 'Tennis courts will be open from May'[31] and the tank traps set up on the Kiangwan golf course, the communists arrived and took over the city. Sir Victor Sassoon lost nearly everything. He heard the news in America. 'Well, there it is,' he said, after a moment. 'I gave up India and China gave me up.'[32]

Lord Bangor quit China in 1936 to spend a legacy from his aunt wandering around Europe. George Stewart departed in 1938 on leave. Sir Christopher and Lady Chancellor arrived in England just in time for the declaration of war. The Foreign Office dispatched Sir William and Lady Hayter to Washington. Tony Keswick came back after the war but, like Victor Sassoon, lost everything in the communist takeover. China, as they knew it, was gone. Lord Bangor said, 'Of all the countries I've been to – and I was working it out the other day, it's around sixty – the one I'd really like to go back to – the one, in fact, I wouldn't mind ending my days in would be China. China as it was during the three years I spent there between 1933 and 1936.' Then he added wistfully, 'Always assuming it was still the way I remember it.'

There is no trace of the spoiling life in modern Shanghai. Paper hunt country is built over, the Family Tree pulled down and the Rubicon filled. There are no more parties, no dressing up and no young men in tails putting out fires. Only an elderly Chinese in hand-knitted mittens who said with an Oxford accent: 'Such a nice university. I was up for three years. Do they still punt on the Cherwell?'

The dentists' villas, so belittled by Sir William and Lady Hayter, still stand behind high walls. After Liberation and again during the Cultural Revolution, peasants moved in from the countryside and took them over, two families or more to a room. The houses depressed me. We are used to seeing a Doric temple or a Crusader's castle in ruins, but not a mock-Tudor home. Grass and flowers were growing between the roof tiles. From out of the windows, on bamboo poles, longjohns, nappies and pink blankets flapped in the breeze like pennants. Stacked up on gutters were pots of plants, pieces of wood, piles of broken tiles, an empty birdcage and a rusty spade or pitchfork. The Chinese had not destroyed or even changed the houses. They had simply adapted them, with complete indifference, to their needs. It increased their forlorn air. A ruin at least becomes part of its landscape. These houses looked lost and forgotten like a doll in a gutter.

The front door of one home stood open. I walked in. Bicycles were propped up against the oak panelling in the hall and rubbish lay in drifts on the parquet floor. It was very cold. I went into the sitting-room. Blankets draped on lines partitioned the room into three. Women were cooking dinner on kerosene stoves. The room lacked lighting or heating. It was as if squatters had moved in and set up camp; but this camp had lasted forty years. I looked up. Communal washing lines, hung with nappies, winter jackets and pieces of smoked fish, crisscrossed the stucco ceiling. From the central garland dangled a chain but no chandelier. A child started to cry. The smoke from the fires and the smell of cooking filled the room and mingled with the stench of urine from the hall. Outside lay a wilderness of rhododendron bushes. I turned to go and saw, set in the wall by the door, a brass buzzer. Every room had them, I had been told. They summoned the servants if you dropped your handkerchief or wanted a glass of water. I hesitated then reached out and pushed. The child stopped crying to stare at me.

The Abattoir of All Human Joys

The happy memories of Lord Bangor and George Stewart tell only half the story. In pursuit of profit, the British created a corrupt, unlovely and pitiless city. That city is now expunged from memory. They talked to me of colonial virtue, of honest institutions and sound administration. But the British in Shanghai were not colonials, they were businessmen. They might have borrowed the plumage of colonial power and dignity but rarely did they fulfil its obligations. Business had given the city its character and its reason for existing. In their eyes business came first and Shanghai second.

British businessmen were a much-labelled species. Known as 'Old China Hands' and suffering from a defect called the 'Shanghai Mind', people remembered them as a group rather than as individuals. One American found it daunting to walk into a room full of them. They knew immediately if you did not think like them and felt it their duty to make sure you did. By chance I received an invitation to meet an example of the Shanghai Mind in his London club.

I was early and the elderly porter insisted I stand under his eye until 'the relevant Member vouches for you'. Mr Arbuthnot introduced himself, a small man with a straight back, sparse hair and watery eyes. 'Glad to see you are punctual,' he said, 'so many women aren't.' He led me to a side room, reserved for lady guests, where he ordered tea and cakes for me ('I hate women who diet') and a whisky and soda for himself.

He pulled out a small notebook and began to enumerate subjects he considered suitable for discussion. He also gave me a list of books. When I told him I had already read them, he appeared at a loss. I took the opportunity to ask if he had visited the French Club, the place Princess Lyuba had declared the centre of Shanghai social life. Mr Arbuthnot frowned. 'I went there once for a New Year's Eve party. Everyone got drunk and made a frightful exhibition of themselves. I never went back again.' Had he travelled around China? 'I took my friends on a couple of motor-car trips but, frankly, after you've seen one pagoda, you've seen them all.' Had he liked Chinese food? 'I only once had Chinese food. I was invited away for the weekend and was forced to eat it. I don't think I have yet recovered from the experience. If I felt like going native, I went to a Hungarian place near me which served solid, manly stuff.' Did he speak Chinese? Mr Arbuthnot looked surprised. 'Chinese was not really in my line of business. If I came up against a Chinese, he could speak English.' He did not have any Chinese friends, then? 'Certainly not. The compradore in our firm asked us out to an annual bash in a restaurant. I never visited his home or met his wife. He was a decent enough chap. He told me the Chinese characters for my name, "Illustrious Pearl", or some such rot, but I had it made up into a name-card. None of the Chinese I gave it to understood its meaning, something to do with the Chinese language, I should say. I am told it's an effeminate and illogical tongue, rather similar to the Chinese character.' He looked me straight in the eye. 'You couldn't trust them. The coolies and my Number One Boy were all right in their place, often very amusing, like children really, but a Chinese official had no decency or sense of honour. He was only interested in using his post to enrich himself. When the Yangtsze flooded and funds were collected in Shanghai to help the victims, I refused to contribute. "Can you guarantee the money will go where it's needed?" I asked. Of course they could not. The refugees never saw a penny. That was China for you.'

The Shanghai businessman understood one equation. In the weakness of China lay the strength of Shanghai. As long as the Chinese were unable to rule themselves, the foreigner could rule Shanghai. A strong and united China would want the Settlements back. The businessman might complain about the Chinese but he did not wish to see them change. At stake was not only the good life that Shanghai offered but his sense of self-esteem. China presented a flattering mirror. Its reflection transformed every foreigner into an emissary of Western civilization. Adventurers, drug traders, the uneducated and the second-rate could examine themselves with confidence. The rough chin turned suddenly smooth, the hunched shoulders straightened, the tattered coat restored and decorated with medals. Unfortunately the transformation did not travel. The foreigner could only impress in the country he despised. In England, the country he revered, he would be nobody. His heart may have been suffused with a beatific vision of Home, a house in the country, riding over the downs; but the Shanghai businessman's sense of his own worth depended on China and the Chinese.

Shanghai's history had left the British with a contempt for the Chinese and a fear of their numbers. The emotions that had made it so satisfying for British sailors to kill unarmed Chinese during the First Opium War remained strong. Many British businessmen, if not wishing to massacre the Chinese like snipe, agreed with Palmerston that 'These half-civilized governments such as those in China . . . required a Dressing every eight or ten years to keep them in order . . . they care little for words and they must not only see the Stick but actually feel it on their Shoulders before they yield.'[33]

The British were responsible for the International Settlement's discrimination against its Chinese inhabitants which ranged from the political to the petty. Before 1926 Chinese could not vote in Municipal elections nor stand for the Council even though the Chinese paid the greater part of the Municipal income. Chinese had to register their property in the name of a foreign friend. A Chinese attempting to enter a foreign hotel, however smartly dressed, found himself directed round to the tradesmen's entrance. The open-air swimming pool in Kiangwan Road only allowed Chinese to bathe if they produced a card of approval from the Shanghai Municipal Council Health Department. The Cathedral Boys' School, Shanghai's foremost British public school, did not offer Chinese as a subject until 1937. A Belgian socialist, visiting Shanghai in 1930, remembered the experience of one European diplomat who held a dinner in honour of the members of the Nationalist government, many of whom had attended American universities. The next day the diplomat ran into a British businessman. 'I heard you invited those so-called members of the government to dinner yesterday,' he said. 'Tell me, in Peking do you also dine with coolies?'

One intrepid woman traveller put the British attitude down to class. 'To those who know nothing of their own native slums Chinese conditions in the poorer city districts may appear unspeakable,'[34] she wrote in 1933 and advised the middle-class British businessman to make a trip to the north of England and Scotland and visit the slums there. She could testify to the same dense over-crowding, a similar lack of daylight and even comparable-sized rats swimming in the open drains. Fifteen minutes from the centre of Newcastle she found a situation identical to Nantao; tenements 'swarming with humanity' dependent on a single tap in the courtyard and an outside lavatory. Some lacked even that. One wonders how many citizens of Newcastle-upon-Tyne would have qualified for a dip in the Shanghai Municipal swimming pool.

By the 'twenties and 'thirties fear of change sharpened British criticism into racialism. The *North China Daily News* took particular exception to those Chinese who had studied abroad and now called for an end to extraterritoriality, no 'Taxation without Representation', admittance to the city's parks (from which Chinese were banned) and the return of Mixed Courts to China. One returned student, stung by the paper's attacks, wrote to it in June 1927,

> If foreign education has merely aimed at making the Chinese students always grateful and submissive towards the countries in which they have been educated no matter how oppressed politically, militarily or economically their brethren are by these same countries, then it is indeed an utter failure on the part of our dear foreign friends, for they have miscalculated the quality of Chinamen who, after all, differ radically from the dumb driven cattle, easily made thankful with a scanty ration.

To which the Editor replied:

> We take pleasure in publishing this letter since it . . . shows more convincingly than anything we could write how radically the modern Occidental system of education has to be revised before it can be of any genuine service to the Chinese student.[35]

By the early 1930s the foreign governments concerned had acquiesced to these demands except for the end of extraterritoriality. 'We Shanghai residents have our backs up against the wall. We are surrounded by unscrupulous enemies who are bent on our surrender and destruction,' declared one leader. In their fear most British ceased to see Chinese as people, even ceased to see them at all. Robert Guillain, correspondent for Agence Havas, the French News Agency, recalled the splendid buildings of the Bund at the base of which, 'unnoticed', people died of cold and hunger. 'The contrast was really very striking.' The *North China Daily News* agreed that something should be done because the Bund was 'our show street' and beggars, 'exhibiting repulsive deformities', represented an unpleasant sight for children 'or for anyone'.[36] The newspaper watched with amazement as the police moved an unlicensed peanut-seller while ignoring an 'appalling bundle of filth and rags' which stretched 'its horrible length . . . on which there was not a square inch of visible flesh that was not foully diseased and there was all too much of it on view'. The paper went on, 'if there is an alternative, peanuts would be preferable'.[37] Even Christmas failed to soften the heart of the *North China Daily*

News. 'It is easy to see that the festive season is here,' it announced. Beggars overran the streets exhibiting 'real or assumed deformities', with children 'a worse nuisance than the grown-ups'. The paper concluded: 'It is pleasant to be charitable when the spirit of Christmas warms the heart ... but there is no excuse for being blackmailed into almsgiving by these hordes.'[38]

The danger of this attitude and its pervasive effect throughout Shanghai's administration is clear from the events which took place in the early hours of December 1st, 1935. The cause centred on another of those 'appalling' bundles 'of filth and rags'.

At 2.30 in the morning a couple of Chinese policemen found a sick beggar on their beat and telephoned to Kashing Road Police Station for assistance. Sergeant Makovetsky, covering for Sergeant Ernest Peters, logged the call. Peters arrived shortly after, slightly drunk, full of the new girlfriend whose passionate demands had caused his delay. As he described these, a young probationary sergeant named Judd walked in. Sergeant Makovetsky suggested he go and look at the beggar. In a fit of ebullience Peters announced his intention of accompanying Judd. As charge room sergeant this was against regulations and a surprising decision for a man already two and a half hours late for duty. The only explanation is an imaginary one. I can see Sergeant Peters digging Judd in the ribs and saying, 'Another bloody Chinese beggar. Let's go and have a bit of fun on this one. Show them what's what, eh?' They left in a patrol car with a Chinese driver.

At the corner of Singkeipang and Point Roads they found a dirty, long-haired Chinese lying on the ground, groaning and frothing at the mouth. They picked him up and draped him over one of the rear mudguards. Judd got into the car and Peters rode on the running-board. The driver, Du Songfu (Doo Sungfoo), started in the direction of Hongkew Police Station where beggars were usually deposited. Peters made him turn around and stop between Yalu and Yuhang Road. Judd and Peters took hold of the beggar and swung him into the creek. A hawker on his way home from a gambling game who saw the beggar's head bobbing up and down in the water shouted *Qiu ming* (Save Life) and woke a boatman 'two Chinese houses away'. They pulled the beggar out, a policeman and an ambulance arrived and the man was taken to St Luke's hospital. A few days later he died of double pneumonia.

The chauffeur confided in a Chinese detective inspector who told Inspector J. G. Bennett, in charge of Kashing Road Station. Peters and Judd admitted they had dropped the beggar over the side but claimed they had lowered him onto a beggar boat that happened to be passing. They were brought to trial.[39]

Apart from Judge Mossop, whose summing up shows he believed them guilty, every other foreigner in court appears to have displayed astonishment that the lives of two young Englishmen, ex-army, 'clean living and sporting', could be put in jeopardy by the death of a Chinese beggar. The trial centred on worth not guilt.

Du Songfu, the driver, appeared as chief witness for the prosecution. Mr Ronald McDonald, the Counsel for the defence, asked Du to describe his reaction when the two policemen threw the beggar into the water. Du replied he felt 'sorrowful in the matter', and had turned his head away. This so surprised Mr McDonald that he interrupted Du to ask a 'delicate' question.

'What religion are you? (I only ask this because you turned your head away.)'

Puzzled, Du Songfu answered, 'I do not understand religion.'

'Have you no religion? Do you believe in any god?' pressed Mr McDonald.

Du repeated that he did not understand.

Judge Mossop, better acquainted with British prejudices, interrupted, 'You are not suggesting, Mr McDonald, that only people who believe in God are kind people, are you?'

Unabashed Mr McDonald replied, 'I tentatively agree with your lordship but prefer to put it in my own way.'

Du said he turned his head because he did not like to see a man drown and repeated, 'I thought no such human being should throw another into the creek.' Mr McDonald, unconvinced either by Du's scruples or his story, pressed him so hard that Du cried out, 'I want to vomit,' and dashed from the room. The Chinese interpreter reminded the court that Du had been standing in the witness box for six hours. And he, translating all that time, was also feeling rather faint.

The interpreter found himself the defence's next victim. Mr Reeks, representing Sergeant Judd, stopped in the middle of a question to point at him and his colleague seated on a bench in front of the judge. 'The interpreters have been continually distracting my attention. I would like them to sit behind me. They are not doing anything improper, but are only distracting my attention.'

The judge, all concern, asked, 'Is anyone else distracting your attention? Is Mr Abbey (the clerk of the court) or am I distracting your attention? We have to sit here, you know. Are they talking?'

Mr Reeks admitted they were not. 'But I feel I am being distracted.' His colleague Mr McDonald added, 'Possibly these two have some hypnotic powers which work on my learned friend and not on us more obtuse people.' The interpreters obligingly moved, their faces 'wreathed in smiles'. It was rare for a foreigner to be brought to trial for the murder of a Chinese, very well executed for the offence. The translators' pleasure in the novelty of the proceedings must have galled Reeks.

The evidence against Peters and Judd proved formidable. Apart from the testimonies from the driver and the hawker, Inspector Bennett himself admitted that the two policemen had panicked when questioned and had tried out a number of stories before fixing on the most plausible. The charge book made no mention of a beggar boat. 'On arrival the beggar had left' was how Peters described their escapade. The prosecution, Mr Victor Priestwood, a dim man with his heart not in the matter, was easily overwhelmed by the eloquence of the defence. McDonald reminded the jury: 'My client is on trial for his life and nothing else. He is a young man, and therefore life possibly means more to him than it does to me.' He dismissed the victim with a brief appeal to Calvinism: 'Mao Debiao (Mau Te-piau) was a beggar, and had possibly been ordained for that position.' Mr Reeks, too clever to call the driver a liar, described Du's evidence as 'invariably embellished', because 'the more uneducated a man was, the more he called into play his imaginative powers. He even came to believe it himself, and then deliberately created those links of evidence necessary to carry conviction in the mind of another person.' Inspector Bennett was less easily dismissed. McDonald took refuge in a conspiracy theory with hints of a 'sinister figure or figures in the background'. When picked up by Judge Mossop on this – 'Do you suggest the police – what are you suggesting?' – he hastily retracted. 'No foreigner. No one in this court. No foreigner.' Peters's only fault, he continued, was, 'Like Samson of old', to dally too long 'with some Delilah that night'. Mr Reeks moved from the biblical to the sentimental. 'And now, on February 10th, 1936 William Alfred Judd, with his father and his mother miles away in England, and possibly a little friend at the back of the court, await your verdict.' It took the British jury less than an hour to relieve the sufferings of the 'little friend' and let the young men off. The crowd, one of the largest ever seen at a local trial, broke into spontaneous cheers and applause.

Judd and Peters, nice enough young men with good records, had, according to the prosecution, committed in fifteen minutes an act 'deprived of all sense of social justice and a total disregard of the laws of humanity'. A remark made by the hawker during the trial sums up the occasion: 'As I was born in Shanghai, I had heard of many curious affairs.'

Basil Duke, a member of Special Branch described the event in a letter to his family. Basil Duke is now dead but by a fortunate coincidence I met his sister, Lady Patricia Maddocks, who had kept his correspondence. This revealed the case to be even more curious than it first appears. The trial had put a stop to Basil Duke's holiday in the Japanese Alps. He wrote with frustration, 'it seems for the moment that the gang of dishonest rats in the Force have caught its finest and most honest man napping.' This is Patrick Givens, head of the Special Branch and the recipient of the Order of the Brilliant Jade. Basil Duke continued,

> the fact that he is honest, a great distinction here, is notorious but in attempting to save one of his men, a sergeant, from a blunder he himself did rather a stupid thing and it was pounced on by his arch-enemy (like himself a Deputy Commissioner) and poor old Pat Givens has been suspended. This Force is more reminiscent of the French Court in the time of Richelieu and Anne of Austria than anything I have yet struck – just a mass of intrigue – masons, Catholics, Scotch, Irish, etc.

When the case came before the Municipal Council, Basil hoped Pat would 'blast his enemies'. He could not believe that the Council, 'even if they are a band of unconvicted crooks themselves, will be such asses as to get rid of one of their few honest employees'. Three months later he reported the 'poor man has just had a premature retirement forced on him and his arch-enemy (and in my opinion, nothing really more than the town's no. 1 gangster) is King of the Castle'. The letter reveals that 'sinister figures' did indeed move behind the scenes. Judd and Peters felt a justifiable indignation. But for the convenience of police politics, the case would never have been brought.

I asked an ex-member of the Shanghai police force for his opinion. He recalled how provoking he found the Chinese. On his beat in Kiangsi Road, a Chinese refugee hawked on to the toe of his boot. Instinctively, he hit the man in the stomach. The refugee suffered from an enlarged spleen and dropped dead at his feet. Had he found himself in court, I wondered. The policeman looked amazed. 'Good Lord, no! I didn't even report it. People were dying all the time on Shanghai's streets.'

Basil Duke arrived in Shanghai the same year as Lord Bangor and George Stewart. As a policeman and a member of Special Branch he did not receive an invitation to drinks at the Long Bar or attend parties in Sassoon's penthouse. There are no descriptions in his letters of early morning rides, Number One Boys or of weekends spent shooting snipe from a houseboat. He spent his time on Shanghai's streets. He carried a gun, kept files on Shanghai's prominent citizens and offers a tour of a violent and disreputable city. A policeman for a guide puts one immediately on the outside of the glittering party, into the dark and wet where things are obscure and menacing. 'Leave truth to the police', wrote W. H. Auden in his verse contribution to the book he and Isherwood produced together on their trip to China. 'We know the Good;/We build the Perfect City time shall never alter.'[40] No one would think the worse of you for preferring to stay indoors for another dance or glass of champagne.

Basil Duke's letters are an account of one particular Shanghai institution. Any police force is a good litmus test for the attitudes and morals of a city and the Shanghai Municipal Police force, an international organization run by the British with a British Commissioner, proves no exception.

By 1941, 4,919 men made up the Shanghai Municipal Police. Apart from the 353 civil staff the force was divided into four branches. The Chinese were the most numerous with over 3,000 men. The Sikh branch, generally consigned to crowd and traffic control, stood at 511 men. The Japanese section of 267 men worked in Hongkew among the Japanese community. The 505 men of the Foreign Branch consisted mainly of British (331 of them) with 126 Russians, 7 Americans and an assortment of 17 other different nationalities including 2 Italians, 6 Germans, 3 Latvians and 1 Hungarian. Fourteen police stations were scattered across the International Settlement from Bubbling Well Station at 172 Yu Yuen Road on the Western boundary to the Yangtszepoo Station at

2049 Pingliang Road over to the East. A British officer and a British senior detective ran each of the fourteen stations.

The police wore a thin blue uniform in spring and autumn, khaki in summer and thick blue for winter. All nationalities shared an identical uniform except for the Chinese who refused to wear shorts in summer. Chinese and Sikh policemen put on thick blue one month earlier than the Foreign Branch. The Sikhs who directed traffic in red turbans, from raised islands at Shanghai's crossroads, looked particularly striking and proved fearsome in a crisis. Basil Duke wrote to his mother,

> We had to keep them more than fully occupied so that they were tired out at the end of each day. If they were given half a chance they would involve themselves in an intrigue of any kind which usually ended up with a fight and both men in court. They had an incurable propensity for lending money out at exorbitant rates and having sex with goats and small boys – or even the more accommodating of their adult Chinese fellow policemen.

The Shanghai policeman received a low wage, an average of SH$300 a month with seventeen days' holiday a year. The force attracted new recruits with a long leave of seven months after every five years of service on full pay plus a free return ticket Home for a man, his wife and two children (the Municipal Council's munificence did not include stepchildren). White Russians – who had no Home – received the cash equivalent.

Recruits required some inducement, for Shanghai had become a dangerous city to police. Armed robberies and kidnappings occurred daily. On average a Chinese rifle went off every five hours. Tony Keswick, when chairman of the Municipal Council, promoted an exchange with the Chicago police force, that other great centre of gangster activity. Five Chicago policemen swapped with their Shanghai counterparts for six months. He went on, 'Our chaps liked it over there and looked on it as a bit of a holiday. They taught the Americans how to fire from the hip and a lot of other useful stuff.' The Chicago policemen found Shanghai a different story. After one month they asked to go home. The dangerous streets unnerved them. G. H. Reynolds, a former member of Shanghai's Special Branch, told me that the Shanghai police force shot more rounds in one month than their Chicago colleagues did in a year. He remembered in what high regard American forces held their Shanghai colleagues. It became a custom for Shanghai policemen to return Home on long leave eastwards because local police forces fêted them the entire breadth of the United States.

The Chinese committed the majority of violent crime, explained Mr Reynolds. Foreigners stuck to fraud. When a police station received news of a robbery, an alarm went off in the men's quarters. Mr Reynolds recalled, 'We didn't quite have a pole to slide down like the Fire Brigade but we dragged on our uniform and ran out to our bullet-proof vans where a row of Chinese constables waited for us.' The first slapped on a steel helmet, the next a bullet-proof waistcoat, the third handed him a Thomas sub-machine gun. Invariably Mr Reynolds found himself in a shoot-out. He was only hit once in his whole career and then by Assistant Commissioner Fairburn who had come along 'for the ride' and shot the heel off Reynolds's boot in the excitement. 'I was more scared of him than the robbers.'

One White Russian member of the Special Branch described to me a typical incident. The Russian was on bicycle patrol with a Chinese helper when a Chinese boy ran towards him shouting, 'Bandits!' The Russian leapt off his bicycle 'like a cowboy' and pulled out his gun. The Chinese led him down a passage and pointed to an iron gate. 'Here,' he said and ran away. The Russian was scared to death. He had already been shot at once and had not enjoyed the experience. He flattened himself against the wall and worked towards the gate. Just as he reached the corner, somebody poked a pistol from the other side into his face. He immediately did the same, his hand shaking so badly that he could not pull the trigger. 'Are you a bandit?' he asked. The pistol pointing at him trembled as much as his. 'No, I am the watchman,' came the reply. The two men put down their guns and faced each other. The Russian left the watchman still shaking and walked into the building where he found seventy people clustered in one room. 'Where's the bandit?' he said. They pointed to a pedlar holding a basket of vegetables. The Russian searched him and found nothing. The boy who had raised the alarm now slunk back. 'Where's his weapon?' demanded the Russian. The boy walked to the window. Down below lay a Mauser decorated in Chinese fashion with a red tail. The Russian ran downstairs and forced an hysterical Chinese woman to unlock the door into the courtyard. He then arrested the pedlar who had killed three people in that building.

147

To keep up British numbers in the police force, the Settlement authorities took twenty new recruits from England every few years. At the age of twenty-five Basil Duke had already spent two years in New Zealand on a Church of England farming scheme and a year in Samoa as a policeman. His plan to marry a Samoan girl so worried his parents that they sent him a ticket to join them in India. In Bombay he worked briefly in an advertising agency before falling from a balcony drunk one night. He broke his hip and returned to England to enrol in the Shanghai Police Force as a probationary sergeant.

His first sight of Shanghai, as he wrote to his mother, seemed inauspicious. 'For the last two or three hours we came up the Yangtsze River, which is quite the filthiest river I've ever laid eyes on, midway between grey and yellow in colour and the country all flat and uninteresting.'

He passed an 'enormous' amount of shipping in the river from Chinese junks to warships of Britain, USA, Japan. His ship stopped down river and 'the disembarkation business was about the most tedious to which I have ever been subjected'. The tender puffed black smoke in their faces and gave 'drum-breaking screeches on its siren, and I have seldom felt the heat so much.' He arrived in Customs to find his new camera had been stolen and that despite paying five cents on every piece of luggage for coolie charges, he had to lump it about himself before 'forcibly capturing' a Chinese official to search it. 'I can tell you I wasn't half in a muck sweat by the time I got outside that shed.'

The new recruits were piled into a police van and the doors tightly closed. 'I think all our hearts rather fluttered at this reception.'

Basil found himself with a White Russian room-mate, which pleased him as it was the sort of thing he expected to have in an International Police Force. He enjoyed the man's limited English which sounded 'amusingly abrupt and harsh' and, whenever the Russian called for a servant, 'I half expect he is going to cut him in pieces with a knout!' Basil Duke's training began immediately and included basic arithmetic, police rules and regulations, local laws, instructions on how to use a .45 Colt automatic and a Jujitsu class once a week. The recruits took their Chinese lessons very seriously as the Terms and Conditions of Service stated that retention in the force depended 'to a great extent' on the ability to learn the language. A class of dedicated men practising the different tones produced a noise 'not unlike a Revivalist meeting with a good many of the opposition hissing'. The force also offered coaching in French, German, Japanese, Russian and Hindustani. Basil studied the last two for, besides helping in his work, proficiency earned an extra monthly allowance of SH$16.85 a language.

As well as attending class, Basil found time to write the lengthy letters expected by his parents in India, a sister in England and another married to a member of the British Consulate in Haerbin. He wrote plaintively, 'The family letter situation really is becoming almost a burden', and explained one silence with the excuse,

> Instead of sitting down in a business-like manner and firmly writing to the 'loved ones' (as funeral directors no doubt would call them) I go into a trance of dreaming and usually decide to dispel the melancholy mood (not necessarily melancholy but sometimes my thought pictures become so vivid I can't stand them any longer) by the, with me, never failing opiate of SLEEP.

He took pains with his correspondence especially when writing to his half Hungarian, half Sicilian and 'altogether delightful' mother. His father, the son of an Irish canon and a failed stockbroker had left for India to try and improve his prospects as a director of industries. Money was always a problem for the Duke family and was responsible for Basil's many changes of school and lack of university education. As he said, the family members made charming individuals but were bereft of 'native cunning'.

Wayward, eccentric and honourable, Basil Duke epitomizes to me the colonial system at its best. After his spell in Shanghai, he became a district commissioner in the Sudan, a job which suited him perfectly. He taught the Sudanese Ancient Greek plays and even built an amphitheatre. By the time he left, sixteen years later, they were producing their own version of the *Medea*. The Shanghai businessman might pretend to admire colonial ideals. In practice, Basil Duke, the epitome of those ideals, never saw the inside of the Shanghai Club.

Basil lived in a '2x6ft. box' so small that he had to give his dog away and lacked both time and money to escape into the countryside. When he did, he wrote gloomily, 'Nature rather forgot herself to start with and man had with a sort of fiendish vigour rubbed it in.' On hearing that a native commissioner in South West Africa had been mauled by a lion, five hundred miles from the nearest town, he thought a similar experience 'would do me the world of good – it would be a pleasant change at any rate from the slower and more painful mauling to which the living spirit is subjected in Shanghai . . . sometimes I feel like just buzzing off defiantly in search of a *vista*'.

He confided to his father that he found some relief in "the three Cs', cinemas, cabarets . . . the third is scored out, no doubt when the letter was forwarded to the rest of the family. Shanghai offered only 'the purely synthetic pleasures of civilization'. Even at Christmas, 'Everyone makes a bee line for the nearest cabaret', where, in the suffocating atmosphere, nothing suggested the approach of dawn, 'except perhaps the even greater impenetrability of the smoke screen around you'. He tried to save £1,000 a year which 'might possibly compensate me for putting in five years in the Abattoir of all human joys but even then I doubt it unless one was certain of a long life'. His efforts at economy meant he rarely socialized except to take a Russian barmaid out, for a steak or to the cinema. Shanghai lacked the facilities provided free of charge in London. 'There are *no* pleasures here that don't cost you *something*.' His letters record an existence far from the 'dim, delicious' nightlife and the fancy-dress parties of the Cathay Hotel.

A visit to Hong Kong on a rugger tour and a dip in the sea restored his faith. Physical and moral well-being were one and the same for Basil. He did not think his family could understand 'what the sight of blue sea and clean sand and hilly headlands feels like to one who for a very long period has seen no water but that which is the colour of water closet water after it has played its part in life and no land but flat land'. He went on, 'Compared with Hong Kong Shanghai is just a corrupt mess and a discredit to all concerned.'

His letters also record the irritations of living on a small salary in a city that combined the abject poverty of China with the unregulated industry of the West. Shanghai was a filthy city. Basil Duke noted that the Chinese knew

more about DIRT and STINKS a thousand years ago than the Indians will learn in the next five hundred . . . although I have always been reputed by the family to have no sense of smell, rarely a day goes by without my being sick in the street.

It's particularly bad in the early morning when what are locally known as the 'HONEY' carts are going about their loathsome business. How any sort of food can smell so badly in its later stages I can't imagine.

The euphemistically named carts contained human excrement collected each morning and sold for a profit by the Municipal Council to Chinese farmers who used it as manure for their fruit and vegetables. The practice made fresh produce dangerous to eat unless cooked. A bite into a peach or a plate of salad became a potential death trap for the foreigner. Raw sewage leaked from the ground into the water supply. No one used tap water, even to brush their teeth in, unless first boiled (they still do not). The foreigner found himself surrounded by almost medieval squalor. The city still boasted a leper colony. The life expectancy of a Chinese in Shanghai stood at twenty-seven, the same as in Europe during the thirteenth century. Dr McDonnal during his stay in 1927 found more dirt and disease in Shanghai than in Calcutta.

Foreign children remembered their mothers' obsession with cleanliness. They were forbidden to play with Chinese children or to eat food from Chinese stalls. Even a piece of water melon was a risk because Chinese vendors injected contaminated water into the fruit to make it look bigger. Rosemary Dale recalled that her mother washed every coin brought into the house before she allowed her children to touch them. When Rosemary won a teddy bear at a party, her mother insisted on sterilizing it.

A moment's thoughtlessness meant a disaster. Rosemary Dale's cousin died at five from rabies. 'We were on holiday and could not get back to a hospital in time. My aunt had to watch her child suffer for two days.' Sir William Hayter recalled one bad typhoon season when Shanghai's streets flooded. A friend of his insisted on walking home through the floods. He caught something from the water and died shortly after. Even the healthy rarely felt so. Every summer found Hallet Abend's chest and armpits raw from prickly heat, athlete's foot between his toes and fingers and his chin and forehead infested with ringworm.

Rosemary Dale came across corpses on her way to school. 'I once kicked a bundle of rags and the bundle fell apart to reveal a dead baby with a blue face.' She found the beggars slouched at her eye level along the pavement almost as upsetting. Adults escaped their attention by gazing over their heads but children had no such option. She recalled vividly the stunted limbs, gouged eyes, putrefying sores and swollen limbs blown up with bicycle pumps. The beggars harangued the foreign children for money and shouted threats when they refused to give any. A beggar with no legs once pursued Rosemary Dale, swinging on wads attached to his hands. 'If you didn't have your amah to protect you, you just fled.'

To the foreign child the life of the ordinary Chinese baffled and terrified. Horrible sights proliferated. In Jessfield Park a man gave foreign children nightmares by pushing a snake into his mouth and letting it slither out through his nose or ears. Rosemary Dale still has bad dreams about the mad girl she once came across tied to a wall. Her grandmother was burning her on the temples to frighten off evil spirits. The girl screamed and screamed. 'My amah shouted at the old woman to stop but she didn't.'

Shanghai was the largest industrial city in the Far East. A short note from Basil Duke to his mother reported that he was in hospital suffering from an eye infection caused by pollution. He blamed the Shanghai Power Co. owned by the Municipal Council.

> Only in a community run entirely for the benefit of vested interests, (the heads of which live elsewhere) would such a menace to health and comfort be allowed to carry on. The smaller fry constantly write letters to the paper on the subject but it does no good . . . the quantity of the black smoke daily belched forth from this Utility Co.'s premises continues unabated. The degree of one's particular discomfort just depends on which way the wind is blowing.

Basil survived the squalor of the city to complete his training and receive an initiation into police politics. A drunken Irish detective sergeant – 'I think he must have been a grocer in former life' – threw his arm round Basil in the police canteen and assured him, 'my superior (?) education did not antagonise him in the least! and that he would always do his best to help me and he expected me to do the same by him'. For all its internationality, power in the Shanghai police force rested with the Scottish and the Irish. The fight against crime appears to have taken second place to the 'age old struggle between the tribes', as Basil puts it. In his five years of correspondence, Basil never mentions crime except for

Sergeant Peters' 'blunder' and then only its bearing on the force's internal feuds. When Basil arrived in Shanghai, the Scots were in the ascendancy. The commissioner himself was a Scotsman while the last remaining Irish chief inspector 'has, I fancy shot his bolt – savouring rather too much as he does of his native bog – not to mention his native whisky – you've never seen such a horror in all your life!' The sight of 'middle aged and thoroughly stupid men who play no games at all but spend all their time in the canteens' had put Basil off drink. It was 'the most awful warning I've ever laid eyes on'. Abstinence did not stop Basil's recruitment, due to his Irish grandfather, into the St Patrick Society. As he wrote, 'it seems the done thing to belong to one side or the other. And if it's a question of a St George or a St Patrick society – I'd certainly choose the latter.' This and his ability on the rugger field drew him to the attention of Patrick Givens, head of Special Branch.

As a Catholic from Cork, Givens belonged firmly in the Irish camp and, until his defeat over the Judd and Peters affair, he employed his considerable power against the Scottish on the force. He sent a 'personal' message to Basil 'to hold my horses and have patience for a better day shortly to arrive'. Givens conducted a simple method of recruitment. He liked a man who played a good game of rugger. Whenever a vacancy occurred in his department, he sent for a list of the force's rugger players. G. H. Reynolds, a member of Special Branch and a rugger player himself, thought this qualification enough, as any game in Shanghai demanded both tact and strength. He recalled one tournament where the Italian Marine Corps drew to play the French Foreign Legion and both sides were searched for knives before the game. He also claimed his team taught rugger to the US 4th Marines once they had recovered their surprise at the lack of protective padding. His nastiest experience occurred during a match against the Italians when he received headful after headful of scented hair-oil.

Givens noted Basil's rugger prowess and invited him to join Special Branch. Basil described his work as almost entirely repression of communism, 'although it does take in anything else political that may come along'. G. H. Reynolds recalled censoring newspapers and films (including *Snow White and the Seven Dwarfs*, considered too strong for British children) and generally performing the same duties as a member of MI5. Basil Duke's first assignment proved a delicate one. The force permitted sergeants to marry after six years' service. A member of Special Branch, in this case Basil, checked the background of every prospective bride, as Basil put it, 'her antecedents, status and the number of times she visits the lavatory daily'. The Council offered special quarters, free coal and SH$7 a day maternity allowance to make up for the many 'inconveniences and indignities' suffered by married members of the force. As a disgruntled probationary sergeant remarked, 'I don't want free fucking coal!' Basil Duke went on to dismiss his investigations as 'a farce in a Force' which lacked 'all esprit de corps or standard of honesty, in which there is corruption from the bottom to the top with one or two exceptions'.

As a member of Special Branch, Basil Duke now enjoyed an insider's knowledge of the city. His letters become both disillusioned and circumspect. He cropped his correspondence of names and incidents but failed to erase their effect upon him. Public school had prepared Basil for service to the Empire but not the free for all of Shanghai society. 'When you contemplate this place you can't help wondering what is the explanation for the difference between the ideals in which British literature is soaked and the dishonesty of which any British political move reeks,' he mused in one letter.

He laid the blame on the British members of the Municipal Council and the big business interests they represented. A glance at the Municipal election of 1936 partly illustrates his point. Of the fourteen councillors, the five British candidates included Tony Keswick, H. E. Arnhold, G. E. Mitchell, Brigadier-General E. B. MacNaghten and H. Porter. Sir Victor Sassoon had taken over but left untouched the family firm of H. E. Arnhold at No. 1 Nanking Road on the understanding that Arnhold, as chairman of the Municipal Council, promoted Sir Victor's interests. Tony Keswick represented his family firm of Jardine Matheson and the Hongkong and Shanghai Bank which forbade its own staff from engaging in local politics. G. E. Mitchell headed Butterfield & Swire, Jardine Matheson's rivals. The other two members revealed the importance the British placed on propaganda whether in the form of the old boy network or a good press. Brigadier-General E. B. MacNaghten of the British-American Tobacco Co., had valuable connections in London as well as a high personal reputation. H. Porter was the director of the *North China Daily News*.

Big business ran Shanghai with one disadvantage. No one voted for them. Annual elections aroused a 'woeful' lack of interest – a direct result, declared J. B. Powell, the American editor of the *China Weekly Review*, 'of the monopolisation of municipal activities by a small clique'.[41] He dismissed the Municipal Council as 'a Select Party of the Top Taipans', who represented not the community but special interests which benefited from the Municipal administration. The ordinary voter felt himself ignored. A letter writer to the *North China Daily News* thought it doubtful if Council members ever met, much less discussed public matters with anyone on a salary of less than a thousand dollars a month which included the vast majority of the British in the city. Another man who signed himself 'Small Fry' refused to vote in protest against the apathy displayed by the British elected each year to the Council. He questioned the virtue of a Municipal Council which allowed smoke to belch from the factories over Central Area, crowded, dirty trams, an unfair taxation system which fell on tenants rather than on landlords (most of whom were Council members) and a fixed water rate which left Small Fry SH$3 a month worse off: 'To the wealthy $3 is probably a mere drop in the ocean: to me it is the equivalent of three picture shows at the Capitol for my wife and myself.'[42]

After the election the Council embarked on a campaign of economic reform. They cut the salaries of their low-paid workers like Basil Duke while leaving the 'enormous salaries' of the highest paid untouched. The Press Information Officer, for example, received SH$23,500[43] in a position 'the necessity for which the newspapers openly question'. In December 1936 Basil Duke wrote, 'One feels that one is employed by a very dishonest organisation which doesn't assist one to go about one's daily work the more cheerfully.' Two years later he departed on long leave to London, never to return.

Basil Duke's letters also reveal that the British discriminated against each other as rigidly as they did against the Chinese. The police belonged to the lower echelons of Shanghai society. Lady Chancellor only knew one because he was 'the young man of my nanny'. An employee of the Hongkong and Shanghai Bank insisted, 'There was a practical reason for what looked like snobbery. Once you opened something to everyone, you ruined the place with numbers.' He recalled the case of his Cricket Club. The Shanghai police asked to join but how, he asked me, could the club contemplate taking on four hundred policemen or four hundred of anybody? He added, almost as an apology, 'One was inclined to feel awkward with people whose background one didn't know,' and admitted he only encountered a wide social group in the Japanese camp during the war. I asked what he had made of the experience. He found everybody rather jolly, especially the White Russian wives of the British policemen who were in charge of the cooking 'and very good indeed. Unfortunately we discovered they were stealing half the food.'

A society based on hierarchy offers at least one consolation. However far from the top you are, there is always someone below you. Basil Duke found himself in a better position than those British born and brought up in Shanghai. British business and the Council reserved their best jobs for men from Home. Low-paid work with no hope of promotion went to the locals. Despite the good education offered by the Cathedral School and the Shanghai Public School, a worthwhile career in Shanghai required a stint in a British school or university. I wondered why the British considered an upbringing in Shanghai so dangerous. Was it eating too much Chinese food? Or speaking pidgin? Or some other, more nebulous contagion, perhaps China itself?

The answer was more prosaic. Only an English public school could produce an English gentleman and only an English gentleman could be trusted. Firms paid young men from England for their integrity rather than for their ingenuity. Banks and firms required transfers of money to be signed by a European, said George Stewart. A public school man's principal occupation was to sit and 'sign a lot of bits of paper'.

The barrier between those from Home and those born in Shanghai still exists. I interviewed two Shanghai families in the same English village. One family lived in the old house by the church; the other on a modern estate. The man on the estate had been born and brought up in Shanghai. The man in the big house worked in Shanghai for four years after Eton and Oxford. The man on the estate knew of the couple in the big house but they did not remember him. I had arranged to see them for lunch and him for tea. As soon as he heard that they lived near by, he invited himself over. 'I am looking forward to reminiscing,' he told me happily. He arrived before me. The couple handed me a drink. He was offered a sherry but, whether through oversight or intention, never received it. He tried to talk of Shanghai but they looked blankly at him. 'We don't remember that,' they said or, 'Oh no, we never went there.' Finally, they remarked, with great sweetness, 'I don't think we ever did meet, did we?' Silence followed. Puzzled and unhappy, the man from the estate stood up and left. 'You never gave him a drink,' said the wife to her husband and then to me, 'He wanted to be asked to lunch but the housekeeper can't manage more than one visitor.' Later, over a hard avocado, the husband looked up and asked, 'What was that man doing here?'

Eric Caulton was born and educated in Shanghai. His father worked as an engineer superintendent with the China Steam Navigation Company. He sailed from England in 1890 and lived in China for fifty years without coming home once. He did not earn enough money to send Eric to school in England. After a 'decent' education at the Shanghai Public School, Eric searched fruitlessly for a job. Finally he persuaded a mining company to employ him as an experiment. They had never before hired a white man in China. Eric reported to an ex-cavalry officer who drank like a fish. 'His job was nothing more than a home for a lost dog, he was so useless,' said Eric. The former cavalry officer took a dislike to the capable youngster, kept him on a low wage and refused him promotion. Eric found the situation 'very frustrating' until the arrival from head office of a new man who recognized Eric's qualities and promptly promoted him. To ensure he made more than the Chinese staff he now oversaw, Eric Caulton received two big pay rises in two years. After three and a half years' experience, he earned £275 per annum. The company paid a new recruit from England £400. I wondered if such treatment had left him bitter against the English. My question amazed him. England was Home, he stated. Before Eric's first visit, an American friend asked why he called England 'Home'. 'I don't know, we just did. It never occurred to me that I would finish up anywhere else.'

Eric Caulton could at least take comfort in the fate of the Eurasian. White Russian, Chinese or foreigner, everybody ostracized the child of mixed blood. Eric Caulton recalled that his parents hesitated to send him to the Shanghai Public School, considered the best in the city, because its pupils included Chinese, Eurasians and Jews. Eric's mother forbade her son to mix with Eurasians. Born and raised in China, she took infinite pains to highlight the difference between herself and her Eurasian neighbours despite their almost identical background and experience. He recalled her irritation when he returned home after a long spell in hospital speaking 'chee chee' – the sing-song English of the Eurasian.

Eric illustrated the general sentiment against the Eurasian with the following story about the founder of a Shanghai shipping line. A rough character, the shipowner had started life as an Outside Customs' man. He had made his money ineffectually searching ships for opium and arms. In one of those curious quirks of Shanghai society, the Inside Customs' men were considered socially acceptable whereas Outside Customs' men, with their reputation for corruption, rarely penetrated respectable drawing-rooms. Success overturned Shanghai sensibilities and brought the shipowner everything except for a son to run his business. He imported a nephew from England – a nice lad, recalled Eric, with a passion for racing. The nephew then fell in love with a Eurasian. All hell broke loose. The uncle had nothing against Eurasians. He even commanded the Eurasian company in the Shanghai Volunteer Corps ('which I would never have been seen dead in,' confided Eric) but with brutal finality, he refused to have the girl in his family. The couple committed suicide. I asked Eric if he had felt as strongly as the shipowner. 'It is an awful thing to admit now,' he said, 'but yes I would have cut my sister out of my life if she had married an Eurasian.'

Lawrence Kentwell provoked a similar reaction from the British authorities. The persecution of this forty-four-year-old Eurasian barrister is an example of prejudice on an institutional scale and the conspiratorial nature in which it was exercised. Kentwell himself, rootless, frantic but imbued with fighting spirit summed up for me something of Shanghai. He took on the British. The city took on China. Neither could hope to win.

In the New Year of 1927 Lawrence Kentwell's life fell apart and only, it seemed, with himself to blame. A suit brought against him for unpaid debts by the Municipal Council and Mr Zhou Guijing, (Chow Kuei-ching) an elderly Chinese financier, led to suspension from his practice and a court case. To many in the British community, Kentwell typified the exasperating characteristics associated with Eurasians. People packed the courtroom in anticipation of an amusing performance. Kentwell did not disappoint them. His hysteria recorded in the court transcripts appears to vindicate British prejudice. The trial was in fact a marvellous piece of stage management by the British authorities.

At first Kentwell refused to attend his trial. Instead he sent 'a most insulting letter',[44] in which he declared his intention to renounce his British citizenship and throw himself 'heartily'[45] into the fight to recover China's rights. Judge Grain saw no point in bringing China's political aspirations into a case about unpaid rates and dismissed the letter as unnecessary. Mr E. T. Maitland, representing the Municipal Council, pointed out that if Kentwell became a Chinese citizen, the case must be retried under Chinese law in a Chinese court. Kentwell had changed his nationality, insinuated the lawyer, in order to avoid his debts.

The Registrar lost his temper. 'I am not going to talk politics, but for many years Mr Kentwell has enjoyed the privileges of British nationality in China, and I use the word "privileges" advisedly. To these privileges are attached certain obligations and one of them is, when he is asked to attend the Court, to attend.'[46] The court issued a warrant for his arrest.

The police caught up with Kentwell the following Sunday. In court he protested that he was now Chinese and therefore the British court lacked jurisdiction over him. He was asked if he was still registered as a British subject. Kentwell declared that he had been to the City Court 'where I renounced my allegiance to Great Britain because of the snobs who have brought disgrace to Great Britain. I am ashamed of them as my nationals and I renounce my allegiance.' He then insisted on speaking in Chinese. 'We don't want English any more,' he declared.

'Oh do let us get on with it a little faster,' begged the Registrar. 'Do try and keep calm.'[47]

That Kentwell could not do. Waving his hand over the closely packed court, he declared, 'Snobs all of them! Shanghai Club and Country Club! I am ashamed of their behaviour as Englishmen!'[48] The Registrar, exhausted and eager to finish, talked hopefully of bail. Kentwell replied he had nothing to offer except his promise to return the next morning. The Registrar took a deep breath then said, 'I try to hold the scales justly and you only try to annoy me. But you won't do it, because I refuse to be annoyed.'[49] Mr Zhou's lawyer now added his protests. The irony of defending China while in court on a charge brought by a Chinese, appears to have escaped the former barrister as he exclaimed to the British Registrar: 'You press me now when you are in the ascendant. You put on the thumbscrews. Wait till we get in the ascendant and will do it tenfold. You remember that Thornton, the Labour member, said the same thing in Parliament.'

To which the Registrar was betrayed in answering, 'And were the Conservative Party frightened?'[50]

At the next hearing, Kentwell offered a 'very stormy interview'[51] with Sir Sidney Barton as fresh evidence. In front of the bemused court, he acted out the confrontation. First he took Sir Sidney's part. ' "Kentwell, you are a traitor to England," said Sir Sidney, according to Kentwell. "You have done England incalculable damage because of your extreme political views and because you have advocated the abolition of extraterritoriality. You have subscribed to the views of the Chinese people." ' Kentwell now switched to himself and explained 'that my extreme views were the result of British snobbery and I asked him if he thought I was going to swallow all these bitter pills'.[52]

The Registrar failed to see the point of Kentwell's charade and called an adjournment. This did not suit the unhappy Mr Zhou. The Chinese naturalization certificate might arrive during the interval allowing Kentwell to escape the British court. The Registrar wondered if Mr Kentwell should go to jail. Kentwell announced he had nothing to give Mr Zhou. 'I have money which I put into a newspaper, but that is just like throwing it into the Whangpoo River. I put in SH$50,000 to fight this arrogant British snobbery.'[53]

He went on to describe his finances with disarming frankness. His newspaper had bankrupted him. Friends gave the odd donation but he lacked enough money even to pay the staff salaries for the New Year. Two years before Kentwell had distributed his savings and his gold coin collection among his six children in England. In retrospect it appeared a symbolic act as if Kentwell had decided to settle accounts with that side of himself and turn back to his Chinese half, so long ignored. Now he was overdrawn at the bank. He had asked his wife who had property in Honolulu for money but warned, 'If I get money from her, I am willing to put SH$50,000 more into the paper to exterminate this British snobbery. I am trying to get it from my wife and if I get it . . . '[54] (the sentence terminated with a blow of Kentwell's fist on the table). He offered Mr Zhou some property deeds instead. There seemed to be nothing more to do but adjourn. Even this proved contentious. Kentwell refused to leave any security. If he did not turn up in court, they could always arrest him again, he pointed out. 'This court has plenty of power. You have battleships and an army here.'[55] His friends were not able to stand bail for him because they too were being terrorized by the British authorities and the Shanghai Club. Francis Zia had even been kidnapped. The Registrar replied, 'Oh, don't talk such nonsense. There is no reign of terror here.'[56]

I almost sympathized with the sorely tried Registrar who believed the court had treated Kentwell with 'the greatest courtesy', and Mr Zhou, still empty-handed. But stronger than sympathy or reason is Kentwell's passion, so extravagant and out of place.

It was the passion of a man who knows himself unjustly defeated. Born in Hong Kong, Kentwell was the son of an English captain and a mother from Guangzhou. Captain Kentwell, unlike most fathers of Eurasian children had not grudged his son the expense of an English education. Kentwell performed exceptionally well, graduating from Oxford with a degree in law. Ten years before the trial he had moved to Shanghai. Those ten years had seen a successful and bright young man turned into an unbalanced bankrupt. He had blamed 'the snobs' and talked of a conspiracy against him. People dismissed him as paranoid and hysterical but in this, at least, he was quite correct.

J. B. Powell reviewed his predicament in the *China Weekly Review*:

Kentwell, although a British subject and probably better edu-cated than the average Briton in this part of the world, has had a difficult time because of his mixed blood. He probably has never seen the inside of any of the clubs maintained by foreigners on these shores and it is also improbable that he has seen the inside of many foreign homes, the reason for this being the damnable social standard prevailing in the treaty ports. As a result of this situation, this mixture of Chinese and English blood in Kentwell's veins and the snubs he has received on the foreign side, has inevitably pulled him over on the Chinese side and has made a radical of him.[57]

The British authorities wanted Kentwell out of the way. His superior education and ability made them uneasy. He knew England at first hand. He had sampled some of its better institutions and met the sort of men that ran them. He was not taken in by the British in Shanghai nor the myths perpetuated in the pages of the *North China Daily News*. He saw their pretence at colonial values for what they were.

Kentwell first made himself conspicuous to the authorities two years before. During the general strike called after police of the International Settlement shot four demonstrators, Kentwell sided with the Chinese. At a meeting of the Shanghai ratepayers, Kentwell stood up and demanded that foreigners allow the Settlement Chinese representation on the Shanghai Municipal Council based upon the taxes they paid. As they paid more taxes than any other nationality, he knew his proposal must be rejected. And it was, almost unanimously.

His greatest friend gave the authorities even more concern. Francis Zia, educated by the Jesuits at St Xavier College in Siccawei, was a well-known journalist, spoke excellent English and had acted as secretary to various British officials. He and Kentwell founded the *China Courier*, described by J. B. Powell as sympathetic to the Nationalist point of view. It showed little patience with communism, received no funds other than from Kentwell's pocket and its circulation barely reached above a thousand copies but it upset the British authorities. They decided to close it down and to silence Kentwell and Zia. In contrast to their plan, Kentwell's vitriol seems as innocent as milk.

The authorities first concentrated on Francis Zia. Shortly after Kentwell's summons to court on January 29th, Zia paid a visit to the *Shenbao*, one of Shanghai's leading Chinese newspapers. It was a Saturday afternoon. As he stepped from the office he was seized, thrown into a car and driven out of the Concession and into Chinese territory. His kidnappers were agents of General Li Baoshen, local Defence Commissioner and a subordinate of Marshal Sun Chuanfang, the warlord who one month later ordered the beheading of revolutionary students in the streets of Nantao. The *Shenbao*'s offices stood in the International Settlement, about a block away from Central Police Station and supposedly off limits to Marshal Sun.

The following afternoon British and American colleagues of Zia called on General Li Baoshen for an explanation. The General said Zia had published an inflammatory article against the Marshal stating that the Nationalist army had put his army to flight. The journalists pointed out that this story appeared by Reuters news service and in all Shanghai's foreign newspapers. They asked why the General had not applied for Zia's arrest in the normal way. If the General could prove Kentwell guilty of a crime, the British police would arrest him and hand him over. The General brushed aside these niceties of law to make an astonishing admission. He had carried out the kidnapping with the full knowledge and consent of the police authorities of the International Settlement. The journalists questioned him hard but the General remained convincing. They took their leave and hurried back to Shanghai where Captain E. I. M. Barrett, Commissioner of Police, declared the General's statement a 'damned lie', but admitted by default that the two men had discussed the possibility for 'I told him I could not permit illegalities even where I sympathized with him in suppression of Guomindang propagandists'.[58]

The General's claim is a plausible one. The Settlement police might even have given him the idea. The latest edition of the *Courier* published on January 26th had earned Kentwell and Zia the personal enmity of Patrick Givens, head of Special Branch. As described earlier, Givens had plastered Shanghai with posters of Chiang Kai-shek depicted as a cobra and a tortoise. The *Courier* noticed the cartoons, guessed who was behind them and wrote, 'it is surprising how poor these posters are as a means of propaganda because they are taken even by the ignorant classes as a sort of joke rather than serious reason'.[59] The paragraph is still carefully preserved in Special Branch's files. Within a week of its publication the Eurasian was in court and the Chinese journalist in jail.

Zia remained under arrest with only the promise from General Li of a deferment of execution 'for the present'.[60] On February 26th the petitions of his foreign friends won him a move to a civil prison from where he wrote them a letter: 'I am making the best of my situation by spending my daily hours according to a sort of time-table of prayer, meals, exercise and reading books and magazines. Thus I have been able to squeeze all of the sourness out of my sufferings.'[61] In the circumstances Kentwell's outbursts appear almost restrained. The snobs had got them both. Mr Maitland who was prosecuting Kentwell, wrote happily to Barrett, the Commissioner of Police, on February 10th, 1927, 'I am glad to tell you that I have strong reasons to believe that I shall be able to deal with him very soon.'[62] The British now turned their attention to the *China Courier*.

The British authorities had called the striking Chinese factories to order in 1925 by turning off all electric power. At the beginning of May 1927 a member of Special Branch tried something similar on a smaller scale. He paid a visit to a Mr Ellis, manager of the Linotype Co. at No. 30 the Bund. This British company supplied the linotype machines used by the China Publishing Company which owned and printed the *China Courier*. The company had taken three machines on a hire-purchase scheme and now owed four months in arrears. The agreement entitled Mr Ellis to seize the printing machinery immediately and without notice. Mr Ellis saw an opportunity for himself. He reassured the inspector that 'from a patriotic point of view'[63] he was prepared to do his bit but the machines were second-hand and, in the present slump, difficult to dispose of. Mr Ellis then named his price. He suggested that *Shaforce*, the Shanghai police magazine, buy the printing machinery which, he added, it 'badly'[64] needed. The inspector decided the pay-off reasonable. In his report he pointed out that without machinery, the China Publishing Co. would find it 'extremely difficult, if not impossible', to get any printing done. He continued, 'There is not a foreign newspaper concern in Shanghai who would produce the *China Courier* and with the assistance of General Yang Hu, it would be an easy matter to prevent any Chinese concern from assisting in the production of this newspaper.'[65] The authorities had put Zia and Kentwell out of circulation and closed their paper. The matter was dealt with.

The British did not get away with it, quite. Few people knew the truth about Kentwell but the prejudice which had embittered him was there for all to see. It affected the Chinese and Eurasian alike as they struggled in their literature, their businesses or just their everyday life to come to terms with the foreign invasion of their city. The struggles left their mark. The British dismissed Chinese over-sensitivity as endemic to the race rather than the result of foreign rule. When they met a Chinese or Eurasian they saw a catalogue of misdemeanours rather than an individual. Were all Chinese cruel and dirty? Did all Eurasians have a chip on their shoulder? It was still no reason for tossing a man's life away like sweet paper or for steadily blighting so many Kentwells just because he and his kind proved infuriating.

The first time I saw the Bund from the Whangpoo occurred on my thirtieth birthday when the Bank of China treated me to a large cake decorated with green icing and two storks and, they promised, 'a nice day on the river'. I imagined rice paddies, water-buffalo and willows. Instead we chugged down the muddy Whangpoo past ship-yards, docks and factories. I caught a brief glimpse of open sea before we turned back. It rained, I remember, all the time. My guide watched a magic show in the hold.

As the boat tied up, I came out on deck. Around and above

me rose the Bund. Its top-heavy buildings still inspire awe but their façades are now festooned with washing-lines and Chinese characters, busy as rust spiders about the stonework. A mere fifty years have reduced the Bund's glory to ridicule, or, if one is kindly disposed, poignance. I wondered what the Chinese made of these buildings. Were they fond of them as one might be of a monster beached up in the wrong place and now turned harmless? Or did they feel merely indifferent? After Liberation in 1949 and again during the Cultural Revolution in 1966, the Chinese crowded into the city from the countryside. Shanghai's past is not their past. In one building, an office worker was letting out a striped awning. It caught the breeze with a sudden flap of colour. The office worker watched it, smiling, then pulled in his head. No one in China makes striped awnings. No one has for fifty years. I imagined that the worker had preserved it all this time to display on special days as a treat for the old beast. Or, rather, as a sign that it was the Chinese, in the end, who had had the last laugh.

A Wonderful Old Racket

Businessmen ran the International Settlement for businessmen. Business permeated Shanghai life. In factories, children worked fourteen hours a day because the Municipal Council, factory-owners themselves, refused to pass a Factory Act. For many years you could not catch a taxi in Shanghai for they might have offered competition to the rickshaw, tramways and omnibus companies run by Council members. It was quite all right, however, to buy an opium pipe or to go dog-racing because members held shares in both. Goodness had nothing to do with Shanghai's business life. Energy, ingenuity and graft had. Like New York and Tokyo today, the only immorality was failure. 'In spite of dark shadows,' wrote Isabella Bird in 1899, Shanghai, 'is a splendid example of what British energy, wealth and organising power can accomplish.'[66]

The flavour of British business life is summed up by one institution. Any view of the Bund shows how its curve hangs like a necklace between two buildings, the Cathay Hotel near Soochow Creek built by Sir Victor Sassoon and, at its other point, the Hongkong and Shanghai Bank.

Today the building belongs to the Chinese municipality of Shanghai. A Chinese soldier stands on guard and when I tried to enter, waved his gun at me. As I walked away the bank's shadow pursued me along the Bund. There was, one felt, no escaping its influence.

The Hongkong and Shanghai Bank was established in 1864 in Hong Kong and in Shanghai a year later. The foreign firms decided a bank would finance trade and stabilize business after the financial collapse that followed the Taiping Rebellion. The arrival of Chinese in the Settlement seeking protection had instigated the city's first real-estate boom; their departure, the city's first crash. Hong Kong's leading firms raised the original capital of five million dollars. So began the Hongkong and Shanghai Bank, the product of over-extension in the past and hope for security in the future.

The building still has the air of a British institution and the role played by the bank during Shanghai's history when it effectively formed 'an arm of European diplomacy'.[67] In China access to foreign capital often ensured a regime's survival. The Chinese dictator, Yuan Shikai, who snatched power from Dr Sun Yat-sen, 'rules today by virtue of the first issue of the reorganization loan,' admitted Sir Charles Addis, the London manager of the Hongkong Bank in 1913. It led to an unhappy association with the British Foreign Office. The cautious banker found himself forced to put politics before profit while earning the reputation, 'as Shylocks and men without bowels of compassion for the poor browbeaten Chinese',[69] complained the bank's agent in Beijing. For his part, the Minister in Beijing grumbled that the bank's attitude was 'real dog in the manger business', and their one aim 'in every transaction is to outdo the Chinese in "squeeze" '.[70]

Profits rose from underwriting the borrowing of the Chinese government and the railways and the new century saw the need for a larger building. The bank first acquired a property on the Bund in 1873, extended in 1903 when the bank bought out its next-door neighbour, MacKenzie & Company. The acquisition gave the bank valuable frontage along the Bund and also added tone for, as Mr Bevis, the then manager of the Shanghai Branch, stated, the firm's business 'of hide pressing and feather cleaning' was 'decidedly a nuisance'.[71]

The large site and the absence of feathers set the bank's directors dreaming of a splendid edifice. They had to wait until the end of the First World War and the arrival of a gang of American currency speculators. The American plan to lure money from the Shanghai business community reckoned without A. G. Stephen, the chief manager of the Hongkong and Shanghai Bank. He bided his time until the Americans over-extended themselves, then moved in and pulled their position apart. The bank was built on the profits. A polite man, he paid the losers a tribute at the opening ceremony, remarking, 'Thanks to the Americans who came out to teach us banking this building stands in our books at $1.'

The directors of the bank decided on the architectural firm of Palmer & Turner whose style was admired throughout the Far East. They eventually designed thirteen of the major buildings along the Bund. The brief from head office in October 1919 appeared equally appropriate as the British motto for Shanghai, 'Spare no expense but dominate the Bund.'[72]

The bank's schemes suffered from one drawback. Shanghai was built on shifting silt. Nothing stayed put in the ground. Coffins buried without lead weight drifted from their places of rest, a fate considered inappropriate for the city's most eminent building and the symbol of business confidence in the Settlement. The Massachusetts Institute of

Technology advised pounding fir pilings down sixty feet and capping the wood with concrete to stop it rotting. A reinforced concrete raft fixed on to the piers served as a foundation. The scheme was first tried out with the Yangtsze Insurance Company building and its success made possible the Bund's distinctive skyline. As construction advanced, the building settled into the mud. John Ritchie of Palmer & Turner recalled the importance of calculating this in advance. The bottom step at the entrance began six foot up in the air. The weight of the building eventually brought it down to the level of the pavement. A surveyor regularly checked the bank's foundations in case the silver coins stacked in its vaults caused the building to tilt.

Tug Wilson, the architect, had to create an imposing building without the advantage of perspective on a site seen in a series of acute angles as the pedestrian or driver travelled down the Bund. He chose the design first used for a public building by Francesco Borromini for the Church of S. Agnese in Agone, Piazza Navona in Rome, the last example of which had been the Old Bailey in London completed by Edward Mountford in 1907. Wilson adapted Mountford's innovation and moved the dome from the centre of the building to the front. The result sacrifices beauty and elegance for authority. A flight of steps leads up to three massive, stone arches. Above them six pillars, rising the height of three floors, support a pediment and large dome. To the pedestrian beneath, the dome appears to topple over with the weight of its own importance. Domination of the Bund is almost physical.

The size and cost of the building expressed confidence in Shanghai in a form everybody could appreciate. Profit followed upon confidence and the bank's owners intended the new building to be as much about propaganda as profit. Nowhere was this double role more apparent than at the opening ceremony.

Punctually at noon on June 23rd 1923, a voluble crowd of elegantly dressed men and women, newspaper reporters and cameramen had gathered on the steps of the new Hongkong and Shanghai Bank to watch her Majesty's Minister, Sir Ronald Macleay, unlock the central gates before following him into the Entrance Hall. The Minister and special guests took their seats on a dais surrounded by the press. Over their heads, supported on eight columns of Sienna marble, rose the dome decorated with symbolic figures in Venetian mosaic to represent the eight banking centres of East and West.

Shanghai, personified by 'Foresight' and 'Sagacity', steered a ship's wheel. After admiring these splendours the crowd moved into the central banking hall to gasp at its marble counter stretching over three hundred feet, the grey marble walls and columns and, above their heads, a huge skylight. In the Chinese department, 'One is arrested on the threshold by the totally unexpected sight of a blaze of Chinese decoration',[73] stated the bank's commemorative booklet. The 'fortunates who have seen the palaces of Peking [Beijing] are immediately reminded of those wonder-halls'.[74] In contrast, the manager's office appeared as British as the British in Shanghai could make it, with coffered, fake-Tudor ceilings, teak panelling and fluted pilasters. The management had provided all the modern comforts. Air-conditioning and heating operated throughout the building; as did old, colonial prejudices. Foreign, Portuguese and Chinese staffs each used separate lavatories.

The Hon. Mr A. O. Lang, chairman of the bank's Court of Directors gave the opening speech. In style and content it represented as unequivocally as the separate lavatories the prejudices of the British. The month before, Chinese bandits had kidnapped a trainload of foreigners during the night. The bandits forced the foreigners from their comfortable berths to a mountain fortress and held them for a month in their pyjamas and nightdresses. After payment of the ransom and release of the foreigners, the bandits were shot and photographs of the corpses sent to the kidnap victims by a contrite Chinese government. This incident, as much as the marvels of the new building, dominated Mr Lang's speech. First he pointed out the purpose of the building. Its heavy cost represented 'visible proof' of the banks's belief in 'this teeming settlement' and 'the great country' of which 'it is the commercial gate'.[75] He then moved to the subject closest to his heart. Like a stern nanny speaking of a wayward charge, he deplored China's present lawless state and went on,

> though conditions look dark now, let us remember that the darkest moment comes before the dawn, and support ourselves with the hope, not only that China has now filled the cup of her folly to the brim, but that the Foreign Powers have awakened at last from their dream of a self-regenerated China. The doctrine that China must work out her own salvation has been tried and found wanting; it is not only derided by most intelligent

Chinese, but has been abandoned by nearly all thinking foreigners.[76]

The time was ripe, continued Mr Lang, to give foreign interference
a trial, not, he quickly assured his audience, 'in any aggressive spirit
but with . . . firm and friendly determination'. The British government must face up to its responsibility and protect 'the immense
interests at stake',[77] or, in other words, the latest investment made
by the bank in its new building. Insistence on essential reforms by the
Chinese government, backed up by an 'unequivocal demonstration of
force', would restore order and be welcomed by the Chinese masses,
'who are suffering, no less than ourselves, from the long-continued
misgovernment and lawlessness of their country'.[78]
For once the Foreign Office found itself in agreement with the
businessman. After complimenting the bank and the architects, His
Majesty's Minister, Sir Ronald Macleay, got to the point. If the
Chinese government wanted to borrow more money it must be
under 'conditions of strict control both over the security and the
expenditure'.[79] The Chinese government had to prove that they
would spend the money to the benefit of China and not fritter
it away on 'swarms'[80] of unnecessary troops who fought among
themselves and, a heinous crime in Sir Ronald's eyes, travelled on
foreign-owned railways without paying their fares. He ended on a
more optimistic note. Amidst the violence and disorder, should the
Chinese 'lose heart at the difficulties which confront them, they can
surely derive comfort and encouragement from the contemplation of
this International Settlement of Shanghai'.[81]
As they left, the appreciative crowd noticed two bronze lions on
either side of the main doorway. One roared to symbolize protection,
the other lay at rest to emphasize security. The Chinese rubbed their
paws for luck. At least, that is what everyone told me except for one
employee who recalled, 'Chinese women preferred to rub the lions'
genitals – quite why, we never discovered.'
Distance creates a different impression of the Hongkong and
Shanghai Bank. I was crossing the Whangpoo on a hot day. Over
the water, the bank lay in shadow except for its green dome. Washed
by sunshine to a translucent white, it appeared to shimmer on its
pediment, too small and fragile for the vast building beneath. One
breath, I felt, would see it drifting like a soap bubble over the city.
The bank's business activities reflect a similar air of insubstantiality.

The principal occupation of a bank is to lend money and secure deposits. The Hongkong and Shanghai Bank also relied on currency speculation for its profits. Until 1932 two currency systems existed in Shanghai: the Shanghai dollar, worth about one shilling and sixpence then or about ten pence today, and the tael, a weight of silver shaped like a tiny shoe. People received their salaries in taels which they exchanged for Shanghai dollars in order to buy goods or pay their rent. All bank business went on in taels. To acquire sterling, for example, people first had to change their Shanghai dollars back into taels. The Hongkong and Shanghai Bank made a profit buying and selling in between. As George Stewart told me, 'It was a wonderful old racket, really, from a banking point of view, but, of course, Shanghai was like that.'

The bank also speculated on the 'very active' currency exchange market in Shanghai. George Stewart explained that he was lucky enough to spend a year in what was called the Books Department where the manager's position was worked out before the market opened next morning. He found this fascinating. 'We knew if we ever told anybody the result, we'd be on the next boat Home. So there was no doubt about it that it was very important.' After the Second World War a Chinese banker visited the Hongkong and Shanghai Bank in Hong Kong. He claimed he had a member of the bank's Chinese staff on his payroll. 'You thought I didn't know your position but I did,' he said with a laugh.

A. S. Henchman, the manager of the Hongkong and Shanghai Banking Corporation in the 1930s became so famous for his currency deals that people called him 'a Wizard'. He dominated Shanghai's exchange position, admitting after his most successful defence of the currency in 1934, 'We had a little behind us to support the currency and the rest had to be made up of finesse and bluff.'[82] Unlike his rivals such as the Mercantile Bank, Henchman had certain responsibilities to Shanghai and the British community. George Stewart explained, 'We were, after all, the premier British bank, and he couldn't go into all those odd deals the Mercantile enjoyed.'

Anyone could start an exchange business. George Stewart shared a house for a time with the owner of one. Nobby Clark used to work for the Hongkong and Shanghai Bank who forbade their employees from marrying until they completed ten years' service. Nobby married before he came out East. When his children started to grow up he thought it better to resign rather than to have the bank discover and sack him. He began an exchange business with a man called P. G. Calcina in Shanghai. At the close of the European and American markets, a certain amount of position remained between the dollar, the franc (still a powerful currency) and sterling. Nobby sold off transactions between American dollars and sterling through Shanghai dollars. After dinner the telephone never stopped ringing with telegrams for Nobby in code. He would spell them aloud, 'A for apple and C for Charlie', then sit down and work out what they meant. Sometimes, if he knew Henchman or the Mercantile Bank – quite a pal of Nobby's – wanted to buy the particular thing he had to sell, he would ring them up there and then. George Stewart sighed. 'Telexes would have made our life together a lot quieter.'

Currency speculation went on throughout the city. Even little boys took part. Lord Bangor recalled the experience of Victor Ginsburger, a successful broker who was born in Shanghai. As a small boy, his father had handed him a Shanghai dollar and told him to go out and make money. Victor soon learnt that the difference between a Shanghai dollar and a silver dollar could fluctuate wildly and that both had an erratic relationship with copper coins known as 'cash' or 'small money'. One Shanghai dollar bought anything between 300 and over 400 cash. Victor took his paper dollar to a Chinese 'cash shop' and changed it into small silver pieces. Next he would buy copper with his silver, wait for a bit then turn it in for small notes. At the end of the day he would return home with as much as one dollar twenty cents. His father was delighted. ' "If you can do that with one dollar you can do it with a million!" he said.'

I asked George Stewart if the bank had invested in the new Chinese businesses which started up in the 'twenties. He admitted that the bank had little knowledge about 'the general run of Chinese businessmen. They didn't even keep accounts with us.' They approached the Chinese compradore rather than the British manager and he personally guaranteed the loan – 'shroff the thing up' was the expression.

The bank dealt principally with British businesses and carried nothing like the bad debt of banks today. The sons of Lancashire textile owners who had started firms in the city before the First World War proved troublesome after 1928 when the Chinese started to manufacture their own textiles. The representatives of the Lancashire firms found themselves penniless. Now in their fifties and untrained for anything except a leisured existence, most held up their hands and admitted defeat. They put the bank in a delicate position. Managers found it embarrassing to be severe with their golf partners while it looked bad for British prestige to declare the whole lot bankrupt. The bank decided to keep them afloat. George Stewart recalled, 'By the time I arrived they were dying out, thank God. Their nuisance value was enormous but really they cost us very little.'

It was possible to make a living simply by virtue of nationality. Captain Donald Ferguson, manager of the Woosung-Hankow Rolets Association, epitomized this side of Shanghai business life. In late September 1927 he attracted the attention of the police after lunch by driving in a 'zigzagging' manner, overrunning a traffic signal before stalling in heavy traffic. The police booked him for drunken driving. In court his counsel pointed out that it was the custom for foreign businessmen in Shanghai to meet during the tiffin hour, discuss business matters and have a few drinks. 'I say that the majority of owner drivers who drive on Bubbling Well Road and other roads during the tiffin hours are under the influence of drink – but, in the best sense.'[83] The judge agreed and dismissed the case.

For the ambitious and hard-working, Shanghai offered fabulous wealth. In the business deal, if nowhere else, foreigner and Chinese met. Together they created a city of extraordinary opportunity. The boom which made instant millionaires of the lucky and the intrepid littered Shanghai's history. The silk boom, the opium boom, the real-estate boom, the rubber boom, the shipping boom, the silver boom, all turned people into gamblers and contributed to the feverish atmosphere of the city. Lord Bangor remarked that Reuters' Shanghai office earned its large revenues through catering to the compulsive gambling urge of foreigners and Chinese. Everybody, men and women, talked incessantly about stocks and shares, about taking a forward position in silver, of selling sterling short, of buying a thousand bales of October Liverpool cotton and selling a load of Chicago wheat. Lord Bangor recalled parties where at around midnight the host would flash the opening New York stock quotations on a screen.

Shanghai citizens gambled on a global scale and, of course, someone worked out how to make money from that. An American brokerage firm called Swan, Culbertson and Fritz took over a large hall, put in comfortable furniture, offered food and drink and lined the walls with boards listing London and New York stocks and bonds, Liverpool and New Orleans cotton prices, and all the commodities dealt with on the floor of the Chicago Board of Trade. Every ten minutes Reuters displayed price changes. Rich Chinese put through their sometimes huge orders for buying and selling on the Western markets which were at once cabled through and confirmed by cable from the other end. This enormous betting shop carried on until the close of the American markets at about 5 a.m. Shanghai time.

Flamboyance, aggression and graft made up the ingredients of the successful Shanghai deal. The Opium Combine is a typical example. At the start of the century 40 million Chinese dollars' worth of opium arrived in China through Shanghai each year. Over 1,500 opium dens existed in the city and nearly 80 shops sold the drug openly. Public opinion abroad and pressure from the Chinese government forced the International Settlement to close its dens. Immediately more shops opened as people wanted to buy opium to smoke at home. When the Chinese government pressed the Municipal Council to prosecute addicts, they refused explaining that to do so was 'incompatible with principles of individual liberty in the Western sense of the word'.[84]

April 1st, 1917 was the date set by the British government for India to cease the export of opium to China. At the same time the Chinese government discouraged cultivation of the drug in the countryside. Their combined efforts sent up the price of the drug and made the fortune of any person with a godown of opium. By 1916 the leading importers of opium were mostly Parsees and Iraqi Jews. They now joined forces and, with financial assistance from the banks, held on to their stocks while making every effort to push up the price. This took the form of a monopoly called the Opium Combine. To enforce the monopoly they exerted pressure on the police to stop the handling, selling or smoking of any kind of opium except the Combine's certificated Indian brand. They made a deal with the Chinese Provincial Officials which halted the import of Chinese opium from the surrounding countryside and also signed an agreement with the Chinese Opium Guild in Shanghai.

As April 1st, 1917 drew closer, they lobbied Westminster hard (most were British subjects) to have the date set back. They failed but as one newspaper editor rather naively pointed out, 'It is one of those paradoxes of fate that the Shanghai opium merchants should have made their greatest profits after the import of opium was prohibited.'[85] Fate had nothing to do with it.

At the beginning of 1917 the Combine planned how to squeeze the maximum profit from their remaining stock. They signed an agreement with the Chinese government on January 28th, 1917. The government promised to buy the two thousand-odd cases of opium at the exorbitant price of Tls.8,200 per case 'for medicinal purposes'.[86] The Combine had ensured the government's excessive generosity by paying a bribe or 'inside squeeze' of Tls.2,500 on every case to a government official. This time the Combine went too far, even for Shanghai. The price caused public consternation. Eventually the Combine lowered the price to Tls.6,200. The Chinese government ferried the drug to Pootung and burnt it in full view of the Bund. After that the Chinese took over growing, distributing and profiting from the opium trade themselves. The warlords used the drug to finance their armies; so later did Chiang Kai-shek. The Combine made the fortune of the opium merchants and paid for their fabulous establishments.

With such huge amounts of money at stake, Shanghai business deals often turned dangerous. George Stewart remembered meeting an arms dealer accompanied by his wife and concubine in the bar of the Park Hotel. He declared himself bankrupt and asked George Stewart to stand them all a drink. He explained that he had acted as a middle-man for a shipment of arms but his buyer had got himself killed. George Stewart saw him a few weeks later wreathed in smiles, both his wife and concubine in new fur coats. Another buyer had turned up and the dealer was back in business again.

I first went to Shanghai just after the fall of the Gang of Four when no one mentioned business without the obligatory preamble of disparagement. I returned a few years later to find the Chinese government all for foreign investment. They even hinted that the Shanghai stock exchange might reopen. I paid it a visit. Washing lines decorated its upper storeys. Down below, makeshift stalls displayed spare bicycle parts, woolly hats and flasks of tea. I asked an old man pulling a cart if he remembered it. 'A stock exchange!' he said, glancing over the peeling and shabby exterior. 'What's that?'

One thing remained the same. It was still impossible to catch a taxi in Shanghai. When I wanted one, I walked to the nearest hotel where taxi drivers sat chatting and chewing melon seeds. 'What's the point of taking you?' asked a disgruntled driver. 'I get paid by the government the same amount if I sit here.' On my last visit things had changed. Trudging back, late at night, I was astonished to find myself flagging down a taxi. The driver was a middle-aged woman. Her son sat next to her. She borrowed the car at night from a friend to make extra money. During the day she worked in a factory. I said how nice of her son to keep her company. She snorted, 'He doesn't come for the ride. He's here to protect me. There's a lot of dangerous gangs of young thugs and ex-Red Army guards about. They hold up and rob taxis late at night. My son frightens them off.' The son bent forward and picked up a plank of wood which he waved cheerily at me. 'Our weapon,' he said.

The next morning I paid a final visit to the Bund. Gone are the peanut-sellers, the beggars with their sores and the refuse of dead babies. Chinese officials now step from Shanghai's most eminent buildings into large, chauffeur-driven cars. Chinese girls in shorts and lipstick giggle at the foreign businessmen standing in clusters outside the former Cathay Hotel. As I made for Garden Bridge a man with long hair, shabby clothes and Central Asian features sidled up to me, hissed something from the corner of his mouth then moved off. From other doorways stepped more men making similar incomprehensible sounds. I was amazed. Nothing like this had happened to me in China before. It was only by the third corner and an encounter with a more audacious type that I discovered my foreign currency to be the object of their attentions. They offered tempting rates. One told me they were Uighurs and that for thousands of years the Uighurs had made the long journey from the north-western province of Xinjiang, known as Chinese Turkistan, down the Yangtze to trade in Shanghai. The Communist Revolution caused a brief interruption but now, forty years on, trade had resumed. Travelling in groups of ten or so for protection, they spent the money they made from illegal currency exchange on television sets and radios which they took back to their villages and sold for extraordinary amounts. The Uighurs said proudly, just as a Shanghai businessman did to Sir Rutherford Alcock, Shanghai's second British consul 140 years before, 'Our business is to make as much money as quickly as we can then go home. We earn enormous sums. We are the richest men in our villages.'

The Uighurs brought home to me the fundamental weakness of British administration in Shanghai. The Municipal Council had fulfilled its original brief and created a city where business could develop with the least possible interference. It had failed to refine beyond that and infuse Shanghai with civic pride. The formidable look of the Bund did not mitigate the businessman's view that Shanghai was a place in which to make money then depart. The building of fountains and the planting of trees were pursuits reserved for Home and retirement. The Municipal Council might have pointed to the many attacks and emergencies Shanghai underwent. Fourteenth-century Florentines, Sienese or Venetians, creating cities in a country described as the 'Cockpit of Europe', could have said the same. Like them, Shanghai's residents were rich, successful and anxious to display their wealth but in Shanghai this took an individual and competitive form; who could build the tallest building on the Bund or own the fastest racehorse. The idea of laying a square where people might sit and enjoy themselves appeared unthinkable. The War Memorial dedicated to the men from Shanghai on the Allied side was the only monument raised by the Shanghailander. Appositely it commemorates an event on the other side of the world rather than one from Shanghai's history as an international city. Unable to inspire a sense of community stronger than national or financial interests, the city had little chance of survival.

Only in the city's final years did the desire for something else take shape. This impulse came not from the Taipans but the British men and women on modest incomes, the 'Small Fry', and is summed up by a letter written in 1932.

Since I arrived in Shanghai some seventeen years ago I have been under arms as a member of the Volunteer Corps on probably a dozen occasions – all, with the possible exception of 1925, in 'defence of the Settlement' because of some change in the politico-military control in the surrounding areas. Always these occasions have meant a cessation of business, a period of anxiety and possible danger, with no benefit whatever to us as a community, but involving much public expenditure and considerable financial loss to many. 'Old stagers' of the mudflat days will smile when one talks to them on the subject and say they have got used to the idea, but are we content to see this sort of thing continue indefinitely through succeeding generations? Is there no desire to hand on something better to our children?

We should organize ourselves as a community with a view to bringing about such a change in the present status that will enable us to live a more normal life with a measure of freedom and security far beyond that which we at present 'enjoy'. It is time the old idea that foreigners come to Shanghai for a few years and then go away with a fortune was entirely abandoned, if it still exists anywhere. It should be recognised that this is a place of permanent residence for most of us, and we have the right to demand that same degree of freedom and security which is the common possession of all civilised communities.[87]

The letter was signed John England and published one day before Japanese shells first exploded in Hongkew.

· FIVE ·

The War Across the Bridge
1932 – The Second Battle

A SHORT WALK from the Bund takes you across Garden Bridge and into Japanese territory. Hongkew was part of the International Settlement. The Americans originally claimed it until they merged with the British to form the International Settlement. In the nineteenth century people considered the eastern bank of the Soochow Creek a desirable place to live. Consulate residences and Shanghai's first hotel, the Astor House, stood there. By the 'twenties Hongkew had become the wrong side of the creek and home to the poorest of Shanghai's thirty-six nationalities, including Japanese, Portuguese and Eurasians (one woman said to me, 'As a child I associated Portuguese so much with Eurasians, I thought it another name for them. After I left China, I was amazed to find they had their own country'.) Wealthy foreigners rarely visited Hongkew except to enjoy its famous market.

A five-storey building on a triangular plot of land and open on all three sides, Hongkew market was said to be the largest in Asia, attracting people from all over Shanghai and the surrounding countryside. It was a real international affair. A polyglot of sounds, smells and sights assailed you on a stroll among its stalls. More than anything else it captured the pungent, cosmopolitan spirit of Shanghai across the bridge.

On the ground and first floor countrymen sold vegetables, fish and meat from booths. At different seasons you found mountains of artichokes, peas, cabbages and new potatoes alongside bamboo shoots, water chestnuts and lotus roots. Javanese mangoes, lichees, pomegranates and persimmons lay in piles with lemons, bananas and pears. Peasants stacked up baskets of brown eggs next to poultry in bamboo cages and hung on hooks every sort of game, including pheasants, snipe and bustards. Tanks of seawater for those who liked their seafood fresh, contained squid, shrimp, mandarin and yellow fish as well as shad and mackerel. Chinese haggled over white-scaled river fish, caught that day and kept cool with chunks of ice. The Japanese insisted that their ocean fish, which had taken twenty-four hours to arrive by boat from Japan, was fresher than the Chinese catch. They displayed slices of tuna and yellow tail in neat rows on bamboo leaves.

Foreigners recalled different things about Hongkew market. Kyoko Hayashi, an eminent Japanese writer born in Nagasaki in 1930, grew up in Shanghai. She described its vast appearance to a child: 'Standing at the entrance was like standing in the mouth of a huge tunnel: far away in the distance, I could just barely see the dim light of the exit.'[1] She accompanied her mother to buy German sausage, Hershey's cocoa and French bread from a White Russian bakery. She did not particularly like black bread but whenever she asked for it the Russian owner beamed with pride and said, 'First prize' in Japanese as he handed it over. Enid Saunders Candlin, on the other hand, recalled the Japanese aspect of the market; the reek of radishes in pickle and prawns fried in batter; the flower market where, among the pails of daffodils, roses, sweet peas, gladioli and chrysanthemums, a Japanese gardener sold dwarf trees and miniature gardens laid out in glazed, oblong pots.

The day I went it rained. The building still stands but food and shoppers appeared scarce. Dirty, wicker baskets held beans and onions, the only vegetables on sale. A few, thin pieces of meat lay on concrete slabs. Two old ladies worked through a pile of prawns. I asked if they recalled the market before the war. They looked vague, as if trying to remember a legend told by their grandmothers

1. Engraving of the Bund by Dr Emma Bormann, an Austrian artist who lived in Shanghai during the Second World War. Born in Vienna in 1887, she took a degree in philosophy before developing an interest in the wood block print. She was fascinated by cities and travelled throughout Europe, America and the Far East. Her daughter, who now lives in Japan, recalled how she liked to present well-known buildings from unusual angles. She would walk through Shanghai exclaiming, 'Oh, I want to get up there. The view must be extraordinary!' then make the first sketch from the roof tops

2. The tree-lined boulevards of the French Concession

3. The Russian Church with Bishop Simon and a group of priests at the gate

4. The poetess Olga Alexeyevna Skopichenko

5. A Russian fur shop

6. Two Russian entertainers; the man was a former ballet dancer trained in Russia

7. A typical sight on Shanghai's streets during the spring of 1927; a Chinese student haranguing a crowd against the foreign occupation of the city

8. A barrier put up by the foreigners between the International Settlement and the Chinese section of the city; it runs down the middle of the road – British troops are closing the barrier to prevent a rush of Chinese (including a rickshaw) into the International Settlement

9. Manuela, the Japanese night-club dancer, doing an impromptu number; her band was made up of German Jewish refugees

10. Koichi Okawa, the Japanese band leader who came to Shanghai after the Japanese military government closed the dance halls in Japan; Mr Okawa has found unexpected fame in retirement – the Japanese recently made a film based on his adventures in Shanghai

11. The Japanese residents of Hongkew celebrating Japan's unification on Memorial Day (now February 11th); every year Mr Okawa's band was invited to lead the parade down North Sitchuan Road to Garden Bridge

12. Sir William and Lady Hayter's servants posed in front of the Hayters' house in the French Concession; they ensured that the Hayters began married life 'with a degree of luxury . . . that we were never to attain again'

13. Basil Duke in the uniform of the International Settlement police force

14. George Stewart

15. The Shanghai Paper Hunt Club, including Sir Christopher Chancellor taking a wade

16. Sir William Keswick after a triumphant race; the race track lay in the centre of the city with shops, office buildings and hotels towering over it

17. Sir Christopher Chancellor dressed for a Paper Hunt on his favourite Chinese pony

18. Lady Chancellor surrounded by Chinese orphans; after the Japanese bombed Shanghai in 1932, she provided a temporary home for Chinese children who had lost their families in the fighting

19. Shanghai Race Club, Grand Stand and Enclosures with the Ewo Stable in the foreground

20. Chinese punters in a mixture of Western and Chinese dress studying the form-book

21. The same punters paid equal attention to divine intervention; after laying their bets, they visited the Chinese altar outside the stable on the race course where they lit incense and red candles and prayed for a win

22. In 1932 war broke out on Shanghai's streets when Japanese marines invaded the city. Here a group of marines in distinctive leggings cover a row of shops from a street corner; they are looking for Chinese snipers

23. Japanese marines behind a barricade of sandbags amongst the ruins of Chapei; the dramatic graffitti advertise a shop which sold a particularly famous sauce

24. The home of a wealthy Chinese in the International Settlement transformed into a dormitory for Chinese refugees

25. A Japanese patrol forcing a Chinese civilian to show them the inside of his hat; they believed that Chinese Communists wore a distinctive sign in their hat-linings

26. Market Place in Shanghai; 'So much life, so carefully canalised, so strongly flowing – the spectacle of it inspires something like terror,' wrote Aldous Huxley of the Shanghainese

27. Lu Xun, Bernard Shaw and Cai Yuanpei (chancellor of Beijing University during the May Fourth Movement) after lunch at the home of Sun Yatsen's widow in Shanghai, February 17th, 1933

28. Emily Hahn with her pet gibbon, Mr Mills

29. Wang Baolian, the bookshop clerk, kneeling with Kanzo Uchiyama on either side of Lu Xun's grave

30. Ruan Lingyu playing a prostitute in *The Goddess*

31. Li Lili, the Chinese equivalent of Marlene Dietrich, posed on a motor bike in *The Queen of Sport*

32. Nanking Road, China's most spectacular shopping street; the photograph was taken by Sir William Hayter with a camera given to him by his wife as a wedding present

33. A Chinese rickshaw man waiting on the Bund for a fare; despite his rags and bare feet he wears a foreign shooting cap

34. A Chinese food seller with his portable kitchen; food sellers were found throughout the city and turned snacking into a Shanghai institution. As Lu Xun wrote, 'Provided your appetite is good, you can eat from morning till midnight'

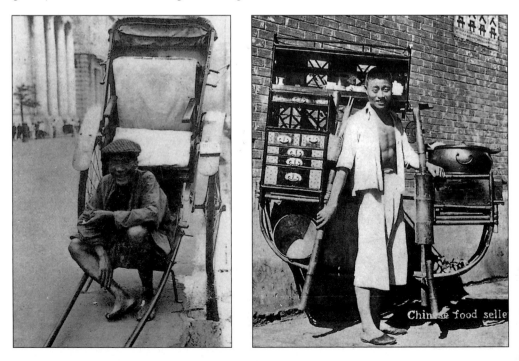

Chinese food seller

35. Chinese dance hostesses in a Shanghai night-club. They wear Western hair styles and cheong-sams split at the side. The fashion began as an expression of freedom rather than a lack of modesty. Chinese women were emulating the high slitted gowns worn by Chinese men and rejecting the trousers traditionally thought suitable for girls before marriage

36. A bridal sedan chair carried through a Shanghai street; the bride remained hidden

37. A Chinese brothel and opium den; the Chinese prostitutes are no more than twelve or thirteen

38. The border of the French and International Settlements, August 1937; the city is all but destroyed

39. Chinese and foreign civilians evacuated from a combat zone under escort by Japanese soldiers; four years later the same soldiers marched the foreigners into camps

then sighed and shook their heads. In the gloom I found a cage of sneezing pigeons, their black feathers fluffed up against the rain.

Around the market stretched street after street of the red brick, terraced houses of Hongkew. In the 1920s a house cost 80–120 taels a month to rent. The landlord sublet to six to eight foreign or Eurasian families, one family to a room. A woman journalist in April 1930[2] happened to glance through the door of one such room to see a typical Hongkew family of a snoring man, a fat woman washing baby clothes, two boys playing marbles, three sleeping babies aged one, two and nearly three respectively, a fourteen-year-old girl smoking a cigarette and a doll-bed containing a much-battered doll. The one window was tightly closed, the steam from the washtub made the room blue while smoke from the girl's cigarette completed the fetid atmosphere.

Hongkew's other name was 'Little Tokyo' after its 30,000 Japanese residents. The Japanese formed part of the International Settlement and the political and social life of the city. Foreigners considered Japanese honorary Westerners. The Japanese occupied two places on the Shanghai Municipal Council. The heads of the great Japanese industrial and shipping firms lived, like their British and American counterparts, in villas in the French Concession. Every spring taipans admired the cherry blossom in the garden of the manager of Mitsui. In summer they attended garden parties on the Japanese Consulate's lawn running down to the river. The Shanghai Club even welcomed Japanese as members, while Japanese schoolgirls could be seen lunching in the Astor House to learn 'foreign table manners'.

Shanghai is under 500 miles from the port of Nagasaki in Japan. As well as Japanese taipans, small traders and shopkeepers moved to Hongkew and set up businesses. The most famous was a shoemaker called Mikawa, a minute, bent Japanese with broken teeth. His shop attracted foreigners and Chinese as well as tourists from the luxury liners, like Mary Pickford who came and ordered thirty pairs of shoes. Enid Saunders Candlin had all her shoes made by him and recalled the process. On the first visit he had picked up her foot, gazed at it silently for some time, made a sketch, measured it, thought some more then asked for pictures of what she wanted. ' "No," he announced, going through them, "you cannot wear this, your instep is too high" or "No, your foot is too thin for such a pump," ' until he decided what would do. 'Then your future,' remarked Enid Saunders Candlin, 'as far as shoes went, was in his small, dry, competent hands, and you never looked back.'[3] Despite his fame, the shop appeared like any other in Hongkew. In winter the only heat came from a few lumps of charcoal in an earthenware jar. Sometimes a child wandered through with a baby tied to its back. 'How many children do you have?' customers asked. ' "I don't know," he answered, "thirteen or fourteen." '[4]

Numbers failed to ensure political power in the Settlement. The Japanese were under-represented on the Council as the majority earned too little to meet the property qualification for voting at Municipal Elections. Instead they organized among themselves. Japanese householders were compelled to belong to the Japanese Residents Corporation and there existed an active 'Association of Japanese Streets Unions'. The standing committee of this organization expressed the Japanese point of view to the Settlement and to its own government in Japan.

Like the White Russians, the Japanese integrated themselves into the Settlement more than the average Westerner. On Broadway, Hongkew's main street and a reminder of the area's American connection, Japanese shops, bars and geisha houses stood next to Chinese traders. As well as Japanese shopkeepers, Shanghai attracted Japanese ostracized by the military regime in Japan such as jazz musicians, dancers, homosexuals and unmarried mothers. For them Shanghai represented a halfway house between East and West. In Shanghai they could eat sushi and enjoy a free society. As one woman told me in Tokyo, 'Nobody asked questions about your past in Shanghai.'

Other Japanese came to study in China. A long history of cultural exchange existed between the two countries. In 1935 Akira Okada was sent by his father to the Tung Wen College for Japanese and Chinese students set up by Prince Konoe in 1895. Mr Okada explained to me that each of the forty-five prefectures in Japan chose and paid for a student to attend. The students competed fiercely for a place. The Chinese, on the other hand, sent rich students whose parents could afford the fees. As well as learning Chinese and English, Okada studied Russian with an elderly White Russian in the French Concession. At the weekend the school authority provided every student with one Shanghai dollar pocket-money. Mr Okada took himself across Garden Bridge where the prices were lower than Central District. There he might enjoy a good Chinese dinner for ten cents then visit the Japan Club on the corner of Chapu Kunghshan Lu before strolling past the cabarets, theatres and cafés along Broadway. 'I and my fellow students would sit for hours in a tiny bar, nursing a drink. Oh yes, we had great fun there.'

North from Hongkew stretched Chapei, a working-class district of factories and warehouses under Chinese jurisdiction. Apart from industry, Chapei was famous for two things: the Commercial Press and the Rokusan Gardens. The Commercial Press had become the largest publishing house of its kind in China and typified the successful Chinese company that flourished in Shanghai. Started in 1896 by foreign-trained Chinese, it supplied three out of every four schoolbooks used in China, published newspapers and magazines and sold paper and games. By the late 'twenties it covered twenty acres of ground in the city with 1,500 agencies throughout the country. Foreigners visited its branch on Nanking Road to buy art books and writing paper, each sheet decorated with orchids and mountain scenes.

The Rokusan Gardens was the sort of eccentric folly Shanghai encouraged and the creation of Mr Shiraishi, an old Japanese resident of the city. I was told about the restaurant by Koichi Okawa, the leader of the best Japanese jazz band in Hongkew. He had visited the Rokusan Gardens as the guest of appreciative fans – 'It was too expensive for an individual like me' – where he enjoyed its mix of Western and Japanese styles along with company heads and military commanders. Mr Shiraishi had decorated each room differently. Some had tables and chairs, others a counter at which customers sat and pointed to what they wanted and still others where they ate on the floor. 'They all served whisky though!' recalled Mr Okawa. Foreigners preferred the traditional Japanese rooms in which Mr Shiraishi took particular pride. The walls were made of paper shoji screens and the floors laid with tatami mats. A vase of flowers or a painted scroll decorated a corner of the room. In summer, maids pulled back the shoji screens to reveal a Japanese garden with stone lanterns, winding paths and carefully clipped flower shrubs. Geishas dressed in sherbet-coloured kimonos played the samisen and sang.

Betty Kato worked for the Japanese Consulate and also enjoyed the Rokusan Gardens. She came to Shanghai as an unmarried mother of a half-American baby: 'You can imagine how popular that made me in Japan!' Now in her seventies, she lives in Tokyo in a one-room apartment overgrown with plants. For our meeting she wore purple ski-pants and talked impatiently of traditional Japanese society. Shanghai had suited her perfectly. She wished she still lived there. It was a good place for a single girl to find work and friends. She had belonged to an international lunch club of twelve working women including American, British, Czech, Portuguese, French and German. She entertained them at the Rokusan Gardens and recalled, 'They used to beg me to take them back before my turn came round again.'

In 1931 events took place which ended international lunch clubs and visits to Hongkew market. Japanese experiments with democracy had grown shaky and the military now tried for control. As a test as much of their own government's strength as of China's weakness, they invaded Manchuria. The Chinese retaliated the only way they could. They refused to buy Japanese goods. The toys, records and bicycles of the small merchants in Hongkew piled up. Chinese firms rejected Japanese merchandise. Chinese banks refused to honour Japanese bills of lading. Seven hundred thousand tons of Japanese cargo littered Shanghai's piers and godowns. Chinese pickets threw passengers boarding Japanese ships into the Whangpoo. Japanese banks and underwriters lost money. Japanese shops and stores had to close. In the streets, posters exclaimed, 'Down with Japanese Imperialism' or, simply, 'Kill all Japanese'.

Japanese freighters did not arrive and the Japanese community could no longer buy their specially preserved ginger in the Hongkew market. Armed police escorted Japanese schoolchildren through Chinese and Japanese demonstrators, shouting slogans at each other.

The unrest in Hongkew led to the Japanese invasion of Shanghai and the first salvo of the Second World War. The Japanese and Chinese governments officially dismissed the event as an 'incident'. They failed to declare war or even break off diplomatic ties. This was a battle, not between nation and nation but between a nation and a municipality. Shanghai had taken on Japan.

On January 18th, 1932 a Chinese crowd attacked five Japanese members of the Buddhist Nichiren sect, a militant order dedicated to Japanese dominance of Asia. They killed one priest. An infuriated Japanese mob set ablaze the Chinese-owned San Yu towel factory. Two Chinese died in the fire. At a mass meeting, Japanese residents called on their government to send additional warships and military units to protect them.

Three days later the Japanese Consulate presented an ultimatum to General Wu Tiecheng, Mayor of Greater Shanghai, demanding the punishment of the priest's murderers and an end to anti-Japanese organizations. The Nanking government and Shanghai's foreign businessmen urged the Mayor to acquiesce. On board the flagship *Azumo*, lying at anchor off the Bund, Rear-Admiral K. Shiosawa reassured the Municipal Council that the Japanese had no intention of trespassing on the neutrality of the International Settlement. On Saturday, January 23rd 500 Japanese bluejackets (marines) landed in Yangtzepoo with more to follow. On Sunday Mayor Wu agreed to reply as soon as possible to Japanese demands. Another of the priests then died of his wounds and Monday found both the British and American governments watching the situation 'with interest'.[5] The Yokohama Nursery changed its name to 'Flower Shop'.[6]

The Municipal Council of the International Settlement was more anxious about the Chinese army encamped outside the city.

A piece of flotsam from the shipwreck of China's politics, the Nineteenth Route Army, a Guangzhou unit of three divisions and 31,000 men, had washed up against the city almost by accident. Like the Nationalist army five years before, its intentions appeared sinister.

The Japanese made overtures to the tall, forty-year-old in charge, Cai Tingkai. General Cai was brave and blunt. He startled all sides with his reply: 'The troops under my command are an integral part of the army of the National Government of the Republic of China by whose orders alone all their activities are directed.'[7] It was a lie. No one directed the Nineteenth Route Army but himself. Certainly General Cai did not represent Chiang Kai-shek who had no wish to fight the Japanese. In Chiang Kai-shek's view, the Chinese communists were his real enemy and always would be. He behaved as if an irritable oracle had predicted every sort of blessing, a talented and beautiful wife, rich and generous friends and the love of the most powerful nation in the world. Only communism could destroy him. In concentrating on its defeat above all else, he fulfilled the prophecy. Chiang Kai-shek suspected the Nineteenth Route Army as much as Shanghai's authorities. The Guangzhou soldiers refused to leave until their wages were paid. Shanghai businessmen started a collection among themselves. Nobody wanted them in the city.

The Settlement's Defence Committee, consisting of the commanding officers of British, American, Japanese, French, Italian as well as the volunteer forces, the chairman of the Municipal Council and the Commissioner of Police agreed that General Cai wanted more than back-pay. Shanghai was even richer in 1932 than in 1927. The young man, like Chiang Kai-shek and countless other Chinese generals before, coveted their city. The Defence Committee ignored the news of the imminent arrival of one Japanese cruiser and twelve destroyers from Sasebo. Even the stated intention of the Japanese to occupy sufficient Chinese territory next to Hongkew to ensure the safety of Japanese residents and their property left them unruffled. The committee considered the Japanese proposal no more unreasonable than their own actions in 1927.

On Tuesday, January 26th the Chinese authorities declared martial law, erected sandbags and barbed-wire barricades throughout Chinese territory and advised foreign residents to evacuate the Outside Roads' Area. Two days later the Shanghai Municipal Council announced a state of emergency. The Shanghai Volunteer Corps took up its positions. The Settlement Defence Committee, still convinced that General Cai posed the real danger, assigned the defence of Hongkew to the Japanese unit of the Volunteer Corps. But defence, as Admiral Shiozawa made clear to Hallett Abend, the correspondent for the *New York Times*, was not what the Japanese had in mind.

Early on the critical night of Friday, January 29th, Hallett Abend took cocktails and caviare with Admiral Shiozawa on board the Japanese flagship. The Admiral dismissed Mayor Wu's capitulation as ' "besides the point" ', and continued, talking slowly and precisely, ' "I'm not satisfied with conditions in Chapei . . . At eleven o'clock tonight I am sending my Marines into Chapei, to protect our nationals and to preserve order . . . you see the army had to protect our interests in Manchuria. There is no Japanese army in Shanghai, so the navy will have to take over a similar job here.'[8]

Abend hurried ashore to file his story and warn the American Consul-General, Edwin S. Cunningham. Half an hour before, the Japanese navy had personally assured the American Consul they considered the crisis over. He begged Abend not to spread 'alarmist'[9] rumours. Unconvinced, Abend prepared for battle. He put a taxi on stand-by and arranged a pile of cable blanks on his desk. Then he sat and waited.

At eleven that evening 400 Japanese marines marched from their headquarters on Kaingwan Road in Hongkew and climbed into eighteen military trucks. In the dingy light of the street lanterns, a group of Japanese civilians cheered them away.

The Japanese trucks and armoured cars headed for the extensive yards, locomotive sheds and warehouses of North Station in the heart of Chapei. Seaplanes hovered overhead ready to flash back news of their success to the Admiral on his flagship. Five hundred yards from the station the Japanese came up against a makeshift barricade of sandbags and barbed wire strung from lampposts and propped up in the centre with the odd table and chair. Behind this unpromising entanglement waited the Nineteenth Route Army. What were they doing there? They had their back-pay. A few had already caught a train from the station. As one Shanghailander said to me, 'We none of us expected the Chinese soldier to stand and fight.'

On the other side of Garden Bridge, Hallet Abend heard two rifle shots followed by machine-gun fire.

The Japanese marched in a blaze of light. Two men carrying torches accompanied each squad, making them easy targets for the snipers dressed in civilian clothes and positioned by General Cai throughout Hongkew and Chapei. The shots Abend heard came from their weapons as they picked off the Japanese. Even when the men hurriedly doused the flames, the Japanese marines stood silhouetted against the glow of lights from the International Settlement. The Japanese command, taken by surprise, ordered armed men on motor-cycles to roar up and down North Szechuen Road shooting out all second- and third-storey windows to halt the snipers' fire. For some reason they ignored the first four blocks of buildings that stretched from the Post Office near Soochow Creek to North Honan Road. These remained lit and open to traffic.

By 11.30 the noise had attracted onlookers from the International Settlement. Cars crowded along the lighted portion of North Szechuen Road. Chattering and laughing groups of Westerners arrived from hotels, theatres and dinner parties to see the fun. They stood around in evening clothes, smoking cigarettes, drinking from hip flasks and enjoying sandwiches and hot coffee from nearby cafés. ' "Hope the Japs will teach the cocky Chinese a good lesson" they said and, "Yeah, Japan is saving the white man the job of bringing the Chinese to reason." '10 As they talked, Japanese marines threw up sandbag shelters on the other side of the road. It was to be the last battle which the West watched in evening dress.

Hallett Abend turned down a side street and found over twenty Japanese crawling forward on their stomachs, pulling a machine-gun behind them. Suddenly a Chinese sniper opened fire. Abend back-skidded his car and made for the lighted part of the road where the crowd in evening dress still enjoyed itself amidst the whine of bullets ricocheting from nearby buildings. 'It was like a grim fantasy; there seemed to be no sense to the whole show.'[11]

Edgar Snow, later one of the first Westerners to understand and write about the importance of Mao Zedong in his book *Red Star over China*, also joined the fun. His wife recalled his 'high spirits' that evening as he found himself under fire for the first time in his life. Returning home, tired, dirty and almost hoarse, he exclaimed exultantly, ' "It has never happened before and it will never happen again . . . that anybody could be so close to a war and watch it safely – all because we're foreigners." '[12]

The Japanese had boasted that they could take the city in four hours. Instead the now three-thousand-strong force found itself pushed back almost into the Whangpoo. Over the weekend Japanese bluejackets and plain-clothes reservists battled with Chinese snipers. In Hongkew the Japanese usurped the functions usually performed by the police of the International Settlement. Their action drew a protest from Great Britain and America.

The fighting continued. Despite the arrival of 20,000 Japanese land troops, bombing from Japanese planes, bombardment from Japanese guns, and constant shelling from Japanese warships on the Whangpoo, 'the heaviest fighting ever witnessed around Shanghai',[13] the Nineteenth Route Army, with no help or encouragement from Chiang Kai-shek, held the Japanese off.

Abend and his assistant Robertson worked twenty-four hours a day. They took it in turn to write and watch, fortified only by sandwiches, scrambled eggs and the occasional absinthe frappé. On the first morning of the battle they stood together and counted sixteen Japanese planes circling overhead in a demonstration flight. Robertson bet they would bomb Chapei. ' "Never!" I ejaculated. "Bomb 600,000 civilians in an unfortified city? Not even the Japs." '[14]

In Chapei tenement houses burned down or collapsed under the incessant shell-fire. Factories, churches, schools, hospitals, cotton mills, a Chinese university, the Commercial Press and its library were all destroyed. Liu Ning, originally from Guangzhou, now living in Shanghai, recalled the bombing of the book company. He was repairing shoes in a small lane when he heard the droning of planes from far away followed by a succession of thunderous explosions 'like lumps of coal being dumped into a wooden box'. The pedestrians panicked. Flames shot up into the sky, black ashes of paper fluttering in the air here and there. Before long one or two cars loaded with mutilated bodies passed by. On the way home he saw flames engulfing the Commercial Press. The fire had extended to the neighbouring houses and lit up half the sky. His sister and her family were waiting anxiously for him with a few bundles of clothes and some cooking utensils. They hurried out and joined the stream of refugees on their way to the foreign Concessions. There they found the big iron gates already closed and they had to stay the night with an acquaintance. The next morning they rented a small room on what is now Huaihai Road. At night Liu Ning slept in the cramped space under the staircase.

The destruction of the Rokusan Gardens broke Mr Shiraishi's heart. He was sheltering sixty or seventy Japanese refugees when the order came to evacuate. The waitresses fled, leaving behind their kimonos as well as the antiques and calligraphies of famous people, including Imperial Princes who had visited the restaurant. Mr Shiraishi moaned, 'All have been stolen or destroyed. Most of which can never be bought with money.'[15] The Japanese razed Chapei to the ground. For the first time in Shanghai's history fighting spread into the International Settlement.

Cai Zhenhuan, a retired engineer who still lives in Shanghai, was one of the many Chinese caught up in the battle. Now wearing a peaked cap over his bald head, he likes to sit in Renmin Park, his briefcase by his side, arranging transactions more from habit than necessity. In 1932 he was twenty and working in the Zhenhua Paint Factory in Chapei. His family lived on Tianmu Road opposite North Station. The Japanese planes attacked the railway lines near his factory. He recalled that the bombs fell like rain, spreading fires whose number overwhelmed the fire-fighters. The Japanese refused to let fire engines through from the International Settlement. A dozen fires sprang up in the neighbourhood of Baoshan Road. By nightfall, they crimsoned half the sky. Flames spread to the most densely populaced section of Baoshan Road and consumed the workers' shacks.

Cai Zhenhuan and his best friend, A Zhang, volunteered to join the Nineteenth Route Army. First they loaded trucks with ammunition and gifts from the Shanghainese. Then they dug trenches a few miles out of Shanghai at Miaotou. During the night the plaintive sound of a huqin fiddle played by a Chinese soldier in a dugout drifted across to where Cai Zhenhuan and his friend lay. Occasionally they heard rifle fire from the Japanese. The next day was one he never forgot.

That afternoon, he and A Zhang worked hard, throwing up great shovelfuls of earth. Pausing to wipe the sweat from his forehead, Cai noticed five or six black dots circling and buzzing overhead. As they flew lower, the red suns on their wings became visible. Someone shouted, 'Lie down!' and the young men threw themselves on to the ground. A Zhang was only two or three paces from Cai Zhenhuan. He heard the noise of machine-guns shooting staccato and a succession of bullets ripping the ground alongside. When the droning of the planes faded away he got to his feet cursing and beating the dust off his trousers. He suddenly noticed that A Zhang lay motionless. He ran up, only to find blood gushing out of a few, tiny holes across his friend's back.

The sight of a city at war riveted the attention of the world. General Sir Ian Hamilton mulled it over at a regimental dinner in Manchester. It surprised professional soldiers, he said, that the Japanese should have selected as a battlefield a crowded city where true leadership, discipline and marksmanship would be lost, and the struggle became one between two blind mobs. Searching his memory, the General could only recall the experience of the Indian mutiny and the fighting in Delhi which had given General Roberts a 'perfect horror' of stopping in a city and losing control of his forces. 'I think he was right too,' concluded Sir Ian. 'That mess-up in Shanghai proves it.'[16] A new kind of war came into being in the streets of Chapei, so alien to the Victorian general, so common to us. Abend, writing in 1943, recalled how the Japanese bombing of Chapei and the slaughter of civilians outraged the civilized world. He finished sadly, 'and now only twelve years later, we have all become so accustomed to barbarities of this kind . . . the Axis Powers have . . . brutalised us'.[17]

Six hundred thousand refugees, fleeing from Chapei and Hongkew to the Settlement for safety, broke like a brown wave across Garden Bridge. Dressed in thickly padded cotton, they carried everything they owned in rickshaws, pushcarts, or tied in small bundles balanced on bamboo poles. Some clutched clocks, one girl in a blue dress held a chicken securely by the wings. Old men carried their birdcages. They spread along the Bund and up Nanking Road looking for a space to shelter. Behind them, night after night, rose the smoke from endless fires.

Some tried to escape Shanghai altogether. A crowd of several thousand refugees inundated the first-class decks, the boat deck and even the bridge of a Butterfield steamer loading alongside the French Bund. They shoved aside or knocked down the steamer's officers and hurled each other to the ground or into the water. Above the shouts, the shrill cries of women and the screams of frightened children separated from their parents and disappearing under foot, the captain's voice rose, unheeded. More refugees appeared every minute. The boat looked set to drift away from the Bund into nearby shipping when the captain managed to call for a naval landing party from H.M.S. *Kent*. They failed to persuade the refugees clutching their bundles, boxes and bedding to move. Any attempt to carry them off by force only added to the noise and panic.

The refugees were trying to escape from an overcrowded city where at night, in every uninhabited or half-finished building, on every roof and every staircase, in every passage and office and even tucked into the corners of storerooms lay bundles of sleeping squatters.

By day refugees with nothing to do clustered in the streets of the International Settlement. Two tents open to the sky presented entertainment against a backdrop of barbed wire on Avenue Edward VII. Each advertised the wonders inside on banners strung across the entrance. Bamboo poles rose over the canvas walls offering tantalizing glimpses of shivering monkeys. Inside, the programmes hardly differed. Three actors in bedraggled finery cavorted with wands and staffs. Two wrestlers never came to grips. A constant drizzle fell on the audience.

Those who stayed in Chapei found themselves trapped without food or water. If they ventured out, they risked meeting the sort of plain-clothed Japanese reservists two British found beating a Chinese near Haining and Chapoo Roads. When the foreigners remonstrated, the Japanese assaulted them with an iron bar and a baseball bat. Members of the Southern Methodist Mission reported seeing a Japanese sailor standing with a bayonet over a Chinese civilian lying across the sidewalk. The Japanese thrust his bayonet into the man's chest. The sailor then withdrew the bayonet, changed its position and thrust it six or eight times into the body until it ceased to move. The sailor then walked to the end of the street unconcerned and joined his comrades on patrol duty.

Chinese women risked another type of encounter. Seventeen-year-old Wang Guise had arrived from Suzhou in search of her mother. Seven Japanese soldiers forced her into a cottage where, according to a doctor's report, she was raped first by one and then by all the others in turn. She told the doctor that she was held firmly by her arms and legs – one man to an arm or leg. When she began to bleed they ran away in fear. 'She was still bleeding when brought here the next morning and on examination the external parts showed no signs of violence, but inside I found a large laceration of the posterior vaginal wall almost through into the rectum.'[18] The police failed to extract any details from her. 'Her mental condition does not seem at all clear which may be as the result of the haemorrhage,'[19] added the doctor with an astonishing lack of understanding.

The doctor's insensitivity reflected how very differently even a sympathetic Westerner viewed the war. No one burnt their homes or probed their buttocks with bayonets. Even members of the Volunteer Corps pursued their duties in comfort. One man in the Light Horse instructed his chauffeur to follow him about with supplies of beer. Another on duty in a pill-box ordered his double bed brought from home. For them, as Edgar Snow's wife and social secretary to the American Consul-General, remarked, the Shanghai war was all 'spit-and-polish, gold braid and festivity . . . but no action beyond tea dances'.[20] The fighting emphasized the divisions in the city.

The Chinese authorities asked Mr Lord, the man who had flown over Shanghai in 1927, to photograph the damage done by the Japanese bombs from the air. To make sure of a good shot, he had to stand up in the plane and lean right over the wings. 'Of course the Chinese gave me nothing for the pictures.'

Foreign journalists also enjoyed themselves. They viewed the battle as 'the perfect story'. Events appeared arranged for their convenience. The Chinese and Japanese provided them with passes covered in the appropriate red seals. They were then able to catch a bus out to the Chinese lines, return for a good lunch in the Settlement before spending an afternoon with the Japanese marines. Between five and seven, the really keen attended the Japanese and Chinese press conferences. Finally in the comfort of an air-conditioned room, free from censorship or shells, they wrote their stories before going to bed with, as Edgar Snow recalled, their conscience, if not their stomach, intact.

Newspaper editors across the world cabled for articles on the unexpected heroes of the Nineteenth Route Army who amazed the journalists when they finally met. The average age of the soldiers was twenty. They wore caps, faded cotton uniforms and tennis shoes. They even fastened their insignia to their shoulders with safety pins. Helen Foster Snow observed them on a train holding hands like Chinese schoolboys: 'as they fell asleep one would hold the other's head.'[21] Edgar Snow took her to an observation point near North Station where she could look into a Chinese dugout and watch two soldiers of about seventeen romping with a black puppy. They laughed and waved at the two Americans. The Japanese, on the other hand, levelled their bayonets at Helen. She noted that the Chinese sentries moved around in the open casually smoking cigarettes, 'but the Japanese kept well-hidden'.[22]

Fifty years later I too wanted to meet soldiers from the Nineteenth Route Army. I was in Shanghai staying at the British Consulate. Trevor Mound, the then British Consul-General, arranged an interview. I wondered what the old soldiers would make of us. In 1949 the Chinese had confiscated the former British Consulate on the Bund. Trevor Mound was the first British Consul-General for over twenty years and the new Consulate, a modest house in the French Concession, concealed an interior unchanged since then with a parquet floor throughout, a panelled sitting room and bathrooms tiled in geometric patterns of yellow, black and turquoise. Trevor drove around Shanghai in a purple London taxi wearing a deerstalker hat and cape. 'I like to promote the best of British,' he said when I queried this eccentricity. He took his passion for all things British rather too far I thought, planning a menu of shepherd's pie and rice pudding for our visitors. 'Old soldiers like rice pudding,' he said, an old soldier himself. For his cook the Chinese authorities had provided a former stoker at the local steel mill. My first meal in the Consulate had consisted of boiled chicken stuffed with tinned macaroni. School dinners, I agreed, might be an improvement.

The two soldiers arrived with their minder, a young man with thick eyebrows and spectacles. He did not think much of me nor of the shepherd's pie which, as a manifestation of Western decadence, he pushed to the side of his plate. He declared himself an expert on the history of the Nineteenth Route Army and instructed us to direct all questions to him. Fortunately he saw no point in talking to a woman. Trevor Mound with his distinguished air and perfect

Mandarin proved a far more flattering prospect. For two hours they discussed economic and political reforms. Occasionally the minder broke off to glare at me or eavesdrop on his elderly protégés. They never looked at him.

Of the two soldiers General Gao Gu was tall and to the point, Professor Zhu Ru, small, plump and loquacious. General Gao wore a neatly pressed Mao uniform, Professor Zhu had discarded his for a fawn three-piece suit and matching socks. General Gao barely changed expression. Professor Zhu's full mouth lay pressed against his face like a piece of fruit. He was the only man I met in China with sideburns.

General Gao Gu's father was a poor teacher. As a soldier, General Gao earned twelve taels a month. 'That's why I joined up,' he explained. Aged twenty-three, he was stationed in the Shanghai Garrison when it amalgamated with the Nineteenth Route Army. Professor Zhu came from a well-off family and attended university where a number of army officers took classes. They encouraged him to join the Chief of Staff. It was not a desk job, he quickly assured me, and described one occasion when the commander dispatched him to Suzhou with a message and a collection of files. The road from Shanghai to Suzhou runs along an ancient canal through rich countryside. When I went there, my taxi was the only vehicle and we drove in the middle of the road honking at the emptiness. In January 1932, Chinese escaping from Shanghai with their possessions choked the highway and attracted bandits from miles around. A group ambushed Zhu's car, killing the American Chinese driver. Zhu bravely if rather quixotically produced his ID card. The result surprised him. When the bandits realized who he was, they saluted him and returned his pistols and filing cabinets. Even brigands, it seemed, respected the Nineteenth Route Army and their stand against the Japanese. I did not ask what he did about the body. 'I drove myself to Suzhou' was Zhu's only comment.

Before the Nineteenth Route Army arrived in Shanghai, General Cai sent a telegram to Chiang Kai-shek requesting orders. The Generalissimo felt compelled to support the Nineteenth Route Army and advised action – but it was only a token support. He really wanted to contain the fighting. When his own soldiers in Nanking asked to join General Cai, he refused permission. The leader of one company ignored Chiang's prohibition and marched to Shanghai, 'but he was the only one to do so,' recalled Zhu.

At first Professor Zhu and General Gao believed Mayor Wu's acceptance of the Japanese terms had averted war. Then the Chinese noticed that the Japanese army was on the move. Professor Zhu went on, 'We were preparing night and day. I had no sleep for ten nights.' The night the Japanese marched to North Station, he was working at headquarters. The next morning he was sent to the front which ran along New Republican Road to the west of North Station. It was Professor Zhu's first battle. The Japanese attacked from the north and south. The Chinese held them off again and again. The professor recalled Chinese jubilation: 'Morale was amazing. It never came into my mind to be afraid or to worry.' General Gao nodded in agreement, adding, 'Some soldiers even played gramophone records behind the barricades and games of bridge. All of us were in high spirits.'

The propaganda battle proved just as absorbing. A former class-mate of Professor Zhu's created a special department to deal with the foreign press and to arrange the nightly press interviews. The fighting also aroused enormous interest among the Shanghainese. Groups of students collected the latest Chinese newspaper reports and distributed them throughout the city. Every day crowds gathered to read the editions. The people of Shanghai sent food and military supplies to the front. When it began to snow, they used the cotton from their winter quilts to make coats for the soldiers, recalled Professor Zhu. He went on, 'a rumour spread that the Japanese would gas us. As we had no masks, people collected cigarette tins, filled them with cotton spirit and attached strings to hold the contraption in place. Actually they were not very useful.'

The stand of the Nineteenth Route Army captured the imagination of the country. The Generalissimo's policy of appeasement had baffled and infuriated his subjects. The battle also made a pleasant change for the Chinese soldier accustomed to fighting other Chinese during Chiang Kai-shek's efforts to unite the country and exterminate the communists. 'We liked fighting Japanese better,' said General Gao.

Ninety student groups from all over China asked to join the Nineteenth Route Army. It was Professor Zhu's job to pick about twenty and organize them into teams relaying artillery and medical supplies to the front. Accomplished bicycle-riders delivered messages. He discovered some to be professional soldiers. Forbidden by Chiang Kai-shek to lend support to the Nineteenth Route Army, they had left their regiments and arrived in Shanghai disguised as students.

I asked General Gao his opinion of the Japanese soldier. Their discipline impressed him. When the Chinese took over Japanese positions they never found wounded or dead Japanese. The Japanese removed them all first. 'We captured one Japanese leader and sent him to Nanjing. At the end of the Second World War, he came back to Shanghai, found the spot where he had been taken and killed himself.'

The equipment of the Nineteenth Route Army consisted solely of machine-guns, mortar and rifles. They fired at the Japanese planes with rifles. I mentioned their leader. General Gao's eyes crinkled with pleasure at Cai Tingkai's name. He lent forward eagerly, for once silencing his companion. He described Cai Tingkai as large for a Chinese, 'so we called him Old Tall Cai. He was only forty-one but we thought that very old.' The youthful soldiers admired Cai's bravery and humour. He was always with them at the front. 'When we got together afterwards he never put on airs and graces but laughed a good deal. He stood no nonsense from his men though.'

As the fighting continued and no reinforcements arrived, the mood of elation gave way to despair. Professor Zhu said, 'We were very down-hearted. We felt completely isolated and forgotten behind our barricades. Chiang Kai-shek treated us unfairly. He even refused to pay us!' Bitter memories and the end of lunch silenced the two old soldiers. We took them downstairs and put them into the purple taxi with the minder. He appeared to have enjoyed himself but still refused to address me. As he made a speech to Trevor, I asked the old men why they had chosen to fight, against all the odds, at that particular time and in that place. Both men looked surprised. They said, 'We loved our country and we hated the Japanese. Our love and our rage overcame our fear of death.'

General Cai was also popular with Helen Foster Snow. 'Newsreel' Wong, the same who had recorded the executions on Shanghai's streets in 1927, offered to take her to interview the General and film the event. Helen wore what she considered appropriate battle-dress – 'my riding outfit and boots, with my foreign-correspondent trenchcoat'.[23] They circled to the rear of the Chinese lines in style with a press car and driver. Suddenly the air exploded a few hundred yards in front of them. ' "That's General Cai's headquarters," exclaimed Newsreel. "I thought it was safe here."[24] His driver started back without waiting for permission, hitting every pot-hole.'

The rather more experienced if less spectacularly dressed Percy Finch had better luck. He was invited with other correspondents to the General's field headquarters, ten miles outside the city, where the General had settled into a small country villa near the Shanghai–Nanjing Railroad. The track was torn and pitted with bomb craters, the steel freight-cars open like sardine cans. Cai's house had not been hit. He showed the foreign journalists his map-lined office, his living quarters and, in the garden, his emergency dugout, reinforced with railroad track. A mile or so away, machine-guns rattled and shellfire shook the green fields.

Cai's frankness impresed Finch. 'Nothing of the double-faced warlord about him.'[25] The General admitted he was unable to hold out much longer without reinforcements from Chiang Kai-shek.

I want the world to know that we are doing our best to resist the Japanese and that we will fight as long as our ammunition lasts. After that, we can do no more. But I hope our resistance will awaken China to the Japanese peril and help develop our national spirit of defiance. If we don't fight here in Shanghai, the Japanese will be like fierce tigers and swallow up our country in a few years.[26]

He made no complaint about Chiang Kai-shek.

Tea was then served, a feast of sandwiches, cold chicken, ham, potato salad, pâté de foie gras, elaborately iced cakes as well as beer, whisky and brandy, all sent by a caterer from the city in a motor truck. As the soldiers and journalists toasted each other in Martell cognac, two Japanese planes hovering overhead caused some alarm before vanishing back behind Japanese lines. Afterwards the General accompanied the correspondents to their cars, shook hands with each other, and made several bows before waving them back to Shanghai, 'his staunch ally'.[27]

The memory of the party stuck in Finch's mind. 'I realize it was Cai's way of saying goodbye to the city.'[28]

For the Nineteenth Route Army could not hope to win. Their sacrifice had merely embarrassed the Japanese army and had caused 14,000 Japanese and Chinese to die. But they had achieved something. They had shown the Japanese up. The Japanese invasion of Manchuria the year before had received scant attention from the West apart from a late and spiritless investigation by the League of Nations. Manchuria was hard to get to and large. Rumours of Japanese atrocities went unremarked. Shanghai proved a different matter.

The world showered Shanghai with support. The Chinese community in the Philippines sent G.$2,000,000 to General Cai. In San Francisco they put on fund-raising plays and organized knitting clubs. Chinese leaders predicted that every adult male would donate at least one month's salary to the cause. The American public reacted with outrage and sympathy to well-publicized accounts from American missionaries of the 'reign of terror' in Chapei and Hongkew. The *Washington Post* declared, 'The Japanese government has either been overpowered by a war machine that is running amok, or is deliberately pursuing a war policy unparalleled in its audacity.'[29] American pilots and machine-gun experts tried to enlist in the Chinese Army to the embarrassment of Chinese consulates throughout the States. In Shanghai the insouciance of the Japanese pilots infuriated an American aviator called Bob Short. He borrowed a plane but was shot down and killed by the Japanese. In Britain, a group led by Maude Royden, the famous woman preacher, offered to form a peace army and place themselves unarmed between the Chinese and Japanese lines. Maude Royden believed 'the existence of the League of Nations hangs in the balance, and this is the moment for us to come forward with help'. She hoped the League would not regard the scheme 'as a mere fantasy'.[30]

For the League it was the beginning of the end. The meeting to discuss the issue in Geneva on February 19th proved to be one of the longest as well as one of the most dramatic ever held. The countries watched in fascination the duel between the Chinese representative, Dr Yan and the Japanese delegate, Mr Sato. As Britain before him, Mr Sato claimed, 'If we had to do with a civilized state our whole conduct might have been different', and reminded the West, 'If we condemned aggressive acts today, it would be necessary to condemn similar acts of other powers against China . . . before.' A Spanish delegate summed up the despair of the assembly when he wailed, 'Where is going the peace of the world? Where is going the Covenant?'[31]

All the world denounced Japan, except the Shanghailander. The *North China Daily News* aptly reflected his sympathies when it greeted the reinforcements of Japanese troops with the confident if misguided prediction that 'Other nationalities will enter fully into the emotions which the arrival from the homeland of these sturdy men of their own race awakened in the hearts of the men, women and children who waved their national flags and uttered their "banzais" in fond greetings.'[32] The paper had always warmed to a parade of soldiers but after the devastation of Chapei and the tales of Japanese brutality their next comment appears extraordinary. The paper declared, 'The Japanese Army has won for itself a well founded reputation for discipline and good behaviour',[33] and went on to assure the new arrivals that 'current controversies will not be allowed to prejudice Shanghai's treatment of them'.[34]

The piece finished with the hope that 'their adventures may have a pleasant ending and give them happy memories to take back with them when the times come for them to go'. This appeared on the same page as a news item describing the Japanese bombardment of a refugee camp, 'an apparent wanton piece of cruelty', the newspaper admitted, the explanation for which would, 'on the face of it, present considerable difficulties'.

The newspaper took refuge in stories of gallant old men and animals; the courage of the eighty-year-old Commander Davis, the English naval captain who refused to leave the Fort Hotel in Woosung which he had built and managed himself while all around was shelled to oblivion: the sight of hundreds of racing ponies walking through the Settlement in single file escaping from burning stables. 'They also had been forced to leave their comfortable homes and each one carried his blankets on his back . . . They . . . knew not whence they were going nor when they would be able to get shelter and their next meal.'[35] The description takes on an almost biblical tone and displays a tenderness lacking from similar accounts of Chinese refugees. When a Chinese soldier shot one pony for its blanket, the newspaper entitled the story 'Extra – Settlement Tragedy'. British readers responded with outraged letters condemning the soldier. The only dissenting contribution came from a Chinese. The piece set him thinking 'of the dying and wounded women and children I see everyday in hospital and thousands of refugees who have lost everything in the world, and never complain'.[36] The soldier had passed many nights in mud and rain. Was it so wrong to kill a pony for its blanket?

It was not a question of wrong or right. It was a question of familiarity. The readers of the *North China Daily News* found it difficult to adjust. For as long as they could remember, Shanghai's wars had followed a set form. A Chinese army arrived, ravaged the countryside, insulted missionaries, starved and tortured thousands of Chinese while holding Shanghai at its mercy. A gunboat or an adroit bribe always saved the day. The foreigner had professed to despise the Chinese way of doing war. Yet the mixture of bluff and chicanery required exactly suited the resources and the mentality of the city. Now here was something different. One of their own had used the Settlement to attack the Chinese. Suddenly the world press wrote up the Chinese, not as cruel and rapacious warlords but as celestials in every sense of the word. The transformation baffled the Shanghailander. A patina of patriotism, table manners and the ability to give a good interview appeared to cover everything. The Shanghailander watched in disgust. He, for one, was not hood-winked. Sooner or later the hooligan would break out.

It was also a question of loyalty. For years the Shanghailander had regarded the Chinese as the enemy and the Japanese as an admired friend. In the 'twenties Japan was a success story. In the dome of the Hongkong and Shanghai Bank, the British architect personified Tokyo by the figures of 'Learning', 'Progress' and 'Science'. Japan possessed a modern army, navy and air force and a parliamentary system. It had looked to Great Britain for advice and help. The pleasure of the *North China Daily News* at its 'wonderful pluck'[37] after the 1923 Tokyo earthquake is expressed in the tone of a happy parent.

Apt imitators sometimes pick up more than they or the imitated bargain for. Japan absorbed not only the fair and civilized image of the Empire but also some of the less pleasant aspects. As a visitor to Shanghai remarked, 'we built up our Eastern supremacy by bloodshed and rapine'.[38] Mr Sato expressed justifiable grievance at the League Council in Geneva. In 1932, Japan contemplated rather less than the Great Powers during the Boxer Rebellion of 1900. The past, however, is always a different story. Apart from Germany and Italy, by the 'thirties the West lacked the will and the money for imperialism. In its place existed a distaste for what could no longer be had. The opposite was true in Shanghai. Japanese imperialism evoked nostalgic memories. The Japanese government was behaving as the Shanghailander wished Britain would do again.

Longing quickly translated into action through the Joint Committee of the British Chamber of Commerce and China Association who represented Shanghai business interests in Britain. In numerous cables they pointed out that the fighting provided 'unique opportunity' to work with the Japanese military, to take over the Outside Roads area and to extend the Settlement. They viewed the Japanese as allies who, on behalf of all foreigners in Shanghai, were ' "pulling the chestnuts out of the fire" ' even if 'in somewhat a crude manner'.[39] One telegram ends with this plea:

> We strongly urge you to do all you can by representation to Foreign Office Member of Parliament and Editors leading Papers to impress upon them vital importance inducing stronger more positive and less unreal policy so that Japan will not be lost when upholding principles of justice, good government and civilisation in this all important region China.[40]

They still believed, even with Chapei in ruins, that the Japanese war machine was a controllable toy and that Japan was a good and docile child.

The British Foreign Office held little patience with such views. Over the next seven years eloquent and passionate appeals by the China Association in Shanghai met with vagueness and, when really pushed, testy advice. It was not 'an axiom', they reminded the Shanghailander in August 1934 over the question of paying Chinese taxes, that 'resistance [to the Chinese government] rather than compromise is in every case the wisest course to pursue'.[41]

The Battle of 1932 reveals why Shanghai, despite its energy and its wealth, was ripe for destruction. Its foreign inhabitants had insulated themselves from the present. In their attempt to recreate the past, they forfeited the future. They might daydream of a city with the personality of Geneva or Venice in the Middle Ages. They might talk of a real international community, a city of cosmopolitan brotherhood, a model city 'for the internationalization of the whole world',[42] but events had shown that Shanghailanders lacked both the will and the imagination for such a project. Their desire to free Shanghai from the enmities taking shape across the world proved as frivolous, fantastic and heartbreaking as Maude Royden's peace army.

The arrival of 8,000 Japanese reinforcements compelled the Nineteenth Route Army to withdraw behind the 20-kilometre limit the Japanese had originally insisted on. The war was over. Chapei lay 'a rubbish-heap', its streets piled with broken stones, bricks and battered bits and pieces. White streamers, the colour of mourning, painted with Chinese characters extolling the names and deeds of the dead, floated from every Chinese house left standing and around the site of the North Railway Station.

By teatime of March 8th the Japanese finally reached North Station and raised their flag. At midnight the departing Chinese soldiers lit a blaze which allowed residents to read a newspaper half a mile away. Over the following days people went out to inspect the dugouts of the Nineteenth Army to find them littered with loot and gifts. Women's purses, bracelets, jade hairpins and jewel boxes hung on pegs driven into the earthen walls or lay hidden among the supports. On the ground, trodden into the mud, a correspondent picked out books in half a dozen languages, photographs, clothing, plates and one 'Sam Browne' belt. Piles of empty lobster, crab and anchovy tins were stacked up with empty brandy bottles and foreign cigarette packets. One officer had provided himself with carpets and a heavy, carved chair and side-table to match. For miles along the road were scattered red and yellow armbands marked with the Chinese characters for 'Nineteenth Route Army'. Some had never been used. The first good weather of the year brought three foreign women out on a sightseeing trip to the fighting area around Kiangwan. They walked alongside the trenches where the dead sprawled three deep. They were struck by the youthfulness of the soldiers; some looked no more than fourteen years old. 'In a shell hole lay one who had died biting his hand in agony. The trenches ran through a bamboo grove. How lovely the grove was in the fresh spring morning and what gruesomeness lay at our feet.'[43]

Admiral Shiozawa threw a party for the foreign press aboard the *Azumo*. Hallett Abend had always thought of him as a kind man. Now he demonstrated an odd combination of apology and defiance. He said with a forced smile, 'I see your American newspapers have nicknamed me the Baby-Killer . . . they should give me some credit. I used only thirty pound bombs, and if I had chosen to do so I might have used the five hundred pound variety.'[44] In the city there erupted a sudden, spontaneous letting off of firecrackers as the Chinese celebrated, unsure why or for what.

Foreigners faced other dangers, mostly from curio hunters. 'What does any sane foreign resident of this Settlement want with an unexploded aeroplane bomb?'[45] asked the *North China Daily News* in exasperation. The golfer appreciated 'the real hardships of war'[46] when he found himself unable to get in his round or two over the weekend. Shell craters on the Kiangwan golf course threatened to rewrite the rulebook. Could a golfer lift a ball out of a shell hole without penalty? And did the same rules apply to a trench as to a drainage ditch? Pony skeletons constituted a further hazard requiring legal definition. The Club House, too, posed a problem. First occupied by Chinese soldiers, it now housed Japanese troops. For the moment a gin and bitters lay off limits.

All that remained was to find peace. Negotiations began over tea in the British Consulate. The one note of sanity and reason came from Sir Miles Wedderburn Lampson, then Minister in China. Pragmatic and something of a fatalist with an immense appetite for work he was sympathetic to the Chinese and critical of any plan to take advantage of Japanese actions to enlarge the Settlement. He had spent over fifteen years in the Far East and was on friendly terms with the Chinese Foreign Minister Luo Wengan, 'a very decent sort of fellow' although inclined 'to drink a bit more than is good for him'[47] and the chief Japanese negotiator. The negotiations were soon imbued with a very Shanghai flavour.

Lampson had to conduct the talks with the American, French and Italian Consuls. He got on well with the American, Nelson Johnson; less so with the French man, Wilden, who was an opium addict; and thought Ciano, whose chief distinction was being Mussolini's son-in-law and a philanderer of Chinese women, very irritating. 'I must confess', wrote Lampson in his diary entry of March 19th, 'I find my colleagues almost more of a trial during these meetings than the Japanese and Chinese.'[48] Two weeks before Ciano had turned up at the morning meeting in the British Consulate, the only person to have any instructions about the proposed conference. 'As usual, he had had a telegram from Mussolini authorising him to take part in any conference about anything whatever happened anywhere – which is very much the usual attitude of Italy.'[49] They failed to understand that 'what is required is infinite and absolute patience'.[50] Lampson believed in allowing the Japanese and Chinese to 'argue themselves to a frazzle' when it might be possible to 'chip in and bring them back to the point'.[51] Wilden had the unfortunate habit of interrupting 'at the most awkward moments' to throw in some suggestion, 'which starts an undesirable hare'.[52]

As negotiations developed, he wrote to his mother-in-law, Mrs Phipps,

> You would smile if you could see the meetings. On one side at the bottom of a long row of tables sit two high Japanese generals, a Japanese admiral and the Japanese Minister: behind them innumerable staff officers, secretaries, A.D.C.s and what not. Opposite them two high Chinese generals, and the Chinese Foreign Under-Secretary: behind these equally innumerable underlings. Then – at a sort of separate desk – myself: . . . To my left, another big table at which (next to me) is the American Minister, and beyond him the Italian and the Frenchman.[53]

The two opposing generals carried on the debate each in his own language. As this was translated, Lampson received a third translation into English. 'Whilst that is being translated into the other, another minion comes up to us and translates it into English for our benefit! Often the Vice-Minister and the Japanese Minister argue freely: and then I take an active part. Everyone smokes, there must be at least thirty people in the room, and the atmosphere gets beyond belief.'[54] It was all, he confided, a matter of face: 'they are quite capable in the pursuit of the said face of losing what they really want'.[55]

Lampson's exertions ensured the signing of the peace agreement. Shortly before, Shanghai's annual Hong List of the city's businesses and probably the best gauge of business expansion came out. It showed business had made a complete recovery. Shanghai returned to its natural state of boom time.

It was also to be its greatest years of disaster. Out in Chapei, Miss Rose Marlowe who taught at the Shung Tak Girls' School, a Southern Baptist Mission enterprise, was inspecting the damage done to the school when two Japanese civilians in white armbands set upon her. One hit her several times with a walking stick while the other struck her in the face with his fist. Miss Marlowe caught the next boat out of Shanghai suffering from a nervous condition. Others should have taken note. The Japanese now liked slapping foreign faces.

Chiang Kai-shek dispatched the Nineteenth Route Army to Fuzhou in Fujian province to chase communists. General Gao explained, 'The Generalissimo planned to kill two birds with one stone. We were too much in the public eye for his liking. Once in Fujian everybody forgot about us.' In 1933, unpaid and ill-equipped, the Nineteenth Route Army rebelled. Chiang Kai-shek had learnt his lesson from the Japanese bombardment of Chapei and now tried the same on Fuzhou. Unfortunately, few foreign journalists reported the results.

Cai Zhenhuan, whose friend had been shot by a Japanese aeroplane, helped carry wounded soldiers as the Nineteenth Route Army retreated, marching all night. At dawn they knocked on the doors of the townspeople, seeking a place to rest before taking a ferry across the lake. Finally he reached Nanjing where he received two dollars for his trip home. He had stayed with the army for three months altogether. 'When I eventually returned to work, the factory foreman sacked me because of the absence. And my father scolded me.'

The stand of the Nineteenth Route Army had brought home to the foreigner the change taking place in China. The unification of the country under the Nationalist party had given the Chinese self-respect. They felt the urge for more equal relations with their foreign occupiers. Shanghailanders were bewildered. Except as a market, they had ignored the Chinese. They knew nothing about the people who were now demanding their city back and who, it was becoming increasingly clear, were to determine Shanghai's fate in the next few years.

· SIX ·

The Chinese

SHANGHAI APPEARED AS alien to Chinese from the interior as to any Westerner. To them it was a foreign metropolis on Chinese soil. Their reaction is epitomized by Old Mr Wu, a character from the novel *Midnight* by Mao Dun.

On a fictional May evening in the early 1930s, Old Mr Wu arrived in Shanghai by boat. He had not stepped out of his country house for twenty-five years. Bandits and communists had finally forced him to leave. At the wharf, he was met by his son, a successful industrialist and carried to one of three waiting cars. As the car moved off, the old man suddenly opened his eyes and cried out with startling vehemence. 'The Supreme Scriptures of Rewards and Punishments!' The car braked. His relatives appeared nonplussed. This was Old Mr Wu's ancient book of divine retribution and his talisman against vice. He had left it behind on the boat and could not face a drive through Shanghai without it.

The book restored to him, the cavalcade of new Citroens set off for the French Concession by way of Nanking Road. Nothing in the tranquillity of the Chinese countryside or in the precepts of his book, of which his favourite was 'Of all the vices sexual indulgence is the cardinal; of all the virtues filial piety is the supreme',[1] had prepared him for what he now saw.

Nanking Road, running at right angles from the Bund past the former racecourse, is still Shanghai's most spectacular shopping street. Fifty years ago, it offered a frenetic, dazzling aberration of East and West. You could buy anything on Nanking Road, from jewelled opium pipes to hot chocolate sundaes, from coolies to Texan chorus girls. International and up-to-date, it epitomized what the Shanghainese (Chinese who lived in Shanghai) admired and wanted. Old Mr Wu had not seen anything like it; neither had the rest of China.

Above the newcomer's head shop-signs crowded in Russian cyrillic and Western script while Chinese characters hung in panels over the pavement. Up and down the road small, open-fronted Chinese shops slipped between the foreign department stores of Whiteaway Laidlaw, Weeks, Kelly and Walsh (the booksellers and publishers), the Chocolate Shop (famous for its milk-shakes, ice-cream and chicken salad), Bianchi the Italian restaurant, Sam Lazaro the music shop and piano importer and Sun Ya, a Chinese restaurant frequented by foreigners. Halfway down Nanking Road, the Chinese-owned department stores of Wing On, Sincere and Sun Sun towered like cliffs on either side of the street. Here customers could ride the elevators, buy duck tongues, skate, look at exhibitions of calligraphy, play billiards or just admire the palm trees growing in the brown and yellow tubs outside Sincere's.

On the street itself East and West met in noise and confusion. American cars skirted barefoot rickshaw pullers. Bicycles jostled against carts loaded with fruit and vegetables, earthenware jars, coal, machinery or bamboo furniture all pulled by men, women and children who survived only because they cost less to use than an animal. Thin, sweating coolies, naked to the waist, pushed wheelbarrows carrying anything from apples to silver bars; or balanced baskets of squawking chickens and geese from long, shoulder-poles while fighting for room with women wearing Paris dresses. Schoolchildren in pressed uniforms picked their way over beggars sprawling like spider monkeys across the sidewalk. The street resounded with car horns, bicycle bells, pedlars calling out their wares, people yelling at each other in half a dozen languages to get out of the way, brass bands advertising shops, dwarfs in top hats crying out, 'Fantastic value! Fantastic value!', the clop, clop of ponies' hooves and, always, in the background, the loud, firm click-click from the Chinese shops of the abacus adding everything up.

The lighted windows of the apartment stores rushed down on Old Mr Wu at one moment then vanished the next. The street lamps on either side of the road came and went at the same alarming speed. The oncoming cars, their horns blaring, rose up at him like a line of black serpents, each with a pair of blinding lights for eyes. A blur of shiny, leaping coloured shapes and hooting, jarring sounds made his head spin and his heart leap. Passers-by dashed along in front of him as if chased by devils.

At a set of traffic lights Old Mr Wu noticed that his daughter's chiffon dress displayed her jutting breasts. In disgust he turned to the window. Drawn up alongside he saw a 'half-naked' young woman seated in a rickshaw, her thighs tantalizing beneath transparent voile. Old Mr Wu's face turned grey. His breathing grew wheezy. The noise of the traffic, the stink of petrol-fumes mixed with the cloying smell of the women and the dazzle of lights trapped him in a nightmare.

Shortly after reaching the French Concession the cars swung into a drive of dark, overhanging trees and drew up before the home of Old Mr Wu's son. Radio music floated from an open window. A woman came out wearing red lipstick and high, clicking heels. She put her arm round Old Mr Wu and led him into the Western house. Her scent overwhelmed him. 'They must be demons or evil spirits, these people!'[2] thought Old Mr Wu.

Holding his book the tighter, his heart beating madly, his throat smarting 'as if choked with chillies',[3] he found himself seated in a large, brightly lit room. His relations chatted and danced around him. To Old Mr Wu the voluptuous mayhem of Shanghai's streets appeared to have infiltrated his son's home. His eyes burnt with rage and excitement. The dancing women wore silk dresses which barely hid 'their full, pink-tipped breasts and the shadow under their arms'.[4] The room appeared to brim with 'countless swelling bosoms, bosoms that bobbed and quivered and danced around him'. All these

quivering, dancing breasts swept at Old Mr Wu like a hail of arrows, piling up on his chest and smothering him, piling up on The Supreme Scriptures of Rewards and Punishments in his lap. He heard wild, seductive laughter and the room rocked and swayed ... 'Devils' cried Old Mr Wu, as golden sparks showered before his eyes ... Something seemed to snap in his head. He turned up his eyes and knew no more.[5]

Old Mr Wu had died, killed by a surfeit of bosoms. Nothing in his experience had equipped him to last one night in Shanghai. He represents traditional China with its emphasis on Confucian virtues, its strict social hierarchy, its framework of family and guild, its restrictions on women and its distaste for the merchant. To him Shanghai was not China nor his relatives Chinese.

Traditional China had suffered the same fate as Mr Wu. The old order had broken down. During the hundred years of Shanghai's existence as an international city, China found itself bankrupt both of ideas to meet the future or rice to feed its citizens. Shanghai offered both. It became the place to find a job, experiment with Western ideas or seek protection from the whims of central government. The result encouraged the modern press, the youth movement, the proletariat, and especially the capitalist to develop in strength. By the 'twenties Shanghai was in the forefront of China's modernization and poised, it seemed, to push old China into oblivion.

Its Chinese citizens possessed all the brash confidence of the self-made. Most came to the city in order to prove themselves outside a tradition that equated success with training in the Chinese classics or the ability to manage land. They inhabited a middle ground neither foreign nor Chinese. They adopted Western dress and habits like horseracing and Christian names. Their houses were furnished with a mixture of Chinese and European pieces. They found themselves at home in 'a place where two civilisations met and neither prevailed'.[6]

Nanking Road represented their contribution to Shanghai. They took pride in its diversity, energy and glamour. They enjoyed knowing people came from all over China to stroll along its pavements and ride the escalators in its department stores. They saw nothing strange in the salmagundi on offer. It never occurred to them that the combination of neon signs and sweating coolies might prove indigestible to the Chinese stomach. The idea would have had them slapping themselves with laughter. They were confident Nanking Road presaged China's future.

Twenty years later it had followed Old Mr Wu into oblivion.

The Most Repellent Kind of Slavery

In 1932 the foreigners watched in awe as a flood of people swept across Garden Bridge. Few had any idea of the conditions in which the majority of Shanghai's population lived or worked.

During its one hundred years as an international enclave Shanghai served as an open city to refugees from China's upheavals. By 1934 one and a half million Chinese lived in the International Settlements while that figure again occupied Chapei, Pootung, Nantao and the Outside Roads Area known collectively as Greater Shanghai and under the control of the Chinese government. Numbers increased all the time for, however bad conditions were in the city, they proved preferable to those elsewhere. The people who sought work in Shanghai's factories had fled market towns like Yiyang in Henan Province, looted seventy-two times over eighteen months by three different Chinese armies, its wells left stuffed with dead. Or they were forced off the land like one peasant outside Shanghai. His landlord had lent him three piculs of rice at such a high rate of interest that after two years he owed forty. Shanghai offered an alternative to people deprived of any other.

Shanghai's sheer numbers benumbed the sensibilities. Displays of sympathy invited such a deluge of need, it seemed safer not to care at all. On July 6th, 1936, a wealthy Shanghainese celebrated his seventieth birthday by distributing twenty-cent coins from the Thibet Residents Association in Thibet Road. Word spread and the next day 30,000 people gathered. The police were called 'for fear of an untoward happening',[7] and the event ended in a brawl with the more aged supplicants knocked down and carried off to hospital.

Numbers mattered in Shanghai. The first decades of the twentieth century witnessed a shift of political emphasis. A series of strikes and demonstrations in 1919 and 1925 had brought home the power of the mob. How to reach, control and make a profit from the ordinary Chinese were questions to absorb the Chinese intellectual, politician and businessman over the next twenty years. Their interest formed a new departure for China. In the past the wealthy and powerful put as much distance between themselves and the less fortunate as possible. When the Emperor ventured outside the Forbidden City, he did so on roads strewn with gold powder and emptied of subjects. Now China's future seemed to lie in those absent crowds and particularly in the urban crowds of Shanghai's streets.

The throng on Thibet Road fell into two groups representing the two sides of poverty in the city. Hongkew's and Chapei's factories had created an industrial proletariat whose potential as a political force inspired the founding of the Chinese Communist party in Shanghai. Their situation was peculiar to the Treaty Ports, most especially to Shanghai. On the other side of the city, among the dank alleyways of Nantao existed the sort of deprivation found all over China. Beggars called wearily. Mothers mutilated their children to attract pity. Their faces reflected the harsh fate of the poor in China. Their numbers reduced each tragic life to a trite reiteration that stupefied the mind. To this category belonged the rickshaw man.

The foreigner had introduced the rickshaw to Shanghai from Japan in the 1860s. As soon as a foreigner stepped from his office or club, the rickshaw men gathered around, jostling to place the shafts of their vehicles as close to the customer as possible. 'He could not help striking a few of them, if he had a stick,' wrote Mr W. MacFarlane in the 1880s. 'They will then go off, and the ones that are chastised are laughed at by all the others.'[8] The rickshaw man was the only contact most foreigners had with Shanghai's poverty. The ensuing guilt produced either a fit of temper (the foreigner never paid the full fare if he had a 'cane handy')[9] or a collective blindness. As one Chinese lady said, 'our rickshaw men are so strong, we treat them like machines'. To the concerned they epitomized, as Enid Saunders Candlin put it, 'the vast insistent need of the country'.[10]

Seventy to eighty thousand men pulled rickshaws day and night around Shanghai. Like the White Russian, everybody recalled the rickshaw-puller. He knew the city intimately. He made Shanghai's back alleys his home; riots, public festivals, weddings and funerals, his entertainment. He reveals an existence limitless in its horror, brief and complete in its pleasures. A full stomach represented happiness. An unlucky stumble or brush with the police meant starvation. He makes the best guide for a tour of Shanghai street life.

Most rickshaw men were farmers driven off their land. Bachelors slept in a loft or shed owned by the rickshaw contractor with five to eight other pullers. Men with families lived in huts built of bamboo, wood, broken mats and scraps of iron on waste ground. The most popular place was the south bank of Soochow Creek, known as Yao Shui Lane where four thousand people squatted without electricity or running water except from the polluted creek. Floods, disease and fire happened regularly. Wu Jisheng was twelve years old and a typical inhabitant. His family came from North Jiangsu. After floods destroyed their land they made their way to Shanghai and moved in with relatives on the bank. Their shack was so small, Wu had to bend to get in. The family suffered continuously from hunger. Soon after arriving his two sisters died. Wu's father was a rickshaw-puller and when he grew up, he would take over from his father.

In warm weather the rickshaw men moved on to the streets as one enraged foreign resident recalled in June 1936. For three summers running, six rickshaw men and their families transformed Park Lane in Hongkew, a 'quite decent' street, inhabited by 'respectable' ratepayers 'into a latrine'. The six families lived, ate and slept on the pavement. The letter-writer who signed himself Mr A. S. Ufferer was particularly incensed by their habit of throwing their leftovers on to the pavement. He continued: 'And amidst this garbage, filth and swarms of green flies, small babies crawl and lie about, watched peacefully by their happy parents, who quite unconcernedly enjoy their siesta.' The writer describes, despite himself and the flies, a scene of fleeting tranquillity. Here is the rickshaw man at the zenith of contentment, the sun shining and his well-fed family about him. A. S. Ufferer remained unmoved. He found it amazing that rickshaw coolies should be allowed to hold family meals, 'right at the very doors of foreign dwelling houses' and threatened to take the law into 'his own hands'.[11]

Rickshaw men without wives to cook for them relied on street vendors for their food. Twenty coppers bought a 'full-to-neck'[12] meal of fried bean curd and noodles made of pea flour taken with dried rice folded into a French patty. Chestnuts fried in a pot either with black sand mixed with liquid sugar or peanuts cooked with white sand cost the same amount. If the rickshaw-puller possessed only six coppers, he spent it on cake and white bread leftovers sold by the apprentices of the 'Da Bing' (Big Cake) shops. Each apprentice carried a tin pot filled with tea into which the coolie soaked his white bread, known as 'foreign meal', before he ate it. Three coppers also paid for congee, a little rice and the water it was cooked in. A dish of salted vegetables or pickles cost six coppers extra. One meal like this, lacking any protein, usually made up the rickshaw man's daily diet. On this he ran round the city. It is not surprising that most were sick or dead by forty.

Only the desperate pulled rickshaws. It cost the rickshaw man one dollar to hire a rickshaw for twenty-four hours. Two men usually shared the vehicle in two shifts of twelve hours each. On average they earned about sixty or seventy cents a shift. At the end of the time the puller often found himself without enough money to pay the contractor and eat. At the depot the contractors beat the money out of the reluctant puller, accusing him of hiding the coins in his clothes. When a rickshaw man failed to earn enough, he borrowed. The average annual interest rate stood at 120 per cent. Between the loan and the rickshaw racket, one puller told Isherwood, 'our life seems to be fastened down with live hooks'.[13]

Foreigners assured me that they did care. Every Christmas they sent contributions to the Shanghai Rickshaw Men's Mission founded by George Matheson, a tall, red-haired Scot retired from the Shanghai Municipal Police Force. The Mission provided food, baths and a place to rest. In summer free kangs of tea equipped with bamboo dippers appeared on the streets for the thirsty puller.

Foreign charity camouflaged the real cause of the rickshaw men's distress; the high cost of renting a rickshaw. Every year the Municipal Council distributed ten thousand rickshaw licences to a monopoly group of rickshaw owners, many of whom were foreign. The registration plate cost five dollars. They were then sold and resold for up to five hundred dollars each. Even at that price contractors made 'huge profits' stated the Rickshaw Committee for the Shanghai Municipal Council in its report published on February 13th, 1931. Contractors, described by one newspaper as 'among the wealthiest foreigners in the city'[14] and 'closely connected' with those in charge of the municipality, blocked any move to lower rentals. In such a situation baths and a spot of tea appeared the best the rickshaw man could hope for.

The hours of running demanded one day of rest out of every three. On his day off, the puller would sleep on the sidewalk, gamble in the teashops or wander over to Nantao, the old Chinese city. Once surrounded by walls to keep out Japanese pirates, by the 'thirties a stroll across the Boulevard des Deux Republiques separated Nantao from the French Concession. It was like going back into China's past. Beyond an iron gate lay a glimpse of cramped houses and passageways winding into a crowded darkness. The rickshaw-puller plunged without hesitation into a world that few foreigners dared penetrate.

The alleyways smelt of sewage and cooking oil. Old ladies with bound feet pushed past beggars and children. On either side, narrow buildings hid courtyards decorated with blossom trees and tubs of goldfish. Balconies met overhead, blocking out the sky. Bamboo poles stuck into the eaves dripped with nappies, trousers and the long, tapering bandages used by women to bind their feet. The alleyways led into San Pailou Road, the main thoroughfare, lined with shops displaying hats, clothes, rice bowls, chopsticks, cooking utensils, canaries, larks, white mice, goldfish, jewellery, sticks of incense and paper money for worship at the temple. The shops advertised themselves with flags or coloured wool blowing to and fro at the end of bamboo poles. The flags carried fanciful claims. One red banner, scalloped in white braid and hanging almost into the middle of the street, belonged to a small and dirty eating house, described as 'The Bright Palace of Summer Relaxation: Has existed since the 5th year of the Republic'. A sumptuous gold and black flag heralded a tailor's, 'The Famous Experts of the Human body, feet and arms, male and female. Most Attractive Prices, Bun Fo Bros'. The small, brown shop next door proved to be 'An Abode for People looking for Peace: Roast Ducks, Goose Eggs, Cheaper than anywhere else', but was easily outshone by its greengrocer neighbour, 'A Pavilion of Abundance: The only Connoisseurs of the Fruits of the Yangtsze Valley'. At the sight of a particular pennant, the rickshaw man might have paused, rubbed his groin then walked on. It promised: 'Round the corner to the left and then upstairs, she is waiting for you.' Sex, like food, was out of his reach.[15]

So was good health. The most splendid shop in the street turned out to be the Chinese chemist. It offered 'All Kinds of Life Treatment'. Laid out on wooden trays were the velvety stubs of antlers, frog skins, toadstools, sea slugs and even small, dead snakes wound in coils. I was taken to one when I complained of sinusitis. The old man behind the counter looked me up and down before fixing his eye on my gumboots, the most practical footwear for China, especially Chinese lavatories. Unfortunately they made my feet appear almost twice as big as those of the average Chinese man. The old man sucked his teeth, glanced at his own slender, felt slippers, then prescribed me a pill the size and colour of a horse dropping. It was very expensive. When I crumbled it up, both he and my Chinese friend expressed disappointment. 'Much better whole,' they assured me. I waited a day then asked for an aspirin. The rickshaw man would have stared at the medicaments, dreaming of longevity, until the owner chased him away.

In the blacksmith's or blanket-maker's, he might have joined the groups of people who had gathered to gossip, lend a hand, eat, or merely watch the owner at work. In the open market he could inspect the dried and fresh fruit, and the fish sold in wire cages. Amidst the crowds, a barber shaved his customer seated on a bamboo stool. Scribes prepared love letters or marriage contracts for the illiterate. Incense and spirit-money pedlars shouted their wares. The rickshaw man hung wistfully round a fortune-teller then moved on.

At the centre of the old city, the sky suddenly opened and the streets turned to a sheet of water covered in lotus flowers. A bridge built in nine zigzags to bemuse evil spirits, led to the Heart-of-Lake Pavilion known as the Huxinting Teahouse. It is still there today, pentagonal in shape with roofs tilting at the corners like flirtatious eyelids over red, painted casements. If you cross the bridge, pushing through crowds dense enough to stop any number of devils, the teahouse reveals men sitting at bare tables drinking cups of tea. Rain scatters through the open casements. The lake is shallow and full of sweet-papers and slime. In the Yu Yuan, the classical Chinese garden beyond, crowds clog the grottoes. Children pee through their split pants on the ancient gingko tree and play around the Exquisite Jade Rock (which the guidebook will tell you is aesthetically perfect being zhou, shou and tou, crapy, scraggy and holey). The shabbiness is reassuring. Here is Old Mr Wu's China, as neglected and out-of-place as the buildings on the Bund. It is also familiar. The air of makeshift, the smell of urine and the flies recall the rickshaw families of Park Lane. Fifty years later their descendants have seen off traditional China as firmly as they have done the foreign ratepayer.

The rickshaw man would pass up the teahouse and the garden for Chenghuang Miao, the Temple of the City God where he could meet friends and enjoy a festival. Outside the temple, flower shows were held three times a year, orchid in spring, chrysanthemum in autumn and plum blossom in winter. At Chinese New Year people gathered here in new clothes to celebrate, their debts paid off and their homes swept clean of evil spirits. In a good year, the rickshaw man might arrive in an overcoat acquired from a pawn-shop and too threadbare even for its former White Russian owner. It flapped at his wrists and hung in folds around his calves. Underneath he wore nothing but a pair of ragged shorts. In this outfit he stuffed himself with dumplings and admired fireworks with names like Lanterns of Heaven and Earth, Flower Pots, Peonies Strung on a Thread, Lotus Sprinkled with Water, Falling Moons, Grape Arbours, Double-Kicking Feet, Ten Explosions Flying to Heaven and the most terrifying of them all, Five Devils Noisily Splitting Apart.

The next day he joined the crowds thronging the alleyways and roads around Nanking Road for the New Year's Fair. It usually snowed. The better-off Chinese huddled in furs or padded robes and fur caps. The noise from the fair put the rickshaw man into tremendous spirits. Actors and female impersonators, singers, clowns, ventriloquists, conjurers and jugglers all yelled as they performed for a mile up and down the pavement. Bellowing wrestlers gripped each other, the snow melting on their bunched muscles. Two men in long blue robes with fur collars, one blowing a trumpet, led a bear on a chain through the crowds. Scenes from plays were acted out in historical dress. A gang of acrobats somersaulted each other into pyramids and towers. A man in black robe and conical hat demonstrated painless tooth extraction. Storytellers beat drums to draw an audience. Singers wailed to lutes while children watched puppet shows, the booths decorated in red for the New Year.

The rickshaw man might squat down on the pavement with friends to discuss the fair, accept compliments on his new coat and perhaps take a bet or two. He would spend any winnings on a visit to an opium den for some 'Chimeng yao', or 'eating dream medicine'.[16] Hongkew boasted dens where a few coppers bought a pipe. The rickshaw man would walk over Garden Bridge, turn into a narrow lane and stop at a small house. It was dark inside and the smell of mould, rotting wood, cooking and unwashed bodies, overpowering. The rickshaw man would feel along the slippery walls of the halls to steps that shook as he mounted. The ceiling sagged so low that he had to drop down and clamber up on all fours. At the top a strip of candlelight burnt beneath the door. The room itself was very small with damp, black walls. Three berths made of planks balanced on bamboo legs appeared the only furniture. On two of them lay men, their bodies almost skeletal through their rags. The owner was an old man who also sold heroin. He nodded at the rickshaw-puller and pointed to the third berth. The rickshaw man took off his coat, placed it carefully beneath his head then lay down. The old man inserted some tobacco into a pipe which looked

like a lady's cigarette-holder with a small bowl at the end. On top
of the tobacco he placed a pink pill which he lit before passing the
pipe to the rickshaw man. The rickshaw man took a whiff, then
another and another. His muscles relaxed. His lids half-closed. He
sighed and stretched himself, smiling up into the smoke as hunger,
debts and lack of women receded into a brief glimpse of light and
happiness.

In Shanghai, as Isherwood put it, 'If you tire of inspecting
one kind of misery there are plenty of others.'[17] The city was
the biggest centre of industry in the Far East, most of it situated in
Hongkew, Yangtzepoo and Chapei. The wretchedness of the Chinese
factory-worker was as much a Western creation as the department
stores on Nanking Road. The majority of Shanghainese spent their
days in factories of Victorian grimness and their nights in rows of
back-to-back houses more reminiscent of something out of Glasgow
or Pittsburgh than the Far East.

Only a few of these areas still exist. Most were destroyed during the bombing in 1932 and 1937. From the heights of Broadway
Mansions you can still see the occasional row here and there like
discarded snake skins.

Before the war the majority of Shanghai's population lived in
a lane, lined on both sides with houses and branching off a main
street. At night the gates leading to the main road were closed,
sometimes guarded by a Sikh. Everybody knew each other in their
lane, watched their comings and goings and heard their family
rows through the flimsy partitions in the evenings. During the
day hawkers came round, sweaty men with bare feet, their goods
slung from a bamboo pole across their shoulder. They advertised
their wares in rousing songs featuring socks, pomade, sesame oil,
bean curd and every type of food. Like New York today, snacking
had become one of the city's favourite pastimes. As one Chinese
writer recalled, 'Provided your appetite is good, you can eat
from morning till midnight.'[18] Stacked up in bamboo baskets
or sold by the bowl, lane-dwellers could choose from pungent, preserved bean curd; noodles in clear sauce; deep-fried cakes with or
without fillings, sweet or salty; dumpling soup; chicken wings and
giblets; dumplings of glutinous rice, wrapped in reed leaves; cakes
of cassia petals and sugar; gruel of lotus seeds; dumplings stuffed
with prawns and pork; bananas, mangoes, Siamese oranges, 'King'
melon seeds, candied fruit, olives and dozens more.

Blind fortune-tellers and mendicant monks also visited the lane. The same Chinese writer, on the point of composing a surrealist poem, found himself disturbed by a horrendous clatter. Rushing to his window, he saw a monk with an iron hook on his chest trailing a chain more than ten feet long. Two other monks followed, beating a drum and clashing cymbals in the hope people would pay them to go away. Life in a Shanghai lane, only forty years ago, possessed a distinctly medieval feel.

Daily entertainment did not make up for cramped living conditions. Shanghai was an overcrowded city with more people than homes. The principal tenant of a lane house subdivided each room to form what the Chinese euphemistically called 'gexiang' or 'dovecots'. He usually took half of the front downstairs room for himself, building a partition towards the back to form a second, windowless chamber. He then divided the chamber again, this time horizontally, to create two dark and airless holes each of which he rented to a family. He divided the upper rooms in similar fashion. The kitchen at the back of the house was either shared by the tenants or turned over to another family. 'The area for each family is unbelievably small',[19] wrote Eleanor Hinder, the chief of the Social and Industrial Division of the Shanghai Municipal Council.

A family had no room for furniture or possessions. Everybody slept on the floor, curled up against each other. They never knew a moment's privacy. Simon Yang and L. K. Tao, authors of a dry report on Shanghai's working class, felt moved enough to break into rhetoric:

> Under such circumstances, where is then family life, the life that has been in existence for thousands of years among all peoples even from the age of hunters? Where indeed is the privacy of life, which any person who wants to lead a decent life must have? Having drudged for more than ten hours in the day amidst noise, dirt, incessant movements and the horrible smell of humanity, where indeed will the worker retire for rest, for comfort, for the enjoyment of that aspect of life which can strictly be called his or her own?[20]

To afford a dark and damp hole, all the family had to labour twelve or fourteen hours a day in one of Shanghai's factories. In 1935 the Shanghai Municipal Council made its first attempt to analyse the numbers of people involved in the city's prosperity. Out of a total Chinese population of 1,120,860, 204,849 worked in industry and 207,455 in trade, finance and transport. Textile trades such as silk, cotton and jute-making employed 75,000.

On Nanking Road stood two of the city's leading silk shops, Lao Kai Fook and Lao Kai Chuang. They stocked in a rainbow hue of colours every type of crêpe de Chine, silk gauze, silk brocade, silk chiffon, striped silks, pongee and Shandong silks and silks interwoven with emblems like the everlasting knot, the double-cash and the lotus. The clerks wore long, grey gowns and pulled down bolt after bolt, shaking out the material in glistening piles upon the counter. They nicked the chosen piece with round-handled, Chinese scissors then ripped the material by hand. Silk for men's shirts cost as little as thirty cents a yard. Taffeta came so cheap people used it for curtains.

Cheap labour permitted this sort of extravagance. Women and children formed the majority of workers in a silk filature as the production of silk required small and nimble fingers and they could be paid lower wages than the foremen or the men in the power house. Each morning the women and children took their places opposite each other in reeling sheds lined with metal benches. For every two women, a child, some younger than seven, worked at a basin into which ran boiling water. The child put its hands into the scalding water, stirred the cocoons then passed the soaked cocoon over to another tray of boiling water in front of the women. One silk thread required the web from six cocoons. The woman worker joined the webs together and passed them through various pulleys over her head to a winding-frame or drum behind. This was driven by machinery which she stopped or started by a foot pedal. Each woman kept five sets going. Steam filled the sheds and the women dripped with perspiration. There was no artificial ventilation. A pungent stench rose from the dead cocoons on the floor. Babies lay asleep under the reeling drums behind their mothers' backs, tucked in so tightly that they could not fall or even turn themselves. Backwards and forwards walked the foreman with a stick, ready to beat a tired child or plunge its elbows into boiling water as punishment. The women worked twelve hours a day, seven days a week. Most suffered from tuberculosis while their fingers turned white with fungus growths.

Lin Lan was a silk factory worker. In 1936 she wrote:

Life is terrible and worst of all are the kids' hunger cries. We are now paid only half our wages. The other half is kept by the factory and we are forced to buy silk with it. This is a pattern since last year apparently because business isn't too good and we have to help improve sales. Yet even the complete wages are not enough to live on let alone half. What's more the factory makes a profit each year. Last year they earned several hundred thousand yuan. I tried to sell the silk to friends but they refuse it. They hardly have enough to eat so why would they buy silk? I think of the landlady's angry look as she asks for the rent, and of my family that have eaten nothing in twenty four hours. I finally manage to get $3 (paper currency) from a pawn shop for the silk. What use are $3? For rent, for heating or for rice? I feel such despair . . .[21]

Jobs like this were in great demand. The worker had to bribe the foreman for a place in the reeling shed and then to pay part of her wage each month to keep it. In these circumstances the workers found it impossible to negotiate for better conditions. Fang Gensai, who worked in a cotton factory, saw her twelve-hour shift increased to fourteen hours. She recalled the reaction when the boss announced the shift had to last sixteen hours.

Everyone was furious. The boss's excuse was that he had no alternative. Hadn't we heard rumours that the factory might have to close? We should willingly increase our working hours for the sake of China's anti-Japanese movement. Surely we wanted Chinese factories to do well and Japanese factories to do badly? Didn't we hate the Japanese? Of course we workers were not convinced by these arguments. We protested but what could we do? The sixteen hour day was implemented.[22]

Even with women and children working, a family never seemed to have enough to eat while what they did consume lacked nutritional value. Half the family income went on food and most of that on white rice. After 1936 prices rose swiftly. Families survived 'by moving the debts',[23] explained one Chinese. The worker found himself forced to take on short-term loans at high interest rates. One man borrowed eight times in three years from a Sikh, a friend, a widow, a liftman, a fellow worker and two chauffeurs. For a loan of $30 from the widow he had to pay back $2 interest per month. The loan had already lasted two years.

At least factory workers were paid. The majority of labourers in Shanghai's workshops received no salary if recruited as apprentices. A man from the city toured the villages in the surrounding country-side. He collected children, promising the parents he would teach the lads a trade and watch over their progress. Once in Shanghai, he peddled the children from workshop to workshop until he found a buyer. A small boy cost SH$5.

Zhu Yinglin came to Shanghai from Ningbo at the age of sixteen and spent three years as a tailor's apprentice. Now old and hunched, his bald head speckled with grave spots, he sits at the entrance of a small lane off the former Bubbling Well Road with his equally ancient sewing machine set up in front of him. He still enjoys working and did not stop while he talked, except occasionally to scratch his head with a needle. He admitted that he had had an easy time compared to most. He lived and worked in a two-storey lane house. The workshop on the ground floor doubled as a bedroom for Zhu and the other assistants. The room above, reached by a shaky, narrow staircase provided a home for the tailor and his family. The front door opened on to the street. During winter, Zhu recalled, it was as cold inside the house as out.

For his board and lodging, Zhu worked from early morning till late at night, baby-sitting, washing nappies, delivering garments, and doing other household chores. He cooked on an old-fashioned coal stove in a corner of the downstairs room then waited on his master and his assistants while they ate. Breakfast and supper consisted of rice gruel with a few pieces of pickled cabbage. For lunch, a 'fairly elaborate' meal according to Zhu, they took rice, one meat dish, two vegetarian dishes and a soup. At night he slept in the shop on an improvised bed of two narrow boards supported by benches. After completing his apprenticeship, he stayed on for two more years, 'as was the custom'. His master paid him two silver dollars a month the first year and three dollars, the second. This was 'an allowance rather than a wage'. After that he set up on his own.

Shanghai's wealth depended on its numerous, small workshops. They explain the city's economic resilience. During a period of unrest, the owner simply rented a lane house elsewhere in the city and started up again. Shanghai lacked any kind of zoning regulation. The owner of a lane house could convert it how he wished. Buffing and polishing of chromium plates, for example, went on in the front room with the chromium vats installed in the kitchen.

The country child sold to a chromium-plating workshop experienced a more typical existence than Zhu. The front room contained six to eight wheels. The older apprentices worked nearest to the doorway and closer to the light and air. They sent the new arrival to the back of the room where he was soon barely visible in the cloud of dust. The machine shaft, attached as it was to a wooden ceiling, set up a vibration which kept the dust in continuous motion. The new apprentice breathed in metal dust and chemical fumes by day and by night when he unrolled his bedding and curled up beneath the machinery. Nearly all the boys suffered from nasal, respiratory and lung complaints.

The plight of the apprentices shocked one American visitor who had spent fifteen years as a famine-relief worker in Shandong and a social-service worker in Beijing. The starving in Shandong, although 'dying by inches',[24] at least had light and fresh air. Above all they were free. The apprentices enjoyed a status indistinguishable 'from the most repellent kind of slavery'.[25] The children looked underfed. Some rolled up their sleeves to display thin arms covered in sores. Many complained of injuries. They worked machines without safety guards in cramped, dark rooms. Accidents happened daily. None recalled going to hospital or even receiving first-aid treatment. The owner shrugged when questioned, remarking that there were 'plenty more'[26] recruits if the child died.

The boys' determination to acquire an education touched the American. In one factory they showed him a cubby hole which they had built themselves in order to have somewhere to prepare their lessons for night-school. They attended school after a 10–12-hour day. Many fell asleep over their lessons.

A constant flow of foreign visitors appears to have been the workers' one diversion. Even Christopher Isherwood and W. H. Auden, surely the most unlikely characters to find in an accumulator factory, noted: 'Half the children have already the blue line in their gums which is a symptom of lead-poisoning. Few of them will survive longer than a year or eighteen months. In scissors factories you can see arms and legs developing chromium holes.'[27]

Their guide was Mr Rewi Alley, a stocky New Zealander with light-cropped ginger hair and a short, rugged nose. A factory inspector with the Municipal Council Fire Brigade, he was also a Marxist and in radio contact from 1934 with the Red Army from his home in the International Settlement. It was he who arranged for Edgar Snow to interview Mao Zedong. Rewi's parents had named him after a Maori chief, Rewi Te Manipoto who had defied the British during the Maori wars, declaring, 'We will fight on for ever and ever.' It proved singularly appropriate as his namesake's motto. After receiving an award for gallantry in the First World War, Rewi Alley returned to New Zealand, tried sheep farming, grew bored and set out for China. He arrived in Shanghai in the spring of 1927 to witness Chiang Kai-shek's slaughter of the communists. He recalled, 'I saw five lads being carried naked and hanging from poles. Right in front of me they were dumped on the ground and an officer got down from a horse and pumped a bullet into the head of each of them. Next day I read in the papers that they were young "agitators", trying to organize a trade union among the silk filature workers.'[28]

Rewi Alley had found a cause and a job. He taught himself Mandarin, studied Marx and became one of the Municipal Council's more unusual employees. He enjoyed limited powers. Chinese and foreign factory-owners resented interference. An attempt in 1925 by the Council to pass a bylaw forbidding children under ten from working failed twice for lack of a quorum. Factory owners viewed with similar suspicion a series of labour laws passed by the Nationalist government between 1927 and 1932. The Japanese members of the Municipal Council summed up the general attitude when they declared the 'real purpose' of the new laws was 'to encroach upon extraterritorial rights through enforcement of this inspection'.[29]

In 1933 the Municipal government managed to give itself the constitutional right to license factories. Inspectors like Rewi Alley could at least insist on certain conditions. Insistence often proved their only weapon. Force of character, respect and repeated visits, exploiting, as one newspaper put it, 'something of a "nuisance value" ' had to make up for the fact that Chinese courts refused to convict Chinese factory-owners. Rewi Alley took the owner of one cotton mill to court three times without success. The man always managed 'to square' the judge.[30]

Rewi Alley's many tours brought before him 'Tragedy, day after day, and most of it easily avoidable. It would be better to have no industry than to compete in this way – bring children into the cities, starving them, working them longer hours than any horse could stand.' His efforts to improve conditions came to a full stop in 1937 when the Japanese destroyed Chapei for the second time. Inflation was out of control, business disrupted and, in the disintegration of the city, no one worried if hundreds of child workers went blind each year from a diet of steamed bread and salted turnips when one egg a week would have saved their sight.

The rickshaw man, the woman in the silk mill and the enslaved apprentice found Shanghai a desperate and indifferent place. Individually they could die on the street without a single passer-by breaking step. In numbers they inspired the cultural and political ferment that overtook Shanghai during the pre-war period.

The Iron House

Shanghai's brief pre-eminence in Chinese history began in the spring of 1926 when fifty university professors left their jobs in Beijing and came to the city, after warlords took over the capital and snuffed out its brief renaissance. Other academics and writers soon joined them. Over the next ten years Shanghai was the cultural centre of China.

Beijing's renaissance dated from May 4th, 1919. For four hours that afternoon three thousand students from the colleges and universities of Beijing demanded Shandong, awarded to the Japanese by the Treaty of Versailles, be returned to China. The protest spread all over the country. In Shanghai over 50,000 workers went on strike. Three months later, the protest had turned into a national debate on education, labour organization and the role of art and the intellectual. The Chinese wanted their culture to broaden its base and be of service to the country. They opened hundreds of new schools and founded numerous magazines. They published books in the vernacular rather than Classical Chinese. Literature was no longer the exclusive property of scholars. Any literate person could read the new magazines or write for them. Foreign works were translated in large numbers. A new form of theatre, called 'Spoken Drama', based on Western theatrical tradition with social reform as its subject, became popular. Film studios were set up and even women writers taken seriously. This tremendous interest in new ideas became known as the May 4th Movement. What had begun with a demonstration against the West had turned into a revolution to reform China along Western lines.

In this atmosphere, Shanghai, the most Western city in China, offered a break with the past and a vision of the future. Its foreign universities, libraries and the occasional visiting philosopher inspired the Chinese to democratize society, liberate women and replace, as one Chinese magazine put it, 'superstition and fantasy'[31] with science and philosophy. Its major publishing houses, numerous newspapers and periodicals all produced forums for intellectual debate. Censorship was less stringent in the foreign Concessions than elsewhere in China (the Ratepayers Association refused in six consecutive years from 1920 to 1925 to approve the Printed Matter Byelaws put forward by the Municipal Council to restrict the press). Extraterritoriality provided security from warlords, and Shanghai's Chinese businessmen, made rich from the boom after the First World War, eagerly invested in a new journal or film studio. The artist and the businessman shared the same aim; how to reach the greatest number of people, how to interest Shanghai's rickshaw men and factory workers. The lively, popular and original work which resulted was unlike anything that has appeared before or since in China. Old Mr Wu would not have approved.

It lasted just as long as Shanghai remained an international city. In 1949, thirty years after the students marched so enthusiastically through Beijing, a strong government once again took control of intellectual and artistic output. The artist found he had merely exchanged the lap of the Confucian scholar for that of the Communist party. Shanghai represented a brief run off the lead.

Artistic life in the city was, as a Shanghainese might have said, a real chow-chow. Like Nanking Road, it encompassed everything. Tsai Chin, the star of *The World of Suzie Wong* and the daughter of one of Shanghai's most famous classical actors, explained to me the incestuous relationship between business, politics and culture. Everyone appeared to know one another, attend the same parties and even sleep together. Gangsters ran the theatres, scholars fell in love with tarts, communists wrote best-selling movies and actresses turned into political leaders. She affirmed: 'It meant we had real gossip in Shanghai, not this silly, modern stuff but really, bad gossip. We believed everything because, in Shanghai, anything was possible.'

Chinese artists and students with their wild, often bizarre experiments, their originality, their political arguments and their courage epitomized something of Shanghai itself between the two world wars. On any tour of the city, they were impossible to miss. They filled tea-houses and coffee shops along North Szechuen Road with noisy debates on the latest literary magazine or the possibility of romantic love. They attended progressive plays at the Golden Theatre and raved over Ibsen's *Doll's House*, starring the future Madam Mao Zedong as Nora. They joined political rallies at the Shanghai College notorious for its communist students and professors. The better-connected took tea with Song Qingling, widow of Sun Yat-sen, in her house in the French Concession and strolled in her garden which appeared transported from an English suburb. The more daring marched in demonstrations alongside Agnes Smedley, an

American columnist, and were hit over the head by Sikh policemen.

Others visited the handsome poet and publisher, Zao Xinmei, at the flat of his American mistress on Kiangse Road, bizarrely decorated with metal bamboo trees and a ceiling spotted with stars. At evening classes in the YMCA building opposite the racecourse, the more committed taught factory workers. Film studios expected them to gatecrash parties for their latest star (sometimes left-wing herself). Even in the Russian restaurants on Avenue Joffre you would have found them taking advantage of the twenty-cent menu of soup, a main dish and all the tea they could drink. They infested the dark, steamy nightclub on the fourth floor of the Sincere Department Store (not the top floor which belonged to the prostitutes); and danced in the dives along Bubbling Well Road where the taxi girls sat in rows around the room and charged one yuan for three dances. They lectured the prettier taxi girls (they always occupied the back row) into the small hours on women's rights, finishing with the inevitable invitation of 'free' love. As dawn broke they handed out leaflets to factory workers stumbling to the morning shift.

On any tour of the city's artistic world, you bump into politics. The two were inextricably linked. The May 4th Movement had declared Art could not exist in a vacuum. It had to raise the people's consciousness and usher in a better era. The work of Shanghai's artists is characterized by doing just that. The struggle of China to assert itself and the violent changes in Chinese society offered novel and dramatic material. Sympathy for the suffering of the ordinary Chinese cast the best work, whether woodcuts, short stories or films, in a left-wing mould. The result transformed the artist from bystander to victim. The Nationalist party brooked no criticism however well expressed.

The early 1930s saw the emergence in China of a central government under the leadership of Chiang Kai-shek. This had immediate consequences for Shanghai. In October 1928 he had been appointed chairman of the National government at Nanjing. His marriage in Shanghai the previous year to Song Meiling had extended his influence through her family to American and Chinese business establishments and had given his regime international respectability. He also had powerful connections in Shanghai's underworld through his membership of the Green Gang. In the 1930s he had consolidated his power over the country and his party. His élite paramilitary organization known as the Blue Shirts worked with the government's Secret Police to neutralize any opposition.

When Greater Shanghai fell to the Nationalist government in 1927, left-wing artists and intellectuals moved hastily into the French Concession or the International Settlement. There they hoped to find security and freedom from censorship absent in the rest of China. The Chinese authorities enlisted the help of Du Yuesheng to extradite the more troublesome. His gangsters snatched the suspect, bundled him or her into a car and drove them to the nearest district under Chinese control where they might be tortured, force-fed their own faeces for example, or shot. The severed heads of journalists turned up regularly in the city's gutters. It was against this background that Shanghai's artists produced some of their best work.

One afternoon in September 1930, Agnes Smedley, the American activist, was standing guard outside the Holland, a small, Dutch restaurant in the French Concession. Agnes had arrived in Shanghai the year before as correspondent for the *Frankfurter Zeitung*. A stocky woman with cropped hair and a passionate if indiscriminate hatred of every form of injustice, she had grown up in a Colorado mining town. Her aunt was a prostitute and her father died of drink. She marched in Shanghai demonstrations, had a tumultuous love life which included an Indian anarchist, and was listed by Special Branch in May 1933 as a suspected Soviet agent. (Special Branch believed her to be 'well paid for her support of the Communist cause'.)[32] Now she and two Chinese friends watched the street. Another Chinese lolled inconspicuously at a bus stop. A fourth slouched on a step across the road. All sweated with anxiety. They had been invited to Shanghai's most dangerous birthday party. Lu Xun, China's foremost modern writer, was fifty. His friends were holding a reception and dinner to celebrate. A hundred of Shanghai's left-wing intellectuals had received invitations by word of mouth. Agnes was on the look-out for the French police or a carload of Du's gangsters.

Shanghai's intellectuals would only have taken the risk for Lu Xun. Famous for his terse prose and for the sardonic humour of work like *The True Story of Ah Q.*, Lu Xun was also admired for his determination to criticize society despite the danger to himself. A great survivor but not a man to compromise, he wrote for the individual in a decade of extreme political groups. How to live with integrity in a time fit only for madmen or butchers was his concern. In his youth he had the more optimistic intention of raising the Chinese spirit from a state of lethargy and backwardness. As he believed in 1905, 'that literature was the best means to this end, I was determined to promote a literary movement'.[33] Success made him reconsider. On March 18th, 1926, in Peking, where Lu Xun worked as a professor of literature at the university, the troops of the local warlord killed forty-seven students during a peaceful demonstration. Two of the students studied under Lu Xun. The news of their death devastated him. Some years earlier he had written to one of the editors of the *New Youth* magazine,

> Imagine an iron house having not a single window and virtually indestructible, with all its inmates sound asleep and about to die of suffocation. Dying in their sleep, they won't feel the pain of death. Now if you raise a shout to wake a few of the lighter sleepers, making these unfortunate few suffer the agony of irrevocable death, do you really think you are doing them a good turn?[34]

He continued to raise the shout but with ever increasing despair. His work is the record of an honest and perceptive man locked up in the iron house of China's revolution.

He makes a good guide. He takes no sides and always has something original to say. He gives an unusual view of the preoccupations of Shanghai's artists, their ambiguous relationship with the Chinese Revolution, Western culture and the Japanese. The danger threatening him illustrates the violence overtaking Shanghai. He never tested the new order after 1949 for he died in the city on October 19th, 1936.

Lu Xun arrived early to his birthday party with his wife, Xu Guangping, carrying their small son in her arms. It was Agnes Smedley's first meeting with the man who became 'one of the most influential factors'[35] during her years in China. She recalled, 'He was short and frail, and wore a cream-coloured silk gown and soft Chinese shoes. He was bareheaded and his close-cropped hair stood up like a brush. In structure his face was like that of an average Chinese, yet it remains in my memory as the most eloquent face I have ever seen.'[36] He spoke no English so he and Agnes conversed in German. A woman of passionate likes and dislikes, Agnes immediately warmed to Lu Xun, declaring, 'His manner, his speech, and his every gesture radiated the indefinable harmony and charm of a perfectly integrated personality. I suddenly felt as awkward and ungracious as a clod.'[37]

Lu Xun moved off and Agnes turned her attention to the other guests. She found herself witnessing one of Shanghai's largest cultural gatherings, 'pioneers' as she put it 'in an intellectual revolution'.[38] Artists, professors, students, actors, reporters, scholars and even two Chinese aristocrats had come to honour Lu Xun. She declared it a 'motley' crowd and fairly representative of Shanghai. The attempt of one group of actors to put on social dramas to rival the more popular works of *Salome* and *Lady Windermere's Fan*, had apparently met with scant success for they looked 'poorly dressed' and 'half-starved'.[39] The students of Fudan University had fared better under Professor Hong Sheng, a director of a Chinese film company. Their productions of Ibsen and even some of the professor's own work obviously earned them at least enough to eat. Another group of left-wing actors, writers and translators gathered round Agnes and proudly described the police raid on their production of *Carmen*. The Chinese authorities had taken exception to the last scene where Carmen hurls her ring at her cast-off lover. They saw it as a political comment on the split between the communists and the Guomindang three years before. Agnes found this absurd but typical of the behaviour of the Nationalist government in Shanghai at that period.

Agnes's attention was next caught by a tall thin student, walking rapidly, all the time glancing behind him. Her friends whispered that he was the editor of the *Shanghaibao*, an underground communist paper 'which conducted a kind of journalistic guerrilla warfare in the city'.[40] He was followed by a man in a crumpled, foreign suit with long, wild hair. Imprisoned for representing the Chinese Red Aid, his family had bribed the authorities to release him. In the midst of all this excitement, Agnes found herself turning to gaze at Lu Xun, her eye drawn to his hand held up in some gesture. As it grew dark, half the guests left and Agnes was relieved of sentry duty. She went inside for dinner.

After dinner came the speeches. The atmosphere grew tense. The Dutch restaurant owner did not understand Chinese but the Chinese waiters listened in earnest. When the man with the dishevelled hair made a report on prison conditions, Agnes watched the waiters carefully in case one left to inform the authorities. The editor of the *Shanghaibao* described the rise of the Red Army and the peasant rebellions. Then a small, sturdy woman with bobbed hair talked on the need to develop proletarian literature. She ended with an appeal to Lu Xun to become the protector and 'master' of the League of Left Writers and League of Left Artists.

Lu Xun gave his attention promptly to each new speaker, 'his forefinger all the while tracing the edge of his teacup'.[41] When they finished, he stood up and in a quiet voice began to tell the history of 'the half-century of intellectual turmoil which had been his life – the story of China uprooted'.[42]

Lu Xun's background was typical of many Chinese who had come to Shanghai. Like a number of businessmen, film directors, writers and even the future communist leader, Zhou Enlai, he grew up in a small town, the son of a once-wealthy family now impoverished, in Lu Xun's case, by his father's opium addiction. The revolution of 1911 barely touched his town. Within ten days the new administration had exchanged their cotton clothes for fur-lined gowns, 'although it was not yet cold'.[43] Power continued to reside with the gentry, the class to which Lu Xun belonged and which he hated. It is not surprising that he, like many others, chose to live in a city that had proved so inimical to the Old Mr Wus of China.

He had been educated in the traditional Chinese classics then became interested in Western culture. Too poor to attend university in Europe or America he went, again like many of his class and generation, to Japan, then enthusiastic for all things Western and sympathetic to the Chinese nationalist movement. Apart from studying medicine, Lu Xun read the Japanese translations of Tolstoy who, he explained to his audience, introduced him 'to social thought and to the power of modern literature'.[44] Later he learnt German and Russian and translated a number of Russian novels and essays. He wished to lay before Chinese youth the best of modern social literature. He had also begun to collect Western classical and modern paintings as well as examples of the graphic arts. Now he was being asked to lead a movement of proletarian literature.

Here Lu Xun's audience must have stirred excitedly. The idea obsessed Shanghai's left-wing writers. They had watched the workers' strikes halt the city in 1925. They could not resist the chance to influence this force. Lu Xun was more clear-sighted. He thought it 'childish'[45] to pretend that he could ever be a proletarian writer. 'His roots were in the village, in peasant and scholarly life. Nor did he believe that Chinese intellectual youth, with no experience of the life, hopes, and sufferings of workers and peasants, could – as yet – produce proletarian literature. Creative writing must spring from experience, not theory.'[46] For the moment, the life of the factory worker lay beyond experience.

His speech failed to impress the radicals in the audience. One young man bent towards Agnes, shook his head and said, 'Disappointing, wasn't it? I mean Lu Xun's attitude towards proletarian literature. It discourages youth.'[47] Agnes, who had a 'lifelong hostility to professional intellectuals', snapped back that she agreed 'entirely'[48] with Lu Xun. So ended the birthday party.

Left-wing writers, like Agnes Smedley's neighbour, believed Lu Xun had forsaken the revolution when in fact he was struggling to define it. 'Revolution is a bitter thing, mixed with filth and blood, not so lovely or perfect as the poets think,' he said, in front of a group of them. 'Romantic dreams' bred disillusion, 'when a revolution is actually carried out'.[49] Such romantic dreams filled the heads of Shanghai's left-wing writers. Within the safety of the International Settlement they could muse on the masses without actually meeting any. They misjudged Shanghai's relevance in the coming revolution. The factory worker might shape China's present but it was the peasant who would dictate the country's future. Few writers ever exchanged the comfort of a Shanghai coffee shop for the communist commune on Jiangxi's wild and mountainous border. Like Shanghai itself, they became, in the end, extraneous to events after 1949.

Their desire to write for the proletariat proved another illusion. The factory worker lacked both leisure and money to read. Out of an annual income of $SH353.29, the average working-class family spent just SH$0.77 on books and stationery. The difficulty of the written language made it almost impossible for an uneducated person to appreciate revolutionary literature or to express themselves 'freely', as Lu Xun pointed out, after even 'ten years of study'.[50] Literature remained a middle-class weapon, written and read by the middle classes. Lu Xun believed the best a middle-class writer might 'hope for', was to achieve works of 'revolt' or 'exposure' of the 'dying class' to which he or she belonged. A 'deep understanding of and hatred for it' would allow the writer to deal 'a most powerful, mortal blow'.[51]

Lu Xun's work was a series of such blows. His artistic progress reveals his efforts to ensure the blows hit home. From 1926 he stopped writing short stories to concentrate on the essay, a form new to Chinese literature. It suited the task he had set himself, to comment, as he put it 'on current events' and lash out 'at chronic maladies by dissecting typical cases'. To Lu Xun good writing made a political statement in itself, for to write well is to write clearly without any chance of misunderstanding. Lu Xun had come to see the short story as a fiction to hide behind. He wanted his pieces to attack. His language is concise and forceful. The essays are tightly constructed beneath a deceptively discursive style, the arguments reinforced with metaphors drawn from Shanghai street life. Lu Xun compared a literary group in the city to the 'blinking dummy which serves merely as an advertisement in an oculist's window'.[52] While he scathingly dismissed the new Nationalist government as being like the worker who saves money, starts a small factory and then treats his workers worse than anyone else. In Lu Xun's last years he exchanged literature for the wood block print as the best medium for reaching the greatest number of people. He financed exhibitions and workshops for young artists.

The strength of his writing and the clarity of his mind set him apart from any literary or political group. It is ironic that the Chinese communists now lionize his memory. He hated Guomindang corruption but never joined the Communist party and quarrelled with the communist literary commissars. If he had lived, I doubt he would have survived Mao Zedong's purges of artists and intellectuals in the 1950s let alone been rewarded with a Memorial Museum in Hongkew Park. By 1927, the International Settlement was the only place left in China where he could publish his work.

Lu Xun's arrival in Shanghai coincided with a period of personal happiness. He had just married Xu Guangping, a former student. A year after they moved to the city, their son was born. They called him Haiying or Child of Shanghai.

Before they came to Shanghai, the couple had led a haphazard, often dangerous, existence. One friend recalled that Lu Xun kept only a bed, a bamboo basket, a chest and a desk in his room. If he had to leave quickly all he had to do was pick up his bed-roll and either the bamboo basket or the chest. In Shanghai his life took a respectable turn. He and his young wife found themselves living in a lane of houses built by a banker for his clerical staff. You can still visit it today.

The row of three-storey, red-brick buildings, each with its own front-yard, lies off Shanyin Road in Hongkew. In this typical home of a middle-class Shanghainese, Lu Xun lived from 1933 until his death three years later. An old lady twitched at a curtain and peered down at me as I passed. Other old people, seated on child-size cane chairs, gossiped in the spring sunshine, their birdcages by their side. The lane appeared clean and peaceful and quite unlike Lu Xun's re-collection of 'buckets of night-soil, portable kitchens, flies swarming in all directions and children milling around'.[53]

Lu Xun's house stands towards the end of the row, its exterior reminiscent of a London suburb. Inside, the prim, nothing-to-hide expression of red brick gives way to an air of secrecy. I found myself stepping into an Oriental home where family and servants relied on their own society and rarely invited outsiders. The front room of Lu Xun's house felt cold and lifeless. The furniture was Western except for a square table made of rosewood. A window at the back looked out on to a similar lane of houses. Upstairs the atmosphere lightened. The small, rear room overspilled with leather trunks, picture frames and Lu Xun's medicine chest. The front room served as both his bedroom and study.

The room is remarkable for its sense of peace. The pink and green panes of glass set in the window filter the light and form a barrier against the outside world. I understood now why the street vendors, singing their wares up and down the lane, made such an impression on Lu Xun. Only sound is capable of piercing its serenity. Against one wall stands Lu Xun's four-poster bed, a contradictory piece of furniture, as contradictory as Lu Xun himself and with most of his characteristics. Made of iron but light and elegant in design, it epitomizes a style which, as my guide informed me sadly, 'did not last long in China'. From the posts hung a white canopy edged in blue and embroidered by his wife with wistaria and roses. Next to the bed an old-fashioned alarm clock, ghoulishly set at the moment of Lu Xun's death, only adds to the air of fragile happiness.

Lu Xun often received visitors. He was fond of young people, admitting in a letter to his wife that he spent 'a lot of time' doing 'odds and ends'[54] for them. Rou Shi, a left-wing writer murdered by the Guomindang, wrote in his diary, 'There were often times when I felt extremely disturbed, without knowing why', but after a meal listening to Lu Xun's mocking humour, 'I would calm down a great deal'.[55] Lu Xun smoked as he talked until the room reeked with tobacco. Then he would smile, stand up and open the window to clear the air. After his visitors left he returned to his desk. He preferred to write an essay in one sitting which meant working through the night. Sometimes he took a nap with his clothes on before starting. At dawn he helped himself to a cup of green tea from a pot still warm beneath the tea cosy embroidered by his wife with grapes and leaves. Then he ate some breakfast and went to sleep.

Lu Xun's house revealed a surprising contradiction. During the period that he lived off Shanyin Road, the ordinary Chinese feared and detested Japan. The Japanese had annexed Manchuria and, just the year before, invaded Shanghai and laid Chapei to waste. At the same time as the Shanghainese boycotted Japanese goods, Lu Xun, China's great patriotic writer, lived in a house replete with Japanese paraphernalia. A Japanese doll in a glass case stood on top of the dresser in the dining-room. A Japanese–English dictionary lay on Lu Xun's desk. In his son's bedroom hung a painting of an acrobat bought by Lu Xun to help the Japanese artist who was dying of hunger. Even the cutlery came from Japan.

The answer lay around the corner at Uchiyama's bookshop on North Szechuen Road. Lu Xun walked there at least once a day, turning right at the end of his row, past 'The Continental Terrace', its name, carved in stone over the entrance to the lane, and down Shanyin Road to its junction with North Szechuen Road. Now Chinese live in 'The Continental Terrace' and the only foreigner in sight was myself. Plane trees lined the road. Between each tree hung a washing line, with pink and red eiderdowns, blue cotton trousers and nappies drying in the breeze. A woman arranged her husband's shirt, nipping the material with careful, proud fingers on to a hanger. She looked up at me and smiled. Above my head wooden balconies sagged with their load of pigeon coops and pots of dead plants. A queue of people waited patiently outside a rice store famous for its quality. In the butcher's, carcasses of meat lay piled on the floor. Fifty years ago, Lu Xun would have paused to buy dumplings for his wife from the vendor on the corner, being careful to avoid West-erners who 'do not use their hands, but stride forward on long legs as if there were no one there; and unless you step out of the way, they will trample on your stomach or your shoulders'.[56] The street vendor is no more and I was quick to step into the gutter when four Chinese students pushed past me.

On the curve of the junction stood Uchiyama's bookshop, now the Shanghai branch of the China Commerce Bank. A plaque put up by the owner's brother commemorates the spot. Before the war it was a meeting place for Shanghai's intellectuals. They came here to buy the latest translations, exchange gossip or hide from the Guomindang in the room at the back which now displayed only ledgers and bamboo baskets of dumplings for the tellers' lunch. Mainly, they came to see Kanzo Uchiyama, the Japanese owner and Lu Xun's friend.

I had asked the Chinese authorities if I might meet someone who had known Lu Xun. I expected an interview of platitudes. The communists have eulogized Lu Xun and overlooked his virtues. To my surprise they introduced me to Mr Wang Baolian, a tiny Chinese with thick eyebrows and a large, humorous face. He was neither a revolutionary nor an intellectual but something far better, the Uchiyama bookstore clerk and eager to talk of the past.

He told me that Mr Uchiyama was a wonderful man. 'I started working there in 1921 when I was fourteen and stayed until his death in 1945 so I should know!' His uncle, a friend of Mr Uchiyama, secured him the job after the death of his parents. In Mr Uchiyama, Wang found a second father. 'When I was sick, he paid for me to stay in hospital for three months!' Mr Uchiyama never fired his staff and extended credit to everybody, especially the students. Wang shook his head. It was his job to collect money at the end of the month and he recalled a stack of unpaid accounts.

Mr Uchiyama was born in Okayama in 1885. At the age of twenty-seven he converted to Christianity. He left for China the following year as a public-relations man for a Japanese eyewash company called Santen Do. He did not think much of the Chinese, remarking with double-edged humility, 'For somebody like me who is less than average, China is the only country where I can succeed.'[57] His job took him all over the country and he saw for himself why the Chinese hated Japan and decided to do something about it, even if only on a small scale. He opened a bookshop in the front of his house and stocked it with one hundred books on Christianity. In his absence, his wife ran the shop with the help of Wang. It soon became famous among Chinese students. In 1924 he expanded, bought the building on North Szechuen Road then gave up his job to work full time selling books.

Ding Jingtang, director and editor-in-chief of Shanghai Literary and Art Publishing House, explained to me the importance of Uchiyama's bookshop in Shanghai's intellectual life. Japan was the centre for progressive thought in the Far East during the 'twenties. Until 1933, the Japanese treated their left-wing writers far more leniently than the Chinese authorities did. The Japanese read and translated Western authors forbidden in China. Marx and Lenin, for example, were translated from the Japanese into Chinese and so the Chinese characters for communism, 'gongchan' (gongchan means literally 'share property'), are derived from the Japanese. Mr Uchiyama sold more books on Marxism, literature and medicine than on any other subject. At that period, many bookshop owners acted as publishers and Kanzo Uchiyama was famous for publishing left-wing works.

Wang recalled how Mrs Uchiyama practised what her husband printed. Every morning she made tea for the rickshaw-pullers – 'up to ten bags a day' – which she left outside for them to help themselves free of charge. Wang explained, 'She felt her fortune was good and that she should share it.'

In the same year that Kanzo Uchiyama exchanged eyewash for literature, he received a visitor. Wang continued, 'One morning at the beginning of October, 1927 there was a knock on the door and in came a sloppy, long-haired Chinese, unshaven and wearing straw shoes. We thought he was a beggar.' The man walked around the store for about an hour, smoking all the time and looking at everything. Finally he came to the counter with books on literature, economics and Marxism worth SH$50. Wang went on, 'We were amazed. We had never taken such a big order in our lives and from such a scruffy individual!'

I like to think that Lu Xun deliberately tested Mr Uchiyama's reaction in a city obsessed with style and consequence. He once wrote:

> If your clothes are old, bus-conductors may not stop when you ask them, park attendants may inspect your tickets with special care, and the gate-keepers of big houses or hotels may not admit you by the main door. That is why some men do not mind living in pokey lodgings infested by bedbugs, but insist on pressing their trousers under the pillow each night so that the creases are sharp the next day.[58]

Mr Uchiyama must have risen to the occasion for after a few weeks Lu Xun returned, this time well-groomed and spent SH$30. He chatted to Mr Uchiyama for about an hour. Wang recalled, 'We were all quite impressed when we learnt who he was.'

Akira Okada, the Japanese student attending the Tung Wen

college, often visited Uchiyama's bookshop at this period. He told me it was a very small shop. The writer with his luxuriant moustache and the bald-headed owner sat in one corner sipping Japanese green tea. Okada recalled Mr Uchiyama's kindness, 'even though we were just boys'. They were allowed to drink as much tea as they wanted. He was equally impressed by Mr Uchiyama's frankness. He spoke his mind on all subjects. Okada explained, 'It is not the Japanese custom and especially not in those dangerous times.' He added that they both looked very poor gentlemen.

The bookshop owner became Lu Xun's close friend and confidant. He also acted as the writer's agent. When Lu Xun went into hiding, Mr Uchiyama collected money owed to Lu Xun and held it for him. During the hostilities of 1932 Lu Xun found himself caught between the Japanese and Chinese armies with bullets flying through the walls of his home. As Japanese soldiers posed a threat to any Chinese civilian, Mr Uchiyama hid Lu Xun in the back room of his shop which few people knew existed. Lu Xun slept on the floor.

Lu Xun was also forced to dodge the Nationalists when Chiang Kai-shek began a campaign against left-wing writers. The Chinese authorities first smashed the windows of Chinese bookshops in the Settlements who stocked these writers. Lu Xun noted, 'The vulnerability of these expensive window-panes made the managers most distressed.'[59] A few days later writers visited the managers and offered for publication stories eulogizing Chiang Kai-shek and the Nationalist party. The managers bought the manuscripts, 'for they cost no more than a window-pane and would avert another stoning as well as the trouble of repairing the windows'.[60] The Central Propaganda Committee now drew up a list of 149 forbidden books including Gorky, Upton Sinclair, Maeterlinck, Sologub and Strindberg. A committee composed of writers censored all new work, 'saving many "men of letters" from unemployment',[61] pointed out Lu Xun. He continued, 'These men are thoroughly familiar with the world of letters, less muddle-headed than mere bureaucrats, better able to understand the implications of any satirical thrust or ironic remark. In any case, polishing is less difficult for a writer than creative work, and we hear the results are excellent.'[62]

As a foreigner in the International Settlement, Mr Uchiyama escaped broken windows and continued to stock books banned elsewhere in the city. He took the precaution, however, of keeping literature on the Russian Revolution upstairs and only handing it out to students he had previously vetted. Wang recalled visits from countless Guomindang spies posing as students. Wang said it was easy to spot a spy. Students wore pins denoting the associations to which they belonged. Spies always appeared too old and well dressed. They came into the shop and just stood around. Wang described one occasion. 'I said, "What do you want to buy?" "Just looking," they said. "You have been looking for two hours," I said. I opened a Japanese book and pushed it under their noses. "Here read this to me!" but of course they couldn't. They just stared stupidly at the Japanese and shuffled about. Finally they left to wait outside by the tram station before coming back again. They wanted to see who were our customers.' Mr Uchiyama told them to get lost. 'I'm a simple businessman not a writer,' he would say. He knew they could not arrest him. As for Wang, 'They couldn't do anything unless I stepped out of the Settlement which I was not going to do in a hurry.' He recalled the head of the Blue Shirts (Guomindang equivalent of Mussolini's Blackshirts), 'a terrible man' who had people picked up and spirited away. 'But no one could interfere with us because we were under the protection of the bookshop.'

The Nationalists' campaign moved from the bookshops to the writers themselves. Lu Xun's pupil Rou Shi, a gentle, eager-faced young man, was attending communist meetings on the third floor of a large house in the French Concession. On the ground floor the members played gramophone records and held mahjong parties to distract the attention of the authorities. On January 17th, 1931 Rou Shi received instructions to attend a less luxurious gathering in the Eastern Hotel on Avenue Edward VII. Someone tipped off the International Police (the gossip at the time blamed another faction in the Communist party). The police raided, arrested twenty-nine men and seven women and handed them over to the Guomindang forces. On February 7th, 1931, a firing squad executed Rou Shi and four other young writers along with a number of communists at Longhua, the city's traditional execution site on the outskirts of Shanghai.

Kanzo Uchiyama heard the news first and hurried to tell Lu Xun who immediately ordered his wife to pack some things as he went through his correspondence, burning everything incriminating. The bookshop owner advised Lu Xun to hide with his family in the Flower Garden, a Japanese hotel.

As the family prepared to depart, Agnes Smedley turned up on the doorstep. She found Lu Xun in his study, unshaven, his hair dishevelled and his eyes 'gleaming with fever'.[63] He handed her an article he had written and asked her to have it translated and published abroad. She warned him that he would be killed if it was published. ' "Does it matter?" he answered hotly. "Someone must speak!" '[64]

It is worth quoting in full.

> In China in the past a prisoner condemned to death was usually led through the busy thoroughfare, where he was permitted to shout Yuanwang, to protest his innocence, abuse the judge, relate his own brave deeds, and show he had no fear of death. At the moment of execution bystanders would applaud, and the news of his courage would spread. In my youth I thought this practice barbarous and cruel. Now it seems to me that rulers of past ages were courageous and confident of their power when they permitted this. The practice even seemed to contain some kindness, some benevolence, to the condemned man. Today when I am told of the death of a friend or a student, and learn that no one knows the details of how he died, I find that I grieve more deeply than when I learn all the details of the killing. I can imagine the awful loneliness that overtakes one who is killed by butchers in a small dark room. When I first read the 'Inferno' of Dante's 'Divine Comedy', I was amazed at its imagined cruelty. Now, with more experience, I see how moderate Dante's imagination was. It failed to reach the depth of the secret cruelty which is common today.[65]

After Agnes's departure, Lu Xun and his family made their escape in four rickshaws. Mr Uchiyama travelled in the first, Lu Xun in the second and his wife and child in the third. Wang came last with their possessions. They stayed in the hotel for 39 days. Mr Uchiyama was the only person Lu Xun trusted with the knowledge of his whereabouts.

Nothing appeared in the newspapers about the execution. 'Perhaps they didn't want to, or didn't think it worthwhile,' wrote Lu Xun.

Constantly in fear of 'the small dark room', Lu Xun also found himself attacked in other ways. He introduced literary magazine after literary magazine only to see each suppressed. He wrote under pseudonyms but censors cut his distinctive style into nonsense. Most horrible of all, his associates disappeared or died. He showed Agnes a letter from an eighteen-year-old prisoner dragged from a Shanghai college and accused of communism because he belonged to a wood-cut study group founded by Lu Xun. The boy described what had happened to him from the day of his arrest until the night he had bribed a guard to deliver the letter. He had watched nails driven under the fingernails of a peasant accused of belonging to the Red Army command. The peasant had knelt in silence, his face like clay, blood dripping from each finger. 'My dear master, when I think of him, ice grips my heart',[66] finished the letter.

I asked Wang if Mr Uchiyama suffered from the anti-Japanese feeling in the city. Wang explained that people appreciated Mr Uchiyama and the good work he did. It made him a popular man. He and Lu Xun simply wanted Chinese and Japanese to be friends. One of Lu Xun's brothers, also a good writer, had married a Japanese and Lu Xun himself was greatly respected in Japan. Many high Japanese officials admired his work. Of course they were both criticized for their stand. Wang said, 'Some people thought Mr Uchiyama an agent of the Guomindang! Many in the Japanese community claimed he had sold out. It was all rubbish.'

He handed me a photograph of himself and the Japanese owner sitting on either side of Lu Xun's grave. Wang Baolian is looking at the camera as if to share a good joke. Mr Uchiyama, a small man with round glasses, glances towards the ground. His kimono hangs around his neck like a great weight or a cangue, the Chinese collar of punishment, forcing his neck forward and his shoulders down with the burden. When Lu Xun died, Mr Uchiyama performed the last rites and placed the announcement of Lu Xun's death in the newspaper. He wanted to preserve the body of the writer in chemicals but Lu Xun's wife refused to have it turned into a relic. Instead Mr Uchiyama invited a Japanese dentist to make a death mask. Shortly afterwards the Guomindang destroyed Lu Xun's tomb. Mr Uchiyama repaired it in secret and told Wang not to tell anyone. Lu Xun's wife visited the bookshop to ask who was responsible. 'I gave a little smile and she understood.'

In August 1945 all Japanese in Shanghai were ordered to return to Japan. Three years later, Mr Uchiyama reluctantly departed. In September 1959 he became the first chairman of the newly-founded Sino-Japanese Society and visited Beijing. He died the day after returning to China and, at his request, was buried in Shanghai.

I asked what Mr Uchiyama and Lu Xun liked doing together best.

'Talking,' replied Mr Wang. 'They talked for hours. I would sit and listen. No, I did not join in,' he laughed. 'I was just the bookshop clerk and had nothing to contribute. They talked about everything under the sun. They were two great men, the greatest men I ever knew. They both had big hearts.'

Lu Xun's opinion of George Bernard Shaw proved as unorthodox as his affection for Mr Uchiyama. The British philosopher and playwright stopped over in February 1933. His visit turned into one of the great events, or rather non-events, of the city's intellectual life. Shaw's host was the Chinese League for the Protection of Human Rights, founded by Song Qingling, Sun Yat-sen's widow, together with Cai Yuanpei, the former chancellor of Beijing National University. Lu Xun heard about the visit from Mr Kanzo Uchiyama in his capacity as the writer's agent. He had received a telegram from the Kaizo-sha Press asking Lu Xun to call on Shaw.

To many Chinese artists and writers in Shanghai, Shaw represented the superiority of Western culture. This, like Shaw himself, appeared to tower infinitely over their own efforts. The translation of Thomas Huxley's *Essays on Evolution and Ethics* in 1896 by Yan Fu had shaken Chinese intellectuals. They began to wonder if their culture, so long considered infinitely superior to all others, did not belong to the dodo category. They gazed at Western achievements rather as the Chinese crowds had watched in awe the demonstration put on by the Shanghai Municipal Council's Fire Brigade. A number concurred with the despondent message of Dr Hu Shi, eminent scholar and former ambassador to the U.S., that 'In a hundred ways we are inferior to others not only in the material way and with respect to mechanisation . . . we are not equal to others politically, socially, or morally either . . .[we must] give up all hope, and go to study others.'[67]

Shanghai was full of Chinese who had followed the doctor's advice. Returned students from Europe, America and Japan boasted of willing Western women and dialogues with famous philosophers. Their bravado often hid a lonely period spent, as Lu Xun pointed out, 'stewing beef in their digs'.[68] I found Madame Papp in an old people's home in Hong Kong. Originally from France, she had met and fallen in love with a Chinese student in Paris who came from the north of China and was tall and handsome. Her mother forbade the marriage and they eloped to Shanghai. On the boat he confessed that he already had a Chinese wife with bound feet. This last detail particularly upset Madame Papp as her own were rather large. 'It made me very self conscious,' she recalled. They settled in Shanghai because it was the most Western city in China and he, after a Western education and with a Western wife, did not feel at ease anywhere else. She found herself snubbed by foreigners and had to make friends from the small band of Western women who had married Chinese. Her husband failed to find a job to match his considerable qualifications. Madame Papp kept them both on her salary as a journalist which he resented. Encouraged by his friends to get back at her, he took a concubine and the marriage broke up. He went up north to fight the Japanese and she never heard from him again.

The air of cultural superiority assumed by many returned students irritated Lu Xun. He dismissed them as 'gentlemen scholars' who 'must speak English – so as to show the dignity of the élite'.[69] They made him eager to meet Shaw as 'I was told he was always tearing the masks from gentlemen's faces', and because, 'China keeps producing men who ape Western gentlemen, and most of them dislike Shaw. I tend to believe that a man disliked by the men I dislike must be a good sort.'[70] Their meeting illustrated the gulf between Chinese and foreigner, even those with the best of intentions.

Shaw had taken to that contradiction in terms, a socialist world cruise. At every port of call he made the appropriate political announcement. In South Africa he had declared many whites 'enervated' and 'without a vestige of intelligence'.[71] In China, he praised the political constitution of the Soviet Union, while in Manila he stopped off to talk with Governor Theodore Roosevelt. In between he enjoyed the *Empress of Britain*'s many amenities; the well-equipped gymnasium, the indoor swimming pool, the star-filled dome of the ballroom and the Mall, a strip of deck bordered with pots of shrubs along which people took their morning stroll. His fellow travellers judged him an excellent man as long as no one disturbed his privacy. One member of the crew said, 'He keeps very much to himself, and we seldom see him in the lounges. Most of the time he spends in a deck chair in his own sheltered corner of the promenade deck, writing away for hour after hour.'[72] Mrs Shaw, who took tea alone in the Mayfair Room, was a 'most likeable and sociable personality', except when it came to questions on the doings or opinions of her husband. These she rebuffed 'sharply'.[73]

On the 17th February Lu Xun joined a crowd of Chinese middle-school students as well as Chinese and foreign reporters and photographers on the Customs pontoon to await the tender from the *Empress of Britain*. Several of the students bore banners and flags, inscribed with slogans like 'Welcome to George Bernard Shaw: Down with Imperialism' and 'Welcome to our great Shaw: Union of Democratic and Cinematographic Workers'. A girl dressed in red handed out anti-imperialist leaflets. A member of Special Branch strolled among the crowds with orders to protect Shaw, renowned for his Soviet sympathies, from White Russian demonstrators. They failed to turn up and the plain-clothes detective passed the time noting that one of the banners misspelt Bernard and examining leaflets. These lacked any connection with communism so 'no notice was taken of the matter'.[74] The foreign authorities, unlike the Guomindang, made a distinction between communism and socialism.

Hours passed and Shaw did not appear. About midday Lu Xun received a note from the ever knowledgeable Mr Uchiyama. Shaw had already slipped ashore, Emperor-like, to avoid the crowds. He was now having lunch with Madame Sun at 29 Rue Molière in the French Concession. Every left-wing dignitary visiting the city hastened to meet Sun Yat-sen's widow, the former Song Qingling.

Lu Xun arrived to find Shaw in the seat of honour, tackling a vegetarian meal with five others. Lu Xun saw no evidence of Shaw's greatness, although it struck him 'that with his snow-white hair, healthy colour and genial expression, he would make a first-rate model for a painter'.[75]

Despite the snide prediction from a White Russian newspaper of 'innumerable attendants',[76] Lu Xun discovered only one cook. Shaw tried chopsticks halfway through the meal, 'but very awkwardly – he could not pick anything up. The admirable thing was that by degrees he became more skilful, till finally he got hold of something quite firmly. Then he looked round to see if the others had noticed his success, but no one had,'[77] except, of course, Lu Xun. It was this persistence of Shaw's which most impressed Lu Xun. Otherwise the playwright did not strike him as a satirist or even as a man who said the unusual. If not mentally overawed, Lu Xun did at least find him physically disconcerted by the Western. After lunch three photographs were taken on the lawn outside. 'As we stood side by side, I was conscious of my shortness. And I thought, "Thirty years ago I should have done exercises to increase my height . . . " '[78]

At two o'clock the lunch party attended a reception held in the Pen Club at the World College. Fifty writers, social stars, theatre magnates and others gathered around Shaw and 'bombarded him with questions, as if he were the *Encyclopaedia Britannica*'.[79] Shaw chose to address Mei Lanfang, China's greatest Peking opera star. 'Will you please tell me,' he asked, 'how a Chinese actor can do anything in the midst of such infernal uproars as one hears on your stage? In our theatre, they put a man out if he sneezes. But you have gongs and cymbals and the competition of half the audience and innumerable vendors. Don't you object?'[80] To this extraordinary remark Mei Lanfang could only murmur how honoured he was to meet such a great man of the theatre. Requests for a speech followed Shaw's second lunch of the day. Shaw stood up and said:

> How preposterous to ask me to make a speech to writers. Now if you were businessmen or labourers, in fact anything but people of my own trade, I could get up and make a bluff, but what is the sense of that with people who are behind the scenes with me? You'll only say I'm sure he stayed up all night thinking out that one . . . After all, I may fool others, but I can't fool you. As for plays, I'm not the fellow who does the work, it's chaps like Mr Mei here, the actors, who do the work. I sit by and take in the money they make for me by their efforts.[81]

After questions about his work and his diet, Shaw said, 'Well, now you've had a look at the bird, I suppose I'd better go along and see these newspapermen who are cursing me for being late.'[82] The meeting resembled a visit to the zoo. 'Now the animal had been seen, that should be enough . . . ' Everyone roared with laughter, 'no doubt taking this, too, for satire,'[83] added Lu Xun.

At that instant, Zao Xinmei ('renowned for his manly beauty'[84] and his American mistress) carried in two large parcels and placed them on the table. Shaw leapt to his feet. 'Hooray,' he chortled, 'I knew I'd get a present; that's the only reason I came.'[85] He unwrapped a stage costume and a glass case containing miniatures of the masques worn by characters in Chinese plays. These he especially liked.

At three they returned to Madame Sun's house for the press

conference. About thirty newspapermen, including one English and one White Russian, arranged themselves in a semicircle around Shaw on the back lawn and 'as a substitute for the world cruise', noted Lu Xun, 'offered an exhibition of reporters' faces'.[86] Again they bombarded Shaw with questions. When requested to give his impressions of China he replied, 'You are just like asking me to write twenty volumes. I am too old to have impressions. I am seventy-seven years old.'[87] When asked what an oppressed people like the Chinese should do, he said tartly, 'they have to solve their own problems . . . Chinese people should organise themselves, and choose for their rulers not an actor or a feudal baron.'[88] He then praised the Russian political constitution. The journalists pointed out that a Chinese would be executed for making this remark. 'I am a foreigner,'[89] said Shaw with a loud laugh. The press conference lasted an hour and a half. Lu Xun thought, 'Shaw cannot really be a satirist if he talks so much.'[90] The reporters stopped writing down every remark he made. When Shaw appeared tired, Lu Xun returned to the Uchiyama Bookstore.

The next morning Lu Xun read the newspapers with pleasure. He found the reports

> infinitely more striking than Shaw's actual conversation. Quite different accounts were given of the same thing, said at the same time and in the same place. Apparently the interpretation of the English varied according to each listener. For instance, on the question of China's government, the Shaw of the English press said the Chinese should choose for themselves rulers they admired. The Shaw of the Japanese press said there were several Chinese governments. The Shaw of the Chinese press said no good government could win the people's hearts. Judging by this, Shaw is not a satirist but a mirror.[91]

Most commented unfavourably on Shaw. 'Everyone had gone to hear satire which would amuse and suit him; instead of which he heard satire which annoyed and injured him. So they all used satire to strike back at Shaw, declaring he was nothing but a satirist. In this contest between satirists, I think Shaw is still the greatest.'[92]

Lu Xun and Shaw had failed to have a proper discussion. When Lu Xun's Japanese editor demanded his impressions of the meeting, the writer admitted to feeling inadequate. Others, he knew, wrote 'as though the subject's heart was laid bare to them the moment they set eyes on him, and I do admire such perspicacity. In my own case, though I have not so much as consulted a manual of physiognomy.'[93] He had formed no impression, or rather he had already revealed it.

Shaw returned to his liner to write and think and sail for Qinhuangdao. Too late by fifty-five years for an invitation to Rue Molière, I look at the photograph taken on Madame Sun's lawn. The impression is of a large, soft man next to a small, sharp man. The one played the role of social rebel, the other, despite an amused and gentle smile, was in deadly earnest.

In his work and his friendships, Lu Xun stood for the sanctity of independent thought at a time when it invariably invited a nasty death. He sums up similar qualities in Shanghai while his duel with the Guomindang reflects Shanghai's increasingly hostile relationship with Chiang Kai-shek. In a talk given to the Social Science Study Group on August 12th, 1931 he imagines a Shanghai where the Nationalist government has silenced debate and criticism. Where in such a society, he asks, is the literature of the oppressors? In his reply, equally appropriate for the communist government now as the Nationalist party then, he points to decrees, news items and court sentences. He used an article from the *Shenbao* as an example. It concerned a woman who accused her husband of buggering her and beating her up. The court found no law forbidding a husband to bugger his wife and as bruising did not count as physical injury, they rejected her case. The man then took his wife to court for making a 'false charge'. Lu Xun went on, 'This is common enough in China today – nothing out of the ordinary – yet I think this gives us a better picture of society than the average novel or long poem.'[94]

Lu Xun's desire to create the best possible picture of society dictated his artistic development from fiction to essay to wood-print. Curiously it failed to endear him to the one medium which achieved this with phenomenal success. At the period he was writing, Shanghai had become the centre of China's film industry. Lu Xun certainly enjoyed his foreign films and went to the cinema on average twice a month. At the beginning of 1935, for example, his diary records he saw, *Cleopatra*, *Tarzan and His Mate* (for the second time), *Treasure Island* and *The Private Life of Don Juan*.[95] Conspicuous by its absence, is any mention of a Chinese film.

That House of Multiple Joys

One morning in Shanghai I found myself in a taxi cab, unable to explain where I wanted to go. The driver and I looked at each other with desperation. Finally, I placed my hands, fingertips to fingertips, under my chin, tilted my head and battered my eyelids. The driver banged the wheel with comprehension. Twenty minutes later we arrived at the Shanghai film studios.

Any rickshaw-puller or factory-worker could have told you about Shanghai films. Film succeeded where the novel, essay and woodblock print failed. It reached into the heart of the worker. For the followers of the May 4th Movement, it was the perfect medium. Both Chinese communists and the Guomindang understood the power of film and sought to control it. Eminent left-wing actors and writers like Mao Dun, creator of Old Mr Wu, produced innovative work of great quality. The chance of influencing large numbers of people attracted the businessman, politician and intellectual to the film industry. By the 'thirties it had become a Shanghai institution reaching into every aspect of the city's life while the films themselves reveal the look and the preoccupations of the metropolis.

The flavour of the film industry is summed up by one building. The Great World's tower, rising in layers like a rickety wedding cake, still dominates the crossing of Xizang Road and Yanan Road, the former Thibet Road and Edward VII Avenue. Now renamed the Youth Palace, single men and women left unmarried by the Cultural Revolution attend functions in its rooms to meet prospective partners, 'in decorous fashion', as my guide said. Before the war its attractions proved more robust. Middle-class Chinese denied all knowledge of the Great World. 'Our maids went there on their day off,' I was told by a Chinese lady, annoyed that I had even asked. She also denied an interest in Chinese films. 'We preferred the foreign variety,' she said. The Shanghai film industry, like the Great World, aimed to attract the ordinary man and woman on Nanking Road who had never read a Lu Xun essay or appreciated a woodblock print.

In the mid-'thirties, Josef Von Sternberg, in search of locations for his film *Shanghai Express*, joined the factory workers and rickshaw men crowding into the Great World.

When I had entered the hot stream of humanity there was no turning back even had I wanted to. On the first floor were gambling tables, singsong girls, magicians, pickpockets, slot machines, fireworks, birdcages, fans, stick incense, acrobats, and ginger. One flight up were the restaurants, a dozen different groups of actors, crickets in cages, pimps, midwives, barbers, and earwax extractors. The third floor had jugglers, herb medicines, ice cream parlours, photographers, a new bevy of girls, their high-collared gowns slit to reveal their hips, in case one had passed up the more modest ones below who merely flashed their thighs; and, under the heading of novelty, several rows of exposed toilets, their impresarios instructing the amused patrons not to squat but to assume a position more in keeping with the imported plumbing. The fourth floor was crowded with shooting galleries, fan-tan tables, revolving wheels, massage benches, acupuncture and moxa cabinets, hot-towel counters, dried fish and intestines, and dance platforms serviced by a horde of music makers competing with each other to see who could drown out the others. The fifth floor featured girls whose dresses were slit to the armpits, a stuffed whale, story-tellers, balloons, peep shows, masks, a mirror maze, two love-letter booths with scribes who guaranteed results, rubber goods, and a temple filled with ferocious gods and joss sticks. On the top floor and roof of that house of multiple joys a jumble of tightrope walkers slithered back and forth, and there were see-saws, Chinese checkers, mahjong, strings of firecrackers going off, lottery tickets, and marriage brokers. And as I tried to find my way down again an open space was pointed out to me where hundreds of Chinese, so I was told, after spending their coppers, had speeded the return to the street below by jumping from the roof. When I guilelessly asked why a protective rail had not been placed around an exit so final, the retort was, 'How can you stop a man from killing himself?'[96]

The Great World had all the glitter and energy of Nanking Road. Its combination of new-fangled exotica, traditional China and pretty girls appealed to the Shanghainese. The strength of the Shanghai cinema lay in its ability to translate the 'multiple joys' of the Great World on to the screen. The Shanghai cinema was essentially popular entertainment which aimed to give people what they wanted.

A tour of the Shanghai film industry, like film-making itself, requires team effort. I have chosen a producer, cameraman, director and actress all famous for their work in the period between the wars as appropriate guides. Together they create a picture of an extraordinary business and its effect upon the city.

Shanghai's most eminent producer and the founder of the Shanghai cinema was Zhang Shichuan. Born in 1889, Zhang like many Chinese in Shanghai came, as Shanghainese invariably replied to any question about their origin, from 'Ningbo more far' – in Zhang's case from the province of Zhejiang where his father was a silk merchant. On his father's death, the sixteen-year-old Zhang moved to Shanghai to live with his uncle, a well-known martial-arts expert. He inspired Zhang to learn English and cultivate an interest in Western inventions. By the age of twenty-one, Zhang had made China's longest feature film. Twelve years later he founded Shanghai's most successful film company.

Zhang presents the Shanghai film industry from a business perspective. The 'twenties saw the beginning of a golden period for the Shanghainese businessman. The May 4th Movement of 1919 had infused the country with patriotic fervour demonstrated by a refusal to buy foreign goods. (It was no accident that the most successful brand of Chinese cigarette sold in Shanghai was called 'Great Patriot', or Da Aiguo.) The First World War had distracted foreign competition and created a demand for raw materials. The Chinese seized the opportunity to start new industries and extend old ones. Shanghai attracted bright, aggressive Chinese who won the city a reputation for sharp thinking and innovation. Y. K. Pao, the well-known shipping owner and a Shanghai success story himself, told me, 'Hong Kong was nothing until the Shanghai businessman moved there after 1949. They soon controlled most of its ocean shipping and textile business.' His remark recalled an encounter I had in Japan with an elderly Chinese wearing a large diamond ring who offered me a lift in his Lincoln Continental. His car and his gallantry, both equally rare in central Tokyo, prompted me to ask if he came from Shanghai. Mr Cheng left the city in 1949 and has run a business in Japan ever since. As we sat in a traffic jam he recalled happier days when his grandfather was a warlord. In the 'twenties he had moved his vast wealth, his wife and seven concubines to Shanghai. 'Then the Shanghai businessmen got hold of his money,' said Mr Cheng. 'He was a man experienced in many things, many things,' Mr Cheng gave me a meaningful look and I remembered the ferocity and greed of Chinese warlords, 'but the Shanghai businessmen fleeced him within the year.' Zhang Shichuan acquired his first lesson in Shanghai business practices from the Great World. It made an appropriate beginning.

Zhang's uncle had built the New World, the city's first entertainment palace and the Great World's predecessor, on the corner of Nanking and Thibet Road. After the death of his uncle, Zhang's aunt quarrelled with her husband's partner, Huang Chujiu. Apart from owning a chain of drug stores, Huang was known for a potion of his invention which claimed to improve the mind. 'Yellow' had sold spectacularly in a city where, as Lu Xun pointed out, 'to live by your wits ... is quite respectable'.[97] The label pictured a Jewish friend of Huang's, implying the customer might hope for a new brain to match that of a Kadoorie or a Hardoon. As everyone assumed Huang Chujiu drunk a bottle of 'Yellow' a day, his adroit handling of the next few months provided excellent, free publicity.

In revenge for the widow's behaviour, Huang Chujiu bought the next-door site, built Shanghai's second entertainment palace and called it, provocatively, the Great World. Zhang's aunt made her nephew a director of the New World and ordered him to put Huang Chujiu out on to the streets. In the teashops the rickshaw pullers exchanged bets on the outcome.

Zhang responded with the grand gesture typical of Shanghai businessmen. He persuaded his aunt to buy the site opposite and to outface the Great World with a New New World offering theatres, operas, ice rinks and pageants. He attracted customers with events such as the 'Queen of the Flower World', a beauty competition of Shanghai's prostitutes. The Great World immediately put on its own 'Battle of the Hundred Flowers'. Zhang's ideas now swelled into the fantastic. He decided to join the New Worlds together so that one ticket gave entrance to both. First he planned a bridge spanning the street but the Municipal authorities refused planning permission. Then he tried to dig a tunnel but the ceiling leaked and customers found themselves scrabbling in filth. Attendance figures fell fast and Zhang's aunt found herself forced to sell up. The Great World went on to become a Shanghai legend.

Zhang Shichuan now applied the painful lessons he had learnt from the War of the Worlds to Shanghai's nascent film industry.

His timing was perfect. The boom in Chinese business had

dramatically increased returns on investments. The Commercial Press paid out 34 per cent in 1919 while the Dasheng cotton mills distributed 90 per cent in dividends to its lucky shareholders. Money-making gripped the Shanghainese imagination while success encouraged speculation in new ventures. In this atmosphere Zhang met his future father-in-law, He Yongcan.

A photograph of Zhang taken at the time reveals a solid man with a pudgy face and obstinate mouth dressed in a Chinese gown. There is no inkling of the charisma which even his acrimonious widow, the chief witness for this period, recalled. He Xiujun, interviewed in China during the Cultural Revolution, which no doubt explains her acerbity, said her father appreciated Zhang Shichuan as soon as he met him. He continually praised Zhang's intelligence and ambition. Here was a young man obviously made for great things and He intended to teach Zhang all he knew.

The same year saw the city swept with a craze for stock-market companies. He Yongcan gave Zhang two thousand yuans to invest. He rented a house in Guizhou Road and announced the 'Datong Stockmarketing Company' open for business. While the authorities tarried over granting him a licence, Zhang changed his mind. What he really wanted, he confided to He Yongcan, was to start a film company. 'Get stuck in,' said the amiable He, 'and if you need more money come to me.' Zhang joined up with four friends and announced funds of 50,000 yuan. 'They only had 10,000 really,'[98] remarked his widow. In March 1922 they painted a new name on the signboard. 'The Mingxing Film Company' meant Bright Star and became Shanghai's most important film company.

Its prospects were hardly dazzling. Its directors did not yet own a studio and shot on some wasteland, the scenery painted on a piece of tarpaulin stretched in front of the camera. Zhang had similar problems with his audience. The Shanghainese refused to pay for anything they could not see. Cinema owners let them in free of charge, ran the picture for a few hundred feet then stopped the film, put on the lights and demanded money which satisfied customers placed in baskets. An interval for tea drinking and cold towels occurred at the end of each reel. The audience threw their towels to an attendant in the aisle who would immediately dip them in iced water before throwing them back. 'The only reliable way to entertain people is to give them what they find interesting,' said Zhang, adding disingenuously, 'but we have no idea yet what that is.'[99]

After three bankruptcies, Zhang applied the formula which had proved successful for the Great World. The Shanghainese adored familiar stories from Chinese legend and opera and made with plenty of violence, Western gadgetry and scantily dressed girls. His films started to make money and film-making replaced stock-market companies as the latest financial craze. Ambitious businessmen joined up with failed writers, hired a hotel room facing south and shot a film in two weeks. Competition became intense. In 1926 the Mingxing was one of fifty companies registered in Shanghai. He Xiujun recalled the atmosphere of panic as everyone chased after money. Zhang first borrowed 3,000 yuan from her then another five thousand. He paid her back then borrowed the money again, paid her back and borrowed it again so many times that she forgot how much he owed her. 'I never kept track of what I handed over and I could not say how much of my own money I went through.'[100] In 1923 they married. He Xiujun became the official owner of the Mingxing company and 'this financial see-saw'[101] a way of life. In comparison Zhang must have looked back on the War of the Worlds almost with nostalgia.

By the end of the 'twenties Zhang's astuteness and hard work had placed the Mingxing amongst the four leading film companies in the city. The company celebrated its importance with a move to new studios in Doumer Street where it doubled in size and turned out two films at once. Success merely exacerbated its financial problems. He Xiujun explained that the more films they sold, the more expenses rose. As owner, she was responsible for debts running into tens of thousands of yuan. Unable to do anything about the large amounts, she still had to cover the day-to-day expenses. One day of filming cost 2,000–3,000 yuan. Only a pawnshop provided such large amounts of cash quickly. Over the years her jewellery and furs went in and out of the brokers 'more times than I can remember'.[102] She even employed a maid especially for the purpose.

The company's image became as important as the films it made. Zhang seized every opportunity to out-dazzle competitors and emphasize the seemingly glamorous existence led by his directors and stars whom, as the company's principal assets, he 'constantly spoilt and sweet talked'.[103] Perks for employees included a small banquet every three days, a big one every five days and something really special for Chinese New Year. As He Xiujun remarked, 'We never let an opportunity slip to demonstrate that Mingxing was a rung above the other film companies.'[104] When things went well they spent a fortune on banquets and parties. When things went badly they borrowed from left and right. She added, 'It was difficult to get a balance.'[105]

Success brought Zhang and his partners the sort of life every aspiring Shanghai businessman dreamed of. He Xiujun employed seven servants including a cook, messenger boy, valet, nurse and gardener. Each director was meant to pay his own expenses but personal and company finances overlapped. As He Xiujun remarked, 'Sheep grow wool in order to have it cut off. At the end of the day it was the company who paid.'[106]

He Xiujun remembered none of the excitement and glamour of the film industry. Life with Shanghai's film mogul proved 'very monotonous'.[107] Zhang devoted his life to film-making. New material for scenarios obsessed him. At night when he returned home he lay down on his bed or locked himself into the lavatory to think up another story-line. His wife insisted he had his best ideas on the lavatory or smoking opium with his partner, Zheng Zhengqiu. He adapted 'trashy' love stories printed in Shanghai's newspapers and cunningly plagiarized American films, taking a bit here and a bit there. He listened avidly to gossip. 'That's a good idea for a scenario!'[108] he would exclaim after overhearing a conversation in the street. He refused to socialize unless on the track of a story, questioning everyone until he was satisfied. Then, in a state of euphoria, he shut himself away and wrote it out.

Zhang possessed the ability to give people what they wanted. He studied his audience with care, particularly its female members, who formed the majority. A film which ended in separation, death or a divided family put off a return to the cinema for some time. On the other hand, women enjoyed a good weep. He therefore chose scenarios which made them cry then laugh. His wife declared that his films were bad and vulgar but even she had to concede their popularity.

Zhang's audience always appreciated his special effects. Flying villains, earthquakes, battle scenes or the giant, hairy hand of the Monkey god holding the hero attracted the Shanghainese as surely as the row of Western lavatories in the Great World. The man responsible for Mingxing's more outrageous efforts was Huang Shaofen, the city's most celebrated cameraman in the pre-war era. I met him in Shanghai. In his late seventies, he is still Chief Engineer of the Shanghai Film Studios and President of the Shanghai branch of the Photographers' Association of China. A small, sleek man with glossy black hair, his over-large hands and feet give him the appearance of an amiable mole. He recalled the difficulties endured by Chinese businesses in pursuit of technical expertise. To avert the problem, many Shanghai entrepreneurs began by working for foreigners or taking a foreign partner (Zhang made his first film with two Americans); then sent their sons to M.I.T. in Cambridge, Massachusetts. Huang was less fortunate.

He had originally joined the Mingxing as a child actor because Zhang took a fancy to his face (Zhang made a star out of his oculist's assistant for the same reason). Huang quickly decided against an acting career. The studio required its actors and actresses to perform death-defying feats 'for real' because of a lack of technical ability. This meant flying through the air on ropes without a safety net or taking part in unrehearsed fights. The studio hired rickshaw men for the battle scenes, provided them with wooden swords and instructions 'to strike out as though they meant it'. Huang shook his head at the result. He saw a number of actors forced to retire from their injuries without compensation or a pension 'and that was a sad end'.

Huang decided to move to the other side of the camera. He apprenticed himself to Mr Liang, the Mingxing's cameraman, and studied engineering in his spare time. He 'itched' to know about camerawork but Mr Liang regarded the small, inquisitive adolescent as a potential rival and refused to teach him. Huang grew desperate. Shanghai lacked a film school and Huang the money to study abroad. His attempts to be 'always' kind and helpful failed to impress the older man. Liang watched over his camera jealously and hid it under his bed at night. The camera was an old American model with a manual starting handle which required a certain knack to get going. Huang pondered how he might acquire that knack when Mr Liang refused to allow him even to carry the 'Ice Cream Maker', the camera's nickname after the Shanghainese had dubbed Zhang's films 'Ice-cream for the eyes'. Finally he found a way. Zhang often invited his family to private viewings and would put Huang in charge of the projection. Before beginning, he took off the belt of the motor and started it by hand. It proved excellent practice. He still had to teach himself every other aspect of camerawork. After five years of surreptitious study, he confirmed Mr Liang's worst fears and became a professional cameraman with the Mingxing at the age of eighteen.

Shortly afterwards Huang found himself in the forefront of a new film movement. In 1932 the Shanghai cinema faced its greatest challenge. The Japanese bombing of Chapei and Hongkew destroyed 16 out of 39 of Shanghai's cinemas. Many small film studios went out of business. Several companies, their studios wrecked and with nothing else to offer, issued newsreels of the battle. They evoked a tremendous response. Suddenly from out of the ruins came a new way to make money: the patriotic film.

Disenchanted by Chiang Kai-shek and enraged with the Japanese, the Shanghainese flocked to see films on social issues, films against Guomindang corruption and the Japanese army. Hardly had the battle finished than the studios rushed out semi-animated cartoons with prophetic titles like, *The Rapid Awakening of Our People* and *Blood Stained Money*. As Huang Shaofen remarked, 'The days of licentious films, fantasies, cops and robbers or films on martial arts were over. People wanted to see something different.'

Zhang Shichuan, sensitive as ever to his audience's wishes, responded with alacrity. The Mingxing had suffered more than any other major company from a withdrawal of capital and damage to its studio. With his customary boldness, Zhang signed up three celebrated left-wing writers, A Ying, Xia Yan and Zheng Boqi. His widow explained, 'No one had any other suggestions to save the company.'[109] Neither a social conscience nor political conviction motivated him. According to He Xiujun he had only one idea in his head when he made films and that was money. She went on, 'His opinion on socially relevant films was quite clear; if they brought in cash, he made them, if they earned less, he made fewer and if they lost money, he'd stop making them.'[110] Left-wing writers wrote over half of the twenty films released by Mingxing in 1933. At their request Zhang replaced the great star of the Mingxing with a flambeau encircled by smaller stars to represent collective action.

The hiring of Xia Yan, who had studied in Japan before coming to Shanghai in 1927 to join the Communist party and work as a trade unionist in Chapei, in particular represented a turning point in the Shanghai film industry. In 1929 the party transferred him to the Left-Wing Writers' League where he began his career as a playwright. Xia Yan ensured that film-making, like the city's intellectual life, was inevitably bound up with politics. Huang

Shaofen, the cameraman, told me, 'Most of us had no idea these new employees belonged to the Communist party: but I knew even then.'

The alliance between capitalist producer and communist scriptwriter resulted in some very good films indeed. They have nothing in common with the 'Ice Cream for the Eyes' of the 'twenties, nor the doctrinaire propaganda made after 1949. Like Shanghai itself, they exist as a magnificent aberration. The artists' scientific observation of people and situations created a new realism that owed little to Hollywood. It is also a record of a city.

The left-wing films of the 'thirties capture Shanghai as no other medium could. The city was made to be filmed. Its extraordinary mix of people, its revolutions and wars, its extremes of poverty and riches produced dramatic material and provided a visually exciting background. Every facet of the city is recorded (every facet but one: I have never seen a foreign face in a Chinese film), from the 'kennels' of the poor to the 'palaces' of the rich; from the fresh, ebullience of the mahjong parlour in *Love's Labours* (*Laogong zhi Aiqing*: 1922), Mingxing's second production and the earliest surviving Chinese fiction film, to the social satire of *Shanghai Then and Now* (*Xinjiu Shanghai*: 1936), set in a typical lane house. Prostitutes, shop assistants, silk factory workers and toymakers could watch themselves on screen. Film celebrated their new importance. They had become the heroes and heroines over whom everybody wept.

The makers of these films formed part of the cultural life of the city. Actors and actresses gossiped with writers and students in the coffee shops on North Szechuen Road or ate in the cheaper Russian restaurants along Avenue Joffre. Their lives hardly differed from the parts they played or the scripts they wrote. Apart from the few stars, they lived in boarding houses and received a modest monthly salary. In the studios everybody mucked in. One actress recalled working as odd-job girl and film-cutter when not required on set. Technicians doubled as bit-part players. As one editor remarked, 'Underground film workers put on no airs – we all ate and rested together.'

Sun Yu, one of the most famous directors of the 'thirties, typifies the left-wing intellectual attracted to film-making during the period. I met him in Shanghai a few years after the fall of the Gang of Four. A tall, cadaverous man, he wore a checked shirt buttoned to the collar under a loose, brown jacket. His face, with its accentuated cheek bones and high-bridged nose, appeared out of some ancient Chinese scroll. His austere manner recalled an earlier age and an idealism untainted by successful revolution. Like many of his generation, he was greatly influenced by the May 4th Movement. He said, 'I wanted to make films about society, films with a social conscience. But I also wanted to make successful films. I was fortunate to work in a time when intellectual films did better than any other sort.'

Born in Chongqing in March 1900, Sun Yu was the son of a scholar historian. Travels with his father around China inspired an early enthusiasm for the arts and led to a doctoral thesis on the poetry of Li Bo at the University of Wisconsin in the United States. He went on to study directing and scriptwriting at Columbia University and take courses in photography, photo-developing and printing. At a New York college, he learnt how to compose a picture, write a scenario and edit. He also attended theatre classes conducted by David Belasco. As he told me, 'I was the first person from China to study film-making abroad.' When he returned to China in the late 'twenties, he teamed up with the nineteen-year-old cameraman, Huang Shaofen, to make *Spring Dream in the Old Capital* (*Gudu Chunmeng*) in 1930. The film created a sensation. Compared to the usual films of that period, it had meaning, 'and that was quite new,' pointed out Huang. *Spring Dream* established the reputations of both men and was a forerunner of the realistic work of the 'thirties.

From 1932 Sun Yu made on average two films a year. 'I liked directing best but I did everything else myself from beginning to end except act. I wrote my own films and did my own cutting. That way I was able to reproduce my own vision.'

Typical of his work and the new realism in Shanghai cinema is *Little Toys* (*Xiao Wanyi*: 1933), starring two of the city's leading left-wing actresses, Li Lili and Ruan Lingyu. It tells how the events of the previous decade affected one family. The family business of toymaking provides the film's central metaphor. Sun Yu explained to me that he got the idea on a trip to Lake Dai where he saw the effect of Japanese competition on local toymakers.

The film begins in the early 1920s in a village near Lake Dai where the Ye family make toys by hand. First caught up in a battle between two rival warlords, the Ye family later lose their small son to professional child thieves who sell him to a rich, Shanghainese couple. The husband dies and his wife, played by Ruan Lingyu, has no choice but to leave for Shanghai with her daughter, played by Li Lili, and other villagers. There, despite sophisticated foreign competition in the shape of guns, cannons and tanks, they set up a primitive, toymaking factory. Ten years pass. In 1932 the Japanese bombard Shanghai. Miss Ye is killed (Sun Yu recalled Li Lili had great difficulty in acting her death. 'She wanted it to be brief, to be understated. Ruan said to her, "While you are dying you should smile," and that was how she did it'.) Mrs Ye is left alone, selling her playthings on the Bubbling Well Road. Before her hesitates a well-dressed boy who stares at her toys as if they are from another world. Neither realize he is her son. As he is driven away in a large car, the sound of sirens triggers off her fear of an air-raid. She stands up in the middle of the road and mad with pain and loss starts to scream. The film ends with her surrounded by a curious crowd, still screaming.

Shanghai audiences immediately recognized the film's themes as their own preoccupations. The threat of foreign competition and Japanese aggression (both political and economic), the flight from the countryside to the city and the disintegration of the family – each detail and character contributes to the carefully wrought picture of hopelessness. The result is a film of extraordinary force. Xia Yan in his role as critic for the *Shenbao* called for: 'More crazy people like Mrs Ye!'[111]

Sun Yu's films also reflect the glamour and panache of the city and Nanking Road in particular. His admiration for Josef von Sternberg's work with Marlene Dietrich (*The Blue Angel* was distributed in China in 1931) sent him on a hunt for the Chinese equivalent. He found Li Lili in the Variety Troupe of the Lianhua company ('we rarely used actors or actresses from outside the company'). He told me, 'She was very young and naive. I chose her because of her naivety.' Innocence, however, is hardly what one associates with her work for Sun Yu. Tony Rayns, in his excellent programme notes to the National Film Theatre's 1985 season of Chinese films, describes her as 'an exotic, exuberant and supremely self-confident sex object'. In a series of left-wing melodramas, she and Sun Yu discovered 'an almost limitless variety of shades, nuances and undercurrents'. Huang Shaofen gave a less flattering verdict. 'She was very active, just like a man.'

The film most typical of her appeal is the *Queen of Sport*, directed by Sun Yu in 1934. Li Lili plays the daughter of a wealthy family who comes to Shanghai to train in a sports academy. The film is a good excuse to see Li Lili's legs in tight shorts while allowing Sun Yu to poke fun at Shanghai's middle classes. There is also a more serious side. Exercise represented a rejection of China's effete past. Students of the May 4th Movement believed a strong body and a strong, modern outlook essential for China's chances of survival. Sun Yu's call for both is overwhelmed by the impervious spirit of Li Lili whose vigorous, sprinting legs seem to presage China's future just as Ruan's screams at the end of *Little Toys* hint at its tragic shortcomings.

In 1936 Ida Treat, an American investigating the Chinese cinema, saw her first Chinese film in Nanjing. A bad copy of a Hollywood movie, it disappointed her as much as the rest of the audience. A Chinese student explained that people high up in the Nationalist government preferred this kind of film. It did not raise unpleasant issues. He advised her to go to cinemas in the International Settlement where extraterritoriality protected the work of the Chinese director just as it had done the essays of Lu Xun. Here she saw *Spring Silkworms*, adapted by Xia Yan from the short story by Mao Dun. Chinese from the neighbourhood filled the cinema and gave the film concentrated and silent attention, occasionally breaking into the guttural 'Hao!' (Good!), the usual sign of approbation in the Chinese theatre.

The new realism in Shanghai's films failed to detract from the glamour of Shanghai's great stars. This small and select band exerted tremendous influence. The Shanghainese followed their lives and discussed their love affairs avidly. Butterfly Wu, the Mingxing's leading actress, became one of the most popular of the period. Her marriage to Eugene Peng (Penn), a Shanghai businessman, in November 1935 attracted greater attention than Song Meiling's to Chiang Kai-shek eight years before. Then, a thousand people had stood outside the ballroom of the Majestic Hotel to watch the bride in her veil of white Chantilly lace. At Butterfly Wu's wedding, the police were called out to control the riot. Four years later a combination of Chiang Kai-shek and the Japanese destroyed the Shanghai pre-war cinema for ever. The wedding of Butterfly Wu marks the height of its influence.

Song Meiling's Western wedding had set a precedent. In the traditional Chinese ceremony, the bride remained veiled throughout. Compared to the procession of wedding gifts and the exultant mother-in-law, she seemed almost incidental to the proceedings. The central importance of the bride in a Western wedding proved much more to a film star's taste – as did the public display. Butterfly Wu insisted that her marriage take place in the Holy Trinity Cathedral on Kiangse Road. Completed in 1893 in celebration of the Settlement's Golden Jubilee to a Gothic design by Sir George Gilbert Scott, it was a landmark of the British community and one of the grandest buildings in the city. Butterfly Wu, who did not speak a word of English, startled the Cathedral's congregation by announcing herself to be a member of the Church of England. As one foreigner recalled, 'None of us had seen her set foot in the place.' A bemused Dean Trivett agreed to officiate.

The wedding also surprised the Shanghainese. Ancient prejudice dictated that a man might make an actress his concubine but never his wife. Before 1911 Manchu law forbade members of the 'le hu', or 'amusement population', from taking the civil-service exam and refused them burial in sacred ground. No other group in Chinese society suffered similar discrimination. It says something for the power of the Shanghai cinema in general, and Miss Wu's personality in particular, that Mr Peng agreed to a ceremony at all, let alone such a public one.

Miss Wu's past also raised a few questions. Shanghai's unscrupulous news-sheets, known as the 'mosquito' press, had exhaustively covered her betrothal seven years before to Lin Shiwan, a former screen actor, and its break-up in a messy quarrel over rings, debts and motor cars. Any story about her, true or false, sold papers. Shanghai's populace felt she belonged to them. They queued up to see her plump, soft beauty and adored the persecuted heroines she played to perfection. The sight of a tear rolling over her round cheek never failed to ravish her audience.

Butterfly Wu was born in 1907, the daughter of a railroad worker. She grew up in North-East China and therefore spoke Mandarin. When the Chinese cinema introduced talking films and set Mandarin as standard cinema speech, Miss Wu, unlike many southern actresses, had no difficulty making the transition. At sixteen she returned to Shanghai with her family and enrolled in film school. Two years later she had made her first film. In 1928 she joined the Mingxing studios and there found fame and stardom. Her ostentatious wedding with its combination of East and West was a real Shanghai affair.

The wedding was due to take place at 11.30 on a Saturday in late November. By 10.30 the crowds had partly filled the cathedral and its compounds. The couple had issued three thousand invitations decorated with butterflies and the Chinese character for happiness. According to Chinese custom, each invitation included the whole household. Guests leant against pillars or found seats in the choir-loft. In the streets around the cathedral police tried to control Butterfly's fans. By eleven the cathedral was packed to its doors. Mr Harvey Gale Duncan, the chief usher, had the unnerving task of finding seats for intimate friends of the bride and groom who arrived late and for government officials who arrived even later. Mr William Peng, another usher as well as the brother of the bridegroom, instructed guests on the appropriate behaviour in a cathedral. The majority behaved as if at a Chinese wedding, gossiping, telling jokes, eating oranges and spitting sunflower seeds in the pews while boys ran up and down supplying everyone with hot towels. At 11.35 the bridegroom arrived in formal morning attire, complete with top hat, spats and a huge boutonnière of red and white roses tied with pink ribbon. He was flanked by two groomsmen, one of whom was Mr Y. Y. Chow, the international walking champion of Shanghai. They took their seats, chatting and listening to the organ programme which Mr J. H. Tebbs, the cathedral organist, had played without break for an hour and a half.

By noon the bride had still failed to appear. The bridegroom wet his lips, ran his finger around his collar and cast furtive glances sideways. More guests arrived. Suddenly a relieved Mr Tebbs broke into the wedding march. The ushers ran up and down the aisle beseeching the men to remove their hats and the guests to stay seated – which everyone ignored. In came the bride, preceded by two flower girls dressed in poke bonnets and baby-blue taffeta dresses ruffled from the knees. Each girl held a silver basket from which she scattered flowers before the bride. The congregation almost broke into applause at the sight of Butterfly Wu. From her shoulders fell an eight-yard train of silk lace. Hundreds of different-sized, white, velvet butterflies covered her tulle veil. As she walked, it billowed up behind, brushing the shoulders of her audience. Her father, Mr Wu Xiugong, wore a Chinese gown with a short black coat. He, at least, had refused to adopt a Western approach to the proceedings. The page-boy and the ring-bearer were in black velvet while the bridesmaid and the maid of honour, both film actresses, remained veiled throughout.

During the ceremony the congregation jostled for a better view and a chance to hear Miss Wu repeat her almost inaudible vows.

As the couple withdrew to the registry, some guests rushed outside to secure good places, others stayed to pelt the leaving pair with rice and confetti. At the sight of the couple at the church doors the crowd went wild. The police could hardly hold them back nor the cameraman obtain photographs.

In the afternoon the bride and groom held a tiffin reception at the Far Eastern Hotel. In the evening management removed the partition walls from one floor of the hotel for the traditional Chinese wedding dinner. The couple had invited over two thousand people, from politicians like Mayor Wu Dezhen and Dr and Mrs V. K. Wellington Koo to artists such as the famous Peking Opera star, Mei Lanfang, and even foreigners like the Count and Countess François Courseulles, Mr and Mrs Chester Fritz (who made a point of mixing with Chinese) and the Iraqi Jew, Mr Denzil Ezra. The bride, dressed in traditional Cantonese style, wore a red skirt embroidered with butterflies and a black coat. During dinner the guests were entertained with selections from Chinese opera, sung in the approved stage manner and dancing from Miss Hu Yunyo, Shanghai's Shirley Temple. The bride and groom followed the Chinese custom and visited each table to receive congratulations and drink a cup of wine. This proved 'no light task'[112] as one reporter remarked. The dinner lasted until morning.

For many days the task of receiving wedding presents occupied Mr Peng's brothers and four of his office staff. They returned gifts from hundreds of fans for lack of space. Even so, red banners, paintings and scrolls, some made by the donors themselves, others the work of famous old painters and writers as well as red envelopes full of money, silver cups, vases, shields, silk and silverware of all descriptions, quite apart from the silver dinner service containing five hundred pieces from the bride's parents, piled up in Mr Peng's home and office. A week later the office staff were still sending out thankyou letters and 'Cumshaw' (a gift of money).

Butterfly Wu's popularity explains Chiang Kai-shek's determination to control the film industry. The cinema became a battleground between communist and Nationalist from the moment Xia Yan persuaded his comrades to pitch themselves into the wicked world of the motion-picture business with its 'entrepreneurs, scoundrels and other rotten forces'. As he himself wrote, 'Films are the sharpest ideological weapon of the class struggle, and the enemy would certainly not let us grasp this weapon easily.'[113] By May 1932 the Guomindang had signed the Shanghai Treaty with the Japanese agreeing, among other things, to suppress anti-Japanese activities. A month later the Guomindang Minister of Propaganda instructed film companies not to disturb the 'atmosphere' of 'calm' with 'provocative films'[114] advocating resistance to Japan. To underline the point, thirty Blue Shirts wrecked a small left-wing studio called Yi Hua (the money to start it had come from a wealthy opium-dealing gangster just the year before). Next morning all Shanghai cinemas received a letter declaring, 'Films . . . that promote class struggle, pit poor against rich – such reactionary films may not be shown. If they are shown, there will be violence and we cannot assure you that what happened to the Yi Hua company will not happen to you.'[115] The letter was signed by the Committee to Destroy Communists.

Guomindang writers now infiltrated the studios as they had done the bookshops and attempted to win over the more moderate directors. He Xiujun recalled that they brought along scenarios and 'added menace to their soft talk'. He Xiujun refused to have anything to do with them but others wavered. 'I cannot tell you how many heated exchanges took place or the battles that went on inside the company.'[116]

In 1933 Zhang received an invitation from Chiang Kai-shek to make a documentary on the eradication of bandits (a euphemistic if not entirely inaccurate term for certain communists) in Jiangxi Province. The result delighted the Generalissimo and he summoned Zhang to Nanjing for an interview. Zhang looked upon the invitation as a mark of favour and set off a confident man.

After a polite opening, Chiang broached the subject of the Shanghai cinema. He said: 'You must realize that the Japanese are not dangerous. Our real enemies are the communists.'[117] He then asked Zhang to name the communists in the film business. Zhang was appalled. As his widow remarked: 'He had got nothing from Chiang except an invitation to shop his best writers and directors.' On the other hand he dared not refuse the General. He stuttered, 'Well, if one at least knew who is a communist . . . ' and left as soon as possible. A friend remembered Zhang coming out of the meeting white-faced and covered in sweat. He had never seen the entrepreneur so shaken.

Zhang had realized that the golden age of business, the days of 'huangjin shidai' (huang-chin shih-tai), as the Shanghainese called them, were over. Chiang Kai-shek persecuted the city's businessmen as vigorously as he did its writers and journalists. Du Yuesheng snatched successful entrepreneurs and held them until their families made a 'contribution' to the Nationalist government. Businessmen found themselves emasculated politically as well as financially and their companies taxed out of existence. In 1929 the city's General Chamber of Commerce which, only six years before, had called so bravely for 'independence' from the central government was placed under the direct authority of the Guomindang. Nationalist officials like Chiang Kai-shek's two brothers-in-law, H. H. Kung and T. V. Song who made no distinction between their public function and their private fortune, took over Shanghai's banks and businesses. After twenty years of independence, the Shanghai businessman found himself back under the Imperial tradition of 'bureaucratic capitalism'.

The propaganda potential of films forced the Guomindang to pursue the Mingxing with more caution than, for example, a business like the Nanyang Tobacco Company. There the takeover had been straightforward. First almost taxed out of existence, it was then forced to 'sell' a third of its stock to T. V. Song and 'invite' Du Yuesheng on to its board. The Nationalists preferred to work indirectly on Zhang through his great weakness: finance. His bank suddenly refused to give him a loan. One creditor took the company to court. The Film Censorship Committee arbitrarily cut his films or left them to sit around on some shelf waiting for a licence. As the company faced bankruptcy, the American Commercial and Exchange Bank, with uncanny timing, offered to buy the Mingxing for 300,000 yuan.

At this critical point Zhang's partner, Zheng Zhengqiu saved the Mingxing. Near to death, he managed, nonetheless, to produce a script entitled *Twin Sisters (Zimei Hua)*. Butterfly Wu played both girls, the one married to a poor carpenter, the other the concubine of a warlord. The film explored the relationship between the classes and the misery of the poor. It was a great success, filling its opening theatre for 60 days before appearing in 28 provinces and 53 towns around China, as well as in Hong Kong and South-East Asia. Its receipts of 200,000 yuan broke all records. Only Lu Xun remained unmoved, remarking with acerbity that the film's message merely instructed people 'to be content with poverty'.

In October 1934 government pressure forced Zhang to sack two of his best left-wing writers, Xia Yan and A Ying. Their departure led to a shortage of good scripts. Zhang secretly instructed his directors to continue to consult the writers 'informally'. Xia Yan recalled, 'We made the most of this opportunity to get our ideas into the film, and made it as socially useful as possible.'[118] This quiet collaboration produced excellent work. In an effort to avoid censorship left-wing writers had to rely on subtlety of characterization and theme to carry their message. Sun Yu recalled one scene in *The Queen of Sport* when groups of young gymnasts from all over China are waving banners representing their areas with the camera lingering on the flags of the six states under Japanese rule. I asked if the Nationalists put pressure on him personally. He shook his head. 'We had no contact with the censorship committee. We did not mix with government officials. They were fearful of film-makers. Fortunately they had reservations about attacking us directly.'

In July 1935 Zheng Zhengqiu died, leaving Zhang more dependent than ever on his left-wing writers. In the spring of the following year the Mingxing moved into larger studios and Zhang devised a scheme for placating the Nanjing authorities. He split the Mingxing into two. Zhang ran Studio One and produced work fit, as his wife scornfully put it, only for the 'petit bourgeois'. Studio Two's relative financial independence attracted left-wing writers and directors – many the former employees of studios bankrupted by the Guomindang. Zhang hoped he could rely on Studio One to keep the company solvent if Studio Two fell foul of the authorities. Studio Two proved impossible for Nationalist writers to penetrate but Studio One bought their acquiescence with good salaries. Unfortunately not even Zhang could solve the problem of the Japanese.

In 1937 the Japanese took over the Mingxing studios and turned it into a barracks. In November 1939 they set fire to the area and burnt the Mingxing to the ground.

The flames destroyed the Shanghai cinema of the pre-war era, and scattered its participants. Zhang Shichuan and Butterfly Wu left for Hong Kong. Sun Yu followed the Nationalist government to Chongqing where he made two anti-Japanese films. Xia Yan moved south to publish patriotic newspapers. Both Sun Yu and Xia Yan stayed in China after 1949, Sun Yu returning from America to take part in the Revolution. Mao Zedong himself, in an anonymous review, criticized the first film he made under the new regime, the *Story of Wu Xun* in 1950. The new leader considered its message irrelevant to the rural audiences of post-revolutionary China and used the film to attack the half-dozen independent film companies left in Shanghai. Three years later they were under state control. The film's failure signalled the end of the May 4th Movement and the emergence of the Chinese government as the sole arbiter of what should and should not be seen. For some time Sun Yu could not direct. He made his last film in 1960.

Many of Shanghai's left-wing film-makers shared his fate. Those who survived Mao's persecution of intellectuals in the 'fifties fell victim to his wife during the Cultural Revolution. Xia Yan, for example, despite heading the Film Bureau of the Ministry of Culture, found his work condemned in 1965 and himself exiled to Chengdu. Zhang Shichuan had correctly predicted of the 'thirties: 'This is the decade everyone will remember.'[119] Never did Chinese directors enjoy such freedom or its audiences exert so much influence again. The communists proved far better censors than the Nationalists, as I discovered at the end of my interview with the cameraman, Huang Shaofen.

Our translator was an elegant young man with curly hair and the face of a youthful Buddha. He had studied in Hollywood and talked only of American cinema. When I asked Huang Shaofen about a particular shot, he questioned the translator with sudden interest. 'He wants to know if you have seen this film,' said the translator. I replied that I had seen many examples of Mr Huang's work. The small cameraman sat back and gazed at me in amazement. I asked why he appeared so surprised. Mr Huang now leant towards me and began to talk, patting my arm all the time. The youthful Buddha could barely keep up with his volubility. Suddenly Huang paused, overcome, it seemed with emotion. The translator explained, 'Films made in the 'thirties are never shown in China, even at a private viewing. I have seen nothing by him before 1949.' It was my turn to stare at Mr Huang in bewilderment. Here was a man whose best work remained unknown to anyone under sixty in his own country. 'Are they any good?' asked the youthful Buddha.

Gossip Is a Fearful Thing

Shanghai's businessmen wooed women as assiduously as they did rickshaw pullers and factory hands. Women offered a new and previously unexplored market. Traditional Chinese society had paid them scant attention. Of all the changes which had shocked Old Mr Wu on his arrival to Shanghai, it was the transformation in the behaviour of his female relatives which did for him.

On Christmas Day 1929, at three o'clock in the afternoon, a Stinson-Detroit took off and circled slowly over the city for more than an hour. Its four passengers included General Liu Beizhuan, his bride Miss Wang Suzeng (Su-tseng), her maid of honour, the aviatrix, Miss Zhuan Zhiyou and the officiating Reverend, Herman C. E. Liu. After celebrating the first inflight Chinese wedding, the couple attended their reception in Hungjao airport. A photograph of the bride and groom show them standing by their plane, looking upwards as their faces break into laughter.

Their happy flight proved the antithesis of the traditional Chinese ceremony. Then the bride and groom saw each other for the first time on the wedding night, the bride conveyed to her husband's home in a red lacquer sedan chair. Miss Wang Suzeng, a graduate of the Shanghai college and a teacher at the Nanjing Girls' Middle School, epitomized the new Chinese woman, as unlike previous generations as the sedan chair is the aeroplane. Her face, beneath the tulle veil and circlet of flowers, is amused and intelligent. She knew that she had achieved the extraordinary. In a tradition which limited a woman's profession to that of wife or whore, she had found both independence and an eligible husband.

Contact with the West had forced the Chinese to reappraise long-held prejudices. Shanghai, as the most Western city in China, moved to the centre of this social revolution, attracting the young and the single woman in particular. In traditional China, power had resided with men and the elderly. Young men obeyed their fathers. Women obeyed men. Unsurprisingly women and students enthusiastically supported those aspects of Western morality which promised independence and choice. Women saw in its uncertain freedoms everything to gain and nothing to lose. Their experiments placed them in the forefront of society's transformation. Chinese newspapers, writers and film-makers concentrated on their emergence and the novelty of their position. The social and psychological difficulties they endured turned them into appealing and exciting subjects.

The China of old Mr Wu regarded a woman as a donkey, or a piece of fruit. They provided labour, sex and, most importantly, sons. Whether wife or whore, they led a prescribed and powerless existence. The law considered wives to be chattels, talkativeness was a ground for divorce, adultery a licence to murder. A daughter had less entitlement to her father's estate than a bastard son. Even then, she could only inherit in her husband's name. A widow's inheritance depended on her chastity. A second marriage meant expulsion from her first husband's family, loss of rights to his estate and severance from their children. Society, on the other hand, expected a widower to remarry and permitted him to keep his first wife's property; his second wife was accepted by his first wife's parents as a stepdaughter. The effect this had on women is revealed in the description of the home against which one managed to rebel.

In July 1925 three examiners in red gowns and ermine entered the largest hall in the University of Paris and took their seats beneath the tapestried walls at a centre table. The hall was empty but for a plump-faced, diminutive Chinese woman dressed in the latest Shanghai fashion. She had rouged her cheeks and lips and wore her hair bobbed. Cheng Sumei was the first Chinese woman to graduate in law from the Sorbonne and the first Chinese of either sex admitted to the French courts in the French Concession of Shanghai. As modern and as Westernized as her haircut, she had already made a name for herself. She had attended the Peace Conference in 1919 as attaché to the Chinese delegation, lectured in Britain and America on China's role in the world and had persuaded – by far the hardest task – the families of twenty Chinese girls to allow their daughters to study in Paris. By 1925, at the age of thirty-one, her biography had been published in the United States and she appointed a judge of the District Court in Shanghai. If her career was a dazzling list of achievements, her upbringing typifies the stultifying existence from which many Chinese women sought to extricate themselves.[120]

Cheng Sumei was born in 1894 to a wealthy, aristocratic Guangzhou family. The Chengs' house lay behind high stone walls and a courtyard of trees, flowers and sweet-smelling shrubs. A flight of stone steps led to the main entrance where a carved, wooden screen across the doorway prevented evil spirits from entering the home. Behind the screen stretched another courtyard decorated with grottoes, artificial rocks, miniature mountains, stone bridges and a lake filled in summer with lotus flowers. From the garden a staircase led to an immense hall paved in marble and containing the family altar. In this room, the family celebrated the marriages, births and religious festivities of the household. Around the walls, Chinese characters recorded the family history. Women were only allowed in here on special occasions.

Next to the hall, a long gallery separated the men of the family from the women. The men shared more comfortable quarters in the main house. The women lived in a series of pavilions outside. Sumei recalled that her two brothers ate, slept and studied apart from her sister and herself and only joined them during recreation hours when all the cousins played together.

The household consisted of 60 family members and 40 servants. The Chengs, like most wealthy Chinese families, kept slaves. A child slave attended every child of the household. After Sumei and her cousins had their feet bound at the age of six, Sumei recalled, 'we were carried to the schoolroom on the backs of our little slaves. They deposited us on our chairs, and when the lesson was over they came back for us, as though we had been so many cripples.'[121] Encouraged by her mother, whose own crippled feet had not kept her husband by her side, Sumei tore off the bandages. Her outraged grandmother pronounced, 'No one will marry her!'[122]

A well-to-do Chinese woman confined her life to the family compound and the homes of other ladies to whom she paid the obligatory round of afternoon visits in a carriage or a chair, the shades of which were always drawn. The visits followed a set pattern. The women first exchanged elaborate compliments then discussed the weather, their clothes, their health, the cost of living and servant problems. Sumei's twenty-five-year-old mother, Mrs Cheng, failed to find consolation in these expeditions. Her husband had left her in the power of his unlikeable mother, while he lived in Beijing with another family, 'quite as though he had forgotten us'.[123] Mrs Cheng's predicament aroused little sympathy. As Sumei remarked: 'In China, when a woman is jealous of her husband, everyone makes fun of her. She is not taken seriously.'[124] The deserted and unhappy mother had nothing to do but keep to her rooms, furnished in typical Chinese fashion, the walls hung with old embroideries, the chairs made of teak. The room looked on to a small garden set about with pots of plants. The gardener replanted the pots each season with peonies, roses, chrysanthemums or sometimes dwarf trees of maple or pine which gave the impression of a tiny forest. At the end of the garden stood a stone altar and Mrs Cheng's sole comfort.

When she was fourteen and living in Beijing, Sumei's grand-mother arranged her engagement. The old woman held a party to which neither Sumei nor her fiancé were invited. From behind a curtain, Sumei watched representatives from her future husband process around the courtyard of her home to a blast of trumpets and the trill of flutes. Eight white horses appeared at the main gates, their harnesses of scarlet leather studded with gold, red-satin scarves fastened across their chests. Their valets wore heavily embroidered livery, surmounted by caps with long plumes. The horses advanced in pairs. Between each swung baskets spilling over with fruits and gifts of every sort, jewels and ornaments in gold and jade, pearl hairpins and presents to bring luck. In the reception room decorated with red silk embroidered in gold characters, family friends prostrated themselves to Sumei's grandmother, enthroned in a large armchair on a raised platform. One by one they touched their foreheads to the ground in the kowtow. Sumei's grandmother sat, radiant with her own importance. Afterwards each of the guests received a piece of the engagement cake to ensure long life. Sumei wrote: 'That night, as I fell asleep, I wondered who had been the real heroine of the occasion? Grandmother or I?'[125]

Twenty years later the authority of the Chinese home appeared a thing of the past. By 1928 the Chinese flapper, surely the antithesis of the crippled and languishing mother of Cheng Sumei, had become a common sight on Shanghai's streets. One newspaper reported, 'She is usually dressed in semi-foreign style with bobbed hair and short skirt ... and powdered face. She attends the movies regularly and expects to be courted in screen lover fashion.' These girls might cause the older generation much worry, but, the paper continued approvingly, 'They lead a wholesome outdoor life and thrive on it. The Chinese flapper has come to stay.'[126] Chinese girls, apart from marrying in aeroplanes, learnt to drive and to ride with foreigners in the Western district. They ran schools and even their own bank, the Women's Commercial and Savings Bank at 392 Nanking Road.

Chinese families no longer hid behind high walls in Nantao. They lived in Shanghai's Western-style homes which could be any-thing from Gothic to futuristic glass with roofs that opened at the touch of a button. In the Park Hotel I met three women who had grown up in such households. They had attended Western schools and played lacrosse. I expected their upbringing to be the same as my mother's. It was some time before I realized that the numerous 'aunties' to whom they referred were, in fact, 'daddy's' concubines.

The Park Hotel proved an appropriate place to find them. Nearly every Chinese I met recalled its glamour. It stands at the point where Nanking Road turns into Bubbling Well Road and looks out over Renmin Park, then Shanghai's racecourse. When it opened in December 1934 it was the tallest building in the Far East and taller than anything on the Bund. Three hundred feet high, its grill room and roof garden offered people a splendid view of the city. The hotel was a Chinese venture, put together by the Joint Savings Society founded in 1923 by four Chinese banks, the Yienyieh Commercial Bank, Kincheng Banking Corporation, the China and South Sea Bank and the Continental Bank. The popularity of the Joint enterprise reflected the wealth of the Chinese community. Funds rose from $1,430,000 at the end of 1923 to $61,627,000 by 1932. In Shanghai tradition, the Chinese business community expressed this new-found confidence with a building as modern and luxurious (and, of course, tall) as anything built by the foreigner.

Its lobby is still splendidly pillared in black and pea-green marble. The former Grill Room once again offers music and dancing at night. Under fairy lights, a young man played the clarinet. Chinese families sat with their children, the smaller ones sleeping on chairs pushed together for the purpose. Across the dance floor, elderly couples circled with dazed expressions on their faces, once again enjoying an activity which the events of the last forty years appeared to have banished for ever.

My three companions were all born in Shanghai, had left during the communist takeover and had now returned on their first visit since 1949. Mrs Wang and Mrs Li were both in their late fifties and lived in Hong Kong. Euphemia Wu came from New York and was twenty years younger. She wore sky-blue leather pants, cut like the bottom half of a parachutist's outfit and billowing with zips and pockets from her waist to her knees. Mrs Li was tall and elegant. She wiped the edge of her glass with a handkerchief before she drank. Her family had been wealthy government officials. Her grandfather came from a town just outside Shanghai and her great-grandfather, whose portrait hung in all their family homes, was a wealthy government official, celebrated for his stinginess. Of his six sons, Mrs Li's grandfather was the playboy. However much he borrowed, it never seemed enough. Her great-grandfather owned a godown where he kept the family fortune in gold and silver taels. Even when old and blind, he still liked to visit the godown once a month, to sit among his fortune and count out the taels. He allowed no one else in, but Mrs Li's grandfather bribed the watchmen. Whenever he needed money for his women or gambling debts he stopped by, carrying with him copper taels to exchange for the gold and silver. Her great-grandfather never noticed the difference. When he died, the family found half his fortune missing. Mrs Li smiled indulgently, 'My grandfather was a very mischievous young man,' she said.

Mrs Wang was short and plump and owned a dress shop in Kowloon. Her father was a Shanghai success story. He had come to the city with nothing and had made a fortune in the construction business. She spent part of her childhood in two lane houses joined together near North Station in Hongkew. After the birth of her brother, Mrs Wang's father had made enough money to acquire a large house in the International Settlement close to the racecourse. Neither her mother or grandmother had bound feet. 'They were far too poor for such frivolities. They expected to work hard all their lives,' said Mrs Wang approvingly.

Euphemia Wu's parents abandoned her in 1952 when she was a few months old. Desperate to escape from communist China but only able to take one child, they chose Euphemia's brother and left her behind in the care of her amah. Three years later her father succeeded in smuggling out both child and nurse to Hong Kong on a fishing boat. Euphemia was put into a convent and her amah dismissed. The Wus had moved to Malaysia and neither made the journey to see their child. Euphemia described the school as a 'dumping ground' for the unwanted daughters of rich Chinese families. When she was eight her mother finally sent for her. She recalled walking into the sitting-room of her parents' house in Malaysia. It was full of elegant women playing mahjong. One got up. 'What are you wearing?' she said. 'That was my mother,' remarked Euphemia drily. 'She refused to embrace me until we had been to the store and I was properly dressed.'

Euphemia's mother interested herself in clothes and mahjong. As Euphemia remarked: 'Most mothers tell their children fairy tales, mine described the dresses she wore in Shanghai.' She had owned cupboards of cheongsams of varying lengths, depending on the fashion, some with inserts of French lace, others embroidered over the shoulders and down one side with dragons or flowers. Her shoes were embroidered to match. She liked lots and lots of embroidery. The more embroidery, the more expensive they looked. Under the cheongsam she wore a corset to coax her waist down to eighteen inches and padding around the bosom. With the cheongsams, she wore a long silk jacket, or fur in winter, with jade jewellery and small, beaded bags. Every spring, servants aired the fur coats for three days then stored them in camphor chests.

'She never worried about the cost of anything. My grandfather kept a drawer full of money. When she wanted some, she just helped herself.'

Mrs Li admitted that she only saw her mother in brief glimpses as she hurried from the house in furs and scent. She rose at noon, made herself beautiful then spent the afternoon and evening playing mahjong. The marriage was an unhappy one. Mrs Li recalled frequent arguments when her father would accuse his wife of neglecting the children and she would complain about his girlfriends.

Mrs Wang insisted that her mother was 'a plain woman' who devoted herself, 'like a proper Chinese wife', to her husband, her mother-in-law and the ten children she had by the age of thirty-six. An outbreak of measles caused a family catastrophe. Mrs Wang's only brother died from the infection leaving a family of nine girls. That seemed enough to me, but Mrs Li broke in to explain the importance of sons to the Chinese father. Only males could worship at the family shrine in the ancestral hall. A dutiful son prayed for his ancestors on birth and death days, lit candles and put out food for his father when he died. Without these observances, a man's spirit could not rest easy.

It was the duty of Mrs Wang's grandmother to find her son another wife. She returned to the small town which she had left years before and bought an eighteen-year-old girl for 300 silver dollars from a poor family. Even at nine years old, Mrs Wang thought her father's new wife looked extraordinarily young when she first arrived in her old-fashioned Manchu dynasty skirt hardly daring to say a word. Mrs Wang's mother treated her as another daughter, 'and in that way they got on'. She used to play ball with Mrs Wang in the garden. She had one son and a daughter and died when she was thirty-four. 'I now live with her daughter who likes to tell people she is my real sister,' Mrs Wang sniffed. 'It's snobbery, I suppose, but I don't contradict her, poor thing, after all she's been through.'

It was some time before the family knew about the third wife. Her father omitted to ask his wife's or mother's permission but set her up secretly in a separate establishment. They only knew of her when he fell sick and she sent a message asking if she might visit him. Mrs Wang's mother burst into tears and refused to have her in the house. A family conference was held. '"For my father's sake let her come,"' Mrs Wang said, adding, 'I always like to be fair.' Mrs Wang's mother stood firm and the third wife never entered the house despite having six children by Mrs Wang's father. After he recovered, the children often visited, but never with their mother.

Mrs Wang finally met the third wife some years later. The concubine was only two years older than Mrs Wang. She assured me that the girl came from a respectable family and continued, 'My father made every excuse for taking her. One of his uncles had no children. "She's not a concubine. She's instead of Number Two uncle's family," he protested. Well, you couldn't take much notice of that sort of remark. When a man was as rich and good-looking as my father he could have what he wanted and think up the reason afterwards.'

I asked Mrs Wang if she was fond of her father. 'No,' she replied. 'With him it was always "Son, son, son" and his concubines. He had too much money and it spoilt him.'

I wondered if it was usual for a man to send his mother to choose his concubine. 'Oh quite,' said Mrs Li. 'A man's mother ran the household. She took all the important decisions and had the power to make life very unpleasant for her son's wives – more, perhaps, than the son himself. That was still true when I was growing up.' Mrs Li's grandmother was something of an exception. The daughter of an official, she had a traditional upbringing culminating in an arranged marriage when she was fifteen to Mrs Li's grandfather. Two years later, after the birth of Mrs Li's father and their move to Shanghai, she rebelled. She unbound her feet, taught herself to read and write and refused to put up with her husband's concubines. He had five officially and numerous others who were unofficial. He sent them as thankyou presents to friends who had done him a good turn. Mrs Li's grandmother demanded a separate establishment and drew the line at further children after their son who adored her. When he married, she moved into his Spanish-style house on Yuen Road.

Mrs Li's grandmother was a severe and dignified old lady but also 'fun-loving'. She took pleasure in Shanghai's mix of East and West and even her morning regime incorporated both. A devout Buddhist, she rose at nine o'clock then spent two hours in her worship room with one of her maids to keep her company while she recited the sutras. Afterwards she returned to her room and switched on the radio. Shanghai had very good radio. Mrs Li's grandmother listened to the daily serialization from an old Chinese novel. Sometimes she tuned to a jazz programme.

Mrs Li continued, 'She wanted happy faces around her. She liked to see people having a good time.' One summer she booked ringside seats for a season of professional storytellers and invited her middle-aged nieces and twelve-year-old granddaughter to accompany her. Mrs Li recalled eating snacks and watching the storytellers perform one after another, each performance lasting for about half an hour. They wore silk robes and carried a fan which they used to make a dramatic point, unfurling it languidly or snapping it shut at a heated moment. By the time they finished, it had grown dark and Mrs Li's grandmother suggested they visit a nightclub. I asked if that was not an inappropriate end to such a traditional form of entertainment. 'Certainly not,' said Mrs Li. 'We all thought it quite natural.' The nightclub possessed a spectacular ballroom and garden. Concealed lights lit up the trees and shrubs and Mrs Li recalled displays of fireworks. Inside she relished watching the men cross the ballroom to where the hostesses sat and ask them to dance or sit at their table. 'It was an education for a twelve-year-old!' She also chatted to a boy, not much older than herself, who boasted that he had run away from home. The son of a rich family, he had spent the last three nights eluding frantic relatives in Shanghai's nightclubs – many of which stayed open twenty-four hours. Towards dawn he curled up on a sofa in the corner and went to sleep. He told the deeply impressed Mrs Li how the dance hostesses fussed over him and fed him titbits. When Mrs Li's grandmother caught her granddaughter yawning, she announced it was time to go. Immediately her nieces stood up and started to flutter about her, helping her to her feet, finding her bag, all anxious to please. She, of course, had paid for everything.

I wondered how the grandmother managed to achieve financial independence from her husband. Mrs Li explained that the Number Six uncle of her father had no children so he adopted his nephew and left the boy all his fortune. Mrs Li's grandmother received a very generous allowance from her son which annoyed her husband but there was nothing he could do about it. She smiled before pointing out the complications of Chinese family finances with any number of wives and concubines as well as their children all fighting for their share. 'Family feuds filled the law courts.'

I asked if her grandparents ever had a reconciliation. 'Of sorts,' she replied, admitting that old age and a kidnapping transformed the erstwhile playboy. Her grandfather owned a chain of hotels in Shanghai one of which he lived in. He preferred it to a house and set up each of his six official concubines in her own suite. Every morning he followed a set routine – stepping into a lift on the ninth floor at nine o'clock sharp. One morning a gangster was waiting for him with a gun. The grandfather's nephew who looked after the hotel received a ransom damand for U.S.$100,000. The cousin did not bother to inform the police – no one did with kidnapping cases. He collected the money, put on a pair of black cloth shoes as the kidnappers had instructed and carried a newspaper to identify himself. Then he drove to a field where he found his uncle in a hut. The old man was very upset, not so much by the kidnapping as by the loss of the money. 'I'll save it all back,' he said.

He was still a wealthy man but he became obsessively mean. He had, for example, always loved cakes. Instead of ordering a dozen or so, he stood outside Shanghai's excellent cake shops staring at the display. After twenty minutes of this he would shake his head and say, 'Very nice but I can't afford it.' He also used to relish chocolates after each meal. Now he bought hard candy instead. After a few sucks on the sweet, he took it out of his mouth and put it back in a tin to save for the next occasion. Miserliness did not endear him to his concubines. One by one they all left (Number Five ran off with his chauffeur) except for Number Four who stayed with him until the end. She and the grandfather moved in with Mrs Li's father and took over Mrs Li's room. Mrs Li's grandmother and Number Four Concubine were very civil to each other. On New Year and festival days she kowtowed to Mrs Li's grandmother as concubines did in old-fashioned households.

A middle-aged Taiwanese businessman now invited Euphemia Wu to dance. He was smaller than her and pressed close as they moved around the floor. Two girls partnering their mothers made up the only other couples. Mrs Wang tried to order another lemonade but the waiters had vanished. When one appeared to give the room a perfunctory glance, he carefully looked over Mrs Wang's head. I recalled the service provided in the Cheng household and asked Mrs Li if her family kept slaves. She was taken aback. 'Not slaves,' she said, 'but it is true we did have a ridiculous number of servants.' (The Nationalist government only prohibited the sale of slaves in 1932.)[127] Each family member had a personal servant, except for the grandmother who had two, one to make her tea and the other to comb her hair. Mrs Li's father had a manservant and all the servants kept assistants. Even the driver was accompanied by an under-driver who stuck his hand out when the car turned and opened the door for the family. The children loved him. He was very young and used to play ball with them. After the kidnapping, the children had to go everywhere with the driver. Afraid that people might mistake him for their father, they insisted on repeating his name loudly and often. Mrs Li also recalled the unusual form of air-conditioning provided by their servants. The family house possessed ceiling fans in all the rooms against the unbearable humidity of a Shanghai summer. The family refused to use the fans at meal times because 'Chinese like their dishes hot'. Instead, at each corner of the square table sat a servant, gently fanning the family as they ate. Mrs Li recalled, 'On summer evenings my maid fanned herself and me until I fell asleep.'

Mrs Li emphasized the close relationship between the family and their servants. It was considered courteous to address older ones as Sister or Brother. If a child forgot itself and screamed abuse, the servant immediately reported the matter to Mrs Li's father 'who gave us hell'. She described a particular incident with the family tailor. Mrs Li enjoyed sitting in his room watching him work. One afternoon, she decided to make up his face. First she crept into her mother's quarters and helped herself to cosmetics then she returned to the tailor. She dabbed his cheeks, painted his lips and finally gave him a thick, black moustache. He continued to sew without a word. At about five, Mrs Li's father returned home. The tailor went to his study and stood patiently in front of the desk. His employer looked up. 'Number Three,' was all the tailor said, meaning Mrs Li, the youngest of the three daughters. Mrs Li's father called her sternly. When she entered the study, he was trying hard not to laugh. 'Never play in the tailor's room again,' was all he said. To mention the word 'make-up' would have piled more humiliation on the man.

The Taiwanese brought Euphemia back to our table. His face

had two deep creases running down the cheeks. He told us he had just pulled off a successful deal with the Shanghai Council, 'I'm in the mood to spread my good fortune around. You ladies are very lucky,' he said pulling up a chair. I was curious and ready to chat but Mrs Li raised her eyebrows and stared across the room. Mrs Wang shifted her small, broad back to him and Euphemia scowled. With one, final, hopeful look at me, he moved off.

In 1929 the National government introduced a Civil Code and a series of laws bestowing certain rights on women. How had these laws affected family life? I asked my companions. They all looked puzzled. I appeared to be talking a foreign language. Mrs Wang said that new laws made little difference because 'One never argued with one's husband or father'. Mrs Li said her father looked on his powers as a natural right and recounted an anecdote to illustrate her point. The son of a rich family, Mrs Li's father never worked a day in his life. He owned almost the whole of Fourth Street in Central district and lived off the rents from its famous bookshops and brothels. Leisure allowed him to pursue the scholarly interests thought appropriate for a Chinese gentleman. He wrote poems and kept a library of classical Chinese texts. He wore the old-fashioned Chinese gown rather than a Western suit and despised any sort of businessman. He was also a stickler for etiquette. In those days, one addressed a superior with an elaborate preamble of honorifics, never by the Chinese equivalent of 'Mr' which sounded curt to Chinese ears. One day an antique dealer called on Mrs Li's father to show him some goods and addressed him as 'Mr'. Mrs Li's father was outraged. He slapped the man on the face. The antique dealer took him to court which ruled Mrs Li's father should pay a large fine to build a street which became known as 'Mr' Street. According to Mrs Li, it still exists today.

Mrs Wang recalled the domestic authority enjoyed by her father. As soon as he began to make money, he invited his brothers and sisters, their husbands, wives and children to live in his house and help run the business. 'That was the Chinese custom. As they depended on him for everything, they did exactly what he said even before he said it.'

Euphemia Wu thought Shanghai women tough and devious, beneath a demeanour admirably adapted to the prevailing source of money and position. She said: 'You can tell a woman from Shanghai even today. They are notorious for their ability to promote themselves and manipulate others. The Song sisters are the most famous example.'

The three women leant together to exchange ancient gossip about the Songs and recall their own escapes from the communists. Mrs Wang left just after the Second World War to study in Hong Kong. Mrs Li got out by a similar piece of luck. After the Japanese invasion of China, her parents finally divorced. In 1949 Mrs Li's mother moved to Hong Kong and invited her youngest daughter for a holiday. Mrs Li was unwilling to go and finally agreed to come for a fortnight. She never returned. The communists confiscated her father's property in Shanghai so he could not buy freedom for himself or his relatives. She never saw her grandmother again. Her sisters and brother have lived in Shanghai all this time. 'I think of them every day. Every time I eat a good meal, go shopping or just enjoy a dip in the swimming pool I think of my sisters and brother and what they have endured. Why was I so fortunate?'

The band stopped playing and the fairy lights went out. The families gathered up their sleeping children and made for the door. As we left, I asked what they thought of Shanghai, 'So overcrowded and dirty,' said Mrs Li. She had visited the family home and found that now it housed fourteen families, including one of five in her father's study. Mrs Wang complained of the rudeness of the Chinese. I said that I found them charming. 'Oh, you're a foreigner,' said Euphemia. 'They're awful to Overseas Chinese because we escaped and they still can't, even now.' Mrs Li did not like to walk in the streets because 'people make remarks'. Mrs Wang's relatives were causing her trouble. 'They all want to get out, every single one of them and expect me to sponsor them. Of course I try and do what I can but they think money grows on trees in the West.'

Mrs Li, Mrs Wang and Euphemia Wu had described the restricted existence led by a Chinese woman with wealth and a family to protect her. The life of a whore proved no less circumscribed.

Shanghai was famous for its brothels. As early as 1869 the Duke of Somerset referred to it in the House of Lords as 'a sink of iniquity'. In 1934 a Chinese newspaper claimed that Shanghai led the world in prostitution and produced some intriguing statistics to support its assertion. In London, one person in 960 was a prostitute; in Berlin, one in 580; in Paris, one in 481; in Chicago one in 430; while in Shanghai as many as one in 130. A visiting Chinese merchant from the interior could buy a guide to the city which included a Red Light section detailing the delights on offer and their price – all deliberately written in archaic language, incomprehensible to an inquisitive wife with her inferior education (in the same way as erotic paragraphs in Western literature were printed in Latin).

Shanghai's Red Light district centred on Fuchow Road, known by the Shanghainese as Fourth Street and running at right angles to the Bund and parallel to Nanking Road. Here worked the city's most beautiful and accomplished singsong girls. At parties held by friends in restaurants, or in the brothels themselves, the visiting merchant enjoyed their singing and playing, was amused by their jokes and gossip recounted in the lilting lisp of a Suzhou accent (girls from Suzhou were meant to be the most beautiful) and finally exalted by their love-making.

All this was done to him not by women but by girls of twelve or thirteen, dressed, to the European eye, like boys, in loose, silk pyjamas with high Mandarin collars. It was not bosom, hips, or even a lovely face that aroused the merchant's interest. Feet, the smaller the better, were the centre of attention and sexual excitement. Three inches long and with swollen instep, they resembled pigs' trotters encased in embroidered silk shoes. Bound feet had belonged to Chinese tradition for centuries. Not only did crippled feet conveniently restrict a woman but also, as readers of the Chinese newspaper, the *Shanghai Press* knew, the smaller the female foot, 'the more wondrous become the folds of the vagina'. Footbinding concentrated development 'in this one place'. Those fortunate 'who have personally experienced this feel a supernatural exaltation'.[128]

Any girl with aspirations had her feet bound. A woman specializing in the business wrapped a bandage of about two inches wide and ten feet long around the soles of a five- or six-year-old. She left the big toe free while forcing the other four in towards the sole. She then wrapped the bandage hard about the heel to push the toes under and into the sole and to bring the sole and heel as close together as possible. The bones slowly broke, the flesh rotted, a toe or two would fall off. It was excruciatingly painful, as one Chinese woman recalled: 'In summer, my feet smelled offensively because of pus and blood; in winter, my feet felt cold because of lack of circulation . . . the heavily-creased plantar couldn't be scratched when it itched or soothed when it ached. My shanks were thin, my feet became humped, ugly, and odoriferous.'[129] Jean McMeekin, an old Shanghai resident, told me that her mother joined the Anti-Footbinding League after living opposite the first Chinese ambassador to Queen Victoria. Jean's mother could not stand hearing the screams of his 'lovely little daughters', having their feet bound for the first time.

The reward was a tiny, fragile foot that aroused in the male that potent combination of lust and pity. In Chinese brothels, men rubbed, smelt, chewed and licked the little feet, love-biting the tiny red slippers while the especially devoted fetishist soaped the naked, unbound foot. As one Chinese official admitted: 'You gentleman know how much time I spend in washing Little White's feet, but you don't know how often I bend down to smell them. I alternate between washing and smelling, sometimes taking as long as forty-five minutes; and I don't let the servant re-enter until the water is cold.'[130]

Manuals even existed to instruct the novice how to hold the tiny foot and extract from it the most pleasure during love-making. The man might ask the girl to rub her feet up and down his penis, 'like two dragons playing with a pearl'[131] as one book put it. Or he might place her on a swing, supporting her thighs with his hands, her tiny feet on his shoulders. Her bowed shoes, 'embroidered and red, slender, pointed, and graceful,' caused him, as they made love with each push of the swing, 'to become mentally intoxicated and spiritually lost'.[132]

The Chinese government declared footbinding illegal in 1911 while a moral-welfare campaign closed down the brothels in the International Settlement. By the late 'twenties, the visiting Chinese businessman had no need of a guidebook. In certain areas of the city, it became impossible to avoid young girls in cheongsams split to the thigh who grabbed customers, as one man recalled, 'with the Chinese equivalent of an American football tackle'.[133] At night on Nanking Road prostitutes of the Third Class (the First reserved themselves for Chinese politicians and officials, the Second for European millionaires) flitted along in rickshaws encircled with a loop of electric lights, their painted faces and silk dresses lit up in the dark, 'like dainty meteors',[134] wrote one Frenchman. Their puller knew exactly when to swerve towards the other side of the road at a hesitating customer. The price agreed, the man hailed another vehicle and the illuminated rickshaw moved triumphantly off, followed by its attendant shadow.

As the Chinese discovered jazz, cabarets took over from brothels in popularity. Even Du Yuesheng, Shanghai's leading gangster, forced his favourite sing-song girls to learn the foxtrot and tango. Clubs fought over the latest singing and dancing star. When one club enticed away two stars from another establishment, the angry owner hired a dozen men and sent them to sit at his rival's tables with instructions to chew gum. On the signal, they spat the pieces on to the dance floor. The stars could not perform their routine and the club lost an evening's take. The victim waited a few months until a particularly crowded night for a return bout. Halfway through the evening his hirelings asked the band to play 'Whistling in the Dark', and dim the lights. In the gloom the men let loose a sackful of water-snakes. Ten minutes later the lights came on and the club was empty.

Shanghai's businessmen competed to acquire a star as a mistress. Important admirers employed gangs to fight the gangs of their rivals. They delivered fur coats and diamonds as regularly as flowers. Euphemia Wu remembered her grandfather's obsession with a particular singer who arrived at one of his parties wearing a dress studded with coloured light bulbs which flashed on and off. She kept the batteries in her handbag. On opening nights, the club stacked flowers from her admirers around the block. Euphemia's grandfather wanted to make her his official concubine but his daughter, whom he adored far more than his wife, took a dislike to the girl. 'Anyone but her,' she said and refused to talk to him until he gave the singer up. The mosquito press followed the love lives of these stars as eagerly as they did Shanghai's film actresses. Who had supplanted whom and how much she got out of him took on an inordinate importance in a city which regarded sex and money as interchangeable obsessions.

In Hong Kong I met a man who still recalled the joys of Shanghai's sing-song girls. We were at a party in the Governor's House to celebrate the agreement between Britain and China over the fate of Hong Kong in 1997. The British boasted of their statesmanship with flushed faces while a few elderly Shanghainese stood in corners making provisional plans for their second escape from the communists in fifty years. My middle-aged companion told me that he had never forgotten the first Shanghai girls he met in Hong Kong in 1949. They had just got out of China, leaving everything behind. He and his friends had survived the war. 'We were all very young and drunk, I suppose, on just being alive.' The Shanghainese appeared wonderfully chic compared to the 'rather frumpy' Guangzhou and English girls. They offered light-hearted relationships, free of guilt and obligation. He went on, 'Of course we bought them presents and paid their rent but it was all, somehow innocent. They fucked, God did they fuck, but no recriminations afterwards, always a laugh, a joke and off to the next party. Some have remained good friends. I still have their telephone numbers.'

Xu Amao, the favourite daughter of a poor family in Pootung, had a rather more typical experience. She did not look like a country girl. She dressed well and cut her hair in the latest Western fashion. Her parents paid for her to attend school where she talked of women's rights and exhibited all the characteristics of a modern girl student. When she was seventeen she fell for a man who encouraged her, saying: 'A woman like you has a right to her own life and shouldn't do anything as old-fashioned as marry. You're made for better things. Come with me to Shanghai and really live.' In the city he took her to a hotel and raped her. He then introduced her to other men and they lived on her earnings until he grow bored and sold her to a brothel-keeper. The owner suffered from bad temper and beat Xu Amao every day for six months. Fortunately, at some point Xu Amao acquired an adoptive father. He felt sorry for the girl and redeemed her from the brothel for SH$300. A new and better life seemed to be opening up when she fell ill with venereal disease and nearly died. After she recovered, her adopted father introduced Xu Amao to an elderly gentleman in Wenzhou. They took to each other. The gentleman handed over SH$300 to repay her debt and made Xu Amao his second wife. She had a daughter. As a concubine she enjoyed no legal status and was expected to wait on her husband's first wife. The jealousy of this woman made life so unbearable that Xu Amao returned to her family in Pootung. The old man wrote to her, releasing her from the marriage and repayment of the SH$300. He wished her well and advised her to find a younger man. His kindness undid her. She grew depressed, refused to eat, then asked a neighbour to look after her daughter. Twice she tried to hang herself but was cut down. Finally she stabbed herself and was found in a pool of blood. She was twenty.[135]

This story with its mixture of initial hope, sexual degradation and financial transaction epitomized the experience of many women in Shanghai. The city, as the most Western and therefore the most 'modern' in China, attracted countless Xu Amaos because it appeared to offer an alternative to the traditional choices of marriage or whoredom. The reality often proved a travesty of both.

In Shanghai a young woman could acquire an education at a Western school and college, pursue a career or make a name for herself as a writer or an actress. Most of all she could enjoy the heady atmosphere of Shanghai's teahouses and coffee shops where people now sought her opinions and debated her difficulties. From languishing in the back pavilions of Chinese intellectual life, she found herself in the equivalent of the ancestral hall. The battle against the old order took place around her. Love and marriage had become the issue of contention between the generations. The rejection of an arranged marriage signalled the first revolt for many Chinese. Those who did so played with the novel concept of romantic love and cohabitation. Their interest even instigated a new genre of literature. Romantic stories, nicknamed by a gathering of writers at a restaurant on Hankou Road in 1920 as the 'Mandarin Ducks and Butterflies school', used Shanghai as a setting. Magazines serializing such stories became immensely popular. Readers waited outside the distributor's shop in Canton Road to collect their weekly copy of *Saturday* magazine. They liked the heroines to be young women from good families, ready to defy their parents for love.

The new arrival to the city led a curious existence. A Chinese girl might wear Western clothes and high-heeled shoes, go to foreign movies, play the part of Nora in Ibsen, smoke cigarettes and take lovers, yet never visit Europe or America, have a single foreign friend or learn a foreign language. The emphasis was all on style or, as Cheng Sumei described it, being 'in the role' and is best summed up by the experience of Li Yunhe, a small-time actress famous in later years as Madam Mao Zedong.

Yunhe arrived in Shanghai in the early 'thirties with dreams of becoming a movie star. Also intrigued by politics, Li Yunhe saw her sexual independence as the cornerstone of her left-wing beliefs. I first visited China a few years after her imprisonment. During my trip to Shanghai I met elderly film directors who had spent the Cultural Revolution in 'the cow-shed', imprisoned in their own studios or sent to work in the countryside. They told me Madam Mao Zedong wanted revenge for the slights she had received forty years before as an unsuccessful starlet. As one director put it, 'She was well-known for her promiscuity and her mediocre acting; and she knew we remembered her hanging around the studios.'

A football star called Li recalled her aggressive behaviour the one night he spent with her. They had met at a reception in the Rich Harvest Gardens on Nanking Road and left together to watch *A Beauty's Heart*, a romantic film starring Butterfly Wu at the Carlton Theatre on Bubbling Well Road. Yunhe turned her 'strange, yearning eyes'[136] on the footballer and pressed her body closer but he was more interested in Butterfly Wu's acting. 'After all I was a man with some prior experience and not bursting with inquisitiveness about sex with a girl. To her fantastic enticements I made no response.'[137]

After the film, they walked along Nanking Road to the Champion Gardens restaurant where they ate an early dinner of fish and rice with a few glasses of sweet red wine. Yunhe's 'ambition and exhibitionism'[138] took the puzzled and now aroused footballer's breath away. They booked a room in Hui Zhong Hotel where the luxurious bathroom and brocade lampshades all created 'a suitable atmosphere for sexual activity'.[139] The moment the door closed, Yunhe leapt upon Li and covered him with kisses, her body 'as hot as a bowl of steamed rice'.[140] She paused to talk a little about his game then, 'all of a sudden',[141] took off her clothes and hopped, 'with a springing step',[142] into the bathroom. Through the open door Li watched her reflection in the mirror over the washbasin. He saw a slender body, good skin, 'flat, lovely eyes',[143] firm breasts and, near her right nipple, 'a pea-sized black mole'.[144] As she climbed into bed, she murmured, 'I am going to give you unsurpassable pleasure',[145] then set to with 'unique skill'. The result left him 'half dead and half lost'. She had provided 'great joy' but not 'complete satisfaction'. Eager to demonstrate her ability, she never forgot herself enough to give total pleasure. He dismissed the experience as a performance. Li recalled, 'She left me with the impression of a promiscuous woman, capable of going to extremes.'[146]

The footballer's attitude is typical of the Shanghainese who shrugged Western mores on and off as easily as a coat. They might put it on for a stroll along Nanking Road but back home they relaxed into more traditional garb. Lu Xun examined the issue in a talk entitled 'What Happens After Nora Leaves Home?', given in response to the popularity of Ibsen's *A Doll's House*. A Chinese Nora eager for an independent existence would have three choices: to starve, to 'go to the bad',[147] or to return home to her husband. 'To put it bluntly, what she needs is money,'[148] he said. Even the successful woman who earned her keep found she had merely exchanged one set of problems for another. She attracted too much attention.

Everybody from Ding Ling, China's foremost woman writer and member of the Communist party, to the most scurrilous of the mosquito press, agreed that women made good copy. They represented society's outposts and the public wanted news from the front, how the soldiers were standing up, what strains were telling most. One never knew, after all, when a wife or daughter might volunteer for picket duty.

Certain professions forced a woman to lead the charge and send back reports. Actresses attracted attention as much for the example they set as the heroines they depicted. One of the most successful and tragic was the film actress, Ruan Lingyu.

Ruan Lingyu acted in some of the best films made in the 'thirties. Their powerful effect relies on Ruan's simplicity, the truth of her interpretation and her intimate, at times almost sly, relationship with the camera. To scenes of deprivation and injustice she adds a powerful sense of melancholy. There is no hint of a Great Leap Forward or of the bright tomorrows which resound through the work of Ruan's boisterous rival, Li Lili. They describe a desolate present and foreshadow a future without hope.

Ruan Lingyu acted the consequences of a woman trying to survive in Shanghai while suffering them herself. The relationship between her art and her personal life riveted her audience. In the end the identification killed her.

Unlike so many of the city's success stories, Ruan Lingyu was born in Shanghai in 1910, the daughter of a low-paid Guangzhou machinist. Her elder sister died when she was one and her father four years later. Her mother went to work as a housemaid and saved up enough to send Ruan to school. While Ruan was living with her mother, the son of the family, Zhang Daming, raped her. She left school at sixteen, determined to support her mother by entering a competition held by the Mingxing Film Company to recruit actresses. 'She tried several times to get into the Mingxing but each time she failed because she was so tense,'[149] recalled Zhang Shichuan's widow. The company had decided to turn her down when she came to the notice of the director, Bu Wancang. Her air of sadness so moved him that he told her to come back the next day to try again. Bu Wancang directed her first film in which she played a widow watching over the coffin of her dead husband. When he came to look at the rushes, he threw the scenario into the air, crying out, 'We have discovered an exceptional talent!'[150] Zhang

Shichuan was less impressed. His widow recalled: 'Ruan Lingyu was a very passionate person and could never hide her emotions. On film she could laugh or cry as she wanted, giving an impression of great vivacity. But as she did not blindly follow the instructions of directors like Shichuan he made no efforts to train her.'[151]

Ruan left the Mingxing to join the Lianhua film company, famous for the quality of its left-wing films, where she came under the influence of Sun Yu. He recalled, 'She did not do so well until she came to us. Then she was a startling success. We liked each other very much. It was never difficult to work with Ruan.' Huang Shaofen also joined the Lianhua where he worked as her cameraman. When they first met, he was twenty-one and she only a year older. They had much in common. They came from the same province, spoke the same dialect and shared the somewhat daunting experience of fame at an early age. Ruan owed her initial popularity to Huang. Her acting skill impressed Sun Yu but he worried about her skin, 'brown like a peasant's', recalled Huang. He tried putting a black silk sock in front of the lens to disguise its rough texture. When that proved too thick, he pulled out some threads, producing a gauzelike effect. He experimented with different densities depending on the shot. For a close-up he used a fine gauze; on a long shot, something thicker. He smiled. 'I suppose I could say I used the first soft lens.'

Her films explored the personal aspect of a woman's life, a theme previously ignored in Chinese literature. One of the most compelling is *The Goddess*, a story of a prostitute, released one year before Ruan's suicide. Written, designed and directed by the twenty-seven-year-old Wu Yonggang for the Lianhua company, the film must be one of the first not to identify prostitution with moral turpitude. Wu Yonggang concentrated on the isolated and precarious existence of the woman rather than on the erotic implications of her profession. The images are deft and the characterization fresh and natural. The film is entirely shot from the prostitute's point of view. We never see a customer. Ruan is not depicted as a hard or sexy woman, merely a very bored one as she stands night after night in her long cheongsam on street corners. During the day her impatience and false smiles turn into animation and tenderness for her son. It is to pay for his education that she goes out each night. One evening she is pursued by a policeman and hides in a house where she is found by a small-time gangster who steals her money. He realizes he is on to a good thing and comes back for more. She changes lodging but he finds her. She tries to get a job in a factory, then as a housemaid, but lacks references. She pawns all her clothes and jewellery. The gangster threatens to sell her child unless she pays him off. She goes back to prostitution. Her son is doing well at school but has to leave when the headmaster discovers how she pays the fees. She decides to escape from Shanghai but the gangster steals her money and gambles it away. When he returns she throws a bottle at him, kills him and is sentenced to jail. The film ends with her in a cell. She has never, one is made to feel, been out of it.

In Shanghainese, 'Goddess' also meant prostitute. Ruan found herself playing both parts in real life. On screen she appeared a modern goddess to her audience, adored and envied for epitomizing the successful and independent woman. Off-screen, society considered her a member of the amusement population and little better than a prostitute. In those days no one had much respect for actresses or the daughters of household servants, explained Huang. Fame meant that she attracted rich and famous men who failed to appreciate her. The mosquito press discussed her love life in lurid detail. She could trust nobody. I imagined the only carefree time she enjoyed was gossiping in a corner with Huang between takes.

Her work became her refuge. Wu Yonggang who directed *The Goddess* recalled, 'During filming she was usually very relaxed, she joked about, sometimes she knitted or nibbled at a bit of food but as soon as she was in front of a camera her feelings, her attitude, her gestures all jelled quite naturally into the part she was playing. With no effort or exaggeration she acted without any preparation or rehearsal.'[152] Huang said, 'She was a complete professional and never got into a bad mood. She excelled in tragedy. Something came from deep within her. The director only had to give a few hints and you saw the feeling slowly well up as she gave herself over to the part. She was not acting, she was suffering the movie.'

That too came under threat. When she became famous, the studio forced her to make two films at once. She grew tense and exhausted from overwork. She also feared the talkies. She had a strong Guangzhou accent and could not speak Mandarin, the official screen dialect. Huang said sadly, 'She thought she would not find work, that she would be poor again.'

The last film she made was *New Women* based on the recent suicide of the film actress, Ai Xia, in February 1934. In the film Ai Xia is transformed into Wei Ming, an educated woman whose husband has left her with a small daughter. She finds work teaching music at a girls' school but, despite gifts of jewels and pity from the school principal, is reluctant to marry again. In debt and with her child sick, she writes a novel which is accepted by a publisher who cannot give her an advance. She needs money quickly and goes to work in a brothel; her first customer is the school principal. In despair she kills herself and, as she lies dying in the hospital, she hears the newsboys shouting outside, 'Famous woman writer commits suicide.' The film opened in February 1935 for the Chinese New Year Festival and was an immediate success. On March 7th friends invited Ruan Lingyu to dinner. After a few glasses she began to behave unlike herself, hugging all the actresses around the table, laughing and talking loudly. As she left she became unhappy and said, 'All parties have an end. I must go. Farewell.'[153] Late that night she took an overdose of sleeping tablets. She was twenty-five.

While her body lay in the morgue, thousands of fans, even more than attended Butterfly Wu's wedding eight months later, blocked the road to see her. The police had to disperse them. On the day of her burial the funeral procession stretched five kilometres. Female fans killed themselves in admiration. A play soon appeared based on her death. In the minds of the Shanghainese, art and reality appeared inextricably mixed. Ruan Lingyu had played the part of a character based on an actress who had killed herself. Now she too was dead and a new play about her was already on stage. The very realism of her films confused the issue. The parts that she took were not separated from ordinary life by glamour or fabulous experience which would have lent distance between her and her audience, her acting and her own life but of the poor or the middle class. She represented the ordinary woman. What she portrayed – rape, poverty, upheaval, suicide – she had also experienced. She brought to the roles an intensity that is extraordinary to watch, even after fifty years.

The obsessive interest of her public drove Ruan to suicide. For months before her death the mosquito press published every detail of the break-up of her affair with Zhang Daming (she had lived with him since he raped her at sixteen), and her move to the tea merchant Tang Jishan who, like Zhang, had no intention of marrying her. Her suicide note said simply: 'Gossip is a fearful thing.'

Two months after her death Lu Xun wrote an essay with that title. He noted the ease with which, 'Brilliant writers dash off big headlines: "More Concupiscent than Wu Zedian"', and the damage they caused women in the public eye. Weak in the face of the strong, the press

> seems strong enough to those weaker than itself; so although sometimes it has to suffer in silence, at others it still shows its might. And those like Ruan Lingyu make good copy for a display of power, because although a celebrity she was helpless. Readers enjoyed these items because it allowed them to think, 'Though I am not so beautiful as Ruan Lingyu, I have higher standards.' Or, 'Though I am not so able as Ruan Lingyu, I come from a more respectable family.' . . . It is certainly worth spending a few coppers to discover your own superiority.[154]

Superiority was not all the reader craved. Her unhappiness re-assured a public made fearful by change. It proved the old ways still retained the power to destroy social rebels. Now dead and harmless, Ruan could be resurrected.

Suicide was the only form of escape for women approved by traditional China. Headlines like 'Intimate Revelations on Ruan Lingyu and Bai the Lanky' melted away as the newspapers turned her into a saint. In death as in life a mask satisfying to her public was cast and fixed. 'She never had an easy time,' said Huang sadly.

The fate of Ruan Lingyu is the fate of Shanghai in the late 'thirties. Like her, its success proved as flimsy as one of Nanking Road's neon signs. Political, financial, cultural or even social innovation is not enough when lights can be switched off and electrical supplies disconnected. In 1949 traditional China, under a new name, did just that. The Shanghainese proved powerless to stop it. They had in fact lost the fight twelve years before.

The turmoil experienced by the Shanghainese during the 1930s was observed with passionate interest by a group of young Americans from the Chocolate Shop on Nanking Road. Over salads and milk shakes, radicals like Harold Isaacs, Agnes Smedley and Edgar Snow (he met his wife in the Chocolate Shop) debated China's future. J. B. Powell, the crusading editor of the *China Weekly Review*; 'Judge' Allman, the hillbilly-turned-lawyer who had presided over that peculiar Shanghai institution, the Mixed Courts; and American businessmen like Carl Crow, the witty and energetic head of an advertising company, joined with American missionaries, chorus girls and the odd conman to enjoy the only ice-cream sodas in the city. In 1935 a ravishing New Yorker caused a sensation when she walked into the Chocolate Shop, her pet gibbon draped across her shoulders.

Nearly everyone I interviewed had an anecdote about Emily Hahn. Men recalled her wistfully; women with vitriol. Now in her eighties, she still possesses a keen mind and the Odalisque appearance that fascinated men as various as Sir Victor Sassoon ('He liked to photograph me naked'), Sir Harold Acton who described her as 'a voluptuous figure from a Moroccan mellah',[155] and the Chinese poet and publisher, Zao Xinmei. Exotic, eccentric and amoral, people associated Emily Hahn with Shanghai in its last years. 'We were all much too physical,'[156] sighed Sir Harold Acton.

She arrived in Shanghai on a cruise with her sister, always intending to leave. She took pleasure in every aspect of the city. She worked for the *North China Daily News*, wrote a book about the Song sisters, attended races in Sir Victor Sassoon's box, inspected Chinese factories, visited White Russian artists and had a new dress made every day. She provides a bridge between the foreigners and the Chinese as events engulfed them both. Unlike many of her compatriots in the Chocolate Shop, she even learnt Chinese.

She caused scandal wherever she went. Enid Saunders Candlin recalled a Greek play put on by Emily Hahn in which the wives refuse to sleep with their husbands until they stop fighting. 'As we suffered from perpetual war in Shanghai, we thought it frightfully unsuitable. I walked out in the middle.' She provoked even more outrage at a dinner party given by a fellow American, Bernardine Fritz. By the mid-'thirties foreigners and Chinese had begun to socialize together. Bernardine was a Founder of the International Arts Theatre and a keen promoter of Chinese and Western friendship. People went to her parties to meet 'interesting' Chinese. No crowd, wrote Sir Harold Acton, could have been more 'jumbled'.[157] Among her guests was Zao Xinmei, famous, as Lu Xun had remarked, for his extraordinary beauty. When dinner ended, Emily and Xinmei got up from the table and left together.

Xinmei took Emily back to his large, old-fashioned house in Yangtzepoo where he lived with his wife, five children and numerous servants and hangers-on. Emily was amazed to see people sleeping all over the place. 'Who is that?' she asked, pointing to a cadaverous Chinese on a sofa. Xinmei looked puzzled then said, '"How was it? Was he the friend of one of my brothers? Did we know his father?

No ... Oh yes, I know!" He turned round, smiling in delight. "Of course. How could I have forgotten? Mr Chou is my jockey."'158 Like other rich Chinese in the Settlement, Xinmei toyed with the idea of owning horses. He had hired a jockey but then grew bored and bought something else instead. Mr Chou had stayed ever since. Emily accepted Xinmei's offer of an opium pipe and so begun one of the most famous affairs in the city.

The affair provided Emily Hahn with a unique insight into Shanghai. Zao Xinmei had grown up in the French Concession and knew the city intimately. A returned student from a rich family, he was a poet who published his own and his friends' work on his private printing press. He revealed to Emily 'a world closed to foreigners'. He took her around 'the back of the scenes' to peer out at the same old Shanghai but, 'through a glow of strange-coloured footlights'.159 He started a magazine with her, invited his friends to her flat and involved her with his chaotic, family life. They even went through a form of marriage ceremony because Xinmei and his wife feared Emily might be lonely. He promised Emily a space in the family graveyard while his wife presented her with two jade bracelets, the colour of mutton fat and the customary present for a new concubine.

Emily lived in an apartment on Kiangse Road – a street previously famous for its American brothels, where ten years before Gracie Gale had entertained foreign businessmen at 'the Line'. Xinmei's friends found the apartment conveniently central. A number of them at any time of the day or night might be found sitting in her green room on green and silver painted chairs admiring her bed piled high by a former tenant with about sixty satin cushions in brilliant shades. Emily recalled her days as various and highly coloured as the cushions. She began her morning arguing with her cook, excellent at his work but foul-tempered. She then spent a tranquil few hours in the offices of the *North China Daily News*. Sometimes she interviewed an Old China Hand or described a bizarre Shanghai sight like the Chinese chemist hung with cages containing sloths from Indochina or the street which only sold pink baby bonnets. At lunchtime, she visited the Chocolate Shop, went shopping for miniature jade screens or sets of tiny, pottery horses, helped Bernardine Fritz entertain a visiting American millionairess or Mei Lanfang, the famous Peking Opera star. In summer she might put on a long dress and a wide-brimmed hat to attend an English garden party in Hungjao. As she said, 'It was all agreeable if you liked people, and I did. There were different flavours to sample . . .'[160]

At night she dined with six or seven young men of the various consular or legation staff, went to the Chinese Opera with Xinmei and his family or enjoyed a foot massage in a Chinese bath-house while listening to stories of Xinmei's youth (he was then only thirty). He described the sing-song girls with improbable names like Abagail and Prudence he had known at seventeen, the red sports car and purple tweed suit he had owned, the pride he had taken in the daily reports by the mosquito press on his affair with an actress, the millions he had inherited at nineteen and lost a few years later and his imprisonment on a false charge during which 'I learned four ways to commit a murder. So the time was not all wasted.'[161]

He introduced Emily to his family, 'the size of which was never definitely described'. In the huge house with its courtyard and windowless walls, the various members came and went, gossiping, sipping tea and playing mahjong. As the servants did exactly the same, Emily admitted, 'I could never tell which was relative and which servant.' Xinmei often had the same trouble. Once in a restaurant Emily pointed out a lovely woman. Convinced she was a sing-song girl, Xinmei asked the waiter to discover her name and invite her over. The waiter murmured something. Xinmei went red. The sing-song girl was in fact his niece. Xinmei introduced Emily to his father, a 'die-hard' rake who had lost large sums speculating and smoking opium. In his youth, he had owned one of the first cars in Shanghai and tried to buy a small, white elephant for Xinmei, then aged four. Emily even met the mother of Xinmei's wife's, a tiny old lady with two round patches of rouge on each cheek, and her occasional companion, a Mr Ku whom Emily first mistook for a cousin. When pressed, Xinmei chose his words carefully, 'No, not exactly, though he is a relative. He was my mother-in-law's lover. For a little while only,'[162] he added with some haste. Xinmei's mother-in-law was a former sing-song girl from Suzhou and one of ten concubines. She had run off in her youth with a Mr Shi but they had no money and she had moved in with Mr Ku only to return to Mr Shi whom she really loved. He never forgave her, even though they lived on Mr Ku's money. Mr Shi, 'a taciturn old fellow with long white moustaches at the corners of his mouth and a black satin cap',[163] picked quarrels with his wife and threw crabs at the mournful and still devoted Mr Ku.

All this, Emily absorbed and wrote up for the *New Yorker* magazine. Tony Keswick asked why she made fun of Xinmei in print. She shook her head and said, 'He didn't understand'. She now showed me a photograph of Xinmei, a slim man with a face like a fawn in a long, Chinese gown. 'He never looked good in Western suits,' she said. I wondered what had become of him. Emily Hahn, I knew, left for Hong Kong and more scandal. Xinmei, she said, stayed in China after the Revolution. The Chinese authorities forced him to take cure after cure for his opium addiction. News of his death did not reach her for years. She said, 'It didn't matter. I knew the day he died.'

Apart from Xinmei, Emily Hahn adored her gibbon, Mr Mills. Fifty years later her office in the *New Yorker* is still covered with photographs of gibbons. She admitted to enjoying a very 'unhealthy' relationship with Mr Mills who wore suits knitted by Emily's amah. Mr Mills refused to let any man touch Emily in his presence. On one occasion, a sinister Japanese nicknamed 'Tiger One Eye' invited her to dinner. The Japanese authorities wished to control, through force or bribery, all Chinese and foreign publications in the Settlement. Tiger One Eye had ambitions both towards Emily and the magazine she had begun with Xinmei. Emily arrived at the restaurant, Mr Mills draped protectively around her neck. Emily explained, 'The only way to get Mr Mills down from a tree was to throw my arms around a man.' After one bite, Tiger One Eye withdrew.

Unfortunately it was going to take more than a jealous monkey to stop the Japanese in 1937.

SEVEN

The War at the End of the Street
1937 – The Third Battle

IN 1934 THE Japanese turned their attention from Manchuria to North China where Chiang Kai-shek, in a series of secret deals, withdrew his troops from the northern province of Hebei to facilitate the Japanese infiltration. His policy proved wildly unpopular among many of his own people. Students and intellectuals, backed by the Chinese Communist party, held demonstrations calling for the end of the civil war between Nationalist and communist and for a united front against Japan. Chiang Kai-shek refused to agree until members of his own party kidnapped him in December 1936. On July 7th, 1937 Chinese soldiers exchanged shots with the Japanese on Marco Polo bridge near Beijing. War broke out between China and Japan shortly after. Public opinion forced Chiang Kai-shek to take a stand against the Japanese. He chose to do so in Shanghai.

Shanghai never recovered. The bombing of the city in 1937 blasted more than lives and buildings. Nanking Road, the Bund and the Great World symbolized the heart, liver and lungs of the metropolis. Greater disasters followed: the takeover of the International Settlement by the Japanese in 1941; the terrible inflation of the 1940s; the arrival of the Chinese communists in 1949. One Chinese worker described how he was paid with wheelbarrows of notes; an American journalist recalled how he survived the Japanese camps and a British businessman told me about his experience of solitary confinement under the communists. Their stories failed to affect me as much as the events of August 1937. Shanghai had taken on for me the characteristics of an old friend. When the friend died, I lost interest.

Summer in Shanghai is rarely pleasant. The rainy season lasts through June, turning imperceptibly into the drenching heat of July and August. In August 1937 the anticipation of war added to the discomfort of the weather. Old China Hands recognized the signs. Outside the city, a Chinese army appeared – this time the German-trained Eighty-eighth Central Division of the National government. In the Settlement rents went up. Rooms that had cost seven dollars now went for twenty-five as the Chinese inhabitants of Chapei, Pootung and Hongkew moved to safety. Those without funds squatted along the Bund or entered the refugee camps improvised by the municipal authorities.

On Friday, August 12th, the Settlement authorities flashed mobilization orders for members of the Shanghai Volunteer Corps on cinema screens across the city. Dimitri Brauns, a White Russian, recalled people applauding young men as they stood up from the audience. The surge of patriotism even persuaded some to join then and there. The companies took up their positions throughout the Settlement. The Shanghai Scottish, the Jewish and the Air Defence Company found themselves stationed in the Union Church with billets in the rowing club. The 'B' Battalion, which included the American, Portuguese, Philippine and American Machine-Gun Companies, occupied the Polytechnic Public School in Pakhoi Road. The 'C' Battalion of White Russian volunteers and regulars manned the blockhouses along Elgin Road. The Japanese Company (members of the Volunteer Corps and quite separate from the invading Japanese army) guarded Boone Road in Hongkew. The Chinese and the Interpreter Company took over the Cathedral Boys' School. Units from the British Army strung telephone lines along Brenen Road. Above the noise of hammers and the dull thump of sandbags falling into place, rose the mooing of cows – evacuees from the Kiangwan and

Chapei areas, now grazing in the fields along Keswick Road.

Two weeks before, Emily Hahn had taken a Japanese admirer out to lunch. 'Mr Shindo admires you intensely,' translated his secretary on their first meeting. 'Unfortunately he has a wife in Japan, and since this is his third marriage he feels he should not make any more changes. But he would be delighted to meet you, any time, in London.'[1] After lunch, Emily was driving him towards Garden Bridge when she nearly ran over a rickshaw man in her new car, a present from Sir Victor. Mr Shindo watched the agitation of the puller.

'Chinese!' he shrugged with contemptuous amusement.

'I can still hear the tone of voice,'[2] she said.

In the early evening of August 9th, Sub-Lieutenant Isao Ohyama, commander of the first company of the Japanese naval landing party, was also motoring in Shanghai, but along Monument Road to the west of the Settlement and in the company of his driver. They intended to 'inspect'[3] the Chinese Hungjao airdrome. Their mutilated bodies were later found filled with bullets.

Ten thousand Chinese soldiers piled up sandbags and blocked the roads around the North Station. Twenty-one Japanese warships moved up the Whangpoo. On Friday, 12th August the shooting began. After a rainy night, Saturday dawned warm and sticky. By late morning the clouds had cleared and the Chinese pilots took to the air in their American-built Northrops. After failing to damage some Japanese cotton mills, they turned their attention on the *Idzumo*, the Japanese flagship on which Abend had enjoyed cocktails and caviare before the start of hostilities in 1932. It lay anchored off the Bund.

The Bund was packed with people. Foreign businessmen leaving their offices at Saturday lunchtime joined Chinese on the rooftops for a better view. Along the waterfront Chinese shoppers, foreign wives meeting their husbands, schoolchildren with their fathers, White Russians enjoying a free afternoon before a night's work, the Bund's usual street vendors, beggars and rickshaw men, all gathered to watch the show. People cheered and booed as the Chinese bombers missed three times, their loads landing harmlessly in the Whangpoo or on Hongkew wharf.

At 4.30 in the afternoon four of the Chinese planes swung towards the Bund. The crowds assumed they were on their way home and began to move off themselves. As the Chinese flew overhead, four black dots appeared below the planes. The crowd watched first with incredulity and then with terror as the bombs smashed down upon them. One exploded on the roof of the Palace Hotel. The other landed across the road at the foot of the Cathay Hotel, Sir Victor Sassoon's showpiece, blasting a crater into the pavement and destroying for ever the myth of the International Settlement's impregnability. Shanghai was no longer a city where foreigners could watch a war in safety. The fighting had landed on their doorstep.

After the explosion came silence. From doorways and hotel windows, people gazed out in shock. A tall European lay on the tramway, his head cut cleanly from his suit of white flannel. Near by sprawled the body of a disembowelled child. A piece of masonry suddenly swayed, broke loose and crashed down on to pavements thick with shards from shattered windows and plate-glass doors. In the lobby of the Palace Hotel victims bled over chairs and sofas. Across Nanking Road in the Cathay Hotel, foreigners sat in tense and silent groups. The only sign of the horror outside was an injured doorman stretched on the floor near the reception desk. The explosion had damaged the telephone lines and no help came for some time. It took two hours to clear the streets of bodies. Furniture vans carried away the dead.

Fifteen minutes later a third bomb fell over the crossing of Avenue Edward VII and Thibet Road and landed on the Great World, 'that house of multiple joys' turned the day before into a refugee camp. Amidst their boxes, bundles and bird cages, a thousand people died and another thousand received injuries.

One of the first on the scene was Brother Shull whose fellow missionaries had rooms over the crossing. He had driven up Avenue Edward VII and had left his car in the middle of the road. The air was acrid with smoke and the smell of burnt flesh. From the ruins came screams, sobs and moans. He could not see a living soul. Those who had not died had fled in terror. He walked through 'streams of blood',[4] sickened by the mutilated bodies of men, women, and children. He gave up hope of finding anyone alive and began to examine the dead for friends and colleagues. At the traffic signal he noticed a line of vehicles caught by the bomb as they waited for the lights to change. Their bodies were scorched and torn, their drivers burnt 'to a crisp'.[5]

George Stewart was in the Race Club when he saw two Chinese planes.

And I remember we were watching as they came over the Great World and somebody standing near me said, 'The bastards have dropped it.' And sure enough it went down and the smoke came up like this. And there was a fellow called Harold Reynell, who a few minutes after that came into the racecourse, and I said, 'Hello, you look a bit upset.' And he was trying to get a drink to his mouth, and he said, 'Yes, I was just driving down, and I saw this bomb drop about two or three hundred yards ahead of me, and I told the driver to come in here.' So that was a terrible business.

Emily Hahn met a Chinese friend in Yuyuen Road. 'He said, "Hello. Some of my friends were killed." I said, "Come on and let me take you home." He got in the car, saying, "Some of my friends were killed. This is going to be worse than 1932. Some of my friends are dead. There's my house – all right, stop here. Miss Hahn, some of my friends were killed."'[6]

Assistant Station Officer Somers was in charge of the first fire engine to arrive at the crossing. Devastated by what he saw, Somers ran into a shop on the Settlement side of Avenue Edward VII to call for ambulances. It was a pay telephone and Somers did not have a 5-cent piece. On the floor a few survivors lay among the bodies. He caught sight of a man with both legs cut off and his right arm hanging in shreds. Somers asked him for change. The man smiled wryly, reached into his pocket with his good hand, took out a 5-cent piece and handed it over. By the time Somers had made his call, the man was dead.

As one side of Avenue Edward VII belonged to the French Concession, the French police arrived shortly after the fire engine. The first intimation of the catastrophe ahead for Slobodchikoff, a White Russian member of the force, was a man's hand lying on the ground, then a thick, grey cloud through which he glimpsed, as in a nightmare, 'crowds' of corpses. He began to separate the dead from the wounded and soon found himself with blood up to his elbows. He loaded twenty-one badly wounded men and women into a truck. An hour later, five had died. He received orders to take the dead to the cemetery in Siccawei. Many of the corpses were torn to pieces. He placed a leg on the ground then waited for someone to come and identify it. The smell was excruciating. He tied a handkerchief around his face but it did not help. 'When I got back to the police station, I was so white my French inspector said, "What's been happening to you?" and he took me into his room and gave me a shot of rum.'

Seventeen-year-old Boris Ivanivitch had lied about his age and joined the French Volunteer Corps three days before. He still had no uniform and went to the accident in a French garbage truck with nothing but a helmet and a stick. He described blood everywhere, 'just like a river', and arms, legs and heads separated from their bodies. 'I didn't eat for a week afterwards.'

Dr D. B. Cater, a junior surgeon, recalled the sheer numbers that filled the casualty ward, the men's out-patients' department and the hospital courtyard where he worked. They arrived in ambulances, motor cars and even furniture vans. The hospital staff dealt with the minor injuries as they came across them. The doctors lost count of how many amputations they performed. Outside the operation room patients screamed for attention. The doctors only took those most likely to survive. The hopeless cases were injected with morphia and left to die in a corridor of the out-patients' department. In the morning all but two were dead. The young surgeon wrote, 'If I wasn't so terribly busy . . . I think I should just sit down and vomit with the horror of it all.'[7]

Four days later, Hallett Abend arrived in Shanghai to find pavements still sticky with clotted blood and the streets smelling like a 'charnel house' despite the sand and disinfectant. Near the racecourse bodies and parts of bodies lay about wrapped in cheap matting. Spatters of human flesh still clung to the billboards and buildings. In the August heat the stench of unburied bodies became unbearable. Night brought a gentle wind from the north but this blew into the Settlement the stinking smoke from the funeral pyres of the Japanese.

The Chinese government tried to explain the disasters as accidents caused by young and inexperienced pilots. 'The Generalissimo is shocked and grieved,' stated Madam Chiang Kai-shek the next day. Other rumours persisted as people refused to accept that mere coincidence had opened a pilot's bomb rack over two of the most crowded spots in the city. They told me Chiang Kai-shek had arranged the bombing in order to bring the Foreign Powers into the Sino-Japanese war. Whatever the truth, the foreign governments failed to react. It was finally admitted. No one was going to save Shanghai.

The bombing presaged the future, made a break with the past and unified the city. This battle proved different from any other in Shanghai's history. For the first time foreigners and Chinese lay dead together. The fighting in 1932 killed less than one hundred civilians in the International Settlement. In 1937, over two thousand died. The foreigners, in particular, suffered from shock. Nothing, they told me, not even the Second World War, was to seem as bad as that afternoon in August. It caught them completely unprepared. They had nothing to compare it with. They could not believe that the mayhem and suffering confined before to Chapei and the Chinese people could touch them.

The British talked of evacuation. The *North China Daily News* encouraged reluctant wives: 'This is where women know how to do their part.' Their presence was 'a positive menace to the lives of their menfolk'.[8] The wives and children dutifully registered at the Shanghai Club and boarded the P. & O. *Rajputana* for Hong Kong.

Those who stayed behind watched the battle develop from the city's skyscrapers. Emily Hahn taught English once a week to a Japanese spy in the Park Hotel. From his room they could see the sky covered in black smoke, a huge yellow moon and, in the distance, buildings glowing horribly. Her pupil wrote down the words as she used them – 'incendiary', 'flare' and 'incredible'. Towards the end of the lesson he sighed and explained the management had asked him to move out. It was a scandal, they said, that a Japanese should stay in a Chinese-owned hotel. He continued, 'If the manager were here – he is a friend of mine – it would not have happened. But he is in Nanjing . . . Yes, the service here is good. It is a pity. Ah, well . . . war is not a paying business, even for the victor.'[9]

Robert Guillain recalled climbing out of a skylight, a drink in hand, to find the roofs around him thick with people, despite warnings from the Shanghai Municipal Council about the danger of flying shrapnel. To the north, hidden behind a horizon of tiles and masonry, the Japanese emptied their bombs over the Chinese trenches.

In Hongkew, Qing Mei also watched the bombs but from a less comfortable distance. A plump, short woman, her grey hair cut in a straight line below her ears, she still lives in the same street where she grew up. Her father worked in a rice store while she, the eldest of five daughters, made joss money from tinfoil (burnt as a gift to the spirits at funerals and sacrifices to ancestors) which she sold to passers-by on the street. During the first Japanese air-raid in August her father was away at work and the rest of the family hid under the kitchen table. The bombing frightened the youngest child so much that she wet her pants and cried loudly. As soon as the raid ended, they heard a hasty pounding on the gate. Mei's mother pulled herself together and staggered to open it. In came their neighbour, Auntie Wang, dragging two children, white-faced and gasping for breath. They had been at lunch when a shell crashed through the roof, bounced on to the bed, broke through the floor and landed in the hall. Luckily it had not exploded. It now lay buried in the hall with its tail showing. Auntie Wang begged Mei's family to leave with her at once as the bomb might go off at any moment. Mei's mother packed some clothes and food into two or three bundles and, carrying a few pots and pans, the family joined the jostling crowds in the streets all making for the Settlement, the aged and the sick in wheelbarrows and carts. Smoke hung over their heads. Flames shot upwards. A constant booming and crackling followed them as they passed alleyways filled with wounded. The whole scene reminded Mei of the 'Palace of Hell' in the Nether Regions.

They reached the foreign Concessions just before the gates closed for the night and stayed with a distant relative of Mei's mother on Ningpo Road. The relative lived with his family in one room on the second floor. Mei's family slept in the kitchen after the other tenants had finished cooking. That night, standing on the roof terrace where the household hung out washing, the little girl watched the northern sky, lit up by the burning buildings of Chapei.

The fighting moved closer still when two Chinese divisions of 20,000 men decided to resist in the old Chinese city of Nantao next to the French Concession. Three hundred metres from the Eden cinema where Marlene Dietrich was playing in *Desire*, the inhabitants of the French Concession could see barbed wire and hear machine-gun fire. The International Settlement and the French Concession found themselves caught between the two armies. Guests in the dining-room on top of the Park Hotel sipped their demitasses and watched Japanese shells from Chapei make their four-mile arc over the roofs of the International Settlement to explode in Nantao, fifty or seventy yards beyond the southern boundary of the French Concession.

The shells sounded to Enid Saunders Candlin as she sat in her garden like invisible, express trains passing overhead. She found she could listen to them with perfect calm, even interest. Some people refused to take the shelling seriously as Emily Hahn explained. An irritating little man, a friend of Mary, the girl she shared a house with, telephoned one day in the middle of a raid. 'I said, "Pingli, wait a minute. We must go downstairs. There's a raid going on. Wait a minute." Mary answered at the downstairs phone and said, "Do you mind calling later? We're being bombed." He said, "Well, what time shall I phone?" She said, "I don't know. Do you mind?" He said, "Will you be there after luncheon?"'[10]

The Settlement still had more to fear from Chinese bombers than Japanese shells. On August 23rd a bomb exploded on Nanking Road, destroying the first floor of Sincere Department store and caving in the side of Wing On. Caught in the hail of shell fragments, between 150 and 170 people died and 470 were injured.

Chan Liu, now a retired engineer living in Shanghai, was sitting in his office at lunchtime on August 23rd when he felt tremors beneath his feet. His British boss declared a half-holiday. They all left, Liu getting a lift from his boss. When they reached the department stores, Liu jumped out and pushed his way through the crowd to have a look. Water shot down from the third and fourth floors of the building, bouncing off the dead and running red into the gutters. Glass covered the street like a crystal carpet. On its glistening surface lay dead bodies, severed limbs and blood, as if someone had spilled a tin of tomato paste. Overhead, the bloody remains of a Vietnamese policeman hung from the telephone wires. When the rescue workers and the policemen arrived, Liu made off, admitting that he had received enough shocks for that afternoon and did not want any more. He still remembered the sick jokes that were soon circulating around the city. One man who had been standing on a hotel balcony when the explosion happened received a box on the cheek from a severed hand flying up from the street. When he recovered, he saw it was a pretty hand with beautifully manicured nails and around the wrist a heavy gold bracelet which he immediately pocketed.

Abend and his assistant, Anthony Billingham, had gone to the Wing On to order a pair of field glasses. Abend had decided to wait in the car and had just lit a cigarette when the bomb exploded with a tremendous lurch accompanied by an explosion so close that it seemed to hurt his eardrums and windpipe.

He sat stunned for as long as four minutes. Nothing moved except rolling smoke and dust. No sound came but for the continued tinkle of broken glass and the rumble of crumbling masonry. After about four minutes the wounded began to moan and shriek and try to drag themselves away; then came the clamour of sirens and ambulances and fire engines and the tempo of shocked life picked up with terrifying rapidity.

He got out of the car and made for the shop. Brick and stone fragments fell around him. He found his legs would not work properly and kept stumbling over dying bodies. The dead carpeted Nanking Road for a block in each direction. At the door of the building 'a human cataract of frenzied, screaming clerks and customers' poured out.[11] Nearly all were wounded, some badly. Inside, clouds of plaster dust and smoke drifted over aisles slippery with broken glass from the showcases. Assistants lay on one side of the smashed counters, customers on the other. Badly wounded men staggered around like aimless drunks. Abend searched fruitlessly for Billingham before finally returning to the car where he saw his friend crumpled on the front seat, covered with blood. The bomb had caught him in a lift with ten others between the ground and first floor. Only he and the twelve-year-old Chinese lift-boy had survived. Billingham received a wound on his left side and had used his right shoulder as a battering ram to knock out the grill of the elevator shaft. Then, hanging on with his right hand, he had dropped down to the ground, the elevator boy scrambling down the grill after him. An artery was severed in Billingham's arm and he had lost a dangerous amount of blood.

Abend immediately started the car to find help. He came across a military ambulance that had nothing to offer the wounded but stretchers. He left Billingham with them and ran into the China United Building in search of his friend, Doctor O'Hara. The doctor had already left so he seized hold of a German doctor, 'a fat little fellow', who was convinced that 'I had lost my mind'.[12] When they got out into the street Billingham, the ambulance and Abend's car had all vanished. The only evidence of Abend's sanity was a pool of blood where he had parked the car. Abend waved down a drunken Scot in a coupé. Together they drove around Shanghai's hospitals until they discovered Billingham. Some passing U.S. Marines had recognized Abend's car, stopped to take a look then rushed Billingham to an emergency dressing station, saving his life.

It was now four in the afternoon and Abend felt awful. He had started the day in the usual summer wear of an American gentleman, starched white duck shorts, white shoes and white, knee-length socks. Blood, turned to a sticky brown varnish, now covered him from head to toe and he felt in need of a drink. Without pausing to change or even wash, he made for the British Country Club where he met Doctor O'Hara who asked him why he was limping. They found a piece of glass the size of a finger embedded in his foot and a two-inch wound on the side of his neck. In the excitement, Abend had failed to notice either injury.

Despite the bombs, the city took care of the Chinese soldier in its inimitable style. The wounded found themselves recovering in nightclubs like the Vienna Gardens, temporarily transformed into an emergency hospital. Hospital cots hid the dance floor, a dispensary had taken over the bar while the nurses' office occupied the orchestra stand. The dance hostesses, described by one visitor as those 'charming slips of femininity',[13] distributed themselves among the men, their hair patriotically styled in the shape of an aeroplane. One fed a soldier fruit out of a tin, another arranged pink carnations in a jar while a third gave a man his first manicure. As the visitor watched, the soldier held up his hand to admire the effect.

Public subscription made up for the lack of funds from the Chinese High Command. As Madam Chiang Kai-shek remarked to Christopher Chancellor, '"Men are cheap but drugs are expensive"', which explains why Sylvia thought China's First Lady 'a bitch and a real stinker'.

Business, of course, continued despite the danger. The same Mr Lord who had flown over Shanghai during the General Strike of 1927 penetrated the war zone as an insurance broker. He said, 'I can tell you one thing, whether they were black, white, or yellow, Indian or Parsee, they always claimed too much.' Mr Lord journeyed to Chapei to verify the more exorbitant submissions. He boasted that he was one of the few civilians to receive passes from both the Chinese and Japanese authorities. On one trip to Chapei he was photographing a particularly expensive machine to prove it had not been destroyed as the owner claimed, when he heard a noise. He turned to find a Japanese soldier pointing a fixed bayonet at him. Mr Lord knew full well that the Japanese forbade cameras in the war zone. He laughed, stepped forward and snapped the soldier. Even now, he said, 'I don't know how I had the impudence'. The soldier motioned Mr Lord to come along and three more sentries appeared. Mr Lord said, 'Hang on a tick,' lined them up and snapped them too. He was then escorted back to the International Settlement. Mr Lord made four enlargements and gave them to a Japanese police superintendent. The superintendent, 'a very likeable fellow', passed the photos on to the soldiers. A few days later Mr Lord received a summons from Japanese headquarters. He grimaced at the memory. 'At that time people did not go there lightly but I said, "Well, it's worth trying," and off I went.' No less than the Commander himself greeted Mr Lord, offered him a cigarette and thanked him for the photographs. The soldiers were delighted and had sent them back to their parents. As Mr Lord was getting into his car, the Commander rushed out after him. '"Wait a minute,"' he called, and presented the astonished Englishman with a bowl of goldfish.

On another occasion, Mr Lord was checking a claim in a Chapei warehouse when shelling shattered the walls and the roof began to cave in. Mr Lord jumped through a window into a next-door store room, explaining, 'I didn't know what was on the other side and I didn't care.' When the shelling quietened down he decided to leave by a hole in the wall. It led into the living room of a Chinese family. At a table sat an old man eating his breakfast; in the corner his wife crouched on a commode. Mr Lord shook his head. 'I popped back again pretty sharpish, I can tell you.'

The fighting between the armies reached its climax towards the end of October. The Chinese received orders to retreat just as Michael Schiller sat his final exams at the Shanghai Public School. When British soldiers took over the school, the pupils had moved to the tenth and eleventh floor of the YMCA building next to the Park Hotel. They had a clear view of the battle as they revised *Macbeth*. Michael Schiller recalled how this lent 'a certain theatricality to events'. He found it an effort to remember that 'this was a live war with real bullets'.

As the boys watched, a battalion of 411 Chinese from the 88th Division barricaded themselves into the godown of the Joint Savings Society. The godown stood across the street from where British soldiers guarded Thibet Road Bridge and the entrance to the Settlement. In the early hours of October 27th, a Chinese sentry on the top floor of the godown noticed twenty Japanese soldiers creeping towards the entrance. He grabbed a dozen hand-grenades to himself, let the Japanese approach then jumped down among them.

The 'Doomed Battalion' soon became as famous as the Nineteenth Route Army in 1932. It captured the imagination of the Shanghainese and expressed the city's need for a show of resistance, however futile. Crowds gathered to watch the fighting and express their support at the barricades. Some asked the British soldiers to pass food and money to the battalion. Sam Ginsbourg, who had first explored Shanghai as a boy during the communist uprising in 1927, recalled an old German woman arriving with a cart full of fresh bread. She waved towards the godown. 'It is for those',[14] she said. When the British stopped the cart, she could not understand why. 'Nein?' she asked.

The British wished to end the fighting. The Japanese had moved up their heavy artillery and could, at any moment, bombard the Settlement in mistake for the godown. The Battalion refused to evacuate without direct orders from Chiang Kai-shek. When approached, Madam Chiang Kai-shek declared, 'They must die that China may live.' The British negotiated directly with both sides (the telephone lines to the godown and the Japanese headquarters still worked) and arranged a truce for midnight. At the last moment the Japanese refused to withdraw their machine-guns. They trained their searchlights on the godown and waited. When the first Chinese soldier appeared they began to shoot. Every time they paused to reload their guns, the Chinese dashed to the safety of a British pillbox.

All over Shanghai, the Chinese soldiers withdrew or gave themselves up, not to the Japanese but to the foreigner. They crossed the road into the International Settlement or the French Concession, laid down their arms and became 'prisoners'. On his return home one night, Robert Guillain saw some Chinese soldiers emerge from the dark ruins of Nantao. Dazed by the street lights, two or three hundred stood surrounded by a handful of French soldiers. They threw down their German guns and their helmets marked with the blue sun of the Guomindang. Their faces shone with tears. Some shook with emotion. Others made strange cries like wounded animals.

The defeat of the Chinese placed the British in an unaccustomed position of vulnerability. Suddenly, it looked as if the Japanese would supplant them as the most important members of the International Settlement. To test their new status, the Japanese proposed a Victory Parade through the Settlement and the French Concession. Tony Keswick recalled the reaction of the Shanghai Municipal Council. Its members had finally understood that the Japanese presented a grave threat rather than 'justice, good government and civilization', as the British had claimed in 1932. Tony Keswick, himself a Council member, explained, 'We didn't want the Japanese setting a precedent that they had the right to march through at any time. And we didn't want them disturbing our one million Chinese who were naturally het up at losing.'

The British made every effort to change the Japanese mind. As head of Jardine Matheson, a firm with long experience in the Far East, and Japan in particular, Tony Keswick conducted negotiations. He found himself unable to play the paternalistic role enjoyed by Sir Miles Lampson during the peace talks of 1932. The Japanese no longer regarded the British as either neutral or superior. He told me,

> When a Japanese comes to talk turkey with you he keeps his sword on. If what he wants is important he takes his sword off and puts it on the chair. If he's talking real turkey to you he takes it out of his sheath and places the blade near your face and asks you to admire it. If you are a Westerner you think, funny, what the hell is he showing me his sword for? If you are in the know, you realize it's turkey and that's very awkward when, like me in 1937, you've got no cards to play.

Tony Keswick appealed to the Japanese respect for tradition; he drew a parallel between the ancient decree that forbade armed troops in the City of London and Shanghai. Tony Keswick arranged for a truck to collect the weapons of the Japanese soldiers as they marched into the Settlement. The rifles were handed back as the soldiers marched out. Tony Keswick went on, 'We soothed them all the way, "The eyes of the World are upon you. We don't want an international incident", that sort of stuff. So that passed off all right.'

During the march, a Chinese civilian hurled himself from a high building shouting, 'Long Live China'. His body hit the pavement in front of the Japanese soldiers led by General Matsui on a bay horse. Then someone threw a bomb. The Japanese immediately cordonned off a section of the International Settlement. Robert Guillain found himself nearly bayoneted by a Japanese marine who shook a blade two centimetres from the Frenchman's chest while screaming at him for taking photographs.

The British all stayed indoors on the day of the Victory Parade. In the evening they watched *The Beggars' Opera*, the prostitutes played by the British community's most celebrated beauties. Sylvia Chancellor mounted the production in order 'to give everybody something else to think about'.

When the Japanese arrived at the French Concession they found the entrance to the avenue blocked by tanks and a determined Admiral Bigot seated on a folding chair between the tram lines. After much discussion, the Japanese passed through disarmed, bereft of flags and escorted by a detachment of French troops.

The Japanese victory accentuated Shanghai's refugee problem. At the beginning of 1937 the foreign settlements contained about one and a quarter million inhabitants. By the end of the year the figure had increased to four million. The continuing occupation of Chapei and Hongkew by the Japanese precluded any chance of a return home. The removal of the fighting into the countryside forced more refugees into the city. A one-armed Jesuit priest, Father Jacquinot de Besange, persuaded the Japanese and Chinese authorities to allow him to establish a safe area for Chinese civilians in Nantao. It stretched for one square mile from the Boulevard des Deux Républiques to Fong Pang Road and became known as the Jacquinot Zone.

Sylvia Chancellor worked for Father Jacquinot. He was an enormous man with a striking beard and a wooden arm which he used to hit Japanese soldiers on the head. She watched him stop Japanese brutality by sheer strength of personality. She went on, 'I saw him stand on the boundary of the Concession, refusing to let some Japanese soldiers through. "There is a Nemesis which will overtake you," he roared.'

Father Jacquinot opened the Zone to refugees on November 6th. A week later, over a hundred thousand refugees had moved in. Father Jacquinot raised funds for food and persuaded the French Concession to lay on light and water. Twice a day he distributed tea and bread or stale cake from the Temple of Mercy at the centre of the old Chinese city.

The Japanese permitted a few foreigners to work with the Jesuit who engaged Sylvia Chancellor as his secretary. The habit of the Chinese Jesuits of talking Latin on the telephone confused her. 'Hic haec hoc, that sort of thing. I went to Father Jacquinot and said, "I can talk French and even some Chinese and I don't mind what I do as long as it's not in Latin." So he took me on.' She stayed for three months.

They set up a hospital in a new house now abandoned by its owner. Despite an imposing façade, it could only hold forty beds. Most of the babies in the maternity section suffered from venereal disease. Franciscan Sisters in their white gowns and winged wimples visited the sick with little to offer besides aspirin, plasters and iodine. A Japanese colonel checked every corpse as the Japanese only permitted dead Chinese to leave the Zone. One Chinese woman developed an infection after giving birth. Without proper medication she would have died. The nuns smuggled her out in a coffin with air holes. When the Japanese colonel asked where she had gone, Father Jacquinot crossed himself and said, 'Elle a rejoint le bon dieu'. After a visit to Hong Kong, Sylvia re-applied to work with Father Jacquinot, 'but he said the Japanese were carrying away women and he couldn't guarantee my safety. I do remember Lady Violet Bonham Carter asking to see me in England to hear my views on the demilitarized zone. It just goes to show how famous Father Jacquinot had become, doesn't it?'

At least the British refugees in Hong Kong were having fun – or so everyone believed. The *North China Daily News* described almost holiday-camp surroundings. Evacuated wives enjoyed excellent food, a wonderful view of the Peak and swimming from the nearby Laichikok beach. One man compared this reported idyll with a letter he received from his wife at the time. She wrote:

> The place is hot at night . . . we have spiders, lizards, centipedes, cockroaches and mosquitoes, there is not a single bath tub, only hoses and we must walk down the stairs across a courtyard to get to them . . . there is absolutely no hot water . . . we have to wash our faces at a tap in the open air . . . there is no sink and the water splashes all over our feet . . . in the bathroom we have to use thick, high, wooden slippers because the cement floors are so filthy . . . and we have no flush and the whole place smells . . . she [their daughter aged three] can't eat the food, it is so poor . . . I am writing the letter on a trunk and am sitting on a camp bed as we have no tables nor chairs . . . there is a beach here but the water is very dirty because nearby there are a lot of dirty boats . . . Oh! I am so miserable I just want to put my head on your shoulder and have a good cry.'[15]

She was, although she did not know it, undergoing a rehearsal for the Japanese camps four years later.

· EIGHT ·

A Bit Like the End of Things
The Fall of Shanghai

SHANGHAI FAILED TO bounce back after 1937 as buoyantly as it had done in 1932. Then the local nature of the hostilities had resulted in a quick recovery. Once China and Japan agreed a truce, the Japanese forces departed and the Great Municipality of Shanghai returned to normal. After 1937, however, Japanese troops pursued the Chinese from Shanghai to Nanjing, devastating the surrounding countryside. In November of the same year the Chinese government stretched booms across the Yangtze at Jiangyin and Qinjiang in order to hamper the Japanese navy but also effectively ending all river traffic. Between July and December trade fell by 76 per cent. It did not recover. Ports elsewhere on the east coast of China increased their share of trade at Shanghai's expense. Shanghai lost what had made it great: the Yangtze and access to the interior.

The Chinese Municipal employees fled, leaving Greater Shanghai in the hands of the Japanese. The Japanese naval and military authorities appropriated the Chinese Maritime Customs and its revenues as well as the Chinese Telegraph Office and the Wireless Administration. Japanese censors installed themselves in the offices of the three foreign cable companies. Japanese authorities took over Chinese businesses and reorganized them to co-ordinate with similar industries in Japan. They closed unwanted factories and shipped the machinery back to Japan for scrap.

The Japanese took over not only Greater Shanghai but also the industrial and most important half of the International Settlement. A ring of devastation encircled the French Concession and that half of the International Settlement still under foreign control. The Japanese surrounded it with a barbed-wire fence and checked everyone going in and out. Across the burnt-out fields and flattened buildings, the skyscrapers of the Bund glinted like a mirage.

Between 1937 and 1941 the Japanese oversaw the destruction of Shanghai. One by one they stripped away the attributes which had made it great. When they finally seized Shanghai itself in 1941, they found the longed-for city no longer existed. The Shanghai of the 'twenties and 'thirties had gone for ever.

For my final tour of the metropolis, I imagined taking one of Shanghai's aviatorial, sight-seeing trips. Distance, I hoped, would give me the writer's equivalent of the aerial photograph I had sought in 1927; the city's confusions and contradictions finally focusing into a comprehensible whole. I imagined making a circular sweep starting in the west from Hungjao airport, flying north to Hongkew then moving south over the foreign Concessions before returning west again to the Outside Roads' Area. I asked Mr Lord who had flown over Shanghai in 1927 and 1932, for recollections of 1937. But he had none, an era had finished for him as for everyone else. Carl Nahmmacher, his flying companion, came down too quickly from ten thousand feet. 'I flew with him on Wednesday. On the Thursday he proposed we try out his new plane. "Sorry old chap," I said, "but I haven't written to my wife for two weeks. Have to give it a miss." Two days later I attended his funeral.'

It was the Japanese and not Mr Lord who provided me with what I sought. Ironically, they only did so as Shanghai was dying. They handed me a city empty of confusion but also of everything else that had made it worth while. Everybody I interviewed had a story about the Japanese. Spread in front of me their recollections resembled a series of snapshots that record, almost incidentally, the end of Shanghai.

From the air Shanghai appeared a pitiful sight in the autumn of 1937. Vast areas were in ruin. To the west, craters filled the fields and villages made black smudges on the landscape. The arched bridges over which the paper hunt had ridden with such dash now lifted charred stumps against the sky. Farmers, unwilling to leave their land, sprawled among the dead soldiers. Armed Japanese pressganged Chinese to dig through the mud around the bodies for cooking implements, window-frames, doorknobs, ploughs, axles, hinges, nails, even screws, to satisfy the Japanese passion for scrap metal. Japanese looters scraped through the debris for money or souvenirs. Here and there the recent rains half-covered steel helmets torn by shrapnel. Across the paddy fields, glutted with unfired grenades, dogs snuffled for corpses while peasants with bags of rice hanging from poles over one shoulder made their way to the city. Only the old and the very young braved the Japanese and travelled three or four days to sell their grain. Sometimes a Japanese soldier stopped them to demand a few coppers or an old woman's worn silver bracelet. At the Settlement boundary they paid a dollar tax on their bundles. An old man with his three grandchildren told a foreigner that nothing remained of his house or his belongings. 'Hai shi you di, hai shi you ni' he added cheerfully. 'The land is still there and the mud is still there.'[1]

In the north Hongkew had become 'a city of the dead', wrote the Reverend A. Baxter after an expedition to check the mission headquarters. As far as the eye could see stretched ruins with only the occasional chimney-pot or telegraph pole left standing. Derelict wires dangled over the wreckage. Corpses rotted in the winter sun. A handful of Sikhs and White Russians examined the remains of their property. The Reverend Baxter found the mission reduced to a few walls and a heap of charcoal. In the tennis court two craters were filling with rain water. He finished, 'One feels a bit dazed trying to get along without a single book and every symbol of a life time . . . When we think in terms of ourselves and the work we have been trying to do, the situation seems to be a bit like the end of things.'[2] The Japanese had taken over the church and refused him entry.

Rewi Alley, the New Zealand inspector who took Christopher Isherwood and W. H. Auden on a tour of Shanghai's factories, also picked through the wreckage of thirty years' endeavour. The fighting had destroyed the factories and workshops which had turned Shanghai into the industrial centre of the Far East. Alley pointed to one former workshop, now no more than a pile of bricks. He recalled the apprentices who had lived there. When the shelling began, their master locked them in and left for the Settlement, returning from time to time to change their food and water. Many boys shared the same fate. Either they died or the Japanese enslaved them. Alley said, 'It wouldn't be so bad . . . to have blown up all this circus, if something better would now take its place.'[3]

The Japanese sentries on the Hongkew side of Garden Bridge personified the new atmosphere of fear in the city. A Japanese proclamation ordered passers by to show respect with 'a gentle bow' and 'a polite good morning'. Liu Ning, the Chinese cobbler who had watched the bombing of the Commercial Press in 1932, recalled the day he forgot to bow. The sentry shouted at him like a mad dog, stepped forward and slapped his face until his nose bled. Qing Mei, who had escaped from Hongkew after a shell landed in her neighbour's hall, admitted all foreigners frightened her but especially the Japanese, 'the most brutal of them all'. She once saw two men carrying a crate of firewood over Garden Bridge. They laid down their load and bowed to the Japanese sentry, then shouldering their crate they started on their way before the Japanese gave permission. The Japanese stopped them, slapped one on the face, and told him to slap the other. After that he arranged them side by side and started slapping their faces till he was tired. Other passers-by watched from a distance, Mei among the rest, holding her breath with fear.

The military treated Hongkew's Japanese citizens with almost equal vehemence. The Japanese Consulate had forced Betty Kato, the former organizer of international lunch clubs, to give up her house in the French Concession and move to Hongkew. As she continued to visit her foreign friends across the bridge, she saw plenty of the Japanese guards. She recalled a sentry hitting one young Japanese woman so hard that he broke her eardrum. She herself was almost killed twice on the bridge. On the first occasion, she had forgotten that Hongkew kept Japanese time, an hour ahead of China. The sentry stopped her one evening for arriving back late. Betty said, '"It's not nine yet."

'"It's after ten!" he shouted.

'"That's your time," I exclaimed.

'As we argued, the Japanese Consul saw me and came over.

"Quiet, quiet," he told me. "Just bow and run away." They all feared the sentries.'

On the second occasion it was raining. Betty's umbrella hid her face as she made her bow. Suddenly a terrible yelling broke out. Betty continued, '"Oh poor person," I thought, "He's caught someone else." Then a bayonet was stuck in front of me. "Why didn't you stop!" he shouted.

'"I didn't know it was me."

'"You looked back twice. You knew!"

'"If it was me I would have stopped." That made him madder. He was just a country bumpkin, no more than twenty-one and he was shaking with rage. I was so furious I did not care if he killed me.' A second sentry summoned an officer who arrived on a motor bike with a side-car. He knew Betty and took the sentry away. Hundreds of people had gathered to watch the incident. By the time Betty reached Bridge House, tears streamed down her face. 'I was so mad at that country idiot, I thought I was losing my mind.'

Bridge House soon became as notorious as the sentries. Originally an apartment block five minutes' walk from Shanghai's main post office in Hongkew, the Japanese converted it into a prison for Chinese and foreigners. In 1937 Betty Kato fell in love with a man seven years younger than herself who had lost his Japanese father and Russian mother in the Russian Revolution. Shortly after they married, the Japanese Military police forced him to work as an interpreter in Bridge House. Betty recalled a car with sirens blasting fetching him away in the middle of the night. Sometimes he remained absent for two or three days. She never knew how long he would be gone. Bridge House drove him 'almost out of his mind'. On one occasion the military ordered him to translate for an elderly White Russian lady. She appeared distinguished and bewildered. '"Why am I here?" she kept on asking. "I never in my life expected to be in a place like this."' She shared a cell with forty other men and women. When she wanted to use the lavatory she had to squat over a box in the corner. She felt cold and always hungry. The night before she had awakened to find a rat chewing her hair. She said, '"I would rather die than stay here."' The Japanese military kept on at him, '"Ask her, ask her,"' but she obviously knew nothing. They hit her and he could not stop them. Betty's husband wept as he told her this: he resigned soon afterwards. In retaliation, the military had

316

him called up although he lacked even basic training. He wrote Betty one letter from his ship. After that she never heard from him again. Betty began to cry. 'He was a beautiful man,' she said, 'and too good for those times.'

Many of Hongkew's original Japanese inhabitants returned to Japan after the fighting destroyed their homes and businesses. A different sort of Japanese took their place: gangsters and adventurers out to exploit the Japanese victory as well as men and women in the entertainment business. In contrast to the shopkeepers and traders, they formed an unsettled population, indifferent to the city and its future. Koichi Okawa is an example of the better sort. I met him in Tokyo, a small, smartly dressed man in a blue blazer with enamel buttons. Fifty years ago Mr Okawa was one of Japan's leading jazz musicians. In 1937 the Japanese government declared jazz music decadent and closed down all the country's dance-halls. Mr Okawa, eleven of his band and his girlfriend, a dancer from Kobe, left for Shanghai. He explained to me, 'It was the nearest Western city to Japan, a halfway point between East and West and very attractive to us.' To Mr Okawa, like countless visitors before him, Shanghai represented opportunity and a chance to escape the repressive atmosphere of home. He fell in love with its eccentric, cosmopolitan nature even as it was disappearing. He and his band were some of the last people to enjoy Shanghai's good times.

Mr Okawa's band found work in the Shanghai Blue Bird Dance Hall on North Szechuen Road near Broadway Mansions. They played from seven to midnight and were paid 200 yen a month each, except Mr Okawa who, as band-leader, received double. At that time a graduate in Japan earned less than 30 yen a month. Mr Okawa's audience consisted of Japanese company heads and senior military officials. He recalled Benny Goodman as a great favourite. The club employed Chinese hostesses who spoke some Japanese. Mr Okawa and his band lived in a building behind the club each with their own apartment done in Japanese style. They bathed together in a hot tub on the first floor. Mr Okawa ate Chinese food because he employed a Chinese maid. I asked if she did not mind working for a Japanese. Mr Okawa smiled and explained he gave his maid presents of peanut oil and soya sauce to keep her sweet-tempered. Few Chinese could afford to eat three meals a day. He said, 'My maid insisted on eating her dinner on the doorstep in order to show off to other Chinese, "Look at me. I am able to have a meal!"'

Mr Okawa enjoyed Shanghai to the full. After work, he and his friends took a rickshaw across Garden Bridge to a Western nightclub like Ciro's or to the Winter Garden to listen to the excellent Filipino bands and meet up with his friend Porris, a Sikh employed by the International Police force. He showed me a photograph of them together. Porris had a thick, black beard, wore a turban and towered over Mr Okawa and his friends. 'Porris enjoyed jazz very much. When a waiter and hostess from the Blue Bird got married, Porris and I went to the wedding.' The unlikely couple spent the night going from club to club, sometimes finishing the evening with a visit to a gambling den. As dawn broke, they returned home, stopping at Hongkew market to eat at one of the many small Chinese restaurants. On their arrival, the Chinese owner called out, 'Do you want pork and soya?' which he knew all Japanese liked. Sometimes rich customers stood him a visit to 'Tsuki no ya', the most famous geisha house in Hongkew. Mr Okawa nodded enthusiastically, 'Yes, that was a wonderful place. Fancy me remembering the name! I don't know how I kept up the pace. I was very happy then. I felt at home in Shanghai. I would be there now if not for the war.'

I asked Mr Okawa if he recalled the Japanese sentries at Garden Bridge. He looked puzzled and shook his head. He remembered sentries on the International side who wore skirts. 'I think they were from Scotland. They looked very funny.'

Hongkew offered a home to other newcomers. Between 1938 and 1941 18,000 thousand German Jews and 4,000 Polish Jews, including the only complete yeshiva (Jewish theological college) to escape the Nazis, made their way to Shanghai. Many settled in Hongkew where, somewhat to their amazement, they found themselves protected by Hitler's allies, the Japanese. They were the last refugees Shanghai made welcome. The readiness of the metropolis to accept all comers had been one of its greatest attributes. Now this too was under threat. The arrival of the Jews marked the end of Shanghai as an open city.

Like the majority of Shanghai's visitors, they came by boat. Sir William Hayter recalled watching them disembark. The Nazis allowed the Jews only a few personal possessions. Many stepped off the tenders beautifully dressed but penniless. The Lloyd Tristino shipping company charged them up to ten times the normal rate. Second class was booked out six months in advance and many Jews bankrupted themselves to buy a first-class ticket.

The Jews came to Shanghai after the rest of the world had refused them. In America the Johnson Immigration Act of 1924–9 gave preference to refugees from Nordic countries and imposed restrictions on everybody else. Other countries followed suit. One man encountered the following difficulties in his attempt to escape the Nazis. In 1933 he left Germany for Spain. Three years later civil war broke out and he went to Italy. He escaped to Switzerland in 1938 but the authorities there issued him with a permit lasting just four weeks. He decided to join relatives in Ecuador and left for Paris to obtain a visa through an agent. Back in Switzerland, the Ecuadorian consul pronounced the visa valid but when he arrived in Ecuador itself he was turned away, as he was in every other South American country. Finally he cabled relatives in Germany for a return ticket. In Europe neither France nor Switzerland would grant him right of entry. Italy permitted him to stay forty-eight hours during which he bought a ticket for Shanghai. To his relief he discovered the city required no visa, affidavit, police certificate or assurance of financial independence. There was only customs to clear and even that was cheap. In his excellent book, *Japanese Nazis and Jews: the Jewish Refugee Community of Shanghai 1938–45*, David Kranzler quotes one woman who wrote at the time in Germany, 'I almost took my life last week. Only this news, that one can get easily to Shanghai, kept me from doing it.'[4]

Peter Berman now works for the *Washington Post*. In February 1939 he sailed to Shanghai from Germany with his family. His parents found a place next door to Astor House, opposite Broadway Mansions. His father started a stationary stall downstairs and the family lived in the flat above. He had managed to bring out his considerable collection of books, each checked by the Nazis before the family left, and now set up a lending library. He had also packed his equally impressive stamp collection which proved popular with the Japanese who liked anything German. Books and stamps kept the Berman family for the next four years. As Peter said, 'Basically that was how we survived.'

Jews, dressed in heavy, European clothes, tramped from door to door in the French Concession and the International Settlement, selling coffee cups, old silver, Bohemian glass, embroidery and fur coats. Enid Saunders Candlin started her married life with German porcelain but, as she said, 'Who wanted things like that in 1939? We had the war in Europe to worry about.'

The Japanese encouraged the Jews to settle in Hongkew in order to revitalize the district. From the rubble, the Jews built new houses equipped with bathrooms (something of a novelty in Hongkew) which they then rented out. Whole streets took on a European appearance and 'Little Tokyo' was replaced by 'Little Vienna'. In the Wayside district and along Chusan Road they opened shops, restaurants and open-air cafés selling milk shakes and ice-cream. Nightclubs like the Roof Garden and the White Horse Inn offered music and comic routines as well as a Miss Shanghai contest. They put on Yiddish plays and published Yiddish newspapers.

At first the city welcomed the Jewish refugees. Shanghailanders set up the Komor Committee, named after its first secretary and administrator, Paul Komor, a Shanghai businessman from Hungary. It turned the Beth Aaron Synagogue into a reception centre and kitchen, feeding 600 refugees a day. When this proved insufficient, Lady Chancellor buttonholed Sir Victor Sassoon. 'I said to him at one of his parties, "Look here, I am sure I can rely on you to find us a building. These are middle-aged, professional men and their families and they need somewhere to live and something to eat and you're the man to do it."' Sir Victor donated the Embankment Building, equipped with a swimming pool but lacking sanitation; a combination of luxury and squalor to forewarn the refugees of what they might expect from the city.

With each new liner, the welcome grew less warm. The official view is summed up in a letter from Cornell S. Franklin, Chairman of the Shanghai Municipal Council to Dr A. J. Alves, the Consul-General for Portugal and Senior Consul of the International Settlement. He was fearful, he wrote, of the already 'acute refugee problem' in the city taxing as it did 'to a grave degree' the Municipal Council and 'private philanthropy'. He asked consuls to take every step 'within their power' to prevent the further arrival of Jewish refugees and to 'bring this view to the notice of interested organizations and shipping companies concerned'.[5] The letter was dated December 27th, 1938 when fewer than 1,500 Jewish refugees from Europe lived in the Settlement. A member of Special Branch gave me the unofficial attitude when he said, 'Hitler did the right thing kicking them out. They were the scum of the earth.'

Franklin's letter had an immediate effect on the governments of America, Britain and France as well as on their major Jewish organizations. Posters and newspaper articles appeared in Germany and Italy warning of the economic conditions in Shanghai. German Jews remained unconvinced. One refugee spoke for all his fellow victims of Nazi persecution when he declared: 'We are going to Shanghai. We know that war is raging in China, that Shanghai is being ravaged, that perhaps there is no place for us, but we are going anyway. Since in face of all other doors closed to us, it was the only one remaining open and our only desire was to flee Germany no matter what happened.'[6]

For reasons obscure to the West, the Japanese continued to encourage Jewish immigration to Hongkew until even their own nationals complained of higher rents and tougher business competition. By May 1939 14,000 Jews had reached Shanghai and their number threatened to double by the end of the year. Even then Captain Koreshige Inuzuka, the Resident Naval Officer in Shanghai and his friend and colleague, Colonel Yasue, hesitated.

They were Japan's 'Jewish experts' in the city. Most Japanese knew nothing about Jews and even fewer had met one. Captain Inuzuka and Colonel Yasue had acquired their expertise when Japan took over Manchuria in 1931 and north China in 1937, between them home to 27,000 Jews. As Chief of Dairen Military Mission, Colonel Yasue kept in constant contact with the Jewish Far East Council from 1938 to 1940. The council even engraved its 'Gratitude and Appreciation' for Captain Inuzuka's 'Service For the Jewish People'[7] on the silver cigarette case which he always carried with him and which saved him from trial as a war criminal in 1946. The Jewish Far East Council might have chosen another form of address if it had known that the helpful captain under a different name, had translated *Protocols of the Elders of Zion* and other notoriously anti-semitic works into Japanese. This apparently paradoxical behaviour has a simple explanation. Colonel Yasue and Captain Inuzuka believed Nazi propaganda – but applied it in a Japanese fashion.

The Japanese government's experience of Jews had been small but decisive. The turn of the century saw Japan anxious to prove itself a modern nation in its war against Russia. Every banker in the West scoffed at their request for money except one. Jacob H. Schiff, a German Jew, was president of the New York banking firm Kuhn, Loeb and Company. Disgusted by Russia's pogroms against Jews, he decided to back Russia's enemies. First on his own and then with two other Jewish bankers, Sir Ernest Cassel in England and M.

M. Warburg and Company of Hamburg, he arranged the flotation of several loans to Japan during the Russo–Japanese War (1904–5) at considerable risk to himself. Among other things, the three Jewish banks financed half of the Japanese navy which defeated Russia's Baltic fleet. The loans made a deep impression on Japan. Schiff was the first foreigner to receive the Order of the Rising Sun and is still remembered with affection by elderly Japanese. His action at the moment of Japan's need confirmed Nazi propaganda. Here indeed was the powerful Jewish banker described so laboriously by Hitler. Better to have such a man as a friend, reasoned the Japanese, than to kill him. In every poor refugee arriving at the city's wharves, Captain Inuzuka and Colonel Yasue saw infinite possibilities. The irony of their policy now unfolded in Shanghai.

In January 1940, Captain Inuzuka pointed out that one-third of Shanghai's Jewish refugees had relatives in America. He believed that grateful American Jews would intercede for Japan while 'utilisation of the Jews who maintain the international press and advertising agencies' would secure 'the betterment of the international feelings towards Japan'. This would prove helpful in the 'international ideological war', and provide a 'prompt'[8] delivery of the raw materials which America refused to supply and which Japan urgently needed. Even if that failed, Inuzuka confidently predicted that once his policy had engaged the sympathies of Jewish financial groups, arms and construction dealers, they would find a way to supply Japan through Shanghai Jews like the Sassoons and the Kadoories, 'who fix their permanent homes and keep their family graves in China'.[9]

This was why the Japanese encouraged Jewish immigration to Hongkew and why they ignored requests from the foreign consuls to stop.

On May 25th, 1939 Sir Victor Sassoon and Ellis Hayim in their capacity as leaders of the Sephardic community explained to Colonel Yasue and Captain Inuzuka that they lacked the funds to care for more Jews. They had already applied to the consuls for help, they said, but only the Japanese with their control of Hongkew could halt immigration. No adverse publicity, they promised the wavering Japanese, would attend the announcement since the Jews themselves wanted it. They added, 'The committee will be satisfied if the influx of refugees be restrained somehow or other.'[10] Only then did the Japanese agree.

The Japanese halted immigration on August 21st, 1939. For

the first time in its history Shanghai restricted its visitors. The unwelcome died in Germany.

Generous relatives in America enabled a few Jews to afford apartments in the International Settlement to the great envy of Hongkew's residents. The other side of Garden Bridge appeared impervious to the change overtaking the rest of the city. The authorities had long since repaired the damage done by the bombs. Sir Victor Sassoon continued to give fancy-dress parties, new nightclubs opened and young Englishmen still arrived at the Bund. Two of these, Christopher Isherwood and W. H. Auden, proved a revelation to the British Community. Left-wing, homosexual and in China to write a book on the Sino-Japanese war, neither young man believed in the formal attire so dear to their hosts. Isherwood, determined to look the part of foreign correspondent, dressed in a beret and a pair of over-sized riding boots. Auden, who had corns, wore carpet slippers on every occasion. They preferred visiting factories with Rewi Alley to playing sport and the city's infamous bathhouses to the Shanghai Club. Was this, the Shanghailander wondered, what home had come to in his absence?

The Settlement was even more a centre of intrigue than ever, despite the break-up of the Far Eastern Comintern spy network after the arrest of Hilaire Noulens and his wife by Special Branch on 15th June, 1931. Spies of every nationality continued to meet at the bar of the Cathay Hotel. The most impressive was Richard Sorge, a stocky, arrogant man who chewed toothpicks, drunk heavily and excelled at liar dice. The journalist Richard Hughes who knew him later in Tokyo described the German as 'the prototype of The Nazi'.[11] In fact Richard Sorge became one of Russia's most successful double-agents. Between 1937 and 1941 he kept Stalin informed of nearly every important German and Japanese military and political decision in the Far East. Betrayed almost by accident, he was arrested in October 1941 by the Japanese and hanged three years later. (Special Branch with its customary thoroughness had listed him as a Russian agent as early as May 1933).[12] Emily Hahn also frequented the bar of the Cathay Hotel, her pet gibbon, Mr Mills, coiled around her neck. After complaints about his lack of house training, he appeared in nappies. People still exchanged the wildest gossip over cocktails if not about 'The Poets' as the British Ambassador, Sir Archibald Clark Kerr, had christened Isherwood and Auden (who suspected he had them followed to the bathhouses), then concerning the British

Ambassador, something of a bathhouse expert himself, and his tiny, blonde, Chilean wife who bicycled around Shanghai in very tight shorts.

Autumn 1937 saw the start of a new paper hunt season. Three Japanese officers asked to join. After some debate the Paper Hunt Committee took them on. Paper hunting depended on the goodwill of the Japanese and the Stewards made every effort, as George Stewart recalled, to get 'pally' with them. They detailed certain members to adopt a Japanese officer and keep an eye on him. 'If he fell off, we had to help him back on his horse.'

The *North China Daily News* reinforced the illusion of normality in the Settlement. War might be imminent in Europe, and actually taking place in China, but nothing affected the calm of its editorials. Long-held prejudices remained intact. The newspaper continued to criticize the Chinese and praise or, at least, excuse the Japanese. Even the Rape of Nanjing failed to convince the paper of its folly.

The Japanese army reached Nanjing in December 1937. Then followed one of the war's worst atrocities. In four days, according to evidence gathered by the Japanese War Crimes Tribunal, Japanese soldiers killed 2–300,000 Chinese (the same number as died in Hiroshima and Nagasaki eight years later) and raped 20,000 women. They bound people together in bundles and shot them or set them alight. They tied others to posts and used them for bayonet practice. They then photographed themselves and their victims and sent the film to Shanghai for development. J. B. Powell, the American editor of the *China Weekly Review*, happened to see the results in his local camera shop. One snap depicted the decapitation of a Chinese. The other, a 'revolting picture',[13] revealed two Japanese soldiers posing next to the body of a Chinese woman they had raped and murdered. The soldiers had requested copies to send to friends in Japan.

The *North China Daily News* printed a more restrained account of the Rape of Nanjing. (The Japanese later imprisoned J. B. Powell in Bridge House, an experience from which he never recovered.) The newspaper admitted that a series of 'deplorable cases' had taken place but hastened to excuse the Japanese soldier. 'The blood lust was upon them, and men in that condition are difficult to restrain.'[14] It reproved a Japanese soldier who had raped and murdered three old women in Hungjao and immediately congratulated itself for doing so. 'These are strong words, but they are written in full realisation of all that they mean.'[15] For real outrage one has to turn to the Letter Page. A month after the Nanjing massacre the Shanghailander was passionately occupied with pigs, in particular, Chinese cruelty to pigs on the way to market. Various readers eulogized the sensitivity of the animals. Toby Gazriloff, for example, kept ten as pets which he taught like dogs to sit down and shake hands. The sight of these creatures, 'pushed, beaten, prodded and crushed bleeding and broken-legged into one lorry', aroused the dismay of gentle-hearted foreigners. Another reader who signed himself 'Porkey's Pal', noted that the coolies practised dance steps on the animals, keeping time with blows, 'and then, this the truth – apparently being sorely in need of a shaving brush for the following morning – they pull out bristles from the pigs' backs. Maybe you will not believe this but there are witnesses.'[16] Of the massacre in Nanjing I failed to find a mention.

Concern for pigs appeared to have blinded the British to the true intentions of the Japanese. They refused to believe that a former admirer might threaten their Settlement. They thought themselves protected by prejudice. Orientals raped and pillaged other Orientals but never Westerners.

The Japanese, of course, displayed a keen interest in the Settlement. From the top of Broadway Mansions, the Japanese generals gazed covetously at the Bund. Still somewhat in awe of the British, they hesitated to take what they wanted. Instead they worried away at the edges, tearing a bit off here, another over there, all the time concentrating their energies on those two peculiarly British institutions, the police force and the Municipal Council.

Their desire to oust the British first became obvious in the Outside Roads' Area. Always a matter of dispute between the Chinese Municipal authorities and the International Settlement, the Japanese Military Police took it over after the Chinese officials fled the city. Foreigners and Chinese filed daily complaints of their brutality. Sylvia Chancellor, who lived in a large house in Hungjao, described to me, with suitable insouciance, the half-resentful, half-admiring attitude of the Japanese. One afternoon Lady Chancellor looked out of her window to see the Japanese army entering her back door, 'So naturally I felt a bit unsettled'. As she spoke a few words of Japanese, Sylvia Chancellor went into the kitchen to find them dirty, hot and tired. '"Want honourable tea," they said.

I thought if I give them tea we'll run out and they'll be angry. So I said "You can't have honourable tea because we don't have any. You can have honourable hot water instead."' Some time later she saw them standing on the lawn. Sylvia Chancellor had put a great deal of effort into her lawn. Without thinking she shouted, 'Get off my grass,' and they all jumped. She explained, 'They liked obeying orders, you see.' An officer then appeared at the door with a questionnaire and asked her age. He invited her to come outside and dispatched his orderly to find a big stone. The orderly came back and put the rock next to Lady Chancellor. The officer stepped on to the stone and the orderly photographed them together. She later received a copy.

Chinese partisans continued to harass the Japanese. Tony Keswick, who lived near the Chancellors, found his house 'right in the battle ground'. He was having tea one afternoon when he noticed fifty Chinese soldiers disguised as coolies assiduously weeding his lawn. The Keswicks represented sanctuary, 'Of course we weren't but they thought we were and the Japanese thought we were which came to the same thing. We didn't disturb them.' Christopher Chancellor recalled standing on his balcony watching a company of Japanese soldiers march by. Suddenly he saw three Chinese soldiers, the first armed with a gun, the second with a stick and the third holding an umbrella, cross his garden and make for the road. 'Sylvia said "Oh, do tell them they're going in the wrong direction!" So I called out. They looked up and were so pleased, each shook his own hand in delight.'

On another occasion Christopher Chancellor discovered the head of a Japanese soldier in the garden. 'We didn't know how it got there or what to do with it but we did know the Japanese gendarmerie would have shot us if they had found it first,' said Sylvia. That night Christopher placed the head in a sack, carried it to the golf course and left it under a bush. Later they watched a Japanese general walk his tiny dog past the sack. The dog stopped and yapped but the Japanese general was in a hurry and pulled the animal away.

Every morning on his way to work Christopher Chancellor had to endure an increasingly acrimonious dispute between his driver and the Japanese sentry guarding the entrance to the International Settlement. His Chinese chauffeur refused to take his cap off to the Japanese. The sentry retaliated by sticking his bayonet through the open window. 'I would push it to one side,' said Christopher Chancellor. 'In the end Sylvia confiscated the driver's cap and that was the end of that.'

In the Settlement itself the law required the Japanese Military Police to ask permission at a Municipal police station before questioning a suspect. A report still exists of one such visit to the Bubbling Well station by a Mr Inouye. The British policeman found himself flabbagasted by the Japanese's 'arrogant and extremely offhand manner', in respect of 'reasonable queries put before him'. The redoubtable Mr Inouye insisted on sitting behind the charge-room desk during the entire investigation and failed 'even to exhibit common courtesy' by rising to meet Mr Aiers, 'obviously'[17] his superior officer. Mr Inouye, it seemed, believed himself already in charge.

In their turn the Japanese asked the Municipal Police to arrest wealthy Chinese officials who had chosen to spend their retirement in Shanghai. The Japanese accused these unlikely suspects of belonging to guerrilla units. Like Chiang Kai-shek before them, the Japanese interested themselves in the wealth rather than the politics of their victims. When they did provide evidence, it too often appeared, as one British superintendent scribbled in the margin of a report, 'a frame up by a dirty rascal'.[18]

The Municipal Council found itself in an equally delicate situation. Tony Keswick, now chairman of the Municipal Council, explained,

> The Japanese could easily have said to me, 'Enough of this nonsense. I have given instructions and 50,000 of our marines are coming through your Settlement and as for your police, we will shoot them.' I couldn't have done anything. You know you don't want bloodshed and that they are stronger. In the old days we were benign shooters. We gave up, I think quite rightly, but once you are not prepared to shoot you've got to have very sharp wits. The Japanese, of course, were ready to shoot. It was not a fact that we wouldn't shoot and they always thought we might.

The last four years of the Municipal Council proved the most dramatic in its history as the Japanese sought control first through the ballot box and then by force.

The Municipal Council consisted of fourteen members: five Chinese, five British, two Americans and two Japanese. The Japanese complained that the ratio failed to represent the 30,000 Japanese residents in the Settlement compared to less than 10,000 British subjects. The leading newspapers of both communities exchanged home truths. The *Shanghai Mainichi* remarked, 'Conditions . . . will no longer allow the Japanese to continue to be humble.' They accused the British of being, 'too much favoured' and 'steeped in memories of their past glory', as well as continually 'boasting of their constructive efforts in the establishment and development of the Settlement'. The newspaper warned that the British lacked 'a true perception of the present and of the future',[19] and accused the Council of general extravagance and incompetence.

The *North China Daily News* admitted the Council suffered from that besetting British sin of 'Let's do something for our old friend who is down on his luck'. It went on to point out the lack of constructive suggestions from the Japanese for the benefit of the community since they had joined the Council in 1916, adding, disingenuously: 'This conclusion has been reached after exhaustive inquiries among older residents.' Japanese criticism, continued the newspaper, smacked more of a desire 'to share some of the succulent plums' than of true reform. It finished with a warning to its own voters not to dismiss the challenge 'hurled down' by the Japanese lightly for 'an ostrich-like attitude in the face of a common danger may be all very well but it exposes that part of the ostrich that remains above ground to a hearty kick'[20] – advice more British institutions in the Far East might have heeded.

The representatives of the two countries fought a bitter election as late as April 1940. A change in the exchange rate had extended suffrage to anyone paying as little as SH$70 in taxes. The Japanese sought to win over the new voters, mostly the German Jewish refugees in Hongkew. The British instructed businessmen and residents to subdivide their property and place each share under a different name with every name entitled to vote. The foreigners won by a narrow margin. The Japanese claimed several of their ballot boxes had not been opened.

The Japanese took their revenge at the next ratepayers' meeting, held at the racecourse in front of 2,000 Japanese and 3,000 foreigners. The episode illustrates for me the end of British influence in Shanghai. The Japanese lashed out with a clumsy, seemingly futile gesture, like a child confronting a bogey man, but they proved their point. The British were no longer invincible. They had lost that aura of superiority which they had relied on to hold the Settlement.

The meeting had been called to raise taxes. The council wanted to finance a larger police force. The Japanese had deliberately encouraged an increase in crime in order to create an unstable situation which they might use as an excuse to take over the Settlement. They, therefore, refused to pay for more police unless the Council agreed to vote in another Japanese member: which suggestion the Council turned down. The leader of the Japanese committee, a man of seventy, made a speech warning foreigners of 'severe trouble'. Unperturbed, Tony Keswick spoke next on the budget. When he finished, a Japanese Council member took his place at the microphone, clutching it with both hands. As he started to speak, Tony Keswick recalled,

> I stepped back and found myself standing in front of the old man who had made the threat. Suddenly there was a bang, bang. I thought the old man had fired a couple of blanks to make the party go. Not a bit of it. He had fired a damned great pistol close enough to burn my clothes. You know unless you are hit badly you don't feel it. One bullet went in here, [he pointed to his back] and, luckily, because his hand shook so much, it came out, perfectly neatly, just above my heart. Another went in here and came out there [he pointed to his arm]. It's very difficult for a bullet to get through clothes but out it came and even took the top three fingers off the little Japanese chap who was standing at the microphone. I got up and flung myself on top of the old man, not heroically but just thinking that he was stirring up trouble and saying, 'You mustn't do that!' Suddenly I realized there was blood all over the place.

Tony managed to walk off the platform to a waiting ambulance. 'If he had fallen, we would have seen a bloodbath,' explained his wife, Mary. 'The Japanese would have gone berserk.' Tony Keswick continued: 'They carried me off to hospital which appeared empty but for a small, Chinese coolie. He knew iodine was the stuff so he got a bottle and said, "Where's the hole?" I said, "The one you can see through," and he poured the iodine until it ran out the other side. That was the most painful part of the whole thing.'

From then on Tony Keswick drove everywhere in a bullet-proof car previously owned by Al Capone. As the car was unbearably stuffy in summer he refused to close the windows, 'so it was pretty useless really'.

Tony Keswick described the shooting as a triumph for the Council and a loss of face for the Japanese. 'One, their head man should not have been firing a pistol. Two, he made a mess of it and, three, they failed to pass the budget because I was rushed to hospital. So another meeting had to be called as soon as they'd propped me up.' I asked if he had not felt afraid. 'Oh no, you see I was a young man in a top job. It was very exciting and we were used to getting our way.'

Apart from Tony Keswick's high spirits, the British had little else to protect them. By 1940 the gunboats and regiments had returned to the war in Europe. One year later, almost exactly one hundred years after the British had routed the Chinese in the First Opium War, the Japanese moved into the Settlement and finally called the British bluff.

The last few years before 1941 saw the city weakened by violence and disorder. Shanghai's success relied partly on a correlation between the respectable and the criminal. The criminal now took charge, promoted himself from contributer to sole editor and produced a very nasty story indeed.

A spate of street murders and assassinations shook the French Concession. In France the co-operative nature of the Vichy government towards Hitler saved the French Municipal Council from the attentions of the Japanese. It failed, however, to prevent the Chinese and Japanese secret services turning the area into their private battleground.

The initial blame lay with General Dai Li, head of Chiang Kai-shek's secret service. A slim man with soft hands who suffered from sinusitis he was, as one American historian put it, 'China's combination of Himmler and J. Edgar Hoover'.[21] Two days after fighting began in August 1937, General Dai Li paid a call on Du Yuesheng, Shanghai's most eminent ganster. Du Yuesheng had demonstrated his loyalty to Chiang Kai-shek in 1927 and the general hoped the gangster might now help him to discourage Japanese collaborators. Du agreed to recruit and train 18,000 men in sabotage and assassination as well as to arm and to pay them.

First the Japanese tried to win over the patriotic gangster. When that failed, they resorted to threats. Ricky Lu, the aged dandy whose father gambled with Du, recalled a Japanese plane circling menacingly over the gangster's home in the French Concession. Du and his fourth wife took the precaution of moving to a friend's flat on Rue

Bourgeat. In November 1937 he left Shanghai for Hong Kong. His departure crushed the French Concession. Disputes broke out, from the highest echelons of the Green and Red Gang down to the night soil collectors who found their monopoly threatened without Du's protection. From his suite in the Peninsula Hotel, Du continued to busy himself with the war in China. He bribed Shanghai businessmen into loyalty or arranged a comfortable exile for them in Hong Kong, visited Chiang Kai-shek in Wuhan (where Du gave an interview to Christopher Isherwood) and kept his men at General Dai Li's work.

The Japanese counter-attacked with a puppet regime under Chiang Kai-shek's former prime minister, Wang Jingwei. In the spring of 1939 Wang set up his own secret service in Shanghai. He too approached Du Yuesheng. When Du turned him down, he picked as a substitute Wu Sibao, a member of the Green Gang and the son of a hot-water seller on Chengdu Road. Wu Sibao was thirty-nine, swarthy and thick-set. He had fought in a warlord's army and worked as chauffeur to Stirling Fessenden, the former chairman of the Municipal Council. As Number One Driver he ran a profitable business selling petrol and tyres stolen from the Municipal garage. He even possessed enough of Du's ruthlessness to earn the nickname Tiny Du. He and General Dai Li now competed to recruit from the streets and arm the city's 'loafers', as the Special Branch of the International Settlement euphemistically called them.

In one month alone, eighteen acts of terrorism took place leaving twenty-one dead and ten injured.

General Dai Li and Tiny Du chose their victims from the two groups of people responsible for much of the city's former vitality: journalists and businessmen. Any unfortunate entrepreneur who joined the Japanese puppet government was liable to find himself axed in his own garden or shot down outside the Cathay Hotel by General Dai Li's men. Tiny Du's loafers hacked off the heads of Chinese journalists who resisted and left the gruesome objects at strategic points throughout the city. When one police sergeant attempted an investigation, he received a finger through the mail.

Indiscriminate violence, inflation and lack of business opportunities finally destroyed the city's reputation for optimism. Most Shanghainese found just staying alive took up all their energy. Zhu, the tailor, recalled the 'dog's existence', he led. He hawked sugar cane, repaired shoes, cooking pots and even toothbrushes to earn enough to buy a little ground corn and dried pieces of sweet potato.

He was always hungry. During the winter he passed dead bodies in his lane every morning and wondered how soon before it would be his turn.

The rich and well-connected found themselves equally vulnerable. Sir Y. K. Pao told me,

That was a very, very bad time. It was an impossible situation. Prices sky-rocketed. I was in charge of the bank responsible for paying the wages of the Municipal staff which included the police. We distributed the wage packets from nine o'clock in the morning, reaching certain branches only in the afternoon. By that time, their pay had lost ten per cent of its value. The Chief of Police came to visit me. 'I want to talk to you,' he said, and put his pistol on my desk. 'This is not necessary,' I assured him hurriedly. 'I can't have my police complaining,' he said. 'What can I do?' I replied. 'I can't hand everyone their money on the dot of nine o'clock in the morning!' It was really the worst position I have ever been in. Another time some very bad men came to my house where I kept the bank's money in a safe. 'We want a loan,' they said. 'Open the safe and give us the money.' I wondered if they could offer some security. They brushed that aside. Then I tried to explain the money was not mine to give. 'You had better kill me or I will have to go to jail,' I insisted. They said they would allow me the night to think it over. In the morning I booked myself into hospital for an appendix operation. Really, I had no choice. By the time I came out, the gang had vanished.

One neighbourhood sums up the debilitating effect this had on Shanghai. The Shanghainese called the district 'Badlands'. It was in the Outside Roads' area between Yu Yuen Road, the Great Western Road and Jessfield Road. As early as 1932 a scrawl in the margin of a Special Branch report noted that 'the Japanese are encouraging the establishment of gambling and drug places'.[22] Like Chiang Kai-shek before them, they were 'in need of funds to meet urgent military expenses',[23] and encouraged every sort of vice to raise them. A description of it presents a final still of the city. It is a harsh picture revealing a metropolis reduced to its vices without the colour or movement of its virtues. Between the focusing and the taking of this last shot, Shanghai's individuality, like some exotic bird, takes wing and vanishes.

You can still walk through 'Badlands' today. Now the streets are lined with factories against which shacks the size of Wendy Houses lean precariously. Half their contents are stacked up on the pavement. Outside one a man ate his supper while his daughter played with a kitten at his feet. From their washing line hung an open, red umbrella adorned with pink ruffles. Fifty years ago, geishas with painted faces and garish kimonos picked their way in split- toed clogs along the same road, then unlit and filled with holes. On the walls posters advertised the latest nightclub or opium den with names like 'Hollywood', 'Peach Blossom Palace' and 'Good Friend'. From the gloom the clubs blazed with neon lights. Guards slouched outside, shouting and fighting among themselves. 'Hollywood', for example, boasted a private army of four hundred men. The grandest clubs occupied the former homes of foreigners on Jessfield Road. Guests drove up driveways still planted with the odd rosebush. Inside, roulette wheels and fantan tables crowded the sitting- and dining-room. Upstairs, in a child-sized bedroom, you could have a girl, smoke an opium pipe or try one of Shanghai's famous, pink, opium pills so pure you sucked them like a sweet.

Behind the mock-Tudor gables of number 76 Jessfield Road, Tiny Du and his exquisite wife (a graduate of one of Shanghai's best girls' school) tortured rich Chinese until they agreed to join the new government or contribute to its upkeep. Fifty years later, the Chinese government have transformed the house into the Jiandong Secondary School. Basketball posts flanking the front door make it look reassuringly suburban. A few doors down at number 94, the 'Jiangsu-Zhejiang-Anhui Opium Suppression Bureau' used to supply drugs to the 'institutions of culture', as the Japanese called their nightclubs and opium dens. From nearby streets erupted the sound of gunfire. At a crossing you might have stumbled on the body of a club-owner, murdered by a rival's guards. Now he lay with his face jammed into the gutter, surrounded by excited geisha.

The 'Badlands' mentality pervaded the city like a noxious gas destroying everything that had been exciting and different about Shanghai, replacing variety with a uniform deadliness. It fingered people for the most trivial reasons, for standing on the wrong corner at the wrong time, having the wrong relatives, or, simply, like Mr Li, the husband of one of the three ladies I interviewed in the Park Hotel, for not buying his own railway ticket. Mr Li's story is Badlands personified. His persecutors happen to have been the Japanese. A few years earlier or a few years later and he might have found himself tormented by Chiang Kai-shek's Blue Shirts, Mao Zedong's Red Guards or the army in Tiananmen Square. Shanghai proved anathema to them all.

In 1940 Mr Li was seventeen and on his way back from Chongqing where he had joined Chiang Kai-shek and the Nationalists in their retreat from the Japanese. Homesick for Shanghai and out of money, Mr Li started the long journey across China with two friends. Before boarding an overcrowded train they befriended an affable, middle-aged Shanghainese who bought the tickets. When they parted in Shanghai, he still had the four ticket stubs in his pocket.

Three weeks later about twenty Japanese military police woke Mr Li by breaking down his door. They took him to a warehouse on Canton Road near the Bund. He recalled a passageway lined with Japanese gendarmes. 'It was a terrible, terrible feeling, I can tell you, to walk down that corridor. It was like going to hell.' He found one of his two travelling companions. A former fancy-dresser who always wore a gold ring, an expensive watch and a flashy pen sticking out of his breast pocket, Mr Li had seen him the night before on Bubbling Well Road in a brown suit and white shoes. He still wore the suit but when he turned around, a whipping had left his back bare and bloody. Interrogators, 'really brutal people', asked Mr Li over and over again why he had gone to Chongqing. They shouted, '"Confess you're a spy for the Nationalists. Write everything you saw and heard. Write down everything you did."' He received no breakfast. 'At lunch I was given rice but I didn't eat anything. I began to write. I was seventeen, what do you expect?'

The Japanese had also picked up Mr Li's other friend whose uncle turned out to be one of Shanghai's biggest collaborators. Unknown to the three boys, the family immediately began to petition for their release. The guards took the boys to a compound with an open corridor down one wall and a makeshift prison in the middle. The prison housed forty to fifty men. It had a tin roof and no sanitation. When the summer temperature rose to over 110 degrees, the stench became overwhelming.

In recognition of the important uncle, the Japanese allowed the boys to sleep in the corridor and use the lavatory. They spent nine days in the compound. Every night they heard the screams of tortured men. Once every two or three days the Japanese pulled a man out of the prison and gave him the water treatment. They tied the victim on his back to a low bench. Then they blindfolded him, raised up his legs and stuck a hose into his mouth. When his belly bloated they stamped on it hard until he vomited so much blood and water, he passed out. Mr Li and his two friends had 'box-office seats' for this. Once they saw the middle-aged Shanghainese dragged from the prison. Mr Li described him as a soft-spoken, refined person. 'I am sure he was not a spy. He probably got shopped to the Japanese for money problems.' They watched as he was given the water treatment.

Mr Li still had little appetite. Late one night, when the temperature cooled, he suddenly felt hungry. The Japanese soldier on duty had a kind face. He sat at a nearby table, his meal box in front of him, practising Mandarin, 'which made me decide he couldn't be all bad'. Mr Li asked how long he had studied the language. They began a conversation, 'ending up with me saying how hungry I was. "Wait," he said and disappeared into the kitchen. Of course I had to wait, what else did he think I was going to do?'

Mr Li suddenly realized how he must appear to the Japanese soldier. His hair had grown long. He had not washed since he arrived and he had been using his shoes as a pillow. The soldier returned with rice, squash and a few, tiny fish. Mr Li made a good meal. They continued to talk and, as a joke, 'for I wasn't brave enough to ask any favours', Mr Li remarked on the hardness of the ground. The Japanese again told him to wait, disappeared and returned with a small, straw mat, 'It's better than a concrete slab,' he said.

The guard changed at eight o'clock the next morning when eight or nine soldiers performed the drill ceremony. The Japanese sergeant caught sight of the mat and asked how it got there. He then called Mr Li's benefactor out of line and, in front of everyone, slapped him for three or four minutes without pause. 'I felt like hell,' said Mr Li.

Each day seemed to stretch a year for the three boys. Mr Li's friend in the brown suit received better treatment for he could barter his rings and pen. Mr Li had nothing. The Japanese continued to threaten: '"Confess or we will send you to Bridge House. Once you go in there you won't ever come out. What more can you write?"' Every day the smell from the prison increased. Every night the screams sickened them. 'Worst of all,' recalled Mr Li, 'was the fear of what they would do to us.'

At 4.30 in the morning of the ninth day a soldier said: '"You have not confessed enough. You will be shot in the compound."' They dragged the boys behind the lavatory and put them against the wall of a ruined building. The boys stood there for three hours. Mr Li went on, 'I wasn't religious but I had been educated by the Jesuits and I started to pray.' They watched the morning drill at eight o'clock. 'This is it, we thought, they'll shoot us straight after.' The drill ended, the soldiers dispersed and the boys were still standing there. 'After a long while, it must have been about ten o'clock, a soldier came up to us. "You are free now. You can go home. Do you want money for a rickshaw?" I said, "No thank you," and we left.'

That same year the Japanese also arrested Mr Wong, a young Chinese journalist who lacked influential relatives to save him. J. B. Powell saw the result as he was going home through the French Concession late one evening. He passed a crowd of people gathered around a street lamp. Several of them were foreigners in evening dress. Mr Wong's head lay at their feet, its bleeding stump resting against the base of the lamp-post. Powell wrote, 'The head had been cut off so recently that there were drops of sweat on the forehead.'[24]

For me Shanghai ends here, among the crowd staring down at the head of the young journalist. Heads had filled Shanghai's streets since it began as an international city. Imperial troops had stacked heads up like water melons after the Taiping Rebellion. The executioners of the warlord carried heads on plates through Nantao in 1927. General Dai Li's men left heads on doorsteps. So why did this particular head mark the close of Shanghai for me? Shanghai had always been a balancing act, its drawbacks only just redeemed by its virtues. Individuality and anarchy, extraordinary vitality and bestial poverty, black humour and blind indifference; the city attracted and appalled in equal measure. Now, as I contemplated the sweat of the young man's terror, it merely appalled.

In retrospect, the pre-war period has an air of unreality about it. One almost wonders if it ever happened at all, so good was Shanghai at creating illusion. Like a Chinese dragon at festival time, you are stunned at how the various parts co-ordinate while the high jumps leave you speechless. As each fresh disaster struck the city, you gasped, afraid the painted cloth must collapse in a heap of scales, tail and twitching eyelids. Finally it did and that is its lasting attraction. Nothing of what made Shanghai great exists today except in a few shabby buildings and in people's memory. The acrobats have emerged from beneath the dragon, picked it up and walked offstage.

Nearly everyone I interviewed affirmed that the period they spent in the city was the best in their life. Sounds, smells and sights exuded a pungency never experienced again. Foreigners talked about those years as reformed drug addicts recall a hallucination. For the Chinese, the deception went deeper. They could not foresee China's past re-emerging from beneath the disguise. They never guessed that their freedom would be as short-lived as the dragon dance.

In the end I can only understand the phenomenon of the city in relation to China. Against the dark nothingness of the country, Shanghai, like a figure in a peep-show, takes on a fragile wonder.

Fifty years later a Chinese jazz band has started to play again in the coffee shop of the former Cathay Hotel. The room is small with a bar and a glass case displaying cakes. Fairy lights are strung across the ceiling and Irish coffee is on the menu. I was sitting with a group of foreigners who live in Shanghai.

The band members played the foxtrots and jitterbugs they last performed before the Second World War. All were in their seventies. Cheng Yueqiang, the drummer, a large man with a sad face, had returned to Shanghai from Hong Kong in 1950 because he believed in communism. During the Cultural Revolution he had had to bury his drumsticks in the back yard. Mr Zhou, the diminutive trumpet player and bandleader kept glancing at his watch. He complained, 'They make us work so hard. Every night, no rest and I am a grandfather!' At exactly ten o'clock and despite calls for more, he packed away his trumpet and went home. Mr Zhou grew up in Wuhan. His mother was killed by the Japanese and his father went to fight and never returned. A rich Chinese adopted Mr Zhou. The man loved music and had imported Russian, American, Filipino and Portuguese musicians to play for him every night. By day they coached orphans like Mr Zhou. A black American called Jimmy Clark taught Mr Zhou the trumpet. Later he came to Shanghai, teamed up with Cheng and played in many of the city's most famous clubs.

During the break, I found Cheng weighing himself on one of the antique machines that stood at the same spot on every floor of the hotel. Before the war I imagined his place taken by foreign women, anxious to stay slim. Now the machines comfort the Chinese that at least they do not starve.

I returned to my table where a Belgian had started a story. In Shanghai to help the Chinese modernize their telephone system, he found himself one day on a station platform with an official as a steam train pulled out. Too late the Belgian attempted a photograph. '"Are you interested in our trains?"' asked the official, flicking his hand at a subordinate. Five minutes later the train shuddered to a stop, shunted back into the station then steamed out a second time. The Belgian got his photograph. 'Nothing in China ever changes,' he said.

The other foreigners nodded in agreement. A German involved in a joint venture with the Shanghai Municipality asked his manager if he might promote a young Chinese. The manager turned the idea down. He explained that the Cultural Revolution had produced two sorts of Chinese; those who pushed people out of windows and those who decided who should be pushed. The government imprisoned the first and kept the second in low-grade jobs. The German's protégé came from the second group. At eighteen he had sent two hundred people to their death. The table shook their heads in horror. An American helicopter pilot said, 'They eat bear paws, you know. They keep the bear in a cage until the last moment. Then they cut off the paws and scoop out the pad. It's meant to be delicious . . .' The band was playing 'Smoke Gets in Your Eyes'. Over his cymbals Cheng winked at me. If China has not changed, neither has the foreigner in China.

An inordinately handsome young man walked up and asked me to dance. He came from a table of equally handsome friends, thin and lithe with dark, curly hair and profiles like Roman coins. We circled decorously around the dance floor to 'Boogie Woogie Bugle Boy'. He told me he was a Palestinian living in Tripoli. 'But I travel to Europe quite often,' he said. The Chinese had offered him 'a working holiday'. I knew that China supports the Palestine Liberation Army and I realized I was in the arms of a terrorist. I did not mention that my married name was Cohen. Nor did I turn and walk away. The outside world seemed suddenly very distant. Between it and us lay China, its vast bulk belittling outrage, its antiquity suspending moral certitudes. In what I now recognized as the true spirit of the city, I accepted his invitation for the next number.

Notes

AUTHOR'S NOTE

I have used the pin-yin system for transcribing Chinese characters phonetically into English with two principal exceptions. The names Sun Yat-sen and Chiang Kai-shek are spelt throughout according to the old system as they are more generally recognized in that form. When referring to streets, shops, places, etc., in the city of Shanghai I have kept spelling used in standard Shanghai guidebooks of the inter-war period.

H.S.

INTRODUCTION

1   Harold Acton, *Memoirs of an Aesthete*, p. 290.
2   Rhoads Murphey, *Shanghai: Key to Modern China 1840–1936*.
3   Aldous Huxley, *Jesting Pilate*, p. 241.
4   Quoted by Pan Ling, *Guide to Old Shanghai*, p. 4.
5   A former member of the International Settlement's Special Branch told me that he had confiscated a number as pornographic material.
6   Josef von Sternberg, *Fun in a Chinese Laundry*, p. 82.
7   Huxley, *Jesting Pilate*, p. 241.

CHAPTER 1

1   The city wall, completed in 1554, was built to protect Shanghai's citizens from Japanese pirates. Japanese and Chinese bands continued to menace China's coast well into the 1930s. One of the last, and more unusual, was Sue Nakawura, a former Japanese primary school teacher who, at the age of eighteen, eloped with a Chinese travelling salesman to Fuzhou where she fell for a buccaneer caled Chen Pailin. Together they cruised the South China Coast raiding ships and towns. Her expert marksmanship won the respect of his men who treated the young woman as a leader. She distributed the spoils and her judgment was never questioned. In the autumn of 1934 she grew homesick, took $35,000 and returned to Hokkaido. The following spring found her restless and she set out for Fujian where she discovered her band dispersed and her lover forced to live in the city's slums for fear of arrest. She tried to resurrect their old life but was caught and imprisoned in Shanghai's Japanese consular gaol in January of 1936. She was twenty-seven.
2   *North China Herald* 30/6/31, p. 463. The *North China Herald* was a weekly compilation of the *North China Daily News*. It is the only form of the newspaper which is now available.
3   Quoted by Murphey, *Shanghai: Key to Modern China*, p. 59.

4   For this brief history I am much indebted to Witold Rodzinski, *The Walled Kingdom: A History of China from 2000 BC to the Present*; Christopher Hibbert, *The Dragon Awakes: China and the West 1793–1911*; Betty Peh-t'i Wei, *Shanghai: Crucible of Modern China* and the patience of Michael Hurst, Fellow of St John's College, Oxford.

5   Quoted by Rodzinski, *The Walled Kingdom*, p. 202.

6   Quoted by Ernest O. Hauser, *Shanghai: City for Sale*, p. 3.

7   Quoted by Rodzinski, *The Walled Kingdom*, p. 185.

8   Hauser, *Shanghai: City for Sale*, p. 43.

9   Murphey, *Shanghai: Key to Modern China*, p. 24.

10   Hibbert, *The Dragon Awakes*, p. 171.

11   Ibid.

12   Dr Medhurst, quoted by Hauser, *Shanghai: City for Sale*, p. 63.

13   Quoted by Jerome Ch'en, *China and the West*, p. 217.

14   Ibid., p. 210.

15   NCH 7/12/29, p. 378.

CHAPTER 2

1   Mao Dun, *Midnight*, p. 239.

2   Viktor Petrov, *Shanghai na Vampu: ocherki i rasskazy*, translated from the Russian for the author by Antonia Lloyd Jones.

3   NCH 26/6/35, p. 524.

4   Enid Saunders Candlin, *The Breach in the Wall*, p. 109.

5   Peter Fleming, *News from Tartary*, p. 26.

6   NCH 27/2/35, p. 457.

7   NCH 23/3/38, p. 455.

8   NCH 4/8/37, p. 193.

9   André Malraux, *Man's Estate*, p. 168.

10   The following is from Valentin V. Fedoulenko, *Russian Emigré Life in Shanghai*, an oral history conducted by Boris Raymond in 1967, Regional Oral History Office, Bancroft Library, University of California, Berkeley, 1967. Courtesy, The Bancroft Library.

11   Shanghai Municipal Police Files F4913 3/1/23.

12   Hallett Abend, *My Years in China 1926–1941*, p. 107.

13   Irene Kuhn, *Assigned to Adventure*, p. 243.

14   Egon Erwin Kisch, *Secret China*, p. 126.

15   NCH 19/1/29, p. 128.

16   NCH 29/1/27, p. 164.

17   SMP File D 6578, 25/5/37 and 26/2/40.

18   The inspectors were very much concerned with the health of the girls and questioned them on the 'prophylactic measures' they took, 'if any'. One girl stated that she allowed 'no man to copulate with her unless he first put two rubber sheaths over his penis'. To which the inspectors commented, 'Possibly she exaggerated a little.'

19   NCH 7/1/28, p. 15.

CHAPTER 3
1   Quoted by Sterling Seagrave, *The Soong Dynasty*, p. 175.
2   NCH 29/1/27, p. 137.
3   NCH 26/2/27, p. 308.
4   NCH 26/2/27, p. 309.
5   Ibid.
6   'Shanghai and the Defence Force', *Lancet*, June 18th, 1927, quoted China Weekly Review 18/2/28, p. 300.
7   John B. Powell, *My Twenty-Five Years in China*, p. 142.
8   NCH 29/1/27, p. 145.
9   SMP IO 7563, 27/1/27.
10   Ibid.
11   NCH 15/1/27, p. 59.
12   Sam Ginsbourg, *My First Sixty Years in China*, p. 47.
13   From a letter dated 20/5/34 written by Harold Isaacs, an American member of the Third International, and enclosed to a colleague in New York on 5/10/34. The letter was addressed to the General Committee of the Chinese Communist party. It reviewed the two-year period of Isaacs' 'extra-organizational collaboration' with the Chinese Communist party in the publication of the magazine, *China Forum*. He describes why he has severed his relationship with the Central Committee, blaming them, among other things, for their 'nauseatingly fawning' praise of Stalin and the débâcle in 1927. He finishes with a salutation to the Communist Revolution in China to which he still remains committed. Both letters were intercepted by the Chinese authorities in Beijing and handed to Gauss at the American legation. SMP 3317. Harold Isaacs' excellent book, *The Tragedy of the Chinese Revolution* (1938), is the chief source of information for this period.
14   NCH 22/12/28, p. 500.
15   Harold R. Isaacs, *The Tragedy of the Chinese Revolution*, p. 132.
16   *New York Herald Tribune*, 20/2/27, quoted by Isaacs, *The Tragedy of the Chinese Revolution*, p. 134.
17   Du's biographical details are from SMP file D 9319, 1939 and 1940.
18   W. H. Auden and Christopher Isherwood, *Journey to a War*, p. 170.
19   Sterling Seagrave, *The Soong Dynasty*, p. 152.
20   Powell, *My Twenty-Five Years in China*, p. 158.
21   Quoted by Pan Ling, *Old Shanghai Gangsters in Paradise*, p. 54.
22   Ginsbourg, *My First Sixty Years in China*, p. 51.
23   Seagrave, *The Soong Dynasty*, p. 225.
24   Letter to Nelson T. Johnson, Department of State, Division of Far Eastern Affairs dated 1/2/27.

25 NCH 2/4/27, p. 15.
26 Quoted by Isaacs, *The Tragedy of the Chinese Revolution*, p. 154.
27 Description of Du's bodyguards from Pan Ling, *Old Shanghai Gangsters in Paradise*, p. 35.
28 Translation from unpublished manuscript by Trotsky, quoted by Isaacs, *The Tragedy of the Chinese Revolution*, p. 161.
29 Pan Ling, *Old Shanghai Gangsters in Paradise*, p. 54.
30 China Year Book 1928, p. 1374, quoted by Isaacs, *The Tragedy of the Chinese Revolution*, p. 181.
31 Ibid., p. 175.
32 Ibid.
33 NCH 16/4/27, p. 103.
34 NCH 9/4/27, p. 143.
35 Letter to Nelson T. Johnson, Department of State, Division of Far Eastern Affairs dated 5/2/27 from A. L. Warnshuis, International Missionary Council, New York City.
36 Jan 17th, 1927 to J. V. A. MacMurray, American Ministry, Peking.
37 Hauser, *Shanghai: City for Sale*, p. 24.
38 CWR 3/1/31, p. 207.
39 Quoted by Ernest O. Hauser, *Shanghai: City for Sale*, p. 15.
40 NCH 31/10/34, p. 175.
41 Ibid.
42 The miscegenation legislation prohibited, explicitly or implicitly, marriages between Chinese and White Americans and penalised anyone who performed such a marriage. Attitudes began to change during and after World War II when U.S. servicemen brought back Chinese wives. In 1943, Congress repealed the Chinese Exclusion Act. Only in 1967 did the Supreme Court invalidate all state laws banning interracial marriages.
43 Powell, *My Twenty-Five Years in China*, p. 20.
44 To the Commander-in-Chief at Shanghai, dated 23/1/27.
45 Ibid.
46 NCH 28/5/27, p. 398.
47 American Consular Papers, January 1927.
48 NCH 17/11/28, p. 266.
49 NCH 28/7/27, p. 279.
50 Ibid.

CHAPTER 4
1 Quoted by Austin Coates, *China Races*, p. 26.
2 W. H. Auden and Christopher Isherwood, *Journey to a War*, p. 237.
3 Coates, *China Races*, p. 26.
4 Ibid.
5 Noel C. Davis, *The History of the Shanghai Paper Hunt Club 1863–1930*.

6   Quoted by Coates, *China Races*, p. 30.
7   Ibid., p. 36.
8   Last four sentences from interview quoted by Coates, *China Races*, p. 267.
9   Quoted by Coates, *China Races*, p. 226.
10   NCH 3/2/37, p. 219.
11   Quoted by Percy Finch, *Shanghai and Beyond*, p. 36.
12   Ibid., pp. 37–8.
13   Ibid., p. 38.
14   Ibid., p. 43.
15   Ibid., p. 44.
16   Ibid., p. 47.
17   NCH 23/7/27, p. 147.
18   NCH 3/9/27, p. 407.
19   Enid Saunders Candlin, *The Breach in the Wall*, p. 54.
20   Irene Kuhn, *Assigned to Adventure*, p. 226.
21   NCH 24/2/37, p. 336.
22   Maggie Keswick, *The Thistle and the Jade*, p. 12.
23   Stanley Jackson, *The Sassoons*, p. 29.
24   Ibid., p. 69.
25   Pan Ling, *In Search of Old Shanghai*, p. 44.
26   Ernest O. Hauser, *Shanghai: City for Sale*, p. 274.
27   NCH 11/8/31, p. 185.
28   Quoted by Hauser, *Shanghai: City for Sale*, p. 274.
29   NCH 8/2/33, p. 239.
30   Signed 'English Woman', NCH 10/2/37, p. 248.
31   Quoted by Stanley Jackson, *The Sassoons*, p. 268.
32   Quoted by Pan Ling, *In Search of Old Shanghai*, p. 44.
33   Quoted by Christopher Hibbert, *The Dragon Awakes: China and the West 1793–1911*, p. 210.
34   Mrs Cecil Chesterton, *Young China*, p. 109.
35   NCH 25/6/27, p. 561.
36   NCH 2/6/28, p. 366.
37   NCH 3/11/31, p. 149.
38   NCH 23/12/30, p. 397.
39   The following taken from trial transcripts in NCH 12/2/36, pp. 278–80 and NCH 19/2/36, pp. 321–2.
40   Auden and Isherwood, *A Journey to a War*, p. 295.
41   *China Weekly Review*, 7/4/34, p. 199.
42   NCH 5/2/36, p. 230.
43   NCH 27/5/36, p. 377, letter signed 'Economy' lists highest-paid workers admitting they give one 'somewhat of a shock'. These Municipal employees also received free medical attendance and hospital accommodation.
44   NCH 29/1/27, p. 162.

45   Ibid.
46   Ibid.
47   NCH 5/2/27, p. 201.
48   Ibid.
49   Ibid.
50   Ibid.
51   Ibid.
52   Ibid.
53   NCH 5/2/27, p. 202.
54   Ibid.
55   Ibid.
56   Ibid.
57   CWR 12/2/27, p. 275.
58   CWR 12/2/27, p. 276.
59   *China Courier*, 26/1/27.
60   CWR 12/2/27, p. 276.
61   CWR 26/2/27, p. 351.
62   SMP 7563, 10/2/27.
63   SMP 7563, report made by D. I. Yorke 20/5/27.
64   Ibid.
65   Ibid.
66   Isabella L. Bird (in this edition known as Mrs J. F. Bishop), *The Yangtze Valley and Beyond*, p. 24.
67   'International Banking and its Political Implications: The Hong Kong and Shanghai Banking Corporation and the Imperial Bank of Persia 1889–1914', essay by David McLean in *Eastern Banking*, H. H. King (ed.), p. 8.
68   Addis to Hillier, November 13th, 1913, HSBC Group Archives, 2/28 quoted in King (ed.), *Eastern Banking*, p. 8.
69   J. O. P. Bland, the British and Chinese Corporation's agent in Beijing, May 25th, 1906 to Addis; enclosed by him to Foreign Office, July 9th, quoted in *Eastern Banking*, p. 10.
70   Alston to Langley, June 2nd, 1913, Alston papers, PRO FO 800/247, quoted in *Eastern Banking*, p. 10.
71   BM March 24th, 1903, quoted in 'Four Major Buildings in the Architectural History of the Hong Kong and Shanghai Banking Corporation' by Christopher Yip, *Eastern Banking*, p. 118.
72   Ibid., p. 123.
73   *The Hongkong and Shanghai Banking Corporation: The Official Opening of the New Building at Shanghai, 23rd June 1923*, p. 72.
74   Ibid.
75   Ibid., p. 24.
76   Ibid., pp. 24–5.
77   Ibid., p. 25.
78   Ibid.

79   Ibid., p. 32.
80   Ibid.
81   Ibid., p. 35.
82   Henchman to J. R. Jones, HSBC, Hong Kong, acknowledging an
      enquiry dated February 18th, 1952. HSBC Archives, biographical
      files. Quoted by Frank H. H. King in 'Defending the Chinese curren-
      cy: The Role of the Hongkong and Shanghai Banking Corporation,
      1938–1941', *Eastern Banking*, p. 283.
83   NCH 24/9/27, p. 538.
84   Hauser, *Shanghai: City for Sale*, p. 118.
85   CWR 26/3/27, p. 93.
86   Ibid.
87   NCH 2/2/32, p. 160.

CHAPTER 5
  1   Kyoko Hayashi, *Rotabo's Alley*, translated by Margret Mitsutani
       (unpublished).
  2   NCH, 8/4/30, p. 55, article by Merriam Griffin.
  3   Enid Saunders Candlin, *The Breach in the Wall*, p. 117.
  4   Ibid.
  5   *North China Sunday News*, War Diary Supplement, 21/2/32, p. 10.
  6   Helen Foster Snow, *My China Years*, p. 48.
  7   Ernest O. Hauser, *Shanghai: City for Sale*, p. 205.
  8   Hallett Abend, *My Years in China 1926–1941*, p. 187.
  9   Ibid.
 10   Quoted in Ibid., p. 190.
 11   Ibid., p. 191.
 12   Snow, *My China Years*, p. 51.
 13   NCH War Diary Supplement, 28/2/32, p. 11.
 14   Abend, *My Years in China 1926–1941*, p. 191.
 15   NCH 9/2/32, p. 186.
 16   NCH 1/3/32, p. 306.
 17   Abend, *My Years in China 1926–1941*, p. 192.
 18   SMP D 3176-A, doctor's report dated 23/2/32.
 19   Ibid.
 20   Snow, *My China Years*, p. 58.
 21   Snow, *My China Years*, p. 49.
 22   Ibid., p. 52.
 23   Snow, *My China Years*, p. 52.
 24   Ibid.
 25   Percy Finch, *Shanghai and Beyond*, p. 247.
 26   Ibid., p. 248.
 27   Ibid.
 28   Ibid.
 29   Quoted in NCH 9/2/32, p. 188.

30   NCH 1/3/32, p. 312.
31   NCH 23/2/32, p. 273.
32   NCH 16/2/32, p. 221.
33   Ibid.
34   Ibid.
35   NCH 16/2/32, p. 224.
36   NCH 23/2/32, p. 284.
37   NCH 12/3/27, p. 405.
38   Mrs Cecil Chesterton, *Young China and New Japan*, p. 82.
39   Copy of Letter from Mr H. E. Arnold to Mr R. E. Wilson, Shanghai, February 11th, 1932, circulated to General Committee members of British Chamber of Commerce and China Association. Arnold was Chairman of the SMC.
40   From Joint Committee, British Chamber of Commerce and China Association, Shanghai, March 11th, 1932, 7.13p.m.
41   Letter from Foreign Office August 28th, 1934. It continues revealingly, 'It will be difficult therefore for British merchants . . . to escape the necessity of estimating for themselves the risks involved in adopting or in maintaining too long what may prove to have been too rigid an attitude.'
42   NCH 23/2/32, p. 292, Letters Page.
43   NCH 15/3/32, p. 419.
44   Abend, *My Years in China 1926–1941*, pp. 192–3.
45   NCH 8/3/32, p. 341.
46   Ibid.
47   Killearn Papers. Peking Archives, Political, Vol. 8, Lampson to Walford Selby, February 10th, 1932 quoted by David Steeds in 'The British Approach to China During the Lampson Period, 1926–1933', one of four papers given at a symposium organised by the International Centre for Economics and Related Disciplines, May 21st, 1980 and published in Ian H. Nish (ed.), *Some Foreign Attitudes to Republican China*.
48   Killearn Papers. Diary March 19th, 1932.
49   Ibid., March 4th, 1932.
50   Ibid., March 19th, 1932.
51   Ibid.
52   Ibid.
53   Killearn Papers. Letters to Mrs Phipps from M.W.L. and others, 1932–4, Lampson to Mrs Phipps, March 27th, 1932.
54   Ibid.
55   Killearn Papers. Peking Archives, Political, Vol. 8, Lampson to Walford Selby, April 24th, 1932.

CHAPTER 6
1   Mao Dun, *Midnight*, p. 6.

2   Ibid., p. 13.
3   Ibid., p. 10.
4   Ibid., p. 13.
5   Ibid., p. 14.
6   Rhoads Murphy, *Shanghai: Key to Modern China 1840–1936*, p. 9.
7   NCH, 8/7/36, p. 107.
8   Ernest O. Hauser, *Shanghai: City for Sale*, p. 135.
9   Ibid.
10   Enid Saunders Candlin, *The Breach in the Wall*, p. 124.
11   NCH 3/6/36, p. 419.
12   L. Z. Yuan, *Sidelights on Shanghai*, p. 57.
13   W. H. Auden and Christopher Isherwood, *Journey to a War*, p. 248.
14   CWR 3/3/28, p. 3.
15   Translation of shop signs, NCH 21/7/31, p. 107.
16   Candlin, *The Breach in the Wall*, p. 240.
17   Auden and Isherwood, *Journey to a War*, p. 246.
18   Lu Xun, 'Snacks', dated 11/6/34, *Selected Works*, Vol. III, p. 56.
19   Eleanor M. Hinder, *Social and Industrial Problems of Shanghai with Special Reference to the Administrative and Regulatory Work of the Shanghai Municipal Council*, p. 44.
20   Simon Yang and L. K. Tao, *A Study of the Standard of Living of Working Class Families in Shanghai*, p. 64.
21   *One Day in China*. This book records Thursday, May 21st, 1936 through nearly five hundred essays sent by ordinary people from all over China. It was put together by the Literary Society founded in 1933. Its editorial board consisted of some of the most famous intellectuals of the time. Its editor-in-chief, Mao Dun, author of *Midnight* and China's leading writer of realistic fiction contended, 'May twenty-first aroused the hearts of almost all those Chinese ... who are eager to know the whole, true face of our motherland which is at this perilous juncture'. Translated from the Chinese by Calliope Caroussis, Section 3, p. 75.
22   Ibid., Section 3 p. 76.
23   Quoted by Hinder, *Social and Industrial Problems of Shanghai with Special Reference to the Administrative and Regulatory Work of the Shanghai Municipal Council*, p. 25.
24   NCH, Letters to Editor from H. J. Timperley, 6/5/36, p. 245.
25   Ibid.
26   NCH 28/7/37, p. 135.
27   Auden and Isherwood, *Journey to a War*, p. 246.
28   Quoted in the *Australian*, 29/12/87, p. 7.
29   NCH 8/7/36, p. 69.
30   Auden and Isherwood, *Journey to a War*, p. 246.
31   *New Youth*, 1919, quoted by Jonathan D. Spence, *The Gate of*

Heavenly Peace, p. 160.

32 Letter from Edwin S. Cunningham, American Consul-General Shanghai dated April 27th, 1935, to the Secretary of State, Washington SMP 10,023.

33 Lu Xun, *Selected Works*, 1/3 quoted by Spence, *The Gate of Heavenly Peace*, p. 100.

34 Quoted by Wang Shiqing, *Lu Xun: A Biography*, p. 97.

35 Agnes Smedley, *Battle Hymn of China*, p. 60.

36 Ibid.

37 Ibid.

38 Ibid., p. 61.

39 Ibid.

40 Ibid.

41 Ibid, p. 62.

42 Ibid.

43 Lu Xun, *Selected Works*, 1/416, quoted by Spence, *The Gate of Heavenly Peace*, p. 120.

44 Smedley, *Battle Hymn of China*, p. 62.

45 Ibid.

46 Ibid.

47 Ibid., p. 63.

48 Ibid.

49 Lu Xun, SW 3/212–13, said in front of the League of Left Wing Writers in the spring of 1930, translation from Spence, *The Gate of Heavenly Peace*, p. 276.

50 Lu Xun, SW 3/112, quoted by Spence, *The Gate of Heavenly Peace*, p. 277.

51 Lu Xun, SW 3/137, 'A Glance at Shanghai Literature', talk given to the Social Science Group on August 12th, 1931.

52 Lu Xun, *A Glance at Shanghai Literature*, SW 3/133.

53 Lu Xun, SW 3/334, essay entitled 'Shanghai Children', August 12th, 1933.

54 Wang Shiqing, *Lu Xun: A Biography*, p. 215.

55 Ibid., p. 235.

56 Lu Xun, SW 3/304, 'Pushing', June 8th, 1933.

57 *Document Showa*, Vol. III, *Shanghai Kyodo Sokai: Jihen Zenya*, published by NHK following their TV series, translated from the Japanese by Kayoko Takai.

58 Lu Xun, SW 3/332, 'Shanghai Girls', August 12th, 1933.

59 Lu Xun, SW 3/152, 'Spooks and Spectres in the World of Chinese Letters', p. 152.

60 Ibid.

61 Ibid., p. 153.

62 Ibid.

63 Smedley, *Battle Hymn of China*, p. 64.

64   Ibid., p. 65.
65   Ibid., pp. 65–6.
66   Ibid., p. 66.
67   Quoted by Jerome Ch'en, *China and the West*, p. 89.
68   Ibid., p. 172.
69   Lu Xun, SW 3/132, *A Glance at Shanghai Literature*.
70   Lu Xun, SW 3/250, 'On Seeing Shaw and Those Who Saw Shaw',
      February 23rd, 1933.
71   CWR 19/3/32, p. 161.
72   NCH 22/2/33, p. 294.
73   Ibid.
74   SMP D4498, 17/2/33.
75   Lu Xun, SW 3/251, 'On Seeing Shaw and Those Who Saw Shaw'.
76   Ibid.
77   Ibid.
78   Ibid.
79   Ibid.
80   NCH 22/2/33, p. 294.
81   Ibid.
82   Ibid.
83   Lu Xun SW 3/252, 'On Seeing Shaw and Those Who Saw Shaw'.
84   Ibid.
85   NCH 22/2/33, p. 294.
86   Lu Xun, SW 3/252, 'On Seeing Shaw and Those Who Saw Shaw'.
87   NCH 22/2/33, p. 294.
88   Ibid.
89   Ibid.
90   Lu Xun, SW 3/253, 'On Seeing Shaw and Those Who Saw Shaw'.
91   Ibid.
92   Ibid.
93   Ibid.
94   Lu Xun, SW 3/140–1, 'A Glance at Shanghai Literature', from
      a talk given to the Social Science Study Group, August 12th, 1931.
95   Jay Leyda, *An Account of Films and the Film Audience of China*,
      p. 97, footnote.
96   Josef Von Sternberg, *Fun in a Chinese Laundry*, pp. 82–3.
97   Lu Xun, 3/318, 'to Live by One's Wits', June 26th, 1933.
98   Both quotations taken from Xiao Feng's interview with He Xiujun
      in 1965, published in China in 1980 and then in French under
      the title, 'Histoire de la compagnie shanghaienne "Mingxing" et
      de son fondateur Zhang Shichuan', in Marie-Claire Quiquemelle
      and Jean-Loup Passek (eds) *Le Cinéma Chinois*, for the retrospec-
      tive of Chinese cinema at the Georges Pompidou Centre, Paris,
      15/12/84 to 28/2/85, p. 47. Translated from the French by Harriet
      Sergeant.

99   Cheng Jihua, *Zhongquo Dianying Fazhanshi (A History of the Development of the Chinese Cinema)*, Vol. I, p. 58, translated by Calliope Caroussis.
100   He Xiujun, *Le Cinéma Chinois*, p. 49.
101   Ibid.
102   Ibid., p. 52.
103   Ibid., p. 50.
104   Ibid.
105   Ibid.
106   Ibid.
107   Ibid., p. 52.
108   Ibid.
109   Ibid., p. 54.
110   Ibid., p. 56.
111   Quoted in Tony Rayns' programme notes to the National Film Theatre's 1985 season of Chinese films.
112   NCH 27/11/35, p. 356.
113   Translated from Xia Yan, *In Memory of Chu Qiubei, Wen Yi Bao (Beijing), no.* 12 (1955) quoted by Jay Leyda, *An Account of Films and the Film Audience of China*, p. 74.
114   Ibid., p. 88.
115   Ibid.
116   He Xiujun, *Le Cinema Chinois*, p. 58.
117   This paragraph, ibid., p. 57.
118   Leyda, *An Account of Films and the Film Audience of China*, p. 92.
119   Cheng Jihua, ibid.
120   Sadly Cheng Sumei went the way of many Nationalists. By the end of the 'twenties Harold Isaacs described her as 'closely connected with the upper and underworlds of Shanghai'. In January 1933 she was accused of misappropriating court funds.
121   B. Van Vorst, *A Girl from China (Soumay Tcheng)*, p. 20.
122   Ibid., p. 21.
123   Ibid., p. 8.
124   Ibid., p. 34.
125   Ibid., p. 68.
126   NCH 28/1/28, p. 157.
127   Most slaves were known as '*mui tsai*', little girls sold by their parents to work as servants. Shanghai's newspapers were littered with stories of their suffering. The following example was reported in the NCH 26/10/29, p. 141: A Chinese woman was arrested at 186 Moulmein Road for trafficking in opium and mistreating her twelve-year-old *mui tsai*. The child testified her family had mortgaged her (i.e. sold her with the proviso that when she was of marriageable age they would pay back the money, take her back and sell her in marriage). Ten days before her mistress had accused her of carelessness, heated

iron tongs over a charcoal fire then burned the girl all over her body. 'It was more painful than I can tell.' As she spoke tears rained down her cheeks. The policeman uncovered her top half to expose such awful burns that 'the spectators could not bear to look at it'.

128 The conservative Chinese writer and intellectual Gu Hongming who viewed footbinding as 'one of China's national treasures'. Quoted by Howard S. Levy, *Chinese Footbinding: The History of a Curious Erotic Custom*, p. 141.
129 Ibid., pp. 27–8.
130 Ibid., p. 142. The practice was known as 'Eating Steamed Dumplings in Pure Water'.
131 'Secret Chronicle of the Lotus Interest', ibid., p. 165.
132 Ibid., p. 159.
133 Percy Finch, *Shanghai and beyond*, p. 11.
134 Francis de Croisset, *The Wounded Dragon*, p. 41.
135 NCH 26/10/29, p. 141.
136 Ross Terrill, *The White-Boned Demon: A Biography of Madame Mao ZeDong*, p. 110.
137 Ibid.
138 Ibid., p. 66.
139 Ibid.
140 Ibid.
141 Ibid.
142 Ibid.
143 Ibid.
144 Ibid.
145 Ibid., p. 67.
146 Ibid.
147 Quoted by Spence, *The Gate of Heavenly Peace*, p. 254.
148 Ibid., p. 255.
149 He Xiujun, *Le Cinéma Chinois*, p. 53.
150 Shu Kei, 'La legende de Ruan Lingyu', in *Le Cinéma Chinois*, p. 149. Translated from the French by Harriet Sergeant.
151 He Xiujun, *Le Cinéma Chinois*, p. 53.
152 Shu Kei, *La legende de Ruan Lingyu*, p. 149.
153 Ibid.
154 Lu Xun, SW 3/193–197, 'Gossip is a Fearful Thing'.
155 Harold Acton, *Memoirs of an Aesthete*, p. 288.
156 Ibid.
157 Ibid.
158 Emily Hahn, 'The Case of Mr Chow', *New Yorker*, 6/11/37.
159 Emily Hahn, *China to Me*, p. 10.
160 Ibid., p. 13.
161 'Jailbird', *New Yorker*, 11/6/38.
162 'Mother-in-law's Joke', *New Yorker*, 2/7/38.

163 Ibid.

CHAPTER 7

1   Emily Hahn, *China to Me*, p. 45.
2   Ibid., p. 46.
3   Ernest O. Hauser, *Shanghai: City for Sale*, p. 308.
4   Mary S. Ogle, *In Spite of Danger: The Story of Thelma Smith in China*, p. 53.
5   Ibid., p. 54.
6   Emily Hahn, *New Yorker*, 9/10/37.
7   *Bombs on China*, War Letters from missionaries. The Livingston Press. Letter from D. B. Cater.
8   NCH 18/8/37, p. 257.
9   Emily Hahn, *New Yorker*, 9/10/37.
10 *New Yorker*, 9/10/37.
11 Hallett Abend, *My Years in China 1926–1941*, p. 259.
12 Ibid., p. 261.
13 NCH 15/9/37, p. 421.
14 Sam Ginsbourg, *My First Sixty Years in China*, p. 109.
15 NCH 15/9/37, p. 462.

CHAPTER 8

1   Edgar Snow, *Scorched Earth*, p. 91.
2   *Bombs on China*, War Letters from missionaries. The Livingston Press.
3   W. H. Auden and Christopher Isherwood, *Journey to a War*, p. 87.
4   Helen Hilsenrad, 'Brown was the Danube', quoted by David Kranzler, *Japanese, Nazis and Jews: The Jewish Refugee Community of Shanghai, 1938–1945*, p. 26.
5   FO S-9460-3-879 (circular 399-Gvii). Annexed Paper (sic), December 27th, 1938, quoted by David Kranzler, *Japanese, Nazis and Jews*, Note 18, p. 165.
6   Ibid., p. 161.
7   Ibid., p. 174.
8   Quotations from ibid., Appendix D, p. 618.
9   Ibid., p. 619.
10 FO KP No. 5, May 1939, p. 1 quoted in ibid., p. 269.
11 Richard Hughes, *Foreign Devil*, p. 30.
12 SMP D4718 dated May 20th, 1933, report entitled 'Suspected Soviet Agents domiciled in Shanghai'.
13 J. B. Powell, *My Twenty-five Years in China*, p. 308.
14 NCH 19/1/38, p. 76.
15 Ibid.
16 NCH 23/2/38, p. 301.
17 SMP D8299, 13/5/38.

18   D8662 1938.
19   NCH 22/1/36, p. 139.
20   NCH 4/3/36, p. 528.
21   Quoted by Pan Ling, *Old Shanghai: Gangsters in Paradise*, p. 84.
22   SMP D3445 2/5/32.
23   SMP D8292A, 28/5/41.
24   Powell, *My Twenty-five Years in China*, p. 334.

Bibliography

Abend, Hallett, *My Years in China 1926–1941* (John Lane, The Bodley Head, 1944).

Acton, Harold, *Memoirs of an Aesthete* (Hamish Hamilton, 1984).

Acton, Harold, *Peonies and Ponies* (Oxford University Press, 1983).

Agel, Jerome and Boe, Eugene, *Deliverance in Shanghai* (Dembner Books, New York, 1983).

Ai Qing, *Selected Poems* (Foreign Languages Press, Beijing, 1982).

All About Shanghai: A Standard Guidebook 1934–5 (Reprinted Oxford University Press, 1983).

Allen, Charles (ed.), *Tales from the South China Seas* (André Deutsch, 1983).

Alley, Rewi, *Peking Opera* (New World Press, Beijing, 1984).

Allman, Norwood Francis, *Shanghai Lawyer* (New York, 1943).

The Anti-Japanese Boycott Movement in China from October 1931 to January 1932 (Compiled by Japanese Press Union, Shanghai, 1932).

Auden, W.H. and Isherwood C., *Journey to a War* (Faber & Faber, 1939).

Ballard, J.G., *Empire of the Sun* (Victor Gollancz, 1984).

Barber, Noel, *The Fall of Shanghai* (Macmillan, 1979).

Barnett, Robert, *Economic Shanghai, Hostage to Politics 1937–41* (Institute of Pacific Relations, 1941).

Baum, Vicki, *Shanghai '37* (Oxford University Press, 1986).

Beasley, W.G., *The Modern History of Japan* (The Charles E. Tuttle Co., 1986).

Bergeron, Regis, *Le Cinéma Chinois 1905–1949* (Alfred Eibel, Lausanne, 1977).

Berry, Chris (ed.), *Perspectives on Chinese Cinema* (Ithaca China–Japan Program, Cornell University, 1985), (Cornell University E. Asia Papers No. 39).

Berry-Hart, Alice, *Ching-a-Ring-a-Ring-Ching* (Rex Collings, London, 1977).

Birch, Cyril (ed.), *Anthology of Chinese Literature* (Penguin Books, 1967).

Bird, Isabella, *The Yangtze Valley and Beyond* (John Murray, London, 1989), (published under married name of Mrs J.F. Bishop).

Blofeld, John, *City of Lingering Splendour* (Hutchinson, 1961).

The Board of Inquiry into Trade and Savings Banks in Shanghai, *The Cotton Industry in Shanghai* (Shanghai, 1931).

Bombs on China: War Letters from Missionaries (The Livingstone Press, 1938).

Boyle, John Hunter, *China and Japan at War 1937–45* (Stanford University Press, California, 1972).

Butterfield, Fox, *China Alive in the Bitter Sea* (Coronet Books, Hodder & Stoughton, 1982).

Cable, Mildred and French, Francesca, *Through Jade Gate and Central*

Asia (Houghton Mifflin Co., Boston and New York, 1927).

Candlin, Enid Saunders, *The Breach in the Wall* (Cassell & Co., London, 1974).

Champly, Henry, *The Road to Shanghai: White Slave Traffic in Asia* (John Long, London, 1934).

Ch'en, Jerome, *China and the West* (Hutchinson, 1979).

Ch'en Yanlin, *Shanghai dichan daquan (A Comprehensive Account of Shanghai Real Estate)* (Shanghai, 1933).

Cheng, Jihua, *Zhongguo Dianying Fazhanski (A History of the Development of Chinese Cinema)* (Beijing, 1963).

Chesneaux, Jean, et al., *China from the 1911 Revolution to Liberation* (Pantheon Books, New York, 1977).

Chesneaux, Jean (ed.), *Popular Movements and Secret Societies in China 1840–1950* (Stanford University Press, California, 1972).

Chester, Wilfred L., *China at Bay* (Kelly & Walsh, Shanghai, 1938).

Chesterton, Mrs Cecil, *Young China and New Japan* (George G. Harrap & Co., 1933).

Ch'i Hsi-Sheng Ch'i, *Warlord Politics in China 1916–1928* (Stanford University Press, California, 1976).

China Association, *Letters from London China Association to Foreign Office and General Committee Papers* (July 1928–September 1941).

China Quarterly, The Readjustment in the Chinese Economy (No. 100, Dec. 1984).

Chinese Information Bureau, *How Foreigners Live and Carry on Trade in China: A Reply to the Statement of the China Association* (London, 1925).

Coates, Austin, *China Races* (Oxford University Press, 1983).

Coble, Parkes M. Jr., *The Shanghai Capitalists and the Nationalist Government 1927–1937* (Council on East Asian Studies, Harvard University Press, 1980).

Cochrane, Sherman, *Big Business in China: Sino-Foreign Rivalry in the Cigarette Industry 1890–1930* (No. 33 of Harvard Studies in Business History, 1980).

Cole, Bernard, *Gunboats and Marines: The US Navy in China 1925–1928* (Associated University Presses Inc., US, 1983).

Collis, Maurice, *Wayfoong: The Hongkong & Shanghai Banking Corporation* (Faber & Faber, 1982).

de Croisset, Francis, *The Wounded Dragon* (Geoffrey Bless, 1937, translated from French by Paul Selver).

Crow, Carl, *400 Million Customers* (Harper & Bros., 1937).

Davis, Noel C., *The History of the Shanghai Paper Hunt Club 1863–1930* (Shanghai, Kelly & Walsh, 1930).

Dehergue, Pere J., 'Israel à Shanghai: Les Communautés Juives', (*Bulletin de l'Université de l'Aurore*, No. 35 (1948).

East China Official Guidebooks, Vol. IV, *China*; Vol. I, *Manchuria*

Bibliography

(Prepared by the Imperial Japanese Government Railways, Tokyo, Japan, 1915).

Endicott, Stanley Lyon, *Diplomacy and Enterprise: British China Policy 1933–1937* (Arthur Barker, 1958).

Eye Witnesses' Reports, *Hell over Shanghai* (1932).

Fairbank, John King, *Chinabound: A Fifty Year Memoir* (Harper Colophon Books, Harper & Row Publishers, 1983).

Fairbank, J.K., *Trade and Diplomacy on the China Coast* (Harvard University Press, 1953).

Farmer, Rhodes, *Shanghai Harvest: A Diary of Three Years in the China War* (Museum Press, 1945).

Fedoulenko, Valentin V., Typescript of an oral history conducted 1967 by Boris Raymond, (Regional History Office, The Bancroft Library, University of California, Berkeley, 1967).

Feuerwerker, Yi-Tsi Mei, *Ding Ling's Fiction* (Harvard University Press, 1982).

Fewsmith, Joseph, *Party, State and Local Elites in Republican China* (University of Hawaii Press, Honolulu, 1984).

Finch, Percy, *Shanghai and Beyond*

Fisher, Lois, *Go Gently Through Peking* (Souvenir Press, 1979).

Fleming, Peter, *News from Tartary* (Macdonald Futura, 1980).

Fleming, Peter, *The Siege at Peking* (Oxford University Press, 1984).

Fontenoy, Jean, *Shanghai Secret* (Paris, 1938).

Friedman, Irving, *British Relations with China 1931–1939* (Institute of Pacific Relations, New York, 1940).

The Future of Shanghai, (collection of articles, Shanghai, 1934).

Galbraith, John Kenneth, *A China Passage* (Houghton Mifflin Co., Boston, 1973).

Gervais, Albert, *A Surgeon's China* (Hamish Hamilton, 1934).

Gilbert, Rodney, *What's Wrong with China* (Frederick A. Stokes Co., New York, 1932).

Ginsbourg, Sam, *My First Sixty Years in China* (New World Press, Beijing, 1982).

Gould, Randall, *China in the Sun* (Doubleday & Co., New York, 1946).

Guillain, Robert, *Orient Extreme. Une Vie en Asie* (Arlea Le Seuil, 1986).

Gunther, John, *Inside Asia* (Harper & Brothers, New York, 1942).

Hahn, Emily, *China to Me* (The Blakiston Co., Philadelphia, 1944).

Hahn, Emily, articles in the *New Yorker*.

Han Suyin, *The Crippled Tree* (Triad Panther Books, Granada Publishing, 1982).

Han Suyin, *A Mortal Flower* (Triad Panther Books, Granada Publishing, 1982).

Han Suyin, *Birdless Summer* (Triad Panther Books, Granada Publishing, 1982).

Han Suyin, *My House Has Two Doors* (Triad Panther Books, Granada Publishing, 1982).

Han Suyin, *Phoenix Harvest* (Triad Panther Books, Granada Publishing, 1982).

Hauser, Ernest O., *Shanghai: City For Sale* (Harcourt, Brace & Co., New York, 1940).

Hayashi Kyoko, *Rotabo's Alley* (unpublished manuscript). Translated by Margaret Mitsutani.

Hayter, Sir William, *A Double Life* (Hamish Hamilton, 1974).

Hibbert, Christopher, *The Dragon Awakes: China and the West 1793–1911* (Longman, London, 1970).

Hinder, Eleanor M., *Social and Industrial Problems of Shanghai with Special Reference to the Administrative and Regulatory Work of the Shanghai Municipal Council* (Institute of Pacific Relations, 1942).

Hong Shen, *Dianying Xiju Biaoyanshu (The Art of Cinema and Theatre Acting)* (Shanghai, 1935).

Hook, Elizabeth, *Guide to the Swire Papers* (School of African & Oriental Studies, 1977).

Howe, Christopher (ed.), *Shanghai: Revolution and Development in an Asian Metropolis* (Cambridge University Press, 1981).

Hsü Shu-hsi, *Japan and Shanghai* (prepared under the auspices of the Council of International Affairs, Chungking). (Kelly & Walsh, 1938).

Hughes, Richard, *Foreign Devil*, (Century Hutchinson, 1984).

Hunt, Jill et al., *A Guide to Shanghai* (China Guides Series, 1985).

Hussey, Harry, *My Pleasures and Palaces* (Doubleday & Co., New York, 1968).

Huxley, Aldous, *Jesting Pilate: The Diary of a Journey* (Chatto & Windus, London, 1927).

Isaacs, Harold R., *The Tragedy of the Chinese Revolution* (Stanford University Press, 1961).

Jackson, Innes, *China Only Yesterday* (Faber & Faber, 1938).

Jackson, Stanley, *The Sassoons* (William Heinemann, London, 1968).

Japan's Military Aggression in Shanghai as seen by Neutral Observers. Information Bulletin No. 2, 20/4/33. Four reports by Committee of Enquiry of League of Nations. (Published by the Intelligence and Publicity Department, Waichiaopu, Nanjing, 1933).

Joint Savings Society, *An Oriental Skyscraper*.

Jones, Francis, *Shanghai and Tientsin with Special Reference to Foreign Interests* (Oxford University Press, 1940).

Jung Chang, *Madame Sun Yat-sen* (Penguin Books, 1986).

Keswick, Maggie, *The Thistle and the Jade* (Octopus Books, 1982).

King, Frank H.H., *Eastern Banking: Essays in the History of The Hongkong & Shanghai Banking Corporation* (The Athlone Press, London, 1983).

Kisch, Egon Erwin, *Secret China* transl. Michael Davidson (The Bodley Head, 1935).

Kranzler, David, *Japanese, Nazis and Jews: The Jewish Refugee Community in Shanghai 1938–1945* (Yeshiva University Press, 1976).

Kuhn, Irene, *Assigned to Adventure* (J.B. Lippincott Co., 1938).

Lee, James Hsioung, *A Half Century of Memories* (South China Photo-Process Printing Co. Ltd.)

Lem, Stanislaw, *The Chain of Chance* (Harvest/HBJ Books, 1984).

Levy, Howard S., *Chinese Footbinding: The History of a Curious Erotic Custom* (Abbeville Press, Walton Rawls, New York, 1966).

Leyda, Jay, *An Account of Films and the Film Audience of China* (Massachusetts Institute of Technology, 1972).

Liang, Hsi-huey, *The Sino-German Connection 1900–1941* (Alexander Falkenhausen).

Lu Xun, *Selected Stories* (Foreign Languages Press, Beijing, 1960).

Lu Xun, transl. Yang Xian Yi & Gladys Yang, *Selected Works* (Foreign Languages Press, Beijing, 1980).

A Pictorial Biography of Lu Xun (People's Fine Arts Publishing House, 1981).

McAleavy, Henry, *That Chinese Woman* (George Allen & Unwin, 1959).

Maillart, Ella K., *Forbidden Journey* (William Heinemann, 1937).

Malone, C. l'Estrange, *The Slavery of China* (Independent Labour Party, Publications Department, London, 1927).

Malraux, André, *Man's Estate* (Penguin Books, 1983).

Mao Dun, *Midnight* (Foreign Languages Press, Beijing, 1979).

Mao Dun et al, *One Day in China* (China Press, 1937).

Masterpieces of Modern Chinese Fiction 1919–1949 (Foreign Languages Press, Beijing, 1983).

Maugham, W. Somerset, *On a Chinese Screen* (Oxford University Press, 1984).

Mendelson, Edward, *Early Auden* (Faber & Faber, 1981).

Miller, G.E., *Shanghai: The Paradise of Adventurers* (Orsay Publishing House, New York, 1937).

Mirsky, Jeanette (ed.), *The Great Chinese Traveller* (Pantheon Books, Random House, 1964).

Moore, Captain W.J., *Shanghai Century* (Burleigh Ltd, 1966).

Murphey, Rhoads, *Shanghai: Key to Modern China 1840–1936* (Harvard University Press, 1953).

Nanking & Hai Chow, *Portraits of China by the American Jesuits in Shanghai* (Shanghai, 1936).

Nien Cheng, *Life and Death in Shanghai* (Grove Press, New York, 1986).

Nish, Ian H., *Some Foreign Attitudes to Republican China* (Four papers. International Centre for Economics and Related Disciplines, London School of Economics, 1980).

North China Daily News & Herald, China Hong List 1938 and 1939. 2 vols.

North China Herald 1927–1941.

Ogle, Mary S., *In Spite of Danger: The Story of Thelma Smith in China* (Washington, 1969).

Pal, John, *Shanghai Saga* (Jarrolds, London, 1963).

Pan Ling, *In Search of Old Shanghai* (Joint Publishing Co., Hong Kong, 1982).

Pan Ling, *Old Shanghai: Gangsters in Paradise* (Heinemann Educational Books (Asia), 1984).

Paton, James, *Wide Eyed in Old China* (R.R. Clark, Edinburgh, 1974).

Petrov, Victor, *Shanghai na Vampu: Ocherti Irasskazy* (Washington D.K.: Izdani Russko-Amerikanskoyo Istoricheskoyo Obschestra, transl. from Russian Antonia Lloyd-Jones).

Petty, Orville A. (ed.), *Laymen's Foreign Missions Inquiry* (Fact Finders Reports Vol. V, supplementary series part 2. New York & London, Harper & Bros., 1933).

Pincher, Chapman, *Too Secret Too Long* (Sidgwick & Jackson, 1984).

Powell, John B., *My Twenty-five Years in China* (Macmillan, New York, 1945).

Pratt, Sir John, *China and Britain* (Collins, London, 1944).

Purvis, Malcolm, *Tall Storeys* (Palmer & Turner Ltd, 1985).

Quiquemelle, Marie-Claire & Passek, Jean-Loup, *Le Cinéma Chinois* (Centre Georges Pompidou, Paris, 1985).

Rodzinski, Witold, *The Walled Kingdom* (Flamingo, Fontana Paperbacks, 1984).

Rossi, Paolo, *Communist Conquest of Shanghai* (Twin Circle Publishing Co. & Crestwood Books, 1970).

Schell, Orvill, *To Get Rich is Glorious* (Pantheon Books, New York, Random House, 1984).

Seagrave, Sterling, *The Soong Dynasty* (Sidgwick & Jackson, 1985).

Shanghai Architectural Society, *Shanghai Jianzhu Xiehui Chengli Jinian Tekan* (special commemorative issue, 1931).

Shanghai Institute of Social Science, *Yingmei Yangongsi zai Hua Qiye Ziliao Huibian* (Compilation of Reference Material of the British American Tobacco Co. in China, 1983).

Shanghai Institute of Social Sciences, *Shanghai Yongan Gongsi de Chansheng, Fazhan he Gaizao* (The Origins, Development and Transformation of Shanghai's Wing On Co., Shanghai, 1981).

Shanghai Civic Association, *Statistics of Shanghai* (compiled 1933).

Shanghai Gonggong Zujie Shigao (A Historical Sketch of the Shanghai International Settlement, Shanghai, 1980).

Shanghai Municipal Police Files, National Archives, Washington D.C., 1919–1942.

Shanghai Waterways Shipping Co., *Lundu jinxi* (Ferries Past and Present, Shanghai, 1977).

Shen, Congwen, *The Border Town and Other Stories* (Panda Books, China, 1981).

Shifan University, Shanghai Teacher Training College and Huangpo region revolutionary committee of Shanghai, *Shanghai Waitan Nanjinglu Shihua* (History of the Bund and Nanking Road, Shanghai, 1976).

Shinobu, J. (sometime Legal Adviser to the Imperial Japanese Third Fleet in Shanghai), *International Law in the Shanghai Conflict* (Tokyo, 1933).

Sitwell, Osbert, *Escape With Me!* (Oxford University Press, 1986).

Smedley, Agnes, *Battle Hymn of China* (Victor Gollancz, 1944).

Smedley, Agnes, *Chinese Destinies: Sketches of Present Day China* (Hurst & Blackett, London, 1934).

Snow, Edgar, *Scorched Earth* Book I (Left Book Club, Gollancz (not for sale to public), 1941).

Snow, Helen Foster, *My China Years* (William Morrow & Co., New York, 1984).

The Sprinkler Bulletin, No. 1511, 30/6/35.

Spence, Jonathan D., *The Gate of Heavenly Peace* (Penguin Books, 1982).

Stephens, Harold, *Asian Portraits* (Travel Publishing Asia, 1983).

Stericker, John, *A Tear for the Dragon* (Arthur Baker, 1958).

Stories from the 30s, Books I and II, (Panda Books, 1982).

Stories of Old Shanghai (Young People's Publishing Co., Shanghai, 1974).

Stuart, John Leighton, *Fifty Years in China* (Random House, New York, 1954).

Sues, Ilona Ralf, *Shark's Fin and Millet* (Little Brown, Boston, 1944).

Tang Diyin, *The Pen and I,* (New World Press, Beijing, 1985).

Tao Juyin, *Gudao jianwen. Kangzhan shiqi de Shanghai* (Information from an Isolated Island: Shanghai during the War of Resistance against Japan, Shanghai, 1979).

Terrill, Ross, *The White Boned Demon: A Biography of Madame Mao Zedong* (William Morrow & Co., 1984).

Thompson, James C. Jr., *While China Faced West: American Reformers in Nationalist China, 1928–1937* (Harvard University Press, 1969).

Thubron, Colin, *Behind the Wall* (Penguin Books, 1988).

Tokayer, Marvin & Swartz, Mary, *The Fugu Plan* (Paddington Press, London and New York, 1979).

Tong Hollington K., *Chiang Kai-shek: Soldier and Statesman* (authorized biography) (Hurst & Blackett, London, 1938).

Townsend, Ralph, *Ways that are Dark* (G.P. Putnam & Sons, New York, 1933).

Tsai Chin, *Daughter of Shanghai* (Chatto & Windus, 1988).

Tuchman, Barbara W., *Stilwell and the American Experience in China 1911–1945* (The Macmillan Co., New York, 1971).

Tweedie, Ethel Brilliana, *An Adventurous Journey: Russia–Siberia–China,* (Thornton Butterworth, 1929).

Twenty Authors from Abroad, *Living in China* (New World Press, Beijing, 1979).

Van Vorst, B., *A Girl from China (Soumay Tcheng)* (Frederick A. Stokes Co., New York, 1925).

Vandervelde E., *A Travers la Révolution Chinoise Soviete et Kuomintang* (Brussels & Paris, 1931).

Varg, Paul, *Missionaries, Chinese and Diplomats: The American Protestant Missionary Movement in China 1890–1952* (Princetown University Press, 1958).

Viollis, Andrée, *Shanghai et le Destin de la Chine* (Paris, 1933).

von Sternberg, Josef, *Fun in a Chinese Laundry* (Secker & Warburg, 1967).

Wan Molin. *Hushang Wangshi* (Past Events of Shanghai) (Taiwan, 1973).

Wang, Adine, *La Chine et la Problème de l'Opium* (A. Pedone, Paris, 1933).

Wang Shiqing, *Lu Xun: A Biography* (Foreign Languages Press, Beijing, 1984).

Ward, Edward, *Number One Boy* (Michael Joseph, 1969).

Wei, Katherine & Quin, Terry, *Second Daughter: Growing Up in China 1930–1949* (Harvill Press, 1985).

Wei, Betty Peh-T'i, *Shanghai: Crucible of Modern China* (Oxford University Press, 1987).

Welch, Denton, *Maiden Voyage* (Routledge, London, 1943).

Wong Su-Ling & Cressy, Earl Herbert, *Daughter of Confucius* (Farrar Straus & Young, New York, 1952).

Wu Hsiu (ed.), *A Survey of Folklore from Shanghai 1930* (Shanghai Trust Co., 1932).

Xian Yan, *Under Shanghai Eaves* (Shanghai, 1937).

Xiao Hong, *Selected Stories of Xiao Hong* (Panda Books, 1982).

Yang, Simon & Tao, L.K., *A Study of the Standard of Living of Working Class Families in Shanghai* (Garland Publishing, New York, 1982, first published Institute of Social Research, Peiping, 1931).

Yip Ka-che, *The Anti-Christian Movement in China 1922–1927* (Columbia University Press, 1976).

Yuan, L.Z., *Sidelights on Shanghai* (The Mercury Press, Shanghai, 1934).

Zhou Erfu, *Morning in Shanghai* (Foreign Languages Press, Beijing, 1962).

Zhu Hu-Xu, Bang Lin, Xing Ge-Sheng, *Shanghai Industry and Labour: Shanghai Change* (Hong Kong, 1939).

Index